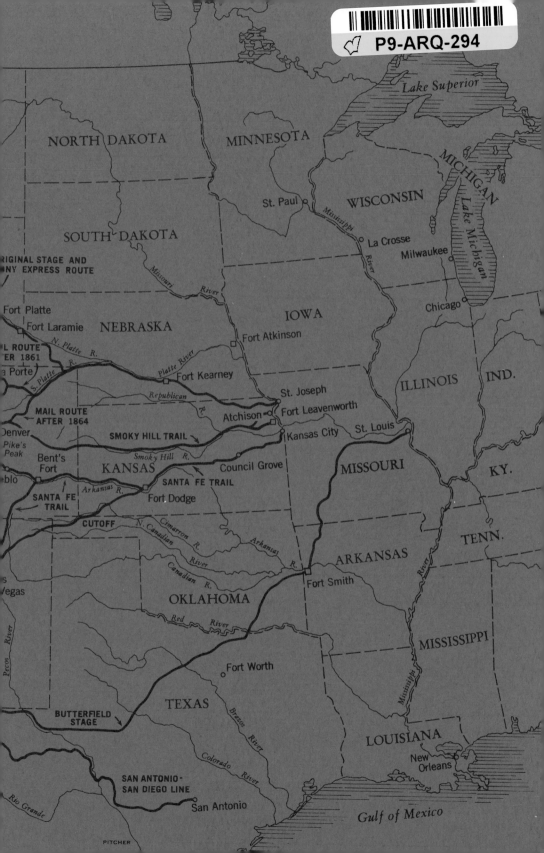

Stagecoach West

California & Oregon Stage Company coach carrying Wells Fargo express, the U.S. mail, and a full load of passengers. (Courtesy, Old Print Shop.)

STAGECOACH
WEST

by Ralph Moody

THOMAS Y. CROWELL COMPANY

New York, Established 1834

By the author

OLD TRAILS WEST

STAGECOACH WEST

*This book is dedicated
to all research librarians, but
particularly to Warren Wickliffe
of Burlingame, California*

Grateful acknowledgment is made to The Arthur H. Clark Company for permission to quote two short passages from *Ben Holladay—The Stagecoach King*, by J. V. Frederick, copyright 1941; and a paragraph from *The Overland Mail, 1849-1869*, by LeRoy R. Hafen, copyright 1926; to Hastings House, Publishers, Inc., for permission to quote two passages from *Gold Camp*, by Larry Barsness, copyright 1962; to Meredith Press for permission to quote a line from *Old Waybills*, by Alvin Harlow, copyright 1934, D. Appleton-Century Company; to Raymond W. and Mary Lund Settle for permission to quote three passages from *Empire on Wheels*, copyright 1949, Board of Trustees of the Leland Stanford Junior University; to the State Historical Society of Colorado for permission to quote from volumes VIII, XII, and XIV of the *Colorado Magazine;* to Stanford University Libraries for permission to quote at length from a manuscript in their Bradford Collection, "Staging in Central California, as Related by Henry Ward"; and to Henry E. Huntington Library, San Marino, California, for permission to quote from six letters in its Waddell Collection.

Acknowledgments

To WRITE this story of stagecoaching in the West a century after its heyday, I have been obliged to gather material from a long list of books, magazines, historical quarterlies, manuscripts, newspapers, and letter files; and to interview men who in their youth were well acquainted with some of the old stage lines, their operators, and the more colorful jehus. I am sincerely thankful to the authors of all the books, articles, and manuscripts I have borrowed from in my research, and to all the librarians and directors of historical societies who have made this material available to me.

I am particularly grateful to Mrs. Alys Freeze, head of the Western History Department, Denver Public Library; Mrs. Laura Allyn Ekstrom, Assistant Librarian, State Historical Society of Colorado; Irene Simpson, Director, Wells Fargo History Room, San Francisco; Ralph Hanson, Manuscript Librarian, The Stanford University Libraries; California State Library, Mrs. Carma R. Leigh, Librarian; Richard Dillon, Librarian, Sutro Library, San Francisco; William R. Holman, Librarian, San Francisco Public Library; Dr. Frank Lundy, Librarian, Love Memorial Library, University of Nebraska; Mrs. N. B. Lacy, Manuscript Librarian, New Hampshire Historical Society; Ernestine Brown, Librarian, University of Washington Library, Northwestern Collection; Thomas Vaughan, Director, Oregon Historical Society; and most particularly to G. Paul Lechich and his staff at Burlingame Public Library.

I am deeply indebted for information and color to Edwin A. Bemis of Littleton, Colorado, publisher of the *Littleton Independent* newspaper for more than fifty years, and who in his youth was a close friend of Bob Spotswood; Clyde V. Smedley of Denver, whose parents were among the first Colorado settlers; S. Omar Barker of

Las Vegas, New Mexico, who was most helpful in supplying me with materials and information about the Santa Fe–Independence stage line; Elmer Kelton of San Angelo, Texas, who helped me with the route of the Butterfield Line; Wayne D. Overholser of Boulder, Colorado, who directed me to much valuable manuscript material; my son Charles, who prepared the original research outline for this book; and to Mrs. Pearl Lee, who has typed and retyped the manuscript with infinite care and patience. And above all others to my wife Edna, who for two and a half years has not only shared the labor of gathering material for this book but has furnished the encouragement and affection that have made the writing a joy.

RALPH MOODY
Burlingame, California

Contents

Illustrations

Maps

All maps in this book are by Donald Pitcher.

1

In the Beginning

EVER SINCE the Stone Age transportation has been the key factor in expanding the limits of the known world, spreading civilization, developing natural resources, and promoting commerce. Although oxen and railroads played a major role for a few decades, until the present century the chief means of overland transportation were the horse, the ass, and their mutual offspring, the mule. Strangely, although separated by more than twelve thousand years, the first and last long-distance equine transportation systems were brought into being for the same purpose: to serve the needs of miners and carry the wealth taken from the mines.

Man made his first effective weapons and tools—spear and arrowheads, daggers, axes, hammers, and hide scrapers—from flint or other hard stone that could be chipped without too great difficulty. But flint was found in only a few inhabited localities, and men who had to travel farthest to secure it were the most painstaking in their chipping. As a result, these men became the most skillful weapon and tool makers, even though they lived at some distance from flint-bearing areas.

It is probable that the early Stone Age men made their journeys in search of flint on foot, as flakes of the stone were hunted over wide areas. Then, about fourteen thousand years ago, they discovered underground deposits, and that freshly dug flint could be chipped with far greater ease and accuracy than sun-brittled surface stone. Flint mining was begun in Belgium and southern England between twelve and fourteen thousand years ago, and mined flint became the most highly prized of all materials.

Archaeological discoveries indicate that the mining of flint led to man's first commerce, for very little of the stone was chipped into weapons and tools at the localities where it was mined, and these primitive implements have been unearthed in widespread regions. Doubtless the stone chippers originally journeyed to the pits and mined their own flint, but findings make it evident that not long thereafter some of the men remained to work the mines while the more skillful chippers gathered into communities to fashion their wares.

Thus the need for commerce and transportation arose. If the most highly skilled men were to devote their entire time to mining or fashioning implements, others must provide them with food and clothing, carry flint from the mines to the artisans, and distribute the manufactured wares. To fill the need, primitive traders came into being, bartering skins, meat, and other foods to the miners for stone; trading this, together with more skins and food, to the artisans in exchange for tools and weapons; and bartering these over wide areas to hunters and food gatherers.

The journeys of these Stone Age traders were longer than had previously been traveled overland, and the loads were heavy, so packs were mounted on the backs of domesticated horses and asses, and the era of equine transportation dawned. Although it is improbable that any of these earliest merchants had more than two or three animals in his train, their hoofs left tracks which were followed by other traders, and the paths they wore became the forerunners of the great trade routes of Europe and Asia.

In the period between 2000 and 3000 B.C. the invention of bronze and the wheel stimulated overland transportation and the extension of trade routes, but their greatest expansion was due to the mining of salt and the Europeans' craving for spices. Salt is a necessity of human life, and salting was the only known way of preserving meat—at that time the chief diet of Europeans—but there were few inland areas where the mineral had been discovered. Furthermore, because their preservation was poor at best in warm weather, Europeans highly prized pepper, ginger, cloves, and other spices as a means of making tainted meat palatable, but these were then to be had only in the Middle East, Africa, and Asia.

About 2500 B.C. a great salt deposit was discovered and mines were opened at Hallstatt in Upper Austria. Archaeological discoveries leave no doubt that this salt was carried to the far corners of the then known world, and was so highly valued that even the peasants of Hallstatt became wealthy from the salt trade. A grave has seldom been opened there that did not contain treasure from distant lands: figures cast in bronze, Egyptian glass beads, ivory carvings from Africa, amber from Scandinavia, pottery from the

Orient, hammered or wrought gold and silver ornaments, armor, or swords inlaid with amber. It is also known that great quantities of spice were brought from Asia and exchanged for salt. As the salt commerce continued from century to century, trade routes were extended to seaports and centers of population throughout Europe and Asia, and a spider web of local roads was developed with its center at the salt mines.

There is little doubt that rude carts with solid wooden wheels were used for hauling salt on the network of roads in the vicinity of the Hallstatt mines, for the wheel and axle were invented early in the Bronze Age. On the trade routes, however, merchandise was carried entirely on the backs of equines or on camels in desert crossings, as the wheel of that time was an efficient load carrier only on firm roads, and the trade routes were merely pack trails.

In 1800 B.C. the much lighter and stronger hub-spoke-and-rim wheel was invented. This led to the development of chariots, the first vehicle designed for carrying men instead of merchandise. About 1700 B.C. the chariot came into use in Egypt, and was quickly adopted throughout the Near East as an instrument of war, the Assyrians and Persians mounting scythes on the wheels to mow down enemy foot soldiers. The Greeks and Romans made little use of the chariot as a war machine. The Romans, however, developed it into a light, sturdy carriage by mounting on broad-tired low wheels a platform that was only large enough to hold two or three standing men, and was circled at the front by a hip-high dashboard. Drawn by four beautifully matched horses, these were the carriages in which military commanders rode when leading their legions forth for conquest and in which conquering heroes paraded triumphantly through the streets of Rome, while their shackled prisoners were herded along behind. By 400 B.C. chariot racing had become one of the most popular events of the Roman games.

Refinement of the chariot, its popularity in horse racing, and its use as a carriage for military officers quite possibly led to the Romans' greatest contribution to wheeled transportation, for the terrain of Italy is rugged and it is extremely difficult for a standing man to keep his balance in a light vehicle that is being drawn rapidly over rough ground. Furthermore, the Romans had learned the science of making cement from lime and clay, and they had an abundance of slave labor as a result of their victorious wars.

Beginning about 300 B.C. they built thousands of miles of paved roads connecting Rome and its most distant provinces. These roads, portions of which are still in use, were usually from sixteen to

An English coach of 1747. (From Stagecoach and Tavern Days, *Alice Earle.)*

twenty feet wide and constructed in four layers. The top layer was thick, flat slabs of hard stone cemented together at the joints. The lower layers were composed of broken stone and coarse gravel mixed with lime and clay and pounded into a solid foundation that in places rose four or five feet above the surface of marshy ground. The Roman roads were built primarily for military use, but over them rolled commerce from all parts of Europe, the Middle East, and Asia, making Rome the hub of the known world.

In 55 B.C. Julius Caesar invaded England, and for nearly five centuries the Romans occupied Britain. During that time they constructed several hundred miles of paved roads very similar to the Roman roads, but their most permanent contribution to transportation was in the development of vehicles and the establishment of a postal system.

The Britons' chariots were somewhat heavier than the Romans' and were mounted on higher wheels, and the platform had a semicircular back rather than a dashboard at the front. The Romans converted this chariot into a carriage by lengthening the platform somewhat and installing a seat for two passengers. In order to control the Britons in the north of England, the Romans built fifteen permanent forts, each a day's journey apart and all connected by a paved road. A postal station was established at each fort, and drivers with carriages and fast horses carried dispatches and military commanders back and forth from one station to another.

To transport supplies and materials between the forts the Romans used trains of heavy carts and a few four-wheeled wagons. One of these wagons was the *carpenta,* a light vehicle for carrying baggage, and some of the *carpentas* were roofed over to keep the baggage dry. A seat or two was sometimes installed, so that a few passengers could be carried when the load of baggage was light. Later this type of vehicle was richly ornamented, equipped with cushioned seats and leathern curtains that could be rolled up or let down, and used in processions or as a conveyance for ladies attending festivals. By the end of the Roman occupation the *carpenta* had evolved into the forerunner of the stagecoach.

After the Romans withdrew from England the roads were allowed to fall into ruins and the postal service deteriorated to a haphazard carrying of letters on horseback by boys called king's messengers. From the beginning of the fifteenth century until the last quarter of the eighteenth, practically all British land travel was on foot or horseback, for the condition of the roads discouraged the use of wheeled vehicles. There were, however, coaches operating in London and a few other localities as early as 1635, although these were clumsy vehicles that jolted slowly along city streets or over short routes between villages. There were also a few stagecoaches operated between cities, but to travel in one of them must have been a harrowing experience. One passenger wrote, "This travell hath soe indisposed mee, y^t I am resolved never to ride againe in ye coach. I am extremely hott and feverish. What this may tend to I know not. I have not as yet advised my doctor."

It was not until 1785 that the first long-distance stage line was established. It operated between London and Edinburgh, a distance of four hundred miles, with way stations at fairly regular intervals for changing horses and supplying meals and lodging to the travelers. The coaches were drawn by six heavy, plodding dray horses at about two miles per hour. They were on the road sixteen to eighteen hours a day, and required from ten to twelve days to make the one-way journey. The establishment of the stage line was made possible by British and Scottish villagers who had improved the primitive cart roads between their villages. If the operation were to continue, however, still further road improvement and some form of government subsidy would be necessary.

[5]

The operation of a long-distance stagecoach line was very costly, as it required many employees, the maintenance of a large number of way stations, and considerable investment in horses, harness, and coaches. To cover these costs, if the coaches carried only passengers and express packages, the operator must charge fares and express rates that were almost prohibitive. The British Government was aware of the situation, and also realized that in order to meet the needs of England's rapidly expanding population, not only public transportation but mail service must be greatly improved.

To accomplish both purposes, Great Britain began awarding contracts to stagecoach operators for carrying mail pouches between the cities and villages along their routes. The payment under these contracts bore little relationship to the amount of mail carried, but was a means of subsidizing the stagecoach operators in order to improve public transportation. To achieve the greatest possible improvement, mail contracts were awarded only to the operators who maintained the fastest and most dependable passenger service.

The mail-subsidy method of improving public transportation soon spread rather generally throughout Europe. To win the coveted mail contracts, stageline operators demanded coaches that were lighter in weight, with enclosed bodies mounted on springs, and horses that combined strength with speed and stamina. As a result, such horse breeds as the German coach horse and the Cleveland Bay were developed. Stagecoach building became an important industry and coachmakers among the most highly skilled and highly paid of mechanics. The British also developed stagecoach driving into an exact science, with precise written rules for harnessing, hitching to the vehicle, and reining either four- or six-horse teams.

In 1785, the same year the London-Edinburgh stage line was established, the first long-distance American line went into operation, running between New York City and Albany. But stagecoach travel was far less important to the early development of the United States than to European countries, with their multiplicity of small villages and rapidly expanding populations.

Until the Revolution the population of the American colonies remained relatively small, and in the 169 years between the settlement of Jamestown and the Battle of Lexington the frontier was pushed no more than two hundred miles inland from the Atlantic. North of Chesapeake Bay the colonists were chiefly mariners, merchants, and farmers who cleared a few acres of woodland and wrested a living for their families from the stony land. Due to greater arability of the soil, a warmer climate, and the introduction

[6]

of slavery, the colonists who settled south of Chesapeake Bay were chiefly agriculturists, many of them owning large plantations.

Here there was little need for public transportation, for there were few towns, each plantation was a community in itself, and travel between them was almost entirely on horseback. Cotton and tobacco, the export crops, were carted to one of the innumerable river branches and rafted downstream to the seaports. In the north the principal cities were situated on large rivers or the coast, and travel between them was almost entirely by boat. Stagecoaches were used to some extent between the inland cities and towns, but no mail contracts were awarded as a means of furnishing Government subsidy, and neither the British type of stagecoach nor style of driving were found to be practicable.

In 1775 Daniel Boone blazed the Wilderness Road from Virginia across the Allegheny Mountains to Kentucky and settled Boonesboro, near present Lexington. Soon afterward, pioneers from Massachusetts pushed westward and settled on the headwaters of the Susquehanna River in northeastern Pennsylvania. During the next decade they were followed by other frontiersmen who pushed still farther westward through New York and Pennsylvania to settle on the shores of Lake Erie.

These early pioneers to the western side of the Appalachians were hunters and trappers. Their westward surge was greatly

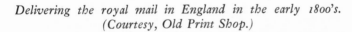

Delivering the royal mail in England in the early 1800's.
(Courtesy, Old Print Shop.)

stimulated by the Louisiana Purchase of 1803 and by the return of Lewis and Clark from the Columbia River with news that there was a fabulous wealth of furs in the Rocky Mountains. Although the westward migration was slowed by the War of 1812, St. Louis had become the fur capital of the United States by 1820. That same year the first stage line reached St. Louis from the East. It, however, did not offer through stagecoach travel from the Atlantic Coast, but carried passengers and express over the most direct route that could be traveled by a combination of coaches and riverboats.

The Great Lakes, the abundance of navigable rivers, and the construction of canals were a deterrent to stagecoaching during the westward expansion period following the Revolution, and the canals had scarcely been completed before the clanging of railroad bells tolled the death knell of stagecoaching east of the Mississippi.

It was far less costly to transport freight by water than to haul it overland, but for vessels from Boston, New York, or Philadelphia to reach the fertile region west of the Appalachians they had to make a voyage of more than three thousand miles: down the East Coast, through the Straits of Florida, the Gulf of Mexico, and up the winding Mississippi and Ohio rivers. To provide a direct waterway between the Atlantic and the region then known as The West, the Erie Canal was completed in 1825, connecting the Hudson River with the Great Lakes. With the assurance of cheap transportation for their crops, farmers by the hundreds of thousands poured into Ohio, Michigan, Indiana, and Illinois. Chicago, a little frontier fur-trading post in 1825, grew so rapidly that it was incorporated as a city in 1833.

The Erie Canal had barely been opened before work was started on a canal to connect the Delaware and Hudson rivers, and to complete the construction in 1829 the builders imported two steam locomotives from England. One of them, the *Stourbridge Lion*, was the first locomotive to run on any American railroad. Thereafter the advancement of railroading in this country was little short of explosive. Within ten years there were nearly forty separate railroads operating in the United States.

In 1836 Narcissa Whitman became the first white woman ever to cross the Rocky Mountains, and her missionary husband, Marcus, succeeded in the Herculean task of taking a wagon over the Oregon Trail as far as the Snake River in southern Idaho. But by that time the Baltimore & Ohio Railroad had been operating trains on regular schedules for two or three years. In making their historic trek of nearly two thousand miles through a wilderness known only to beaver trappers and often hostile Indians, the Whitmans were unharmed, but that same fall a mother and her child were killed in a train wreck on the Columbia Railroad in Ohio. And before a passable wagon road had been opened between Independence, Missouri, and Portland, Oregon, a railroad had been built to within a hundred and fifty miles of Chicago.

By 1840 the days of the stagecoach were rapidly drawing to a close in the East and Midwest. But a decade later the golden era of stagecoaching dawned in the West, making it possible within a single generation to settle and develop the natural resources of the vast region lying between the Mississippi Valley and the Pacific Ocean.

On February 2, 1848, the Mexican War was brought to a close by the Treaty of Guadalupe Hidalgo, ceding to the United States all of present California, Utah, and Nevada, most of Arizona and New Mexico, and the portions of Colorado and Wyoming lying west of the Continental Divide. But, unknown to the signers, gold had been discovered two weeks previously in the foothills of the Sierra Nevada mountains, about a hundred miles northeast of San Francisco Bay. It was fall before news of the California gold discovery reached the East Coast, and a winter crossing of the Rockies was at that time considered impossible, but in the early spring of 1849 thousands of gold rushers stampeded westward. The more practical of them joined together and made up wagon trains, while the impractical set off for the frontier by train, canal boat, or any kind of public transportation on which they could get aboard.

Among these argonauts were men who had been stage-line operators before being driven out of business by the rapidly expanding railroads. It is not surprising that some of them believed they saw an opportunity to regain their fortunes when they reached St. Louis, for there was no public transportation beyond that point. Knowing little or nothing about the country west of the Mississippi, they formed stage-line companies, gathered whatever vehicles, harness, and horses or mules they could get hold of, and advertised for passengers to California.

Although there were few if any coaches among the vehicles and no means of securing fresh teams west of St. Louis, most of the firms advertised impossibly fast stagecoach transportation. Early in May 1849 the Pioneer Line advertised in the St. Louis papers that its fast coaches would make the twenty-five-hundred-mile run to the California diggings in seventy days, at a fare of $200. There were plenty of would-be argonauts who in their eagerness to reach the gold fields rushed to buy tickets, and on May 8 a procession of Pioneer Line vehicles set out westward along the swampy Missouri River valley.

The following, taken from a letter to the publishers of the *St. Louis Republican,* gives a good description of the futile first attempts at transcontinental passenger transportation:

FORT KEARNY, INDIAN TERRITORY, June 10, 1849.
Dear Sirs: The Pioneer line of *fast* coaches reached here on the 8th, advertised to go through in 70 or 100 days, I forget which—the end of one month finds them about 300 miles on the road. The passengers were loud in denouncing all *fast* lines and the Pioneer Line in particular. A strong feeling of discontent prevails throughout the entire company ... . and the chances are thoroughly in favor of a general explosion. The devil himself would find it difficult to give satisfaction to an incongruous crowd of 120 persons, drawn from all parts of the world and thrown together for the first time as is the case on the Pioneer Line. There are to be found lawyers, doctors, divines, gentlemen of leisure, clerks, speculators, &c. &c. tumbled in together and obliged to stand guard, cook victuals, bring wood and water, wash dishes, and haul wagons out of mud holes.

The failure of stage lines in their attempt to transport forty-niners proved beyond doubt that successful passenger transportation across the vast uninhabited region west of the Missouri River could not be carried on without way stations at frequent intervals, a reasonable semblance of roads, and Government subsidy in the form of mail contracts or otherwise.

But California presented a unique situation in 1849, and public transportation required no Government assistance. Men who had struck rich panning were spending gold dust as freely as if it were sand, and the Johnny-come-lately would pay outrageous fares for fast transportation in hope of getting to the diggings before all the good claims were gone. As a result, stagecoaching leaped twenty-five hundred miles westward at a single bound.

Until outmoded by railroad and motor vehicle transportation at the close of the century, stagecoaches sped over the primitive roads of the western prairies, deserts, and mountains, drawn by hustling four- or six-horse teams, and driven by the most skillful reinsmen the world has ever known. This, the last long-distance equine transportation system, was, like the first, brought into being primarily to serve the needs of miners and carry the wealth taken from the mines. The golden era of stagecoaching in America was strictly a thing of the West, but the glorious heights it attained could not have been reached without the craftsmanship, ingenuity, and creative genius of New England Yankees.

2

Yankee Ingenuity

A LARGE PART of New England is a terminal moraine laced by forested mountains and strewn with great boulders left by melting glaciers as the Ice Age receded northward. When in the mid-1700's good farm land became scarce along the coast, frontiersmen pushed inland, following the rivers that flowed down from the mountains and clearing farmland in the fertile valleys. Their roads were simply wheel ruts twisting snakelike around swamps and boulders and straddling the stumps of trees that had been felled to open a passage through the woods.

The English stagecoach, although ponderous and heavy, was not strong enough to withstand the punishment of such roads, and Yankee passengers were unwilling to stand the punishment inflicted by the steel springs upon which English stagecoaches were mounted. If they were strong enough to support a fully loaded coach, they afforded no flexibility when it was lightly loaded, so the vehicle might as well have been springless. Springs that provided flexibility for a full load on relatively smooth road would permit the body to crash down upon the axles with bone-crushing force when a wheel dropped into a pothole. The lateral rigidity of the British springs caused the top-heavy coaches to capsize if a sharp curve were rounded at a brisk trot, and because they allowed no back-and-forth movement the passengers were often thrown from their seats when a wheel struck a stump or boulder. Furthermore, the steel springs of that time would often break under such stress, leaving passengers stranded in the wilderness.

Soon after the Declaration of Independence was signed, Yankee carriagemakers began experimenting with stagecoach designs. Their aim was to develop a vehicle that was light enough to be drawn rapidly without undue strain on the horses, rugged enough to withstand New England roads, flexible enough to spare passengers as much jolting as possible, and enclosed to protect them from inclement weather. It must have ample auxiliary space for carrying baggage, express, and mail. The driver's seat must be high enough to give him the greatest possible foot leverage on the brakes, unobstructed vision, and rein room for handling a four-, six-, or eight-horse team.

No one knows to whom the greatest credit belongs, but these ingenious carriagemakers designed and developed the egg-shaped body which, in conjunction with thoroughbraces, brought American stagecoach building to the forefront the world over, made long-distance travel endurable for passengers, and, together with New England reinsmanship, did more than anything else—with the possible exception of mail contracts—to promote the great stage-coaching era of the middle 1800's.

To avoid the shortcomings of steel springs, the Yankee coach builders suspended the bodies of their vehicles on leather thoroughbraces. A heavy undercarriage was mounted on stout axles in the same manner as for a freight wagon. At the four corners of this frame iron standards about a foot high were mounted and securely braced. To the top of the pair on each side was shackled a six- or eight-ply belt of thick bull-hide leather about four inches wide, forming a cradle upon which the body of the coach was suspended.

These carriagemakers had been brought up on farms and knew that a hen's egg stood on end would support more than a hundred times its own weight, so they were well aware that a thin shell had tremendous strength if properly curved. It is not surprising that in trying to attain the greatest possible strength with the least possible weight they designed coach bodies in the shape of an egg. But this shape when combined with the use of thoroughbraces had a much greater advantage than strength alone. By curving the sides of the body out, the center of gravity was placed squarely between the wheels, minimizing the chance of capsizing on sharp curves or when crossing unbridged streams. The long curve from front to back gave the body a rocking-chair action when resting on the thoroughbraces. Shackling the body to the leathers limited the amount of rock, but allowed enough play to absorb much of the shock when one of the wheels hit a stump, boulder, or hole—not only for the passengers and driver but for the horses as well, for it cushioned the blow transmitted to their shoulders through a jerk on the traces.

There was little actual spring to the thoroughbraces, but by suspending the body of the vehicle and keeping it from direct contact with the running gear, they gave it a motion somewhat akin to floating, minimizing jolts and shocks as much as possible. Strong and durable as the egg-shaped body was, it had numerous disadvantages. Except at the center, there was little head room inside, the seats at front and back were narrow, and nothing could be carried on the oval top. So that these coaches could carry baggage the builders hung a platform at the rear of the body. To the front end of the oval they attached a boxlike unit open at the front. The top served as the driver's seat, the somewhat extended bottom a footrest, and the space between provided a convenient carrying place for mail bags or express. Because of the shape of these early appendages the driver's seat on a stagecoach was invariably called "the box."

In 1813 Lewis Downing opened a little wheelwright shop in Concord, New Hampshire, and began making freight wagons. Although he was an expert craftsman and a perfectionist, none of the innovations which so vastly improved American stagecoaches during the first quarter of the nineteenth century can be credited to him, for until 1826 he produced only heavy wagons and a few two-wheeled chaises, never employing more than a dozen journeymen and apprentices. That year, possibly because his father-in-law was one of the best-known New England stage drivers, Downing decided to go into the manufacture of stagecoaches. As his assistant in the new venture he took in J. Stephen Abbot, a twenty-two-year-old journeyman chaise builder from Salem, Massachusetts. A year later Abbot had become Downing's partner.

There is good evidence that Abbot was an inventive genius, for soon after the Abbot-Downing partnership was formed the firm moved into the forefront of the industry as the most progressive builder of fine stagecoaches and specialty vehicles in America. Before midcentury, Concord coaches had become world famous, the envy of every stage driver in this country, and they were being exported to Europe, Canada, Australia, Africa, South America, and Mexico. There is little doubt that the firm's phenomenal success was attributable to Abbot's continual design improvements, together with Downing's uncompromising insistence upon perfection in craftsmanship and use of the finest materials obtainable.

In building their Concord coaches, Abbot and Downing adopted the thoroughbrace suspension and all the advantages of the egg-shaped body, but eliminated the disadvantages. To retain the rocker action and keep the center of gravity equidistant between the wheels, the lower third of the body was built in the form of a modified oval with curved panels at the sides but with the ends widened enough to allow seating for three passengers. The sides and ends were then continued upward with a very slight curve to the height of eight feet six inches above the ground.

The top, bulged only enough to insure quick drainage, was surrounded by a stout iron railing at the back and both sides. This provided space for carrying several hundred pounds of express that could be exposed to the weather and permitted three passengers to sit behind the driver if necessary. The platform at the back of the coach was enlarged, its outer end supported by straps attached to the corners of the roof, and the whole enclosed in black oiled leather to form a weatherproof boot for baggage, fragile express, or mail sacks. The driver's seat was raised to within two feet of the roof, allowing greater leverage to be applied on the brakes and permitting better control of a six- or eight-horse team. The seat was extended across the full width of the redesigned coach, providing space for two passengers beside the driver and doubling the size of the box beneath.

Until the middle of the nineteenth century bridges were scarce. Even the famous Boston Post Road was little more than a pair of deeply worn ruts winding through meadows and woodlands, skirting marshes and tide flats, plunging through unbridged stream beds, and detouring around stumps, boulders, and potholes. In spring and fall the roads were often a continuous bog of deep mud, in winter they were drifted high with snow or frozen into ridges of ice, and in summer the ankle-deep dust was sometimes hot enough to fry eggs. Such conditions were devastating to wooden wheels, for there are very few types of wood—and those only if thoroughly cured and seasoned—that do not swell in dampness and shrink in dryness.

In spring and fall it was not at all uncommon for the spokes and fellies (rim segments) to swell far beyond their normal size. Their circumference confined within an iron tire, they warped out of shape to such an extent that the wheel often left a track in the shape of a wriggling snake. If not soaked at frequent intervals during the hot, dry weather, the wood in such wheels would shrink proportionately, and ordinary iron tires expanded in the high temperature of summer road dust. No longer held tightly in place by the spokes and fellies, the tire was very likely to slip off. The wheel would then collapse, often upsetting the vehicle and dumping its load at the roadside.

Another form of failure, particularly in the wheels of early stagecoaches, was caused by centrifugal force. When a heavily loaded coach rounded a sharp curve at speed, the lateral thrust against the hubs of the outside wheels was tremendous. If the spokes and fellies were shrunk or warped even slightly, the wheel had a tendency to cave outward and collapse. In stagecoaching, such a failure was often disastrous, for it invariably caused the coach to capsize.

Whether it was the most elegant stagecoach or the lowliest mud wagon, every vehicle that rolled out of the Abbot-Downing shops was built to withstand the most severe road and weather conditions imaginable. The size, weight, cost, and elegance of bodies varied widely, but with only a few minor exceptions the running gear was the same regardless of model: the sturdiest, safest, and most dependable that could be produced by flawless design and craftsmanship from the finest materials available.

To save weight, iron—always hand forged from the best Norway stock—was used sparingly, mainly for axle bars, tires and hub collars, thoroughbrace standards, brake rods, fittings, etc. All the rest of the running gear was made from flawless straight-grained ash or white oak lumber, seasoned for at least three years and sun-warped in every direction until any tendency to warp had been completely worked out of it. During the firm's early years its only machines were a circular saw and a band saw, both operated by horse power. When in the late 1840's the demand for Concord vehicles had increased beyond the capacity of a single shop, the partners separated, took in their sons, and operated under the names of J. S. and E. A. Abbot and Company, and Lewis Downing and Sons. The most modern woodworking machinery on the market was then installed, but 90 per cent of the joinery was still done with simple carpentry tools in the hands of expert craftsmen.

The art of hand-tooled joinery reached its peak in the mid-1800's. There are few finer examples of its perfection than the Concord wheels that still survive after more than a century, some of them having endured fifty years or more of constant use over rough roads. The rear wheels of a Concord stagecoach stood exactly five feet one inch high, and those at the front three feet ten inches. The latter was the height at which the body was mounted on the thoroughbraces, and since the sides were curved well in at the bottom there was ample room for the low front wheels to fit beneath, allowing extremely sharp turns to be made.

Each spoke was shaped with a drawshave not only to the exact measurement but to the exact weight of every other spoke in that particular wheel, thus insuring perfect balance. It was then mortised into the hub so accurately that a man could not pull it out with his hands. The mortises were so cut that the spokes inclined slightly toward the outer end of the hub. This resulted in a wheel that was dished inward at the center to provide solid bracing against the thrust of centrifugal force. The fellies were band-sawed to an exact arc, width, and thickness, then balanced in weight and mortised accurately with hand tools to the spokes. When all the segments had been set, the wheel was an exact circle and perfectly balanced on the forged-iron axle bearing. So tightly were all the pieces joined that no bolts or screws were needed, and hammering and prying were required to take them apart.

When the joinery had been completed, a tire, very slightly smaller in circumference and three-eighths of an inch thick, was forged from a bar of Norway iron. After its diameter had been expanded by heating it to a cherry red, the tire was quickly slipped into place around the wooden rim and the wheel dipped into cold water before the wood had been more than singed. The quenching shrank the iron back to its normal size, binding the entire wheel together as tightly as if it had been squeezed in a powerful vise.

If kept properly painted these wheels were impervious to water, drought, extreme desert heat, fifty-below-zero cold, or stresses that would collapse wooden wheels made by any other manufacturer. One Concord coach was lost near shore in a shipwreck and salvaged after lying three months on the ocean floor. The running gear was put into service without rehabilitation of any kind and used regularly for more than fifty years over rough mountain roads.

Because of their rugged construction and the additional leverage afforded by the very high seat, the brakes on Concord coaches were extremely powerful. The beam, suspended from the frame of the running gear, was connected to a long wooden foot lever at the right-hand side of the driver's seat. With both hands free to control his team, the driver could apply enough pressure on the brake shoes to drag the rear wheels of a heavily loaded coach in descending the steepest hills.

The Concord stagecoach of the 1840's was designed for use along the eastern seaboard and over such roads as led westward to the Mississippi Valley. Lightness of body coupled with strength and elegance were in demand, and the Concord coach met the requirements admirably. The framework of the body was small-dimension, straight-grained white ash; each piece was steamed pliable, bent to the exact curve required, and then kiln dried until it was tough as rawhide and stronger than most iron of the time. Thin poplar panels were steamed, shaped and dried on templates, then hand tooled to fit snugly into the grooved framework, thus attaining the egg-shell ratio of strength for weight.

On each side there was a door with a glass window that opened by lowering the sash into a pocket between the panels. At either side of the door there was an unglazed window. These were fitted with leather curtains that covered the openings snugly against cold,

Arrival of a coach at an old stage station.

rain, or snow. If the weather was pleasant they were rolled up from
the outside and held in keeper straps at the window tops.

There were three leather-cushioned three-passenger seats in the
standard light Concord coach, those at the front and back facing
each other, and the one in the center facing forward. The end
seats had deeply padded back cushions, but if the three occupants
were also deeply padded they became very close traveling com-
panions, for there was barely fifteen inches of seat space apiece.
The middle seat was a three-section bench, the center segment
bolted solidly to the floor and an extension hinged to each end.
These folded up to provide passageway between the doors and
rear seat. The backrest was a broad leather belt suspended on
straps from the ceiling, its ends attached by hooks to the door
frame. Passengers on this seat were allowed a bit more hip room
than the others, but if one of them faced a long-legged traveler on
the front seat they had to interlock knees.

From the earliest days of stagecoaching, the drivers, particularly the more colorful and dashing, were regarded by Americans
with much the same idolatry as that of the Romans for their chariot
racers. Unless the weather was bad, the most coveted seats on a

Concord coach were the two beside the driver. Bestowing this honor was his jealously guarded prerogative, and heaven help the pushy passenger who tried to take one of those seats without invitation.

If a judge, congressman, or other important man were among the passengers, he was likely to be awarded the outside seat. But if there was a young, charming, and unattached lady passenger, the driver was certain to assign her the seat next to himself, and getting her up to it was no small part of his prerogative. The seat was seven feet above the ground, and there were only three step plates leading up to it. The lowest was at the height of the front wheel hub, the next at the top of a thoroughbrace standard, and the third at the base of the box. To make the ascent, a lady in the voluminous skirts and petticoats of the mid-1800's required considerable helping, and the driver was never niggardly with his assistance.

When a Concord coach left the factory it was not only unequaled for durability, design, joinery, and smithing, but was a complete work of art. Multiple coats of paint had been applied, rubbed down with pumice, and covered with two coats of spar varnish, making every surface as smooth, hard, and highly polished as a fine mirror. The body was usually red, with an exquisite landscape painted on each door, and most of the paneling decorated with the ornate scrollwork of the time. The name of the purchaser was often lettered in gold leaf above the doors. If he carried packages for one of the express companies, its name might be lettered on both sides of the driver's box. Or if he had a mail contract the lettering might be U. S. MAIL. The steps and top railing were shiny black, the running gear usually yellow, with fine red lines on the wheel spokes. At each side of the coach a square brass-and-glass candle lamp was mounted, more for ornament than light.

The light Concord stagecoach of the 1840's weighed about twenty-five hundred pounds and sold f.o.b. factory for about $1200. These coaches were the envy of every stage driver, but they were too expensive for many operators and impractical for other than predominantly passenger transportation. To meet the situation, Abbot and Downing built vehicles called "celerity" and "mud" wagons, far less elegant and expensive than a Concord coach, but equal to it in durability and workmanship. In both vehicles the body was cradled on thoroughbraces above the same basic running gear as the coaches, but the suspension was somewhat different. Mud wagons were designed, as the name implied, for use in deep mud or over extremely rough roads, and celerity wagons were for fast runs with mail and express on lines where passengers were few. Appearance and comfort were therefore secondary to utility, stability, and dispensing with every unnecessary pound of dead weight.

In order to lower the center of gravity, the thoroughbraces were not suspended from standards. Near each end the multiple bands of leather were looped over a low crossbar and the shackles were attached with adjustable eyebolts at the extreme ends of the under-carriage. The body was flat-bottomed and attached to an iron frame that looked like a low sled with the runners curved up two or three inches at front and back. The frame sat atop the thorough-braces and was shackled securely to them at both ends. This con-struction, though far less comfortable for passengers, allowed enough floating action to cushion road shocks for the teams and greatly increased stability.

Instead of being curved, the lower sides of the wagon bodies flared out at an angle; the front and back rose straight from the floor. The driver's seat was mounted high on the front, supported by wooden side panels, and had a footrest that extended well out above the tails of the wheel team, providing a large front boot for carrying mail or express. At the back there was a canvas-covered baggage boot nearly as large as that on a light coach.

Both wagons were equipped with a pair of upholstered seats facing each other from front and back, and provided space for six not-too-stout passengers. There were no doors or windows, but the side openings were relatively the same as those in the Concord coach. In bad weather they were covered by canvas cur-tains that were carried rolled and strapped at the top of each open-ing. The roofs were also of canvas, stretched tightly over ash bows. The two vehicles were very much alike, except that ruggedness was stressed more in the mud wagon and lightness in the celerity wagon. Each sold for $500 f.o.b. Concord.

During the half century or more that Yankee craftsmen were evolving the clumsy, rigid British mail coach into the graceful, flexible Concord coach, Yankee reinsmen were evolving an art equally graceful and flexible from the famed and formalized four-in-hand driving taught by the British school of staging.

When New England pioneers pushed westward into the rugged hills of New Hampshire and Vermont their greatest need was for a horse strong enough to pull stumps and a plow, but with speed enough to get over the roads rapidly in case of emergency. Nature soon filled their need exactly by producing a mutant, a horse like no other before him, and with such marvelous prepotency that his characteristics were transmitted to offspring so distant as to carry

[19]

only one thirty-second of his blood. The colt, foaled by a driving mare belonging to a schoolteacher named Justin Morgan, was given his owner's name and became the sole foundation progenitor of the Morgan breed of horses. Although short-legged and weighing less than a thousand pounds, he could outpull any other horse on the frontier and outwalk, outtrot, and outrun any horse ever matched against him.

In 1788, Messenger, the Thoroughbred to which all American record-holding trotters and pacers trace ancestry, was imported to New York from England. When Justin Morgan repeatedly beat Messenger's fastest offspring, a rivalry sprang up between the New York and New England horsemen that resulted in the world's fastest harness horses and most skillful reinsmen.

The skill of New England drivers was refined by bigotry in the churches. Horse racing was condemned as a sin, but the devout could not keep two men with fast Morgan carriage horses from matching one against the other. To save face, the parsons amended their definition of sin to exclude trotting and pacing matches that were not run on racetracks and on which there was no wagering. They were careful to look the other way if a man put his hand in his pocket, but got antiracetrack laws passed in all the New England states.

Without racetracks, the New England horsemen were obliged to course their fast Morgan trotters over tortuous country roads in training them for races against Messenger's offspring on New York tracks. In doing so they developed extraordinary horsemanship, but there were a few men who stood out head and shoulders above the others. These were steady-nerved, determined, confident men who had the ability to transmit to a horse their slightest desire through the touch of their hands on the "ribbons" and to inspire a response to the very limit of the animal's ability. One generation of New England reinsmen followed another in family lines, fathers teaching their sons the art of reinsmanship from early boyhood.

When stagecoaches came into use in New England these reinsmen were experienced only in driving single horses or pairs, but knowing that multiple-span driving had been developed into a formal science in England, they sent for the manual of rules and regulations prepared by the British school of staging. It stressed trimness and snugness and had been developed on the theory of attaining the greatest possible controllability through unity. In a six-horse-hitch the wheelers (back span) were harnessed snugly to the rigid coach pole that controlled the turn of the front wheels.

The tugs and the breast-straps that attached the collars to the neck yoke at the end of the pole were adjusted carefully to eliminate any untidy slackness.

This method of hitching held the pole firmly centered between the wheelers, allowing the front wheels to make no more than the slightest deviation from a straight line unless the horses turned. A swing pole, its purpose to hold up the doubletrees of the lead team, was attached by means of a stout hook to the end of the rigid pole, and the middle (swing) team was harnessed to it with no slackness in breast-straps or traces. The reins were in turn held snugly by the driver so there would be equal pressure on the bits of all six horses and they would be reined as a single unit.

Just as Yankee wheelwrights found the ponderous British mail coach with its stiff steel springs too heavy and rigid for efficient use on American roads, Yankee reinsmen found the British four-in-hand methods of hitching and driving multiple-span teams entirely too inflexible for effective handling of spirited horses on the tortuous New England roads. But their greatest objection was to the punishment it inflicted upon the horses.

When the glaciers melted they not only strewed the surface of New England with great boulders but left buried beneath the surface billions of rocks that were roughly round and varied from the size of a football to that of a wash tub. The deep frosts of winter heaved these rocks upward and the spring thaws settled gravel and dirt under them, each year pushing them nearer the surface or above it. As a result, many New England roads were studded with protruding rock domes. When a front wheel hit one of these, stopping its progress momentarily, the end of the wagon pole was wrenched violently to one side because the axle being pivoted at the center. If the wheel and swing teams were hitched snugly to the poles they could be thrown off stride when a wheel hit a large rock. But if the rock were small the sidewise jerk was only enough to cause the breast-straps to twist the collars on the horses' shoulders and necks. With a hundred or more small rocks to the mile, it was not long before the twisting collars wore off patches of hide.

Not only were snugly hitched horses restricted in their action but, in order to stay in the roadway, the wheelers had to brace themselves against the side pull of the team ahead whenever rounding a bend; and on the narrow, twisting New England roads they wasted a great deal of energy. Then too, under the British four-in-hand method of hitching and driving, all six horses were reined as a unit, minimizing the driver's control of individual spans.

To New England's finest reinsmen, who were masters at transmitting their will to a horse through a touch on the reins so slight as to be almost imperceptible, the British four-in-hand method was entirely unacceptable, so they devised and perfected a method as flexible, graceful, and uniquely American as the Concord coach. And the foundation on which the method was built was the same as that on which the body of the Concord coach rode: the thoroughbrace suspension.

No man can have the empathy with horses that enables him to draw out their finest qualities unless he has sufficient admiration and affection for them that his first thought is to save them unnecessary hardship. The first aim of the Yankee reinsmen was to rid their horses of the punishment inflicted by the British system. The second was to devise a method by which each span could be reined entirely independent of any other with no drag on the horses' mouths or the driver's arms and with a touch barely strong enough to transmit his will. To accomplish this the wheel and swing teams had to be hitched loosely to the poles; but, of course, the wheels of the vehicle had to be kept on the narrow roadway, and only the action of thoroughbraces made this possible with a loosely hitched team.

Unless the pole was held in position by the horses, a heavy vehicle with steel springs would turn off a narrow road when a front wheel struck an obstacle. Also, if the obstacle was of any appreciable size there would be a hard jerk on the horses' shoulders when the forward motion of the wheel was suddenly stopped. If, however, the body of the vehicle was mounted on thoroughbraces there would be neither jerk nor turn, because of inertia: when the forward motion of the wheel was retarded, the body rocked forward on the thoroughbraces in a straight line, thus lifting the wheel over the obstruction and keeping the vehicle from swerving aside.

Although the pole flailed back and forth a few inches each time a front wheel struck a rock, there was no need for the horses to hold it rigid in order to keep the vehicle on its proper course. There was therefore no need for neck yokes, so the New England stagecoach drivers discarded them, lengthened the breast-straps, and buckled them directly to a ring at the tip of the pole, allowing plenty of slack. This allowed the end of the pole to flail as much as a foot from side to side without putting the slightest twist or jerk on the horses' collars. It also provided enough slack in the traces to cushion ordinary road shocks, give the horses freedom of action, and permit individual reining of each span.

The New Englanders held the reins for a six-horse-hitch in the conventional manner, those for the leaders between the fore and middle fingers of each hand, those for the swing team between the middle and third fingers, and those for the wheelers between the third and little fingers. The ends of the "off" or right-hand reins were allowed to hang down from the heel of the right hand, but the ends of the "near" reins were looped up over the left thumb before being allowed to hang. The whip was grasped between the thumb and forefinger of the right hand, with the butt held securely by the heel of the thumb. But from there on the Yankee method of rein handling differed entirely from the British.

The Yankee method of reining a six-horse-hitch was a combination of finger and brake manipulations. The artistry, skill, finger dexterity, and practice necessary to a top-flight reinsman was about equal to that required by a concert pianist, and very much akin to it. Each rein was manipulated by "climbing" it—gathering it in by alternately drawing with the finger on each side of it—and by separating the fingers just enough to let it slip out the desired amount.

It is not too difficult for a novice to "climb" a rein between the middle and fore fingers of his right hand, or to let it slip back. But try to climb one between the third and little fingers of your left hand while holding another stationary between the third and middle fingers and at the same time letting still another slip an exact distance between the middle and fore fingers. The New England reinsman who was considered worthy of the name had to be able to manipulate all six reins simultaneously, each one absolutely independent of all others, and with the same dexterity and apparent effortlessness with which a great pianist plays a Bach concerto.

A passenger sitting beside him might almost believe that he was actually telegraphing his instructions to the horses through the reins, for they hung a little slack, and his hands rested, seemingly motionless, across his knees. But although seldom seen by the passenger or felt by the horses' mouths, the fingers beneath those upturned knuckles were moving as the need arose, the tendons and muscles that controlled them as flexible as silk threads and as strong as spring steel. At a flick of his wrist the tip of the whip lash might flick out and snap with a report like a pistol shot above the back of a loafing lead horse, but there was no tightening or loosening of the lines held in the whip hand. If the whip touched a horse it was never in punishment; it was only a light sting to get his mind back on his business.

Although a heavily loaded coach might require six stout horses to pull it up a steep hill at a slow walk, it rolled along easily where the going was fairly level and the roadway reasonably hard packed. If the teams were hitched to the poles in the loose Yankee fashion, the horses would trot along freely at such times, tugs a bit slack and singletrees swinging. The New England reinsmen took advantage of this slack in perfecting the technique of their art.

For instance, with the horses swinging along a narrow road at a brisk trot, the coach might be approaching an equally narrow crossroad onto which the driver wished to make a left-hand turn. With the teams at a trot, all the reining had to be done within a fraction of a second if the coach were to be kept in the narrow roadways. The lead span had to continue straight ahead until it was past the center of the intersection before starting its turn. Otherwise the side pull against the end of the swing-pole would turn the second span too soon unless it were reined firmly. Then while the lead span was being turned to the left, the swing span had to be held straight ahead by reining slightly to the right until it too had passed the center of the intersection. And as the swing span was being reined into the turn the wheelers had to be reined to the right, for if they were allowed to turn too soon the coach would cut the corner, always with the chance of an upset.

As much as a hundred yards before reaching the corner the driver would begin working his fingers, adjusting each rein in relation to the others exactly as it should be at the moment of starting the turn. But in the adjusting he would take up so little of the slack that a passenger watching him intently would never notice it, and no horse would feel the slightest pull on a bit. Casually, the reinsman would reach his right foot out and rest it on the pedal of the brake shaft. Then, at the exact moment the heads of the lead span reached the center of the intersection, the foot would press down lightly. Instantly the ears of every horse in the team would spring to attention in anticipation of the reining that always followed the sound of a sliding brake beam.

The amount of pressure put on the brakes slowed the coach barely enough to take the slack out of the traces. It also took the slack out of the reins, drawing them up just enough to put a pull on the bits that was no stronger than could have been exerted with a cotton thread. At the moment their tails reached the middle of the crossroad the left-hand corners of the lead span's mouths received the turn signal. At the same time the swing and wheeler spans were feeling a signal at each corner of their mouths, but the one to the right was slightly stronger, holding each span straight ahead until the right-hand rein was permitted to slip an inch or two through the driver's fingers. As a result, the coach swung smoothly around the corner without a wheel leaving the ruts, and with a minimum loss of momentum. The corner was no sooner turned than the brake was released, slackening the tugs and reins, and the horses again picked up the spanking rhythm of their trot.

Many a passenger sitting beside the driver on such a turn gave all the credit to the intelligence of the horses. Most of the others were convinced that the horses had been over the road so often that they made the turn from habit and that its machinelike precision was due to instinct. Few passengers would believe that the driver had anything to do with it, for throughout the entire maneuver he had sat with both hands resting seemingly motionless across his knees. The closest possible scrutiny would not have enabled them to see the slight separation of fingers that permitted a rein to slip a trifle when pressure on it was no longer needed.

The fine New England reinsmen invariably used the brake in conjunction with reining, for by this method they could control each span in a six-horse team with absolute independence of other spans. And to a very great extent they could control each horse as independently as if driving only him.

When horses are in a pull hard enough to keep their traces tightly drawn they are almost always moving at a walk, so reining is seldom needed. If it is required there is plenty of time for even the most inept driver to adjust the lines. In such pulls the true reinsman always let out additional slack, then took it in again as soon as the pull was completed, so that the feel of the bit in each horse's mouth would always be the same unless he was intentionally being reined. When a team was being brought to a stop the pressure on the lines was slightly, though not much, firmer than in other reining, and was applied equally on all six horses. But the driver made no move with his hands; he simply hit the brake a little harder, to let the team know what was expected of it.

There were several reasons for this light-touch method of driving. One was that a horse's mouth, like a man's hand, becomes calloused by hard use. If more than light pressure is kept on it for any extended length of time it becomes insensitive to any moderate pull on the bit, and the horse is said to be "cold mouthed." A cold-mouthed horse is not only difficult to control but wastes a great deal of his and his driver's energy by "boring" against the pull of the reins.

By the deftness of their hands and their method of driving, the

New England reinsmen kept the mouths of their horses so "sweet," as it was called, that the animals would instantly answer a touch on the lines that was scarcely more than a hint. With a six-horse team hitched so loosely as to frighten a British stage driver and with the horses trotting at a fast clip, an expert reinsman could swerve the wheels of a Concord coach so accurately as to miss a stone in the roadway with no more than a couple of inches to spare. But he seldom bothered to swerve around one unless it was large enough that it might cause an accident. The action of the thoroughbraces would lift the wheel over and spare the horses any jerk or strain, and passengers in those days were used to a little jolting.

This apparent disregard for the comfort of passengers was, however, a precaution for their safety. Horses not only can see better in the dark than men can but have an instinct that enables them to follow, even in pitch blackness or a blinding blizzard, a trail or road with which they are familiar. By reining around inconsequential obstacles a driver would accustom his team to depending upon

On to the West—Concord coaches carrying passengers, baggage, and mail. (Courtesy, Union Pacific Railroad Museum Collection.)

him at all times for guidance, and such a team would be very likely to run off the road some black or fogbound night when the driver couldn't see to guide them.

But there was still another reason for loose hitching and loose reining. Horses are nervous, high-strung, sensitive creatures, and like humans they become fatigued far more quickly under nagging and undue restraint than otherwise. Although horse for horse they might be inferior in size and quality, a loosely hitched team in the hands of a master reinsman could always outrun and outlast a close-hitched team with a rough-handed driver, regardless of how skilled he might be otherwise.

Some of the finest New England reinsmen never gave a team verbal commands of any kind, and no driver worthy of the name yelled or shouted at his horses. But some of the most skilled and colorful of the old-time reinsmen kept up a fairly constant chatter in the tight spots, singing out to one horse or another by name—urging him on, encouraging or steadying him, as the need might be. Every stage horse knew his own name, and although he couldn't understand English he could and did understand every shade of meaning in the driver's tone. Other drivers were amazingly skilled whipsmen, and often inordinately vain of their accomplishment. These men never touched a horse with the lash of a whip, although they might let the shaft drop lightly on a loafing wheeler's back, but when a team was in a spirited run the rawhide thongs at the end of the lash would be kept popping like firecrackers. Much of this chatter and whip cracking had a double purpose, for it entertained the passengers and steadied their nerves as much as it steadied and encouraged the horses.

Reinmanship was an honored art in early New England, for only through years of practice could all the reining techniques be learned and the necessary finger dexterity be acquired. Fathers spared no effort in coaching sons who showed an aptitude for it, and from the age of seven or eight the boy devoted several hours a day to practice at a reining rig.

The rig was a rather simple affair. A seat with an adjustable footrest and a brake shaft at the right-hand side—very much like the "box" on a Concord coach—was attached to a barn wall about five feet above the floor. About ten or twelve feet in front of it was the "ribbon rack." This was a frame made of two-by-fours, about three feet high and five feet long, hinged to the floor and so rigged that the top would rock away from the "driver" when pressure was put on the brake shaft, then spring back when the pressure was removed.

Attached to the top crossbar were six "horses," three at either side. These were pieces of hardwood lath approximately eighteen inches long standing in an upright position against the far side of the bar and hinged to the top of it so that about six inches projected above. A rein was attached to the upper end of each lath and a weight to the lower end, its heft varying with the age and strength of the boy.

For a year or so the little fellow practiced with only two light reins attached to very lightly weighted horses. He was first taught to climb a "ribbon" between the fore and middle fingers of either hand, tipping the horse's head forward and lifting the weight to any desired height, then letting the rein slip back through the fingers with sufficient control that there was no "slap" when the lath came to rest against the back of the bar. When he became adept with one rein he would learn to climb a pair simultaneously. After becoming dexterous enough so that his fingers would perform the manipulation without conscious thought he was taught to hold one rein or let it slip exactly the amount desired while climbing the other at varying rates of speed.

A second year of practice was usually required to educate the other fingers, making it possible for the boy to manipulate a pair of reins with equal dexterity regardless of which two fingers they were held between. He was then allowed to practice with four reins, and at least another year was needed to learn the technique of manipulating each one with absolute precision and entire independence of every other one. Not until a boy had mastered the art with four reins was he allowed to practice with six. Then, as he became proficient with the full complement, the heft of the weights on the horses was gradually increased to build up the strength of his fingers, wrists, and arms.

During the final year of a boy's training—usually when he was in his middle teens—he was taught the artistry of loose-rein driving, schooled in it on a Concord coach with a spirited six-horse hitch, and his handling of the whip was perfected. When his father at last considered him to be a thoroughly accomplished reinsman, he usually presented the boy with a handsome whip, handmade to exact specifications and perfectly balanced, the handle often inlaid with silver. A stage driver's whip, although never used for punishing his horses, was the symbol of his profession, and often his most cherished personal possession. For that reason a top-flight stagecoach driver was generally called a "whip," although in the West he was called a jehu if he was noted for particularly fast driving.

3

Dawn of the Golden Era

AN ANNOUNCEMENT of what was probably the first "stage line" west of the Missouri River appeared in the *Oregon Spectator* of October 29, 1846:

TELEGRAPH LINE
Eight Ox Power

The subscriber begs leave to announce to the public that he proposes to run an express—rain or no rain—mud or no mud—load or no load—*but not without pay*—from Oregon and Linn Cities to Tuality Plains during the ensuing season—leaving the two former places on Mondays and Thursdays, and the Plains on Wednesdays and Saturdays. The "cars" will be covered and every accommodation extended to passengers. For freight or passage, apply to the subscriber, proprietor and engineer, at Linn City.

Oct. 29, 1846   S. H. L. MEEK

John Whistman is generally credited with operating the first stage line in California and Alexander Todd with being the first expressman, but the following advertisement appeared in the San Francisco *Alta California* in June 1849.

MAURISON & CO'S EXPRESS AND MAIL LINE. *For the transportation of Passengers and Baggage from Stockton to the Stanislaus Mines.* Through in Twelve Hours!—The undersigned respectfully inform the public that they have established a line of Stages between Stockton and the Stanislaus Mines, for the accommodation of passengers and baggage.

A STAGE will leave Stockton every other day for the mines, at 4 o'clock, A.M., and arrive at the other end of the route in 12 hours. Returning, a Stage will leave the mines at the same hour on the intermediate days, and arrive at Stockton at 4 o'clock, P.M.

MAURISON & Co. Stockton, June 25, 1849.

[29]

Since the first stagecoach to reach California would not arrive for another year, the stage referred to in the ad was probably a wagon. And since the distance from Stockton to the Stanislaus mining camps was little more than forty-five miles and a round trip would require two days, it is probable that there was only one wagon, that Maurison was the driver, and that the "& Co." was window trimming.

Alexander Todd arrived in San Francisco a few days after Maurison's ad appeared. He went directly to the diggings but could not endure wading in ice-cold streams to pan gold dust. After a month of luckless panning he quit the sand bars and set about establishing a mail service for the miners. There was no Government mail service to the mining towns, and many of the men were homesick and sure there were letters for them at the San Francisco Post Office, but to inquire for them they would have to make a round trip of more than two hundred miles.

Todd went from camp to camp along the southern end of the Mother Lode, listing the names of miners who wanted him to inquire for their mail and bring it to them. He charged them a dollar apiece for listing their names and an ounce of gold dust for each letter he brought them. When he brought out the first batch of mail the merchants and more successful miners asked him to take back their gold dust for deposit in San Francisco banks, since there were no banking facilities nearer. For this service he charged 5 per cent of the dust entrusted to him. Within a few weeks he had the names of more than two thousand miners on his list, and on one trip to San Francisco he carried—in a butter firkin that he took down the San Joaquin River and across San Francisco Bay in a rowboat—gold dust worth more than $200,000. He went on to become California's most successful individual expressman.

In late August or early September 1849 John Whistman began operating a stage line between San Francisco and San Jose over El Camino Real—The Royal Highway.

For three-quarters of a century El Camino Real, extending from San Diego to San Francisco along the route that is now U.S. Highway 101, had been the main artery of travel in California. But for all its impressive name, it was nothing more than a bridle and pack-animal trail, for the Spaniards and Mexicans had used no wheeled vehicles in California. Nor was it a single trail, but a skein of trails. During the rainless summers, travelers and pack-train drivers avoided rugged creek gorges among the hills by following trails through the valleys, and those that skirted the margin of the tide flats along San Francisco Bay. But in the rainy season, when the low

Sutter's Mill, site of first gold discovery in California. (From Marvels of the New West, *William M. Thayer.)*

lands became knee-deep bogs of sticky mud, trails along the lower reaches of the hillsides were used.

Monterey had been the Spanish and Mexican capital of California, but following the Mexican war—and much squabbling among the American citizens of the new territory—San Jose was chosen as the territorial capital. The town became even more important during the gold rush, as it was on the direct land route from San Francisco to the diggings. By the summer of 1849 El

Camino Real had been widened into a wagon road from San Francisco to San Jose, but the widening amounted only to wearing a pair of wheel ruts along the trails that were not too rugged or boggy to prohibit the passage of vehicles. The first three miles out of San Francisco the ruts passed through a shifting sea of loose sand. It was under these conditions that John Whistman started operating his stage line.

There are few authentic records of the very early stagecoaching in California, but fortunately Henry C. Ward, one of Whistman's drivers, later wrote a few pages of reminiscence. They have been preserved and are in the Bradford Collection in Stanford University Library under the title "Staging in Central California, as Related by Henry Ward." Excerpts from it are quoted here—although not always in the sequence written—for it is believed that Ward's is the best eyewitness report in existence of the difficulties encountered by the early stage-line operator in the West. It is probably because of Ward's opening sentence that Whistman is usually credited with being the first California stageman.

The first Stageing in this part of California was done by John Whistman and was run between San Francisco and San Jose in the fall of 1849. . . . The stock was Mules and Mustangs and badly cared for—turned out to grass for feed, and an open coral for stable. Any kind of a spring waggon that was large enough was a stage, [among other vehicles] Whistman had an old French omnibus. The first drivers were Tom Calloway, Dawson Calvin & Ward. Time about 9 hours—Not regular. Passenger [fare] was $32.00 or two oz gold dust.

[Whistman] was compelled to haul off after the first rain as there was No settled roads in the country. The stock was then put on from San Jose to Alviso (the head of San Francisco bay distance 8 miles); passengers went from there to San Francisco by boats.

Early in the spring of 1850 Whistman stocked the San Francisco road again and Ackley and Morrison [Maurison, who started the Stockton-Stanislaus line] put on an opposition Stage. The drivers were Stanley and Morrison. In the summer of 1850 Waren Hall, William Hall, and J B Crandall, all from the National road runing betwene (Very Cruz and the City of Mexico), bought the Whistman Stageing, and soon after contracted to carry the Mail daily to San Jose and try weekly to Monterey. . . . Before Hall & Crandalls time the st[a]geing was poor.

Hall & Crandall commenced improving the stock and establish stations and put feed on the road. Hay and Grain from Austraila (plenty of wild oats but Nothing to cut them with). They put four teams on each side. Two six horse teams out of San Francisco and two out of San Jose and four five Mule teams on the Middle route.

The first thourbrace stage wagons were brought across the plaines by William Beeks in 1850 and bought by Hall and Crandall with twenty head of big emigrant horses. The waggons were fourteen passenger Mud waggons [not Abbot-Downing] seating twelve passengers inside and two outside with the driver. Dickey seats were put on back and front Makeing seats for twenty passengers. The first drivers (other than the proprietors) was Jhon Dillon and Jhon Jenkins. Dillon was from Mexico.

Some of the very best stage drivers displaced by the building of railroads in New England had been driving in Mexico for several years before the discovery of gold lured them to California. The reason for their being there was that Mexicans were inept reinsmen. They could handle six-horse teams only by mounting a driver on one animal in each pair, which tired it unduly. When Don Jose Saratuso contracted to carry the Mexican mail between Veracruz and Mexico City, he sent to the United States—probably to Concord—for coaches, harness, and the best stage drivers that could be found. At that time two dollars a day was considered good wages for a New England stage driver, but to get the best Don Jose offered a hundred dollars per month and all expenses. This, however, was barely more than chicken feed for a California driver in 1850, for Ward wrote:

Drivers salery on the San Jose and San Fran road was $300.00 per Month but that was a small part of their income as the perquesetes was big. There was No Mail or Express at the time [1849 and 1850] and drivers received pay for all letters & packages besides one per cent for all Money caried by them; letters left at the office 25 cts, if delivered

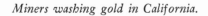

Miners washing gold in California.

[33]

$1.00; an erand Nt less than $1.00; passenger way fare $1.00 or less went to the driver. Passengers riding on the seat with the driver was supposed to treat the driver to drinks and cigars on the road. Drinks was free to drivers at all stations but it was seldom that driver drank on the road.

Ward was, no doubt, truthful in writing that drivers seldom drank on the road, but, if other writers of the time are to be believed, the drivers were few who passed up a free drink or two at the stations.

There are reported to have been hundreds of thousands of wild horses in California at the time of the Mexican War, but very few of them were of any value for stagecoaching. There were several reasons for this. The wild herds were descendants of the original stock brought from Spain by the early explorers and conquistadors—and some horses certainly were descended from mares brought to the West Indies by Columbus. Since the only vehicles used by the Spaniards in the New World were ox-drawn carretas and since mules were used as beasts of burden, all the horses brought to Mexico were saddle stock. In the temperate climate and lush pasturage of southern Mexico the horses multiplied rapidly, particularly so because the Spaniards preferred stallions for war horses and were opposed to castration.

As the number of horses increased beyond need they were allowed to run loose, and only the finest young stallions were caught and broken. This left the poorer ones to sire the colts, so the quality of the herds gradually degenerated, and with each generation the horses became wilder. Then too, horses have the ability to adapt to conditions more quickly than most other animals. In areas where feed is scarce, successive generations will steadily diminish in size. In the century it required for horses to migrate northward to semiarid Sonora (the source of the California stock) their average weight had diminished to no more than nine hundred pounds, and many of them were so wild as to be unbreakable.

In his reminiscences, Ward tells graphically of the way in which Hall & Crandall secured and converted the best of the wild mustangs into good stage-line horses.

There was not enough broke horses in the country . . . and they was compelled to use wild ones. At this time it was considered a disgrace by the Spanyards to use Mares for any thing but breeding. There were thousands of wild mares in the lower part of the State. The price from $4.00 to $6.00 per head; but as we were pressed for time and wanted onley the best we contracted with Don Juan Foster to give us the pick of all the wild Mares in the country and deliver them to us in Los Angelus for $20.00 per head.

John Forster was an Englishman and brother-in-law of California's former Mexican governor, Pio Pico. He was one of the largest foreign-born landowners in California, having acquired the lands which belonged to Mission San Juan Capistrano before secularization in addition to the mammouth Rancho de la Nacion near San Diego, and Trabuco near Los Angeles.

We tried to get Mares about six years old and weight about eleven hundred. . . . Foster delivered to us five hundred Mares and fourteen Stalions. In twenty days we had them on Hall & Crandalls ranch (Mountainview) and commenced to break them to harness. They had Never been lassoed by the Neck (ranchers lasso them by the forward feet and throw them as they are caught to brand and cut the hair from there tails & Manes), and when caught by the Neck Made a fight for life. They were coraled in the Morning, twenty or thierty were lassoed and tied down and the ballance turned out. Then a strong rope halter with a blind attached is put on and with about twenty feet of strong rope they are tied, a stake drove in the ground and they halterbreak themselves. After a few days at the stake they were harnessed; and—three wild Mares with [a] gentle or broke horse in the Near lead, with the off Mare straped to his hame ring—the Mare[s] was blindfolded and hitched to breaking waggon. When all was ready [we] raised this blind and let them go. They are frightened to Make them start, but when they find they can go they Make things lively. As soon as they learn to start they are put togather in four or six horse teams until they are used to the bit and being guided by lines. They [Hall & Crandall] then put on a line from San Jose to San Fran (other than the Mail) with six horse Mustang stock with two drivers on each coach and No stops betwene stations. They was kept at work in that way and by the Midd[l]e of June 300 or 400 was stage horses. They were generaly worked in six horse teams. . . . Some of the Mares were crippled and a few killed but those that was good stage horses Never forgot to leave a station in a run.

Ward's being careful to make a special note that half-broken mustangs were not used on coaches carrying mail is particularly interesting. A mail contract was the envy of every stage-line operator; since runaways and upsets were common when untamed mustangs were used, few operators would risk acquiring a bad reputation with the Post Office Department by losing a sack of United States mail. But passengers rode at their own risk, and in the early years of the gold rush the demand was for speed, not safety.

There is no record of other early California stage-line operators going to the expense of securing and training the best mustangs available. But there were few who did not use them, for these tough little broncos had endurance and speed far beyond that of

[35]

mules or most horses brought from the East by pioneers and gold rushers.

Ackley & Maurison's advertisement in the *Pacific News* leaves no doubt that they forced John Whistman to sell his decrepit line by reducing the fare and using fast mustangs with which they claimed to have reduced the running time by a third.

THE UNITED STATES MAIL line of Stages will, on and after this date leave the EMPIRE HOUSE, San Francisco, daily, (Sundays NOT excepted,) at 8 o'clock, A.M., for SAN JOSE. And from the Mansion House, San Jose, daily, at 7 o'clock, A.M., for San Francisco.

This line is furnished with the best stages and horses the country can produce, and carries passengers through the whole distance—60 miles, in about Six hours.

The Proprietors have reduced the rates of fare so as to enable all who desire a trip over one of the most beautiful roads in the world, to do so at a very small expense, and hope thereby to receive such patronage as the enterprise merits.

For further particulars inquire at the office.

ACKLEY & MAURISON

The ad also shows that Maurison had lost none of his flare for window trimming, as the firm had no mail contract, the only road was a skein of bumpy wheel ruts between the hills and the mud flats, the distance was only fifty miles, and the time was still nearly nine hours. Although the advertisement was placed in a rival newspaper, Maurison was careful to curry the goodwill of San Francisco's *Alta California*, for on April 12, 1850, it gave the following article prominent space:

STAGES TO SAN JOSE. We are glad to learn that a line of Stages has been established between this place and San Jose, by Messrs. Ackley & Morrison. The Stages leave the St. Francis Hotel, at 7 A.M., three times a week, and go through in about nine hours. The proprietors have placed us under obligations by taking charge of despatches from our reporter and promptly delivering them.

After buying out Whistman and changing the name of the line to Berford & Co., Hall & Crandall were not long in meeting Ackley & Maurison's challenge, and in their announcement proved themselves fully as gifted in the arts of ad writing and window trimming.

BERFORD & CO'S LINE

OF EXPRESS MAIL STAGES,

HALL & CRANDAL, Proprietors,

Are now running every morning to San Jose, leaving Berford & Co's office in the plaza, at 8 o'clock, A.M., and the City Hotel in San Jose at 7 o'clock, A.M.

The reduced rate of fare puts it in the power of every one to visit the beautiful and healthful valley of Santa Clara. There is no more charming drive in California than that from San Francisco to San Jose, and as one is whirled rapidly through the oak openings and across the level plains under the skillful driving of Professor Dillon or Crandal, who drive their own coaches, he finds that pleasure is united with business, and wonders he has never made the trip before.

The great advantage this line possesses over all others is that the Stages were bought expressly for the road, and with a particular attention to *safety*, while the drivers, who have served a long apprenticeship from New England to Mexico, make the *quickest* time and *never meet with accidents*, which are so likely to occur with the old fashioned stage coaches. We invite our friends to give the line a trial.

BERFORD & Co.

It will be noticed that Hall & Crandall set their departure time from each end of the line at the same hour as their competitor's, and articles in the local newspapers indicate that many a spirited race resulted from it. The most famous was the race to be first in arriving at the capital with news that California had been admitted to the Union. Peter H. Burnett, the state's first governor, recorded it in writing his *Recollections*.

The State of California was admitted into the Union September 9, 1850. It so happened that I arrived in San Francisco, on my return from Sacramento City, the same day of the arrival of the steamer from Panama bringing the welcome intelligence of this event. . . . Next morning I left for San Jose on one of Crandall's stages. He was one of the celebrated stage-men of California, like Foss and Monk. He was a most excellent man, and a cool, kind, but determined and skillful driver. On this occasion he drove himself, and I occupied the top front seat beside him. There were then two rival stagelines to San Jose, and this was the time to test their speed. After passing over the sandy road to the Mission, there was some of the most rapid driving that I ever witnessed. The distance was some fifty miles, most of the route being over smooth, dry, hard prairie; and the drivers put their mustang teams to the utmost of their speed. As we flew past on our rapid course, the people flocked to the road to see what caused our fast driving and loud shouting. . . . I never can forget Crandall's race. He beat his competitor only a few moments.

Although the first Concord stagecoach to reach California had arrived at San Francisco by clipper ship around Cape Horn on June 24, it is not believed to have been used in this famous race. In May 1851 the firm of Hall & Crandall was awarded a four-

[37]

Wagons pass Pilot Knob, en route to the goldfields. (Courtesy, Old Print Shop.)

year contract to carry the U.S. mail three times a week between San Francisco and San Jose. The contract required that four-horse coaches be used, and the compensation was $6000 per year. The firm started the service with the mud wagons brought across the prairies by Beeks in 1850, but soon after the contract was awarded Warren Hall went to Concord, New Hampshire, to confer with Abbot and order stagecoaches specially built to meet the unique California requirements.

Inspired by Alexander Todd's phenomenal success, scores of

expressmen had sprung up throughout California's Mother Lode country. And as roadways were hacked out of the mountains, stage lines were established between the various mining camps and Sacramento or Stockton. An expressman seldom operated a stage line, and many of them served a single mining camp, collecting gold dust from the miners, taking it to San Francisco for deposit in one of the banks, and bringing back the mail. Instead of using a butter firkin, as Todd had on his famous rowboat trip down the San Joaquin River, they usually carried their collection of gold dust in a stout wooden box. As there were then few fair damsels riding stages in California, it was customary for the expressman to sit beside the driver, and it was only natural that he kept the precious box between his feet.

In the East a traveler usually had baggage, often weighing half as much as himself, which was carried on the rear platform of the stagecoach. In California there was little baggage to be carried, for few miners had much clothing beyond what they were wearing. As a result of the heavy load on the front and little or none on the back, the standard Concord coach had a tendency to tilt forward on the thoroughbraces. Rumors of a new discovery would bring Johnny-come-latelies rushing to a camp in thousands. At such times thirty passengers might crowd into and onto a vehicle built to carry a maximum of fifteen, often breaking it down when a wheel dropped into a particularly deep hole. Also, the glass window in the doors of Concord coaches was almost certain to be shattered.

To meet these conditions, Abbot designed a special coach, later known as The Wells Fargo. The coupling beams were suspended below the rear axle rather than being mortised through it. This not only strengthened the axle but lowered the back mounting of the thoroughbrace standards about four inches, offsetting the tendency for the body to tilt forward when heavily loaded at the front. To further strengthen the running gear the fellies and tires of the wheels were widened to three inches. Heavier standards were used for mounting the thoroughbraces, the leather belting widened, and an additional twenty feet or more added. To insure control of a grossly overloaded coach when descending a precipitous mountain road, the entire brake assembly was strengthened and the blocks increased to a size that put twelve inches of braking surface against the tire of each rear wheel.

Without the slightest loss of grace and beauty, the framework of the body was increased in dimension to the point where, without strain, the coach could carry as big a load of passengers as could possibly crowd inside and onto it. Glass was replaced by leather curtains in the door window.

The driver's seat remained the same as on the light eastern coaches, but the platform beneath it was enlarged and hinged to the body not far above the base. The front end of the platform, projecting well out above the tails of the wheel horses, was turned up at an angle of about forty-five degrees to form a footrest, and was supported by stout, adjustable leather straps attached to the corners of the seat. The sides were covered with thick black leather, forming a large "boot" for carrying expressmen's gold-dust boxes. A leather "apron," which could be attached with snaps to the front edge of the footboard and sides of the coach, was provided to cover the legs of driver's-seat passengers in bad weather.

The size of the rear platform was enlarged, and its outer end supported from the roof corners by stout chains instead of straps. This triangular space was covered with black cowhide leather, forming a weatherproof boot for carrying mail sacks, express packages requiring protection, and baggage. The leather for one of these western coaches required the best part of the hides from fourteen cattle. During the 1850's and 1860's hundreds of stage-coaches were built at Concord and shipped around Cape Horn to California.

With the mail contract secured and special Concord coaches ordered, Hall & Crandall announced that the fare on their line between San Francisco and San Jose was being reduced to sixteen dollars, just half the rate that Whistman had charged. The reduction was by no means made through altruism or because Hall & Crandall felt that its patrons were being overcharged, but to drive their competitor, Ackley & Maurison, off the road. Then, on July 2, 1851, the firm published an announcement that its line was being extended to Monterey, by way of Gilroy. Stages would leave San Jose at five o'clock each Monday and Thursday morning, reach Monterey that evening, and make the return trip next day.

Failing to jar Ackley & Maurison loose with a sixteen-dollar fare, Hall & Crandall cut the rate to ten dollars in October. That did the trick, and with a monopoly on the San Jose business the rate was still high enough to make the Hall brothers and Jared Crandall wealthy.

While the Halls and Crandall became wealthy by stagecoach-ing on the peninsula, James Birch and Frank Stevens were doing equally well in the Sacramento Valley and the foothills of the Mother Lode. Both were from Providence, Rhode Island, and both were twenty-one years of age when, in the early spring of 1849, they joined a California gold-rush party. The party crossed the continent with a caravan of ox-drawn wagons and must have made amazingly good time, as it reached Sacramento in August, far

Off for the mines. Passengers crowded onto stages at the rumor of a new discovery. (From Marvels of the New West, *William M. Thayer.)*

ahead of most overland argonauts from the Atlantic Coast. But it is much more amazing that these two boys should have joined an ox-drawn caravan, for they were not only horsemen but reinsmen and the descendants of New England reinsmen.

Both James Birch and Frank Stevens had become accomplished reinsmen and been awarded their whips in their teens, both had been top-hand stage drivers for Otis Kelton of Providence, Rhode Island, and both had fallen in love with the boss's stepdaughter, Julia Chase. It is probable that their reason for joining the gold rush in the spring of 1849 was that each hoped to make a fortune, then return to win Julia's hand.

If that was their purpose, both succeeded, although neither of them entered the actual gold rush when they reached California. Birch is believed to have had very little if any capital, but Stevens must have had a few hundred dollars. In any case, he rented or bought a wooden shack in what is now the slum area of Sacramento, painted a sign on the front of it reading "Rest for the Weary and Storage for Trunks," and went into the hotel business.

James Birch, the more aggressive and brilliant of the two, was quick to see that for a man of his experience the potential profit from stagecoaching was far greater than from any gold strike he might expect to make at the diggings.

There is no record of the date on which the Providence caravan reached Sacramento, but it could hardly have been before late

August. On September 1 Jim Birch pulled up at the landing where a riverboat from San Francisco was unloading argonauts just arrived by clipper ship from New York. His stagecoach was a springless farm wagon with boards cleated across the top for extra seats and he was driving four frightened mustangs probably bought from some Mexican for three or four dollars apiece; they were wearing an assortment of secondhand harness that might have been picked up from some stranded emigrant for a five-dollar bill. But argonauts who could afford clipper passage around Cape Horn should have money in their pockets, and they would certainly be in a rush to get to the diggings. As they came down the gang-plank Jim Birch is reported to have called out, "All aboard for Mormon Island! Forks of the American River! All aboard!"

Birch's was the first public conveyance out of Sacramento, and his judgment proved good, not only regarding the demand for fast transportation, but as to the destination chosen and what the traffic would bear in the way of tariff. Mormon Island was near the site of James Marshall's original gold discovery, the forks of the American River was understood throughout the East to be the very center of the great California bonanza, and the clipper ship passengers were willing to pay any price to get there in a hurry. Birch set the fare at thirty-two dollars, about twenty times as much per mile as stagecoach fares in the East, and had no trouble in getting as many passengers as his wagon would hold. There is no record of the number that he carried on his first trip to the diggings, but it is certain that he collected fares enough to pay for his entire investment many times over.

There were probably no more than two or three days between the time that John Whistman drove his dilapidated French omnibus out of San Francisco on his first trip to San Jose and Jim Birch's pulling out of Sacramento on his first trip to Mormon Island. In fact, there is no proof that Whistman was ahead of Birch. If so, he didn't stay there long.

Henry Ward, in his reminiscences, left no doubt that Whistman put every possible dime of the fares he collected into his pocket, reinvesting nothing to improve the quality and condition of his livestock and equipment or to better the condition of the roads. There is little doubt that his shortsightedness, rather than the rainy season, forced him to reduce his line to eight miles in the fall of 1849, and that this, rather than competition from Ackley & Maurison, drove him out of business in the spring of 1850.

Jim Birch, on the other hand, was a farsighted promoter—aggressive, dominant without being domineering, sound in judgment, and possessed of extraordinary business ability for a boy of twenty-one years. Although the length of his line was some-what shorter than Whistman's, the terrain was far more rugged and the roads infinitely worse. His first trip to the diggings must have been rough on both passengers and horses, and no faster than a man could have walked, for the mustangs had to cover the entire distance without rest and their combined weight was probably less than that of their load. But as fast as Birch took in fares he put the money right back into the line, getting the road into passable condition for winter travel, bridging the worst gullies, building relay stations at ten-mile intervals, and stocking them with feed and horses.

Instead of being obliged to curtail his operations when the rainy season set in, Birch extended his line, bought the best vehicles and harness he could find, and hired drivers who had learned to handle the reins in New England. By February 10, 1850—when John Whistman's operations had been reduced to an occasional eight-mile trip between San Jose and Alviso—Birch was advertising "through-in-daylight service, daily including Sundays" from Sacramento to Sutter's Mill, nearly twenty miles beyond Mormon Island up the rugged American River canyon.

An article appearing in the *Sacramento Placer Times* a month later indicates clearly that young Jim Birch was not only a first-class stage-line operator but a gifted public relations man, and that his horsemanship was nothing short of superb:

We made an "experimental trip" in one of Mr. Birch's stages a few days ago, which proved highly satisfactory. The horses had never been harnessed but once or twice before, yet they dashed through sloughs and gulches in a remarkably knowing style. These California horses seem to know about as much as most folks. The appearance of the country in the vicinity of the Fort [Sutter's] is very pleasing: flowers being in bloom and cultivation going forward with a good deal of activity. The party returned highly delighted with the hour's ride, and fully satisfied that Birch's Line was *the* line to get to the Mines in a hurry.

But in spite of the reporter's eulogy of California horses, and unlike Jared Crandall, Jim Birch did not believe that good stage horses could be made from even the best Mexican mustangs. In order to stock his line he bought the best eastern stage-type horses brought to California by emigrants and quite a number that had been shipped in from Australia, paying as much as a thousand dollars apiece for particularly fine animals. As he improved his stock he cut the running time on his line, and as the patronage increased he reduced the fares without waiting for competitors to come in and force him to do so.

But Jim Birch's success was too apparent, and the demand for rapid transportation to the mining towns that had sprung up throughout the foothills east of the Sacramento and upper San Joaquin valleys was too urgent to be neglected. By the fall of 1850 a dozen stage lines, most of them with only one vehicle, were operating out of Sacramento. Almost without exception the owners did the driving, using half-broken mustangs and any sort of conveyance they could get hold of, but William Beeks had evidently come to California with the fixed intention of going into the passenger transportation business. After selling Hall & Crandall an unstated number of mud wagons and twenty eastern horses, he ran the following advertisement in the *Sacramento Transcript* of October 19, 1850.

SACRAMENTO AND NEVADA CITY EXPRESS LINE. THROUGH IN 12 HOURS. The Undersigned, having a very choice Lot of Spring Wagons and a splendid stock of Horses, have established a Daily Line of Stages between Sacramento, Rough and Ready, and Nevada cities, and confidently rely upon the patronage of the traveling community. Being well aware that a single trip will convince one and all that, in point of safety, comfort and speed, this line is unequaled in the New State of California. Stage leaves Iowa House at 6¾ o'clock A.M. and Crescent City Hotel at 7 o'clock each day.
  Wm. A. BEEKS, Proprietor, R. O. SELFRIDGE, General Agent.

It is doubtful that anyone other than Beeks brought a caravan across the country in 1849 or '50 with the intention of going into the transportation business in California. But the amount of freight required to build the mining towns and supply the miners was enormous. During the summer and fall of 1850 hundreds of prairie schooners and ox teams were put to freight hauling from the Sacramento docks when their owners found freight rates high and worthwhile mining claims hard to come by. Following Jim Birch's lead in improving the roads to aid his own business, the freighters improved them in order to carry heavier loads. By the spring of 1851 the Mother Lode country of California was laced with a network of roads that, though rough and often precipitous, could be traveled by wheeled vehicles.

Meanwhile California's newly elected senators, William McKendree Gwin and John Charles Frémont, were in Washington demanding that their state immediately be connected by railroad with the rest of the Union, that it have equal mail service, that the Federal Government construct post roads at once to connect California's principal cities and towns, and that sizable mail-carrying contracts be awarded to stimulate and improve passenger transportation.

[44]

4

Stagecoach Center
of the World

SINCE the Missouri Compromise of 1820 there had been a growing hostility between the North and South regarding the extension of slavery in the territories. With the annexation of Texas the hostility was aggravated to a point where it threatened a split in the Union.

When, in 1849, California sought admission as a free state the Senate of the United States was equally divided between pro-slavery and antislavery forces. Both factions agreed that California with its great wealth and rapidly expanding population was entitled to statehood, but the South bitterly opposed its admission as a free state. It was finally accomplished, but only by the Compromise of 1850, which provided for the organization of Utah and New Mexico territories and stipulated that each should have self-determination regarding slavery when ready to be admitted as a state.

In fact, the citizens of California had been fairly evenly divided on the subject of slavery. When choosing their first senators they had elected William McKendree Gwin, a native of Tennessee who was strongly sympathetic to the southern cause, and John Charles Frémont, an uncompromising abolitionist and son-in-law of Missouri's powerful Senator Thomas Hart Benton.

When Gwin and Frémont introduced their bill proposing the immediate joining of California with the rest of the Union by railroad there was no lack of agreement in the Senate that the project should be carried out with the least possible delay. But the Senate was still equally divided, and the embers that would eventually flame into civil war were already smoldering. The pro-slavery senators insisted vehemently that the railroad must be built entirely through the South, and the abolitionists were equally ada-mant that it should be built through the North. The result was that no Pacific railroad bill was passed.

The senatorial vote in California had, however, encouraged southern senators to believe the new state might be swung to their cause in the event of a split in the Union. Furthermore, the northern senators were not too sure the Californians would remain loyal if disgruntled with their treatment by the Federal Govern-ment. Both factions were therefore anxious to mollify their new constituents, and passing the proposed postal bills seemed the best way of doing it—short of a transcontinental railroad—for the great-est complaint from California had been concerning the lack of mail service.

Regardless of the fact that there were only thirty-four post offices in the entire state and even though no provision was made for the construction of post roads, legislation was passed for wide-spread awarding of mail contracts to California stage-line operators. In addition, a contract was let to Colonel Samuel H. Woodson for carrying mail once a month from Independence, Missouri, to Salt Lake City. Then, in the early spring of 1851, a contract was awarded to Absalom Woodward and George Chorpenning to carry mail monthly between Salt Lake City and Sacramento, thus setting up an overland transcontinental mail service.

Without mail subsidy, the profits from California stage-line operations had been far from unattractive in 1850, for a stage seldom pulled out of Sacramento for the diggings without as many passengers as the conveyance would hold, and the fares averaged better than fifty cents per mile. Then too, before the end of that year there were more than a hundred expressmen serving the mining camps, all glad to pay high rates for having their "treasure" boxes carried. With the added prospect of winning a lucrative mail contract, every enterprising man who could handle a six-horse team and had the price of horses and equipment set about establishing a stage line in the spring of 1851, or in expand-ing the one he already had. Frank Stevens quit the hotel business, bought the best horses and vehicles he could find, and founded the Pioneer Stage Line between Sacramento and Hangtown, now Placerville.

Most of those who rushed into the business in the spring of 1851 started a line to the newest diggings in the foothills, equipping it with half-broken mustangs and any sort of a light vehicle that would carry eight or ten passengers. Only Jim Birch, Frank Stevens, Jared Crandall, Warren Hall, and a few others had the foresight to realize that mail contracts would not be awarded to operators serving only a few mining camps. They would fall to those with lines operating between the principal towns and cities on fixed schedules over routes sufficiently important to be considered post roads, and with first-class equipment. That was Hall & Crandall's reason for buying and training so many large mustang mares and for buying mud wagons and heavy coach horses from William Beeks, ·and why Warren Hall went to Concord, New Hampshire, to have special coaches built.

Newspaper articles and advertisements of the time indicate clearly that before the end of 1850 James Birch had begun shaping his business definitely for the acquisition of mail contracts, and that he had ordered both Concord and Troy coaches. It is also evident that he had written to reinsman friends in New England, offering them big wages and telling of the high prices that stage-type horses were bringing in California. In any event, some of the finest New England reinsmen, including Charlie Parkhurst, arrived with the 1851 caravans and began driving stages for Birch or Stevens. Furthermore, there were hundreds of excellent Morgans, Cleveland Bays, and Kentucky road horses brought across the plains.

On October 5, 1850, an advertisement appeared in the *Sacramento Transcript*:

NOTICE. The subscribers inform the public that they have purchased all the interest of JAMES BIRCH in the SACRAMENTO AND COLOMA STAGE LINE. They respectfully solicit a continuance of the patronage which was so liberally bestowed upon the late proprietor.

WILLIAM COLE, JR., ANSON BRIGGS.

Though famous as the site of Marshall's first gold discovery, Coloma was only a small town, and the probability of a mail contract being awarded to the line was even smaller. Birch set up a line to Marysville, the principal city north of Sacramento, and to Nicolaus, the head of navigation on the Feather River for steamers from San Francisco, both of which would certainly be mail centers.

Apparently he was still doing a good public relations job, for on February 18, 1851, the *Transcript* published an article that came very near being a eulogy:

NEW LINE OF STAGES. Mr. James Birch, extensively known in this vicinity, has established a line of stages between Nicolaus and Marysville, in connection with the steamer Gov. Dana. He has fifty of the finest horses and the best coaches in California, and the way he puts through his passengers is a caution to slow teams. He has an abundance of passengers as the Gov. Dana has carried one hundred passengers daily for the last two weeks. Mr. Birch, we believe, is the first man that established a stage line in this country. He is endowed with great perseverance and integrity, and if any person deserves success it is James Birch.

Two months later the *Sacramento Union* announced that Birch had established the Telegraph Line of U.S. Mail Coaches, "running between this city and Nevada, the largest and most important mining town in California."

But James Birch was far from alone in opening new stage lines. By the summer of 1851 Sacramento had become the stagecoaching capital of California; lines radiated from it like threads from the center of a spider's web, and twenty-seven mail contracts had been awarded. Hall & Crandall had bought out and re-equipped a line between Sacramento and Marysville originally started by a Bear River farmer. Baxter & Monroe, with hopes of securing a California-Oregon mail contract, had opened a stage line to Shasta City, 180 miles north of Sacramento, hacking out a roadway over the trail blazed up the Sacramento Valley by Jedediah Smith in 1828.

In 1852 stagecoaching in California was given an additional boost by the entry of Wells, Fargo & Company into the express business. Adams Express Company, one of the largest in the East, had established a banking and gold-dust-buying subsidiary office in San Francisco in 1849—Adams & Company—and had since opened branch offices in Sacramento, Stockton, and some of the larger towns. With Wells, Fargo & Company in the field, keen competition sprang up between them. The businesses of individual expressmen were bought up by the score, and banking offices were established throughout the Mother Lode country.

On the main street of the larger mining towns the bank building stood out like a fortress. The thick side and back walls were usually built from rough slabs of hand-split mountain stone, but the fronts were often the fancy brickwork of the period. A pair of heavy cast-iron shutters covered each window, while the street and vault doors were made from plates of half-inch steel. In the smallest camps the offices were merely slab shacks or log cabins, with a steel safe weighing several hundred pounds anchored to the floor.

At these offices the miners could sell gold dust as they washed it from the sand bars, receiving drafts payable at New York, Boston, or Philadelphia. Or, if he chose, the miner could deposit his dust with the express company and for a small fee have it transported to the firm's banking house at San Francisco for safe keeping. The express companies had strongboxes made for transporting the treasure by stagecoach. Some of them were simply stout, metal-bound wooden or leather boxes with hinged and padlocked lids. But for a shipment of considerable value, the box was usually made of steel and sometimes bolted to the bottom of the boot beneath the driver's feet. Contrary to popular belief, neither Wells, Fargo & Company nor Adams & Company operated stagecoach lines during the California gold rush. Instead, they contracted to have their treasure boxes carried and paid high rates, but they, like the Post Office Department, awarded contracts only to the most reliable and well-equipped operators.

The actual gold rush was fairly well over by 1852, but California's population continued to grow at an amazing pace, for each man working in the diggings had to be backed up by a variety of nonminers elsewhere: builders, farmers, bankers, freighters, merchants, clerks, and tradesmen of every description. As the population increased and more mail contracts were awarded the stagecoaching business expanded and the service improved. But lines had already been established between all the cities in central California and to almost every town and camp in the mining area, so the operators were obliged to compete with one another. In some cases as many as five individuals or firms were running coaches over the same line, each trying to outdo the others in speed and excellence of equipment. As might be expected, this resulted in a good many spirited races.

Several factors have combined to create in the public mind a glorious but entirely false conception of stagecoach driving in the West. First there were European tourists and newspaper editors from the East who crossed the continent by stagecoach in the late 1850's and early '60's and then hurried home to write glamorized articles and memoirs. Few of them failed to include a stagecoach careening down a snakelike, precipitous mountain road hacked from the sheer granite walls with six horses galloping wildly, the driver flailing them with his whip and shouting at the top of his voice to urge them on while the skidding wheels struck sparks and "hurled rocks into the awesome canyon thousands of feet below."

Then there were the magnificent and highly imaginative paintings by Frederic Remington and Charlie Russell of Indian attacks on stagecoaches, the horses running frantically and the driver pouring on the leather.

The third factor was the western novel, stories of a romantic, glamorous, imaginary West that never was, with violence and fast

An early California stage drawn by two horses. (From Harper's Weekly, *February 1855.)*

action the chief ingredients used to achieve suspense and drama. In these sagas of the fantasy West no cowboy ever rode and no stagecoach ever rolled at less than an all-out gallop.

To complete the misconception, the movies, and now television, have firmly fixed the image, presenting visually this West-that-never-was, where every stagecoach is driven up hill and down at a breakneck gallop.

One may form a fairly good idea of the speed at which stage-coaches generally traveled throughout the West by making a few comparisons. A hundred and fifty miles a day—equal to six and a quarter miles an hour—was considered excellent cross-country time. This, of course, included stops for meals and for changing teams at relay stations, but a man has walked at the rate of six and a quarter miles per hour. Ten miles per hour—six minutes to the mile—was bragging time for a stagecoach run over reasonably good non-mountain roads, but men can run a mile in under four minutes.

In the spring of 1852 Hall & Crandall decided to compete with Baxter & Monroe for the anticipated California-Oregon mail contract, so they stocked the old Hudson's Bay trail from Colusa (the head of navigation for river steamers on the Sacramento) to Shasta with Concord coaches and the best of their mustang mares. Not to be outdone, Baxter & Monroe moved their best reinsmen and their finest eastern road horses onto the line. To no one's surprise, this resulted in the fastest long-distance race in California stage-coaching history.

The famous 160-mile race was from Shasta to Colusa, a slightly downhill run over the stoneless, floorlike Sacramento Valley in the rainless summer of 1853 when the road was firm and unrutted, and there were relays of fresh horses at frequent intervals. The Baxter & Monroe driver won the race in the extraordinarily fast time of eleven and a half hours, approximately four and two-thirds minutes to the mile, while the norm for a Standardbred trotting horse is two minutes to the mile.

The reason for the seemingly slow time of stagecoach travel was that there was seldom a route without at least a few hills to be climbed, stretches of deep sand to be crossed, or boggy places where the wheels cut deeply. These had to be traversed at a walk, and the number of horses used depended entirely upon the weight of the load and the horsepower required to get it through the hardest pulls without too many "breather" stops.

On downhill stretches the drivers tried to make up lost time, though it is doubtful that any but the most foolhardy allowed their horses to travel faster than a smart trot. A trotting horse has two feet (diagonal front and hind) on the ground nearly all the time, so can maintain good balance even when traveling down a steeply pitched road that is rough and winding. But it is very dangerous for a galloping horse, as he is supported by only one leg or entirely airborne more than half the time, and to retain his balance when rounding curves he must keep his outside forefoot in the lead, making it necessary for him to take skipping steps frequently in order to change leads.

Almost every western stagecoach driver was a showman by nature, and few of them failed to bring their teams into town at a smart trot or even a gallop if the footing was good, but out on the road every good driver husbanded the strength of his horses to fully equal the distance to the end of their relay.

By the fall of 1853 the capital investment in stage lines operating out of Sacramento alone was estimated at $700,000, but the competition had become so keen that a rate war seemed inevitable. To head it off, James Birch got the operators together and worked out the plans for a consolidation. As a result, the California Stage Company, a joint-stock concern with a capitalization of a million dollars, was organized in December 1853 and went into operation on January 1, 1854. It combined at least five-sixths of all the stage lines in California, and had 111 stagecoaches or mud wagons operating over fourteen hundred miles of road. Birch was elected president of the new firm, and Frank Stevens vice-president.

Almost the entire one-sixth of the state's stagecoaching that had not been merged into the California Stage Company was in the Los Angeles area, where another twenty-one-year-old had been the forerunner. He was Phineas Banning, who was to become one of the most famous reinsmen in the United States.

Banning had come to Los Angeles from Delaware in 1851, shipping by way of the Isthmus of Panama. There is little doubt that he was an accomplished reinsman at the time, for the first stage line in southern California was just being started and Phineas got the job of driver. The twenty-two-mile line operated across the prairies between the newly incorporated city of Los Angeles and the seaport village of Wilmington on San Pedro Bay. In all probability its total assets amounted to no more than Jim Birch's had when he made his first run to Mormon Island. In any case, young Banning became a partner in the business, and very soon acquired sole ownership.

Since the Mother Lode country extended little farther south than the tip of San Francisco Bay, Los Angeles had no gold-rush boom. Consequently, Banning had no such opportunity as the early Sacramento stagemen to make a fortune in a single year. He must, however, have prospered from the start, for in 1852 he joined with D. W. Alexander to establish a stage line between Los Angeles and San Diego. It followed El Camino Real, the trail originally blazed by Portolá in 1769. In the spring of 1853 they followed the Royal Highway of the Spaniards northward, establishing a stage and freighting line to San Buenaventura (now Ventura), Santa Barbara, and San Luis Obispo.

In the summer of 1854 gold was discovered on the Kern River, in the mountains about forty miles east from the present site of Bakersfield. Although the deposit was small as compared to many of the discoveries in the Mother Lode, a two-and-a-half-pound nugget was found, causing a short-lived gold rush. The argonauts were desperately in need of provisions and supplies but between them and Los Angeles stood the mile-high Tehachapi Mountains without so much as a pack trail over them, for the gold rushers had come down the San Joaquin Valley from the north. The only known way of crossing to Los Angeles was over an extremely rugged trail blazed by the first American beaver trappers to invade California and seldom traveled since Kit Carson guided Frémont, the "Pathfinder," over it in 1844. As was his custom, Frémont had left his name on the most spectacular pass in the mountains, where the trail plunged steeply down to the San Fernando Valley.

Los Angeles merchants were anxious for the business from the mining camps, and Phineas Banning was determined to open a road across the Tehachapis in order to get the staging and freight-hauling business. Probably driving a six-mule team hitched to a mud wagon, he set out with several merchants to explore a wagon route and open trade with the miners.

The climb to Frémont Pass was so steep that the passengers had to walk, and the descent on the far side so precipitous that they didn't dare ride. Their judgment proved to be good. The hill was too steep and rough for the brakes, so mud wagon, mules, and driver rolled in a tangled mass to the bottom of the canyon. But such a trifling accident didn't discourage Phineas. He patched up harness, righted the wagon with the help of his passengers, and went on to cut the first wheel tracks of what is now the four- to eight-lane U.S. Highway 99: through San Francisquito Canyon, up the thirty-mile climb to Tejon Pass at the summit of the range, and descending more than three thousand feet in the next fifteen miles down twisting Grapevine Canyon to the San Joaquin Valley.

A few weeks were required to fix up the most dangerous spots on the road, and then Banning & Alexander began sending ten-mule freight wagons and six-horse passenger stages over the Tehachapis on regular schedules, carrying capacity loads at every trip. A few miles north of the summit the U.S. Government built Fort Tejon, for which the firm was awarded the freighting contract at four and three-quarters cents per pound. During the building and at the height of the gold rush the hauling business required a train of seventeen wagons, and the running time for stages was cut to fourteen hours. But the expected bonanza proved to be a flash in the pan. By May 1855 only a few hundred men remained at the new diggings.

Banning & Alexander had, however, made considerable hay while the sun was shining. By the time the Kern River gold rush collapsed they owned five hundred mules, forty enormous freight wagons, an unknown number of horses, and fifteen stagecoaches. They had contracts for hauling the greater part of the army supplies to Fort Yuma on the Colorado River. Their stages ran daily to San Bernardino, and in the winter of 1855 long trains of their freight wagons, each pulled by eight or ten big mules, continued eastward across Cajon Pass, the arid Mojave Desert, and northward to Salt Lake City, wearing deep wheel ruts over the route that is now U.S. Highway 91.

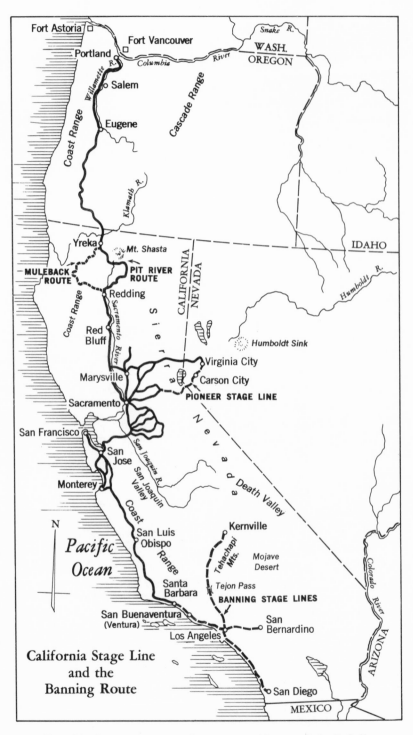

Fort Astoria

Fort Vancouver

Portland

Columbia River

WASH.
OREGON

Snake R.

Willamette R.

Salem

Cascade Range

Eugene

Coast Range

Klamath R.

Yreka

Mt. Shasta

PIT RIVER
ROUTE

IDAHO

MULEBACK
ROUTE

CALIFORNIA
NEVADA

Humboldt R.

Redding

Sacramento River

Coast Range

Red
Bluff

Sierra

Humboldt Sink

Virginia City

Marysville

Carson City

Sacramento

PIONEER STAGE LINE

San Francisco

San
Jose

Nevada

San Joaquin R.

Death Valley

Monterey

San Joaquin
Valley

Coast

N

Kernville

Range

Pacific
Ocean

San Luis
Obispo

Tehachapi Mts.

Mojave
Desert

Colorado River

Santa
Barbara

Tejon Pass

BANNING STAGE LINES

San Buenaventura
(Ventura)

Los Angeles

San
Bernardino

ARIZONA

California Stage Line
and the
Banning Route

San Diego

MEXICO

By 1861 Sacramento was the stagecoaching capital of California. A year later Wells Fargo entered the express business.

Meanwhile the state capital had been moved from San Jose to Sacramento, a railroad was being built between that city and Folsom, and under Jim Birch's management the California Stage Company was more than keeping pace with the expanding population. At the time of the merger there had been great concern that, with a monopoly, the new firm would curtail service, raise rates, and generally gouge the public. But within six months every newspaper in northern California was shouting the company's praise.

The races, which had resulted in speeding up travel during 1853, were stopped, but the running time was further reduced by improvements in the facilities of the combined lines. Poor-quality horses were replaced with the finest that could be bought, extensive roadwork and bridging was done, and inferior rolling stock was replaced by Concord coaches on the principal lines or with thoroughbrace-mounted mud wagons on the rougher mountain roads. As many as ten coaches a day were scheduled between the principal cities, and for most of the smaller towns semiweekly schedules were replaced by daily service. In making an address to the state legislature on January 5, 1855, Governor John Bigler said, "California today can boast of stage and coach conveyance equal, if not superior, to any of her sister States."

Less than two months later the state was plunged into devastating panic. On February 18 the steamer *Oregon* brought news to San Francisco that Page and Bacon Company, one of the largest banking institutions in St. Louis, had been forced to close its doors. The news started a run on Page, Bacon and Company, the firm's San Francisco affiliate, and on February 22 it made an announcement in the *California Chronicle*, saying in part, "We must suspend. We cannot raise coin on our bills. The coin is not in the country."

The poorly chosen wording of the announcement touched off a full-blown panic. Mobs of frightened depositors rushed to Montgomery Street, the Wall Street of San Francisco. They stormed the offices of Wells, Fargo & Company, Adams & Company, and the smaller banks along the street, fighting each other for a chance to get in and withdraw their money before these banks too should fail. They were soon joined by the riffraff of the city, who turned the stampede into a riot, hoping the bank vaults might be broken into.

Adams & Company on the west side of the street, and Wells, Fargo & Company on the east, put shotgun guards at their doors, let depositors in a few at a time, and paid off in U.S. currency or gold dust as fast as the tellers could count and weigh it. By closing time Adams & Company had paid out over $200,000 and their vaults were nearly empty. The next morning the firm failed to open its doors.

Telegraph lines between San Francisco and the larger towns and cities had recently been completed. News of the rioting and Adams & Company's failure was flashed over the wires, and panic rushed like a tornado throughout the state. Some of the more fortunate Adams & Company depositors at Sacramento and Stockton were paid off before the doors were closed, but the less fortunate got little or nothing. At Auburn and Sonora the mobs broke into the Adams vaults, cleaning them out to the last grain of dust, although little of it went to the actual depositors.

With the failure of Adams & Company the rioters in San Francisco went wild. Wells, Fargo & Company and a few of the small private banks were still paying off depositors, but it was no longer safe to continue. Shops, stores, and wholesale houses locked their doors and barricaded their windows. Even the courts adjourned.

Wells, Fargo & Company not only weathered the storm but won the complete confidence of the Californians and a near monopoly on the express-banking business of the Far West. The following fall Louis McLane, a young retired United States naval officer, was appointed general agent in charge of the firm's California business. He was an extremely able man, and his appointment had as great an influence upon stagecoaching in the West as upon the express business.

Many firms throughout the state were ruined by the panic, but the California Stage Company was affected very little, partly due to the continued influx of population but more particularly because it had its business affairs in as excellent condition as its staging operations. Throughout 1855 it went ahead with an expansion program that extended its lines almost the entire length of the state. The panic was no sooner over than the firm set about building relay stations and stocking a line between San Francisco and Los Angeles. The route followed the course of the old padres' trail, El Camino Real, almost the entire distance, and is now U.S. Highway 101. The opening of the line in early summer provided the first direct stage connection between northern and southern California.

In 1853 Hall & Crandall had established a mail and passenger service between Marysville and Yreka, twenty miles south of the California-Oregon boundary. The roadway their coaches wore northward along the Sacramento Valley is now part of the same automobile route that Phineas Banning pioneered over the Tehachapi Mountains: U.S. Highway 99. At Redding the valley pinches off between the Cascade and Trinity mountains, and the river then flowed through an impassable gorge, now covered by Shasta Lake. As Jed Smith had done when he blazed the original trail, Hall & Crandall turned northwestward at Redding toward what appeared to be a low gap in the Trinity Range. And, like Jed, they found the gap to be a V-shaped rock-walled canyon barely wide enough to let a single horse or mule through. A road could be opened no farther than French Gulch, twenty miles beyond Redding. There passengers and mail had to be put on muleback for a trek of sixty miles over the rugged Trinity and Scott mountains to Callahan's Ranch, near the foot of Mount Shasta.

As soon as the Los Angeles line had been put into operation, the California Stage Company started work on a roadway from Redding to Yreka. Highway 99 now continues due north from Redding, slicing through granite shoulders of the Cascade Range, crossing Shasta Lake on multimillion-dollar bridges, and following the Sacramento River to its headwaters at the foot of mile-and-a-half-high Mount Shasta. Lacking money, equipment, or engineering skill for such a project, the stage-line operators turned their road to the northeast. They hacked out a route through the foothills of the Cascades, blasted a roadway wide enough to get stagecoaches through the wild Pit River canyon to the east side of the range, and then swung back to the northwest between Grizzly Peak and Mount Shasta, opening what is now State Highway 89 to the headwaters of the Sacramento. From there to Yreka they again opened road that is now part of U.S. Highway 99. The modern highway with its deep cuts, high fills, wide curves, and 5 per cent grades does not, of course, exactly follow the old stage road, but parallels it rather closely.

The new route was put into operation in the summer of 1855, completing direct stage-line connections of 850 miles between San Diego and Yreka, while other lines were extended farther to the east and south from Sacramento. At the same time daily stagecoach service was inaugurated between Shasta and Sacramento and the fare reduced to twenty dollars—one-quarter of the rate per mile originally charged by Jim Birch on his Mormon Island line.

The Federal Government had built no post roads in California, and the state no highways, but as the California Stage Company and Banning & Alexander extended their lines, they opened and improved more than fifteen hundred miles of California road that is now part of eight major U.S. interstate highways.

Even with the improvements, the roads were for the most part only dirt tracks; the worst spots were graded a little with picks and shovels, sloping chutes were dug into overly steep creek banks, and unavoidable bogs were corrugated with brush or saplings. In the spring of 1854 Pine Creek, near Tehama, was in flood from recent rain in the mountains. Unaware of the flood, the stage driver on the Shasta line attempted to ford the stream in the dark. The coach upset in the swift current, drowning five passengers and four horses. The driver and five other passengers were swept downstream and managed to save themselves by clinging to brush on the creek bank.

Near Marysville a wheel of a stagecoach carrying twenty passengers dropped into a washout one dark night, upsetting the coach, breaking the driver's leg, and tumbling the passengers into a gully. None was seriously injured, and the occurrence was accepted as one of the inevitable hazards of night travel.

Instead of blaming the stage company, the newspapers printed such articles as this one from the *Shasta Courier*: "We join most heartily in the praise bestowed upon the California Stage Company by the *Marysville Herald*. We have not heard a single word of complaint against the line for months past. Indeed there is not the slightest possibility of anything of the kind at this end of the line."

By 1856 Sacramento had become the largest stagecoaching center on earth and the California Stage Company the largest stagecoaching firm in the United States, even though it had released several of its lines to stockholders and numerous independent operators had entered the field. It was operating twenty-eight daily stage lines over 1970 miles of road; had contracts for carrying the U.S. mail about two-thirds of that distance; owned 1500 horses and 205 Concord stagecoaches and mud wagons; and employed 300 drivers, agents, relay station keepers, hostlers, and others. The total distance traveled by the firm's stock and equipment was in excess of a million miles per year, equal to more than 250 round trips between Sacramento and St. Joseph, Missouri.

5

On the Santa Fe Trail

WHILE stagecoaching was making such tremendous strides in California it was barely limping along in Kansas and New Mexico. The Santa Fe Trail, the first road west of the Missouri River, had been in use for nearly three decades but was still the most dangerous road in America.

Under Spanish rule, Americans caught south of the Arkansas River were imprisoned, but in 1821 Mexico won independence. That summer William Becknell set out from Franklin, the western outpost in Missouri, driving a few pack horses loaded with cheap, gaudy merchandise for trading with the Cheyenne Indians. He followed the Missouri upstream to the present site of Kansas City, then continued westward along the Kansas and Smoky Hill rivers to what is now central Kansas. There he turned southwest, reached the Arkansas at its great bend, and followed the north bank to the point where La Junta, Colorado, is now situated. There a network of Indian trails crossed, and he learned that the Cheyennes had gone south of the Arkansas to steal horses from the Mexicans.

Unaware of Mexico's independence but unwilling to lose a year's trading, Becknell decided to risk being caught by Spanish soldiers and crossed the river, following an age-old Indian trail—now U.S. Highway 350—to Raton Pass in the Sangre de Cristo Mountains. He was descending by a trail that is now U.S. Highway 85 between Denver and Santa Fe when he was surprised by a small company of Mexican soldiers. They were overjoyed to find that he had American merchandise, told him Mexico had won independence, and urged him to take his goods to Santa Fe for sale. He found the Santa Fe Mexicans well supplied with Spanish silver dollars and as delighted with his merchandise as the soldiers had been. The señoritas fought with one another to pay two dollars a yard for New England calico that cost six cents in St. Louis, and a paper of needles brought twice as much.

The profit was fantastic, and Becknell hurried back to Franklin, his saddle bags loaded with Spanish dollars. He was joined by other frontier merchants in organizing a caravan for the next spring. There is no record of the value of the cargo that left Franklin in May 1822 or of the number of pack horses in the caravan. But it was the most important ever to move over the Santa Fe Trail, for Becknell and two of his associates took their merchandise on wagons, the first wheeled vehicles to roll westward from the Missouri.

Believing the Sangre de Cristo Mountains to be impassable with wagons, Becknell crossed the Arkansas River near present-day Dodge City. He struck southwest for nearly sixty miles across a flat, waterless desert to the great bend of the Cimarron River, pioneering the route that is now State Highway 45. He followed the Cimarron River across the southeastern tip of Colorado, the end of the Oklahoma panhandle, into northeastern New Mexico. Continuing to the southwest he intersected his trail of the previous year, then followed it around the foothills of the Sangre de Cristo Mountains to Santa Fe, a distance of 970 miles from Franklin.

The route was a hundred miles shorter than by way of Raton Pass, and wagons could be hauled over it without difficulty, but it had some disadvantages. There were no landmarks to guide by on the crossing between the Arkansas and Cimarron rivers, the summer heat was scorching, water and feed for animals had to be carried, and travelers losing their way were almost certain to die of thirst. Furthermore, the route along the Cimarron and across northeastern New Mexico was through the hunting grounds of the Comanche and Kiowa Indians, among the most dangerous on the continent. Because of this, the merchants were obliged to band together, taking their goods over the trail in large, strongly armed caravans. Even these were harassed by the Kiowas and Comanches, but the trade grew rapidly, for there was an insatiable demand for American goods in Santa Fe and the profits were enormous.

In the spring of 1824, 81 men left Franklin with 156 horses and mules, 25 wagons, a small cannon for frightening away Indians, and merchandise that cost about $35,000. It sold in Santa Fe for $155,000 and beaver pelts worth $10,000, but the caravan was constantly harassed by the plains Indians, several men were killed, and nearly a hundred horses and mules were stolen.

The killings and plundering increased steadily during the next four years. Then, in 1829, Charles and William Bent quit beaver trapping and entered the Santa Fe trade. They quickly won the friendship of the Cheyenne and Arapaho Indians for white men, and used seasoned mountain men for guards when moving a caravan through Comanche and Kiowa country. For nearly twenty years the Bents dominated trade in the Southwest and travel over the Santa Fe Trail.

In 1834 the brothers built Bent's Fort at the point on the Arkansas River where Becknell had turned southward to hunt the Cheyennes in 1821. Soon afterward they opened a wagon road over the old trail he had followed to Santa Fe. Although the road was rough, the pull up the mountains to Raton Pass difficult, and the distance from Independence, Missouri, to Santa Fe a hundred miles longer than by the Cutoff, the route by way of Bent's Fort became the main line of the Santa Fe Trail. It not only avoided the dangerous waterless crossing between the Arkansas and Cimarron rivers, but a far more dangerous running of the gantlet through the Kiowa and Comanche hunting grounds.

With the Cheyennes and Arapahoes friendly and the Kiowa-Comanche territory circumvented, travel over the Santa Fe Trail became reasonably safe. Small wagon trains could make the journey from early spring until late fall, the Mexicans' demand for American goods remained strong, and the trade increased from year to year. In the spring of 1846 more than four hundred great prairie schooners rolled westward over the trail: loaded with goods worth more than $1,750,000, drawn by nearly eight hundred draft animals, and accompanied by more than five hundred men.

Texas had been annexed the previous December, and war with Mexico was expected to break out at any time. In the summer of 1846 General Stephen Kearny led the Army of the West, including 1750 mounted dragoons, over the trail from Fort Leavenworth to Santa Fe. The dragoons were volunteers, the flotsam of the frontier, and G. F. Ruxton—the great eyewitness historian of the early American West—described them as "the dirtiest, rowdiest crew I have ever seen collected together."

The few Regular Army officers were unable to enforce discipline, and every dragoon's trigger finger was itching for a shot at an Indian or buffalo. Although hunters had been sent ahead to supply meat for the troops, the dragoons shot thousands of buffaloes for sport and left the carcasses to rot on the prairies. Indians who came within musket range were sniped at, and those at a distance were frightened away by cannon fire. These were Indians who for

*Indians attacking a wagon train—a frequent peril along the
Santa Fe Trail. (Courtesy, Old Print Shop.)*

more than a decade had been the white man's friends, but after the
Army of the West had passed they were his bitter enemy.

Kearny's conquest of New Mexico is called bloodless because
the Mexicans surrendered without a shot being fired, but the after-
math was far from bloodless. While the general spent a month
being entertained by the elite, his dragoons were reveling in the
hospitality of the Santa Fe señoras and señoritas, of whom one of
the officers wrote, "They do not seem to know what virtue is . . .
and are very fond of the attention of strangers."

The husbands of the generous señoras acquired a deep and lasting hatred not only for the drunken, swaggering dragoons, but for
all Americans. They bided their time until, after appointing
Charles Bent governor of New Mexico, Kearny moved on with
part of his army toward California. Then, in January 1847, the disgruntled husbands aroused the already infuriated Indians. Governor Bent and twenty other Americans were murdered by an angry
mob, and the rebellion quickly spread throughout the Southwest.

No caravan passed over the Santa Fe Trail without being attacked. Forty-seven American traders were killed, 330 wagons were
looted and burned, and more than 6500 horses, mules, and oxen
were slaughtered or stolen. For the first time, Bent's Fort was

attacked and trade in the Southwest was brought to a standstill. United States troops on the Santa Fe Trail were no safer than civilians. A company of cavalry carrying the army payroll to Santa Fe was attacked, five men killed, six wounded, and a large number of horses stolen.

With thirty-five hundred U.S. troops in Santa Fe, the supply line had to be kept open. Cavalry posts were established along the route, and heavily guarded military freight transports and merchants' caravans continued to roll, but few if any crossed the prairies without being attacked. The fabulous Indian trade that the Bent brothers had built up was ruined. In 1849 William touched a match to the arsenal and blew the great landmark of the western prairies into a heap of rubble.

Such were conditions when the Post Office Department awarded Waldo, Hall & Company a contract to carry the U.S. mail between Independence and Santa Fe. The service was to start on July 1, 1850, with monthly deliveries in both directions, and thirty days were allowed for making each trip. Little is known of the enterprise, but it is evident that the firm was determined to provide first-class passenger as well as mail service in spite of the Indian danger, for the Independence *Missouri Commonwealth* reported:

The accommodating contractors have established a sort of base for refitting at Council Grove, a distance of 150 miles from this city, and have sent out a blacksmith and a number of men to cut and cure hay, with a quantity of animals, grain and provisions; and we understand they intend to make a sort of travelling station there, and commence to farm. They also, we believe, intend to make a similar settlement at Walnut Creek next season. Two of their stages will start from here the first of every month.

The stages are gotten up in elegant style, and are each arranged to convey eight passengers. The bodies are beautifully painted and made water-tight, with a view to using them as boats in ferrying streams. The team consists of six mules to each coach. The mail is guarded by eight men, armed as follows: Each man has at his side, fastened in the stage, one of Colt's revolving rifles, in a holster below one of Colt's long revolvers, and in his belt a small Colt's revolver, besides a hunting knife, so that these eight men are ready, in case of attack, to discharge 136 shots without having to reload. This is equal to a small army armed as in ancient times, and from the look of the escort, ready as they were either for offensive or defensive warfare with the savages, we have no fear for the safety of the mails.

The *Sacramento Transcript* of October 2, 1850, reprinted the article, adding the comment: "That sounds exceeding like fudge."

[63]

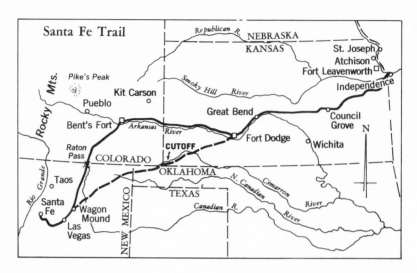

The Santa Fe Trail, the oldest road west of the Missouri River, had been in use since 1821.

In any event, the Independence reporter was overconfident. Although the article indicated that two stagecoaches would travel together, it is evident that only one was used on the first trip and that there were no passengers, but two drivers and eight guards. That summer Alexander Majors was hauling freight to Santa Fe for the army. When his caravan reached Wagon Mound, New Mexico—the landmark where the cutoff met the road by way of Raton Pass—Majors found the burned coach and "the bones and skeletons of some of the horses that drew it, as well as the bones of the party of ten men, who were murdered by the Indians." Signs showed that the Indians had been Kiowas, armed only with bows and arrows against the guards' formidable array of Colt's firearms.

No further report is found of the "beautifully painted and watertight" stagecoaches, but there were irregular mail stages, probably a wagon or two that accompanied a heavily guarded caravan. In August 1852 William Lane, recently appointed governor of New Mexico, traveled from Independence to Santa Fe "with the mail stage," accompanied by a military escort. The Indians had, however, been brought under fair control by that time. Travel north of the Arkansas River was reasonably safe, and although the Kiowas and Comanches were far from friendly they were becoming cautious of white men's rifles.

The best description of "stage" travel over the Santa Fe Trail in the early 1850's is that of W. W. H. Davis, District Attorney for New Mexico in 1853. On November 1 he took the "mail stage" from Independence to Santa Fe, kept a diary, and later wrote of the trip in *El Gringo*, a book of his experiences in New Mexico.

The stage which the district attorney traveled consisted of three wagons: one for mail and baggage; one for hauling feed, water, and provisions; and an "ambulance" (a spring wagon with seats and a canvas top) for passengers. The fare was $150, including meals, and forty pounds of baggage were carried without extra charge. Each wagon was pulled by a six-mule team, and in addition to the driver there were two outriders—men who acted as guards, whipped up the lazy mules, and herded along a dozen or so extras for relays. Davis was the only passenger, and although he gave no such detailed description of the firearms as the *Missouri Commonwealth* reporter of 1850, he wrote that all ten men in the party were heavily armed.

Waldo, Hall & Company, as the *Missouri Commonwealth* article reported, established a stage station at Council Grove, but Davis found it only a "filthy old cabin, windowless and doorless," though the blacksmith was still there. There was no other stage station on the entire 860-mile route, and no inhabitants other than Indians for 600 miles beyond Council Grove. Before dark each evening, camp was made at some spot where there was water, grass for the mules, and the least danger of a surprise Indian attack. The wagons were pulled into a triangle to provide a little fortification in case of attack, and the mules were picketed close by to graze. A fire was built, beans boiled, salt pork fried, and corn bread baked in the fat. While two-man relays stood watch through the night the others rolled in blankets and slept on the ground with their feet to the fire. At noon a dry camp was usually made, the mules given a small feeding of grain, and picketed out to graze for an hour or two.

On November 10 the mail stage reached buffalo country at the great bend of the Arkansas. The herds had already been so reduced by hide hunters that Davis wrote that "their roads and wallows were all growing up in grass." The outriders, however, brought in plenty of meat, and roast buffalo hump was a welcome change from beans and salt pork. The party reached the cutoff crossing on November 13 and stopped two days to fill water casks, cut hay for the mules, and soak wheels before starting the fifty-mile waterless *jornada* to the Cimarron River. They made the crossing in fifteen hours of hard driving, and reached the present site of Satanta, Kansas, on the sixteenth.

There the party entered the Comanche-Kiowa hunting grounds,

[65]

and the outriders must have laid their whips sharply on the backs
of the mules, for they struck a fifty-mile-a-day pace, extremely
long mileage through rough country with no relays of fresh animals. On November 21 the mail stage rolled past Wagon Mound,
where, three years earlier, Indians had burned the Waldo-Hall
stagecoach and massacred the crew. The mules were evidently
nearing exhaustion and the zone of danger considered fairly well
passed, for two days were spent in making the twenty-five-mile
crossing of the Turkey Mountains to Fort Union, the first habitation of white men seen since leaving Council Grove.

Fort Union, 110 miles out of Santa Fe, had been built following
the Indian massacres of 1847 as quarters for cavalry guarding the
trail between Santa Fe and Bent's Fort. Davis noted that it had
"little the look of a fortification. Its houses are of pine, arranged
in streets, and it has neither breastworks or stockades."

From Fort Union the trail was reasonably safe, and the mail
stage on which Davis traveled pulled into the plaza at Santa Fe
on November 26, having averaged thirty-three miles a day since
leaving Independence on the first of the month—good time under
the circumstances.

In 1854 Congress awarded Jacob Hall a four-year contract at
$10,980 per annum for monthly service each way in six-mule stage-
coaches, each trip to be completed in twenty-five days or less.
The coaches had no sooner been put on the line, however, than
the Indians again went on the warpath, and Hall appealed to
Congress for military protection and damages to cover the losses
already sustained. Instead of allowing damages, Congress increased
the compensation to $22,000 per year, retroactive to August 1854.
The military protection was inadequate, and doubling the compensation failed to cover the losses from Indian attacks, so the service
continued to be irregular.

By 1858 the firm had become Hockaday and Hall, and was
awarded another four-year contract, this one at $39,999 per year
for semimonthly service. It is evident that Hockaday and Hall
restocked the line with stagecoaches and mud wagons, but that
no relay stations were built, for the following advertisement was
run in the Independence and Santa Fe newspapers:

Santa Fe Traders and those desirous of crossing the Plains to New
Mexico are informed that the undersigned will carry the United States
Mail from Independence to Santa Fe for four years . . . in stages drawn
by six mules. The Stages will leave Independence [Mo.] and Santa Fe
on the first and fifteenth of each month. They will be entirely new and
comfortable for passengers, well guarded, and running through each way

in twenty to twenty-five days. . . . Provisions, arms and ammunition furnished by the proprietors . . . No passenger allowed more than forty pounds of baggage in addition to the necessary bedding . . . Packages and extra baggage will be transported when possible to do so, at the rate of 35 cents per pound in summer and 50 cents in winter.

The advertisement went on to say that the fare would be $125 in summer and $150 in winter, and that in all cases the "passage money must be paid in advance." The service, however, remained irregular for several years and was often interrupted by Indian trouble. Before the close of the Civil War, towns had pushed westward into central Kansas, relay posts were established at reasonably frequent intervals on the eastern portion of the line, and the running time from Kansas City to Santa Fe was cut to thirteen days and six hours. Concord coaches were used for the first and last hundred miles or so and mud wagons the rest of the way.

In 1863 the first steel rails were laid westward from Wyandotte, Kansas, across the river from Kansas City. Because of the war and Indian attacks, the progress was slow, but by 1866 the tracks had reached Junction City, Kansas, a hundred miles west of the Missouri. To meet them, stagecoaches and freight caravans from Santa Fe veered northward at the great bend of the Arkansas. Year by year the rails crept toward the Southwest, and the Santa Fe Trail terminated at each new railhead. By 1872 the rails reached the point on the Arkansas where, half a century before, Becknell had crossed the river to pioneer the Cimarron Cutoff route. Thereafter the cutoff fell into disuse and all traffic again moved over the road the Bent brothers had hacked out of the mountains between their fort and Wagon Mound.

For a year the railroad terminus of the trail was at Kit Carson, Colorado. Then the Kansas Pacific extended a branch line to the approximate site of Bent's old fort, and that remained the railhead for the stage line until Raton Tunnel was completed and the first train rolled into Santa Fe in 1880.

6

Aaron Brown and
the Overland Mail

WHEN IN 1850 the Government invited bids for carrying the mail monthly between Independence and Salt Lake City, the high bid was $45,000 for providing service with four-horse stagecoaches. The low bid was $19,500, submitted by Samuel Woodson, but specified no particular means of transportation. Woodson's bid was accepted. The contract became effective July 1, 1850, and required that each one-way trip be made within a time limit of thirty days.

Although the Oregon Trail was a well-traveled road by 1850 and the Indians along it were peaceful, Woodson had contracted for more than he could deliver. The length of the route was more than fourteen hundred miles, a third of it over mountains, and there was no settlement between Salt Lake City and Fort Kearney, a distance of a thousand miles. To maintain a thirty-day schedule the mails—often containing three or four hundred pounds of Government printed matter—would have to be carried a minimum of forty-seven miles per day, an impossibility even in good weather unless relays of fresh horses and mules were stationed along the way. As was to be expected, the service was irregular in summer and almost nonexistent in winter.

In the meantime California had been admitted to the Union and its senators were demanding rapid overland mail service. To appease them the Government advertised for bids to furnish monthly mail service between Sacramento and Salt Lake City, to connect there with Woodson's service to Independence. There were numerous bids. One was for four-horse coach service with a guard of six men, at $135,000 annually. The lowest bid, by Absalom Woodward and George Chorpenning, was for muleback service "by the then-traveled trail, considered about 910 miles long," at $14,000 per year. Their bid was accepted in April, and on May 1, 1851, Chorpenning with several men and a string of mules left Sacramento with the first overland mail. They were sixteen days in getting over the summit of the Sierra Nevada through deep snow, and reached Salt Lake City on June 5. On the way Chorpenning staked out a quarter-section of land on what is now the site of Genoa, Nevada, for establishing a mail station.

The Indians of the Great Basin, abused by forty-niners on their way to California still felt hostility to all white men. When Woodward took the November mail east, going by way of the California and Oregon trails through southeastern Idaho, he was killed by Indians on the Malad River in northern Utah. Chorpenning was unable to get over the Sierra Nevada with the December and January mails because of deep snow. In February he found a way through the Feather River canyon, but all his horses froze to death on the way. He and his men reached Salt Lake City with the letter mail in April, having walked the last two hundred miles. The March mail, and that of the following winters, was sent by ship to San Pedro, then by pack mule over the Old Spanish and Mormon trails to Salt Lake City.

The situation for Woodson and his men was no better. With the November mail they were lost in a blizzard in the vicinity of South Pass for several days, then struggled through deep drifts for a month before reaching the Wasatch Mountains. Unable to get their exhausted animals across, they were obliged to abandon them, cache the printed matter, and drag the letter mail forty miles over the mountains on foot.

Brigham Young, then governor of the territory, wrote to Utah's delegate in Congress, "So little confidence have we in the present mail arrangement that we feel considerable dubiety of your receiving this or any other communication from us." And in June 1853 the *Deseret News* reported that twenty-four heavy bags of mail had been cached en route during the past eight months, as it was impossible to get them through deep snow or across flooded streams.

Obviously, the mails could not be carried across the country with any regularity and in reasonable time until there was a transcontinental railway or a well-bridged and improved highway, together with a Government mail subsidy large enough to enable the contractor to build, stock, and maintain relay stations at frequent intervals.

From the time of California's admission to the Union her senators, Frémont and Gwin, had been constantly pressing the demand for a transcontinental railway. The need for it, emphasized by the inability of Woodson and Chorpenning to get the overland mail through with any regularity, was fully recognized in Congress. In the winter of 1852–53 the Senate gave more attention to that subject than any other. But in the equally divided Senate every proposal was deadlocked over the question of route; the proslavery forces insisted that it be through the South, and the abolitionists that it be by way of the central overland route.

In an effort to break the deadlock, Senator Gwin introduced a bill for the construction of a railroad on approximately the route of present U.S. Highway 66 from southern California to Albuquerque, New Mexico, then continuing eastward along the Red River between Texas and Indian Territory (now Oklahoma). Since this route led directly into the South it was unacceptable to the North.

When it became clear that no agreement could be reached on any route, the Army Appropriation bill of March 1853 was amended to provide funds for the survey of such railroad routes to the Pacific Coast as the Secretary of War deemed expedient. It demonstrated the South's legislative skill, for that same month incoming President Pierce had appointed Jefferson Davis as his Secretary of War. Davis set army engineers to exploring five transcontinental railroad routes, but it is not surprising that most of them favored a southern course.

At the next session of Congress the railroad route controversy was further complicated by the question of establishing the area that is now Kansas and Nebraska as a territory of the United States. The southerners, led by Jefferson Davis, fought relentlessly for the extension of slavery to the proposed territory and for the construction of a railroad from the Mississippi Valley to California entirely through the South. The antislavery forces demanded that the area be established as free territory and that the railroad be constructed wholly through the North with Chicago as its eastern terminus.

In May 1854 the territory dispute was settled by passage of the compromise Kansas-Nebraska Act, leaving the question of slavery to be settled by a vote of the territorial settlers, but the matter of a transcontinental railroad route still remained deadlocked. In an effort to break the stalemate, Illinois Senator Stephen Douglas introduced a bill for the construction of three railroads to the Pacific Coast—one through the North, one through the South, and one by a central route. The bill passed the Senate, but not the House of Representatives.

Frémont had served as a California senator only one short term in 1850–51, but his father-in-law, Missouri Senator Thomas Hart Benton, had vigorously carried on the fight for a transcontinental railroad via a central route with St. Louis as its eastern terminus. When Douglas' bill failed, Benton gave up hope for a railroad in the reasonably near future and announced that he would thereafter lend his efforts to the construction of a military wagon road from the Missouri to California. In March 1855 he attached to the General Post Roads bill a clause calling for a mail route between St. Louis and California by way of "the mouth of the Huerfano; Pueblo, Colorado, and the Little Salt Lake [Utah Lake] to Stockton on the San Joaquin." This route, now U.S. Highway 50 through the Rockies, had been "explored" by Frémont in 1853, although Kit Carson had guided the "Pathfinder" to California over it in the fall of 1845.

Benton's attachment failed to pass, as did an overland-mail bill introduced by Senator Weller, Frémont's successor from California. Even though they failed, they had great influence upon overland transportation, for they stirred the Californians to action. Petitions to Congress for a wagon road and adequate overland-mail service were circulated throughout the state during the remainder of the year and were signed by seventy-five thousand citizens.

The Californians had their petitions bound into two large, impressive volumes and sent to the East Coast by steamer; they were presented to Congress in mid-April 1856. California was a wealthy and doubtful state, 1856 was a presidential election year, and both factions were anxious to win the support of the "golden state." Even so, no single route could be agreed upon, for it was generally believed that the transcontinental railroad, when eventually built, would follow the route of the post road. An act was passed, however, appropriating funds for two post roads: $300,000 for the construction of one from Fort Kearney, Nebraska Territory, through South Pass to the eastern boundary of California, and $200,000 for the construction of another from El Paso, Texas, to the California boundary at Fort Yuma. The bill required that streams be bridged, wells dug, cavalry posts established, and freight depots constructed along each route. But no provision was made for mail service over these roads when built.

Road construction was barely under way before bills were

An Indian assault on a mail carriage. The lead horse lies dead on the trail.

presented for the establishment of fast semiweekly mail-and-passenger service to California. Again a deadlock resulted as each faction insisted that only one federally subsidized means of rapid transportation be provided, and that over the route of its choice. After a year's wrangling, an ingenious solution was worked out in a conference committee between the House and Senate by adding the following sections to the Post Office Appropriations bill:

Sec. 10. And be it further enacted, That the Postmaster-general be, and he is hereby, authorized to contract for the conveyance of the entire letter mail from such point on the Mississippi River as the contractors may select, to San Francisco, in the State of California, for six years, at a cost not exceeding $300,000 per annum for semi-monthly, $450,000 for weekly, or $600,000 for semi-weekly, at the option of the Postmaster-general.

Sec. 11. And be it further enacted, That the contract shall require the service to be performed with good four-horse coaches or spring wagons, suitable for the conveyance of passengers, as well as the safety and security of the mails.

Sec. 13. And be it further enacted, That the said service shall be performed within twenty-five days for each trip; and that before entering into such contract, the Postmaster-general shall be satisfied of the ability and disposition of the parties bonafide and in good faith to perform the said contract, and shall require good and sufficient security for the performance of the same; the service to commence within twelve months after signing the contract.

Again the South had outmaneuvered the North, for Aaron Brown, an ardent proslavery partisan from Tennessee, was Postmaster General. Even though the legislation gave the contractor his choice of starting point on the Mississippi and specifically named San Francisco as the California terminus, it gave Brown unrestricted choice of contractor, regardless of low bid or experience, and therefore absolute control of the route over which the California mail would be carried.

The Post Office Appropriation bill was passed by Congress on March 3, 1857, and on April 20 the Post Office Department advertised for bids. Separate proposals were invited for semimonthly, weekly, and semiweekly service, and the bidder was required to specify his starting point on the Mississippi and the route over which he proposed to operate.

It was well known that James Birch would enter a bid, for he had plenty of capital to finance such a venture, and no man in the country could match his accomplishments in organizing and operating successful stage and mail lines. He had several times been called to Washington for consultation when the California post road and overland-mail controversies were raging in Congress. During those visits he had won the confidence and friendship of many legislators and Government officials, among them the Postmaster General. Furthermore, he had married, resigned as president of the California Stage Company, and built a magnificent home in Massachusetts, from where he could keep in close touch with the overland-mail situation in Washington.

Few other bids were expected, since a vast amount of capital would be required to build relay stations two-thirds of the distance across the continent and to equip, stock, and man such a line. Nine bids were received, however, for it was believed that the profits would be enormous if the Postmaster General could be induced to grant a contract for semiweekly service with a $600,000 annual subsidy.

The lowest bid—$520,000 per annum for semiweekly service—specified St. Louis as Mississippi River terminus and the proposed route as the still uncompleted $300,000 central overland post road between Fort Kearney and the California boundary. The highest bid was $1,000,000 for carrying the California mail once a week for one year from Gaines' Landing or Vicksburg, Mississippi, although no specific route to California was proposed. This bid, being in excess of $600,000 per annum was, of course, unacceptable under the terms of the act passed by Congress.

An unexpected bidder was Butterfield and Company, a group of seven New Yorkers headed by John Butterfield, who was one of the founders of the American Express Company and a personal friend of President Buchanan. Butterfield's associates were all executives of the four giant express companies of the United States: Adams, American, National, and Wells, Fargo.

Possibly to avoid winter snow in the Rockies, but more probably because of his friendship with the President, Butterfield designated a route which, although far more expensive to equip and somewhat longer than the central overland post road via South Pass and Salt Lake City, would offend neither North nor South. He specified St. Louis as the firm's Mississippi River point and proposed a route by way of the Santa Fe Trail to New Mexico, thence to California from Albuquerque along the 35th parallel, now the route of the Atchison, Topeka, & Santa Fe Railroad. Further reasons for Butterfield's proposed route were that St. Louis had direct rail connections with all the large cities of the East, and tracks had already been laid more than a hundred and fifty miles westward across Missouri. It was his intention that mail and passengers be carried as far as possible by train and to start his coaches from the various railheads as the line was extended westward. This would not only reduce the firm's operating expenses, but materially add to its passenger business, as western Missouri and eastern Kansas were already well populated.

Most of the other bidders were hastily organized firms, and it was no secret that Aaron Brown would strongly favor a route entirely through the South with Memphis, his home city, as the eastern terminus of the line. Even though Memphis had no rail connections with the East, three of the bidders named it as their Mississippi River terminus and specified their route as the one Senator Gwin had proposed in 1853 for a transcontinental railroad: along the Red River and through Albuquerque to southern California, then northward to San Francisco through the San Joaquin Valley.

Postmaster General Brown could hardly reject St. Louis as an eastern terminus, that being the most southerly railroad center on the Mississippi, but he would not risk it as the sole eastern terminus. In direct violation of the act, he specified the only terminals and route he would accept: "from St. Louis, Missouri, and from

Throwing out the mail. (From Harper's Weekly, *July 4, 1874.)*

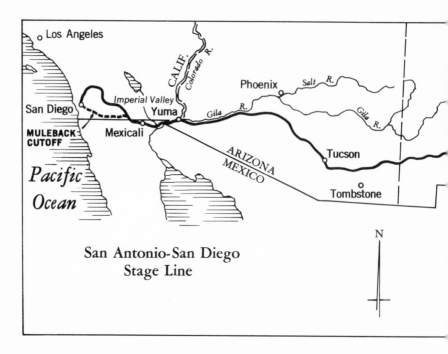

Los Angeles

CALIF.

Colorado R.

Phoenix

Salt R.

Imperial Valley

San Diego

Yuma

Gila R.

Gila R.

MULEBACK CUTOFF

Mexicali

ARIZONA
MEXICO

Tucson

Pacific

Ocean

Tombstone

San Antonio-San Diego
Stage Line

N

*One writer described the line between San Antonio and San
Diego as going "from no place through nothing to nowhere."*

Memphis, Tennessee, converging at Little Rock, Arkansas; thence,
via Preston, Texas or as nearly so as may be found advisable, to
the best point of crossing the Rio Grande, above El Paso, and not
far from Fort Fillmore: thence, along the new road being opened
and constructed under the direction of the Secretary of the Interior, to Fort Yuma, California, thence, through the best passes
and along the best valleys for safe and expeditious staging, to San
Francisco."

At news of Brown's action a howl of protest went up from the
North, but most particularly from California. Scores of citizens'
committees and newspaper editorials demanded mail service over
the direct central overland route, pointing out that thousands of
tons of freight were being hauled over it annually and that it was
being used by 90 per cent of the overland emigrants to the West.

In justification of the route he had specified, Brown wrote in
his annual report that repeated failures of the Salt Lake City mail
to maintain a regular schedule because of deep snow in the mountains "put that route entirely out of the question." As for the route

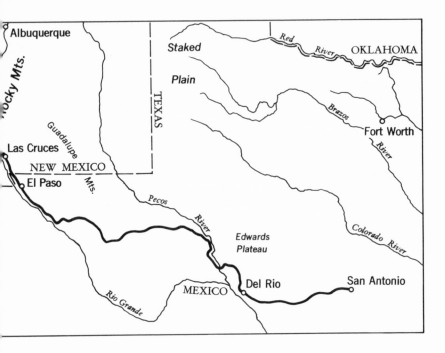

through Albuquerque and across the New Mexico and Arizona plateaus to southern California, he cited War Department maximum and minimum temperature records at Albuquerque as proving the climatic conditions on such a route to be unsatisfactory. After extolling the superiority of the route he had specified, he wrote: "The Department supposed Congress to be in search of a route that could be found safe, comfortable, and certain during every season of the year, as well for the transportation of mails as for the accommodation of emigrants and the future location of the railroad to the Pacific."

It was true that the greater portion of the route would be practically snowless during months when the central route through the Rocky and Sierra Nevada mountains might be closed to wheel travel. Little else, however, could be honestly claimed for it. The distance over it from St. Louis to San Francisco was more than seven hundred miles greater than by the central route. The cost of building and supplying relay stations would be nearly double, and there would be no local passenger business, as more than 80 per cent of the route lay through entirely uninhabited territory. Between Little Rock and El Paso lay eleven hundred miles through an almost trackless wilderness, the western two-thirds of it arid Comanche Indian country. What Brown had referred to as "the new road being opened and constructed" between El Paso and Fort Yuma was neither new nor being constructed, but was the most dangerous six hundred miles of wheel tracks in North America.

That section of the route, known as the Gila Trail, had been an Indian thoroughfare for centuries before Coronado marched over part of it in 1540 when hunting for the Seven Golden Cities of Cíbola. Under command of Colonel Philip St. George Cooke, the Mormon Battalion of Kearny's ill-fated Army of the West had, with incredible hardship, taken the first wagons over it in 1846.

Cooke, guided by an old-time mountainman who was half Cherokee Indian, led the battalion down the Rio Grande from Santa Fe to within about eighty miles of El Paso, then turned westward to the vicinity of present Lordsburg, New Mexico. Straight to the west was the Mexican settlement of Tucson, through which the battalion must pass, but between lay a hundred and fifty miles of deserts and mountains, the homeland of the Chiricahua Apache Indians, the most dangerous tribe on the continent. Rather than risk either the waterless wasteland or an encounter with the Apaches, Cooke made a three-hundred-mile detour southward around the Chiricahua Mountains. From Tucson he followed the route over which Father Garcés had guided Anza to California in 1774, roughly the present line of the Southern Pacific Railroad along the Gila River to Yuma, then northwest across the deserts and mountains to San Diego.

In 1849 the army had opened a passable wagon road between San Antonio and El Paso, Texas. The first wagon train of gold rushers to come over it was conducted from El Paso to Tucson by Colonel Jack Hays, hero of the Texas War of Independence and recently appointed United States Indian Agent for the Apache region. Hays led the wagon train up the Rio Grande past Fort Fillmore (near present Las Cruces), intercepted the wheel tracks left by wagons of the Mormon Battalion, and followed them to the point where Cooke had started his detour. There Hays continued on westward through the heart of the Chiricahua Apache stronghold, opening a wagon road over the route that is now U.S. Highway 80 between Lordsburg and Tucson.

The San Antonio-El Paso military road and the Cooke road, shortened by the Hays cutoff, made up the first transcontinental thoroughfare in the United States connecting the Gulf of Mexico with the Pacific. It was, nevertheless, nothing more than a set of rough wheel tracks with chutes cut in the steepest stream banks and rock-walled mountain passes hacked wide enough to let a wagon through.

The route had the advantage of being passable in winter when wagon travel over the central route was blocked by snow in the mountains, but in the searing heat of summer the suffering from thirst, lack of grass, and Indian depredations were almost unimaginable. During the early years of the California gold rush more than thirty thousand argonauts passed over the road, leaving its course through the deserts lined with thousands of horse and oxen skeletons, hundreds of abandoned wagons, and an untold number of graves.

Congress had authorized nearly twice as much per mile for road construction between El Paso and Fort Yuma as between Fort Kearney, Nebraska, and the California boundary on the central overland route. Little had been or would be done, however, except to dig a few wells along the way, somewhat reduce the worst mountain grades, and install a ferry for crossing the Colorado River at Fort Yuma.

Whether or not there was a prior agreement between them, James Birch entered a bid for carrying the California mail by way of the exact route specified by Postmaster General Brown; it was for semiweekly service at $600,000 per annum.

By the Constitution of the United States, Congress was given power "to establish post offices and post roads." Although the Postmaster General had authority to start service on a route as soon as it was established, he was not obligated to do so unless a specific appropriation of funds had been made, and it was customary not to begin service until it became apparent that the approximate cost would be covered by the expected revenues. For that reason senators and representatives in the mid-1850's used the Postal Route bill (always long, kept on a handy table, and never printed) largely to keep voters in their districts happy. If a group of constituents petitioned a congressman for the establishment of a mail route that seemed to him unjustified, he added it to the bill and notified the proponents of the action he had taken in their behalf, but introduced no appropriation bill to provide funds for starting service over the route.

In the fall of 1856 the San Diego *Herald* republished "the resolutions of the people of El Paso county, Texas, in which is advocated the establishment of a tri-weekly mail coach line from some point on the Gulf of Mexico, by way of San Antonio and El Paso, to San Diego, California. The resolutionists, regarding the road by this route as a national military and mail road, resolve to instruct their Senators and Representatives in Congress to urge the project upon the Government."

The resolutionists must have carried out their resolve, for the Postal Route bill enacted by Congress on August 18, 1856, established a mail route "from San Diego, via El Paso, to San Antonio, Texas," but no appropriation for service over the route was made.

It seems apparent that Aaron Brown had as well as promised Jim Birch the California mail contract if he would accept the specified route, but that there was a little "horse trading" between the Postmaster General and the President in mid-June 1857. Brown was convinced that railroads would soon be built along any mail route to California over which service had been established, and he was determined that there should be a line entirely through the deep South. President Buchanan was evidently as determined that his friend Butterfield should have the $600,000 California mail contract, and was willing to bargain.

In any event, Brown suddenly decided to establish service on the San Antonio-San Diego route authorized by Congress in 1856. On June 22 he awarded James Birch a four-year contract at $149,800 per annum for semimonthly service over the route, beginning July 1, 1857, with thirty days allowed for making each one-way trip. Soon thereafter, "looking at the respective bidders, both as to amount proposed and the ability, qualifications, and experience of the bidders to carry out a great mail service like this," Brown ordered that a six-year contract for semiweekly Mississippi River-to-San Francisco mail service be awarded at $600,000 per annum to The Overland Mail Company, a $2,000,000 joint-stock company which Butterfield and his associates had organized and of which he was president.

When word reached New York that the contract was to be awarded to Butterfield, the *New York Times* was scathing in its criticism. An editorial of July 7 was particularly biting:

We charged no corruption when we expressed our belief that despite bidding, it had been decided to award the contract to Mr. Birch. . . . Mr. Birch is a gentleman of large capital and much experience, and is more competent, perhaps, than any other single man in the United States to execute this great mail contract. He has influential friends, too, who urged him on the Postmaster General; and we repeat today—and Mr. Birch will not deny it—that he had reason to believe three months ago that he would certainly get the contract. . . . We repeat that it was the

Postmaster General's determination to give it to him down to a very recent period. . . . So much for our position. The President has overruled the determination to give the contract to Mr. Birch.

That Aaron Brown had made a commitment to Birch and was buying out of it with Government funds is rather apparent when the terms of the two contracts are compared. The distance from St. Louis to San Francisco by the specified route was approximately three thousand miles—half of it with scarcely a wheel track—and semiweekly service each way would require well over six hundred thousand miles of travel per year, so the compensation would be less than a dollar per mile. Furthermore, the act passed by Congress required that the contractor furnish service with "four-horse coaches or spring wagons, suitable for the conveyance of passengers" and that "the said service shall be performed within twenty-five days for each trip." To maintain such a schedule fifteen hundred miles of road would have to be opened, and at least two hundred relay stations built, supplied, manned, and stocked.

On the other hand, the distance from San Antonio to San Diego was only 1475 miles, so semimonthly service would require little more than 70,000 miles of travel per year, making the compensation per mile more than double what Butterfield and Company would receive. Moreover, there was already an established road over the entire route, and thirty days were allowed for making each trip. With a schedule requiring only fifty miles of travel per day there was no need of establishing more than fifteen relay stations, eight of them at existing military posts along the route.

In fact, there was so little excuse for establishing mail service between San Antonio and San Diego at all that one writer called it the line "from no place through nothing to nowhere." With the exception of Tucson (which probably had less than a score of inhabitants who could read or write English) the only town or city on the entire line was El Paso, then on the Mexican side of the Rio Grande. It already had service by a mail-stage line between San Antonio and Santa Fe that had been established in 1854. Also, when the Butterfield stages went into operation they would carry mail from El Paso to within a hundred miles of San Diego.

Nevertheless, Aaron Brown had provided the impetus that would usher in the great era of overland stagecoaching.

7

Stage Lines Through
the Deserts

WITH only eight days between the time James Birch was awarded
the San Antonio-San Diego mail contract and the date on which
service was scheduled to be started, he had no time to lose. He
engaged as superintendent for the new line Isaiah Woods, a thoroughly experienced stage-line operator and expressman. Probably
by steamer from New York to Galveston, Birch hurried Woods
away to San Antonio with eleven Concord coaches and celerity
wagons, harness, etc. He was to buy mules (as it was not believed
that horses could endure the desert heat), hire men, and get the
first mail away for San Diego as quickly as possible. Birch then
set out for San Francisco by way of Panama to wind up his affairs
there.

Although there were six frontier cavalry posts strung along the
military road between San Antonio and El Paso, no traveler in
western Texas was safe from Comanche attacks. While Woods
was buying mules and hiring men in San Antonio the famous
frontiersman and explorer Edward F. Beale was on his way there
from El Paso, and on July 7 he noted in his journal:

We were passed on the road this morning by the monthly El Paso
mail on its way up, by which I received . . . a box about two feet square,
for which the modest charge of twenty dollars was made! The dangers
of this road, however, justified any price for such matters. Scarcely a
mile of it but has its story of Indian murder and plunder; in fact from
El Paso to San Antonio is but one long battle ground.

On July 9 Woods started the first mail sack off for San Diego on a pack mule. He sent along a crew of guards and keepers with a herd of mules for establishing relay stations at the various cavalry posts along the way to El Paso. At Devil's River the party was attacked by Indians, and although a troop of cavalrymen came to their assistance, one keeper was killed, one wounded, and more than twenty mules were stolen.

On July 24 Isaiah Woods, knowing nothing of the attack, accompanied the second mail out of San Antonio in two wagons, one a celerity wagon for guards and the sole mail sack, the other a canvas-covered spring wagon for hauling water, provisions, and mule feed. Woods encountered no Indian trouble and overtook the first mail as the remnant of the mule train neared El Paso on August 7. That same day James Birch reached San Francisco on a steamer also carrying copies of *The New York Times* in which the editorial stated flatly, "The President has overruled the determination to give the contract to Mr. Birch."

His business affairs put in order, Birch took a steamer from San Francisco on August 20 for his return to New York. Eleven days later Major Woods arrived at San Diego with the first direct overland mail from the East. The city—still little more than a Mexican pueblo although it had been incorporated as a city in 1850—went wild with joy. The people thronged the plaza, shouting and cheering, bells and "a hundred anvils" were rung, and an old cannon roared out a welcome as long as the powder lasted.

The most difficult part of the entire trip, although safe from Indian attacks, had been the last 220 miles from Fort Yuma across what is now the rich Imperial Valley but was then a waterless desert of shifting sand, northward to circle the Laguna Mountains by way of Cooke's wagon road—up rugged Vallecito canyon, past San Pasqual where Kearny's exhausted Army of the West was all but annihilated in 1846—and then southward over what is now U.S. Highway 385 to San Diego.

Major Woods spent more than a week in San Diego setting up the western headquarters of the line, appointing an agent, arranging schedules, hiring men, and buying mules and equipment for establishing relay stations at Fort Yuma, Tucson, and Fort Buchanan—a cavalry post near Apache Pass in the Chiricahua Mountains.

Mail and passengers were scheduled to leave both ends of the line at 6:00 A.M. on the ninth and twenty-fourth of each month. The fare was set at $200, including meals on the road and thirty pounds of baggage, exclusive of blankets and firearms; any additional baggage was a dollar per pound. The service would be in

[83]

stagecoaches with six-mule teams, and each coach would be accompanied by six mounted guards.

Sending the mail sack ahead on muleback under heavy guard, Woods established seven relay stations along the line as he made his return trip to San Antonio, stocking each of them with hay, grain, provisions, and a score or more of the best mules he could buy, and putting in charge a keeper with three or four men to serve as guards and stablemen. In doing so he obligated James Birch for many thousands of dollars, not knowing that he had been lost at sea when, on the night of September 12, the steamer *Central America* went down in a storm on the Atlantic.

When word of Birch's death reached the Southwest, creditors began clamoring for payment of the obligations Woods had incurred in stocking and equipping the line, but the Birch estate was tied up in probate court and no funds were available. In an effort to straighten the matter out, Woods appealed to the Postmaster General. By agreement, the contract was transferred to George H. Giddings, operator of the mail route between San Antonio and Santa Fe, the southern portion of that route discontinued, and the section between El Paso and Santa Fe awarded to another bidder. Giddings and R. E. Doyle formed the firm of Giddings & Doyle to operate the San Antonio-San Diego line and retained Isaiah Woods as superintendent.

With the gold rush to California past there was almost no travel over the southern route, and the amount of mail to be carried was woefully small. Even so, it is probable that if James Birch had lived he would have maintained the best possible stagecoach service in discharging his obligation to Postmaster General Brown. Giddings & Doyle, however, were concerned only in getting the mail through within the specified time in order to forestall cancellation of their contract. After the first few trips the mail was regularly carried through within thirty days or less, but no passengers are believed to have been carried until October and the service given them was hardly up to the standard Birch had set in the California Stage Company.

In January 1847 Cooke had followed an old Spanish pack trail in leading the Mormon Battalion across the California mountains from the desert to San Diego. They had found the rock-walled pass between the Vallecito and Laguna mountains so narrow and boulder-strewn that it took four hundred men two days to hack out an eight-mile opening wide enough to get wagons through. The argonauts who had come over the Gila Trail during the gold rush had continued northward to the vicinity of San Bernardino before crossing the mountains, and few wagons had been over the Cooke road from the time the battalion opened it until Isaiah Woods arrived with the first mail from San Antonio.

The first passenger known to have traveled over the line was a correspondent for the *San Francisco Herald*, who made the trip from San Diego to Tucson in November 1857. It is probable that the vehicle he traveled in was not a Concord coach, that the driver was not a highly skilled New England reinsman, that the mules were the usual headstrong variety, and that the road through the mountains was barely passable. In any case, scarcely a mile was traveled without a breakdown of some kind.

After the better part of a day had been lost, the mail sack was transferred to a packsaddle on one of the mules that had been herded along as a relay team. Taking the rest of the spare mules for remounts, the guards pushed ahead to get the mail to San Antonio on time, leaving the stage driver and his lone passenger to get through as best they could. The next mail had passed Fort Yuma before they got there, having been brought across the mountains from San Diego on muleback by way of a recently discovered pass that is now the approximate route of U.S. Highway 80. Stopping every few miles to make repairs or to graze the mules where a bit of grass was found, the driver and his passenger made their way eastward along the Gila River, across a forty-mile waterless desert to the Pima Indian villages south of present Phoenix, and southeast to Tucson over what is now Highway 84, completing the 470-mile trip in twenty-three days—a few more than it would have taken a man to walk the same distance.

The second passenger to write of his experiences in traveling the line was Charles F. Hunning, who made a trip eastward from San Diego the following month. Although the California mountains were crossed on muleback—from which the route acquired the name of the Jackass Line—Hunning was only one day less in reaching Tucson than the *San Francisco Herald*'s correspondent had been. But again the mail was sent ahead on muleback and reached San Antonio within the thirty-day time limit. At that time the Apaches in Arizona and the Comanches in Texas were in a particularly hostile mood. Hunning wrote that eastward from Tucson "we had a very good coach, plenty of mules, and seven men well armed with Colts and Sharp's rifles," not to mention two quarts of whiskey taken along by the guards.

Even though the route was as far south as one could be and still remain in the United States, winter nights on the desert could be bitter cold for camping out. And although half a dozen guards would be provided for each trip, they might go ahead with the mail sack and leave the passengers to defend themselves. So that his readers might be properly prepared when making a journey over the line, the editor of the San Diego newspaper published a list of the clothing and equipment a passenger should carry:

One Sharp's rifle and a hundred cartridges; a Colts navy revolver and two pounds of balls: a knife and sheath; a pair of thick boots and woolen pants: a half dozen pairs of thick woolen socks; six undershirts; three woolen overshirts; a wide-awake hat; a cheap sack coat; a soldier's over-coat; one pair of blankets in summer and two in winter; a piece of India rubber cloth for blankets; a pair of gauntlets; a small bag of needles, pins, a sponge, hair brush, comb, soap, etc., in an oil silk bag; two pairs of thick drawers, and three or four towels.

The editor's thoughtfulness did little to convince travelers to the East that it would be more enjoyable to go by the overland route than by steamer and the Panama Railroad, particularly since the fare by sea was less and the time shorter.

During the Indian uprising the Comanches in Texas raided relay stations and military posts, stampeding and driving away scores of cavalry horses and stage mules. In Arizona and New Mexico the Apaches plundered nearly every ranch and settlement between Tucson and the Rio Grande. The *San Francisco Herald* reported that forty Apaches had tried to stop the eastbound mail, but that "the mail travels so rapidly that the Indians have no means of making any combination to stop it." The chances are ten to one that the mail was on muleback, for few Indian ponies could keep pace with a frightened grain-fed mule unhampered by coach or harness.

With the coming of spring the Indian trouble subsided and stage-coach service between Fort Yuma and San Antonio improved, although there were seldom more than one or two passengers and the mail was often sent ahead on muleback. Since the stations were more than a hundred miles apart, it was customary to herd along an extra relay of mules, but there was no fixed routine for traveling. If the mail had been sent ahead the stage driver might stop to graze the mules wherever he found good grass and cover no more than ten or fifteen miles in twenty-four hours. Or if the moon was bright when he was crossing Apache or Comanche territory he might drive straight through the night, for Indians seldom attacked between twilight and dawn.

The mail time from San Diego to San Antonio was cut to twenty-seven days or less, and as competition from Butterfield drew nearer the Jackass Line made a bid for more passenger business. In the fall of 1858 it advertised in the *San Francisco Herald*:

OVERLAND TO TEXAS ! ! !

THE

SAN ANTONIO

and

SAN DIEGO MAIL LINE,

Which has been in successful operation since July, 1857, are ticketing passengers through to San Antonio, Texas, and also to all intermediate stations.

Passengers and Express matter forwarded in NEW COACHES, drawn by six mules over the entire length of our Line, excepting from San Diego to Fort Yuma, a distance of 180 miles, which we cross on mule back.

Passengers GUARANTEED in their tickets to ride in coaches, except the 180 miles, as above stated.

Passengers are Ticketed from San Diego to:
Fort Yuma,
  Maricopa Wells,
    Tucson,
      La Mesilla,
        Fort Fillmore,
          El Paso,
            Fort Bliss,
              Fort Davis,
                Fort Lawson,
                  Fort Lancaster,
                    Fort Hudson,
                      Fort Clark and
                      San Antonio, Texas.

The Coaches of our Line leave Semi-monthly from each end, on the 9th and 24th of each month, at SIX O'CLOCK A.M.

An ARMED ESCORT travels through the Indian Country with each mail train, for the protection of Mails and Passengers.

Passengers are provided with Provisions during the trip, except where the Coach stops at Public Houses along the Line, at which each passenger will pay for his own meal.

Each passenger is allowed thirty pounds of personal baggage, exclusive of blanket and arms.

Considering that Maricopa Wells was only an Indian village, and La Mesilla a tiny Mexican settlement just outside Fort Fillmore, a passenger's outlay for meals could not have been great.

The advertisement brought little if any new business, and the Jackass Line "from no place through nothing to nowhere" was

[87]

gradually cut back until, before the outbreak of the Civil War, nothing remained except 367 miles of route between San Antonio and Fort Stockton, Texas. Even though it is possible that no more than a hundred passengers rode the line during its entire existence and the cost to the United States Government was in the neighborhood of sixty-five dollars for every letter carried, the operation stands as a landmark in American history, for it was the first transcontinental passenger-and-mail facility.

While Isaiah Woods was setting up his landmark in the far South, Postmaster General Brown was awarding mail contracts with what a great many people—except Californians—denounced as reckless abandon.

On September 16, 1857, two months after service had been started on the San Antonio-San Diego line, the Postmaster General awarded the California mail contract to John Butterfield and his associates, a few concessions having been made on both sides. Service was to begin one year from that date and Butterfield agreed substantially to the route specified by Brown, but with a few alterations.

At the eastern end of the line, stagecoaches were to start simultaneously from Memphis, Tennessee, and Tipton, Missouri (railhead of the Pacific Railroad, 160 miles west of St. Louis), and were to meet at Fort Smith, Arkansas, where the Memphis passengers and mail would be transferred to the Tipton coach.

With the signing of the Butterfield contract the proslavery forces in Washington had good reason to believe they had all communication between California and the rest of the nation well under their control. Not only would both transcontinental mail and passenger lines be through the deep South, but the Secretary of the Interior had taken precautions against any competition from the central overland route. The $300,000 post road authorized by Congress between "Fort Kearny in Nebraska Territory via South Pass to the eastern boundary of California" had been turned away from the Humboldt River in northwestern Utah Territory (now Nevada) to reach the California boundary in an uninhabited mountainous wilderness a hundred and fifty miles northeast of Sacramento.

But even before the ink was dry on the Butterfield contract the Mormons had upset the control, forcing the hands of Congress and the pro-South cabinet of President Buchanan.

The Mormons—their homes burned, their founders murdered, and driven from first Missouri and then Illinois—had migrated to Utah in hope of finding isolation in the wilderness. They had no

Brigham Young, the leader of the Mormons, called upon his people to defend their territory against "Gentile" intruders.
(From Leslie's Monthly Magazine, *June 30, 1877.)*

sooner settled in Salt Lake Valley, constructed irrigation systems, and established prosperous farms, than the discovery of gold in California brought thousands upon thousands of "Gentiles" swarming through their "Promised Land."

The Mormons distrusted and resented the intrusion of all Gentiles, but particularly those from Illinois and Missouri, and antagonism mounted steadily during the 1850's. In 1857 President Buchanan declared that a state of rebellion against the United States Government existed in Utah, and sent troops to put it down. Brigham Young at once called in Mormon settlers from throughout Utah Territory to defend their Promised Land. As a result, antagonism against the Gentiles was fanned to fever pitch among the more fanatical Mormons.

A week before the Butterfield mail contract was signed in Washington a large party of emigrants bound for California from Illinois, Missouri, and Arkansas encamped in Mountain Meadows, near the southwest corner of present Utah. They were attacked by a strong band of Paiute Indians. The tribe was friendly with the Mormons, and it is quite possible that they had been set on by zealots. For three days the emigrants defended themselves against the Indians' spears and arrows from behind a barricade of overturned wagons. They were then approached by Mormon settlers who offered to protect them in a retreat to Cedar City. The Mormons told them they must go on foot and unarmed in order to avoid further attack by the Indians. The emigrants did as they were advised, and 140 of them—all but a few small children—were massacred.

When news of the massacre reached Washington there was great apprehension that the Mormons might join with the Paiutes to cut California off completely from the rest of the Union. There was also apprehension that the troops then on the march to Utah would not be strong enough to withstand a Mormon attack, so it was decided to send additional forces in 1858.

At that time the mail between Independence and Salt Lake City was still being carried somewhat irregularly once a month, at a compensation of $32,000 per annum. In summer the mail and an occasional passenger were taken through by wagon; in winter the letter mail only was carried, on muleback. West of Salt Lake City the California mail was being carried once a month regularly at $30,000 per annum, but a full thirty days were required, for the mail was taken on muleback over the Mormon Trail to Los Angeles, then sent to San Francisco by sea.

With the buildup of armed forces in Utah the War Department was in need of much better communications from both east and west, so Congress instructed the Post Office Department to improve materially the mail service on the central route. Consequently, the contract for service between Salt Lake City and Independence was canceled and bids were invited for furnishing weekly service with four-mule wagons or carriages and a twenty-two-day time limit for each trip. In the early spring of 1858 a two-and-a-half-year contract, commencing May 1, 1858, at $190,000 per annum, was awarded to Hockaday & Company—the John Hockaday who, with Jacob Hall, had been the most successful of the numerous mail-stage operators on the ill-starred Independence-Santa Fe line.

George Chorpenning, who still had the Utah-California mail contract, was summoned to Washington in April. He offered to furnish weekly mail-stage service on a twelve-day schedule between Salt Lake City and Placerville, California, for a compensation of $190,000 annually. His offer was rejected, and he was given a contract for semimonthly service on a twenty-day schedule at $34,000 per annum. A provision was included in the contract, however, that if more rapid or frequent service were later required an additional $30,600 would be paid for a sixteen-day, $45,600 for a fourteen-day, or $60,600 for a twelve-day schedule, the total compensation to be doubled if weekly service were ordered.

Aaron Brown was evidently fearful that construction of the

transcontinental railroad through the South might be jeopardized by this improvement in service on the central route. He more than offset it by additional service south of Kansas, which, under the Kansas-Nebraska Act, might become abolitionist territory.

All post office and post roads bills passed by Congress since 1850 included innumerable routes without the slightest intention that service should ever be started on them. Two of these caught Postmaster General Brown's fancy in the winter of 1857–58. One was for a route between Neosho, in the extreme southwestern corner of Missouri, and Albuquerque, New Mexico, then little more than a Mexican pueblo on the mail route between Santa Fe and El Paso. The second was a route from Kansas City via Albuquerque to Stockton, California.

The first Stockton mail left Kansas City, no doubt in the same coach with the Santa Fe mail, on October 1. It was a month later, however, that the first stage for Kansas City pulled out of Stockton. According to the *San Francisco Bulletin* there was a great celebration at Stockton when a six-mule team galloped out of town with the eight-passenger Concord mud wagon "filled with blankets, provisions, and camping utensils, while the driver and guard were well equipped with Colt's persuaders. . . . A mail of some fifty or sixty letters was forwarded." There were, however, no passengers and no relay posts, and it is evident that no spare mules were driven along for relays, for the driver set a very slow pace.

No finer driving conditions could be found than those in the San Joaquin Valley during fall, but less than twenty-seven miles per day was averaged in reaching Fort Tejon. There it was learned that a party of emigrants had recently been massacred by the Mohave Indians. Next day the stage went on, but the driver and guard lost courage after reaching the desert. They returned to Fort Tejon, pleading for an escort of cavalry, and were still there when the first stage from Kansas City pulled in, having been unmolested by the Indians. Failing to secure an escort, the eastbound stage turned back with the westbound, both reaching Stockton on November 24.

Only one other mail was brought through from Kansas City, that in May 1859, but the Postmaster General's report for that year stated that four eastbound mails had been carried. Even so, the cost to the people of the United States for mail service over this useless line was at least ten times greater than the sixty-five-dollar-per-letter cost on the San Antonio-San Diego line. Nevertheless, it was a bargain as compared to the per-letter cost on the farcical Neosho-Albuquerque line.

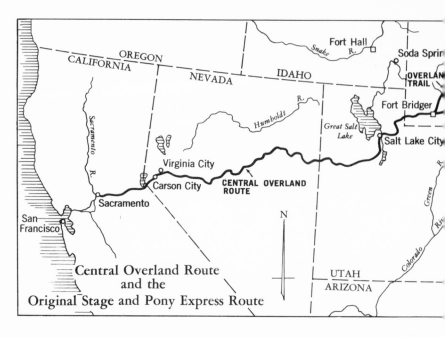

The central overland route was the shortest and fastest way from the Mississippi to California. But it was politically op-

A contract at $17,000 per annum for monthly service with six-mule wagons over a route following as nearly as possible the 35th parallel between Neosho and Albuquerque was awarded "through the intercession of Hon. John S. Phelps, Representative in Congress from the Neosho district, and from the supposition that it would aid in determining the best route for the future Great Pacific Railroad."

U.S. Highway 66 now follows the proposed route: southwest to Oklahoma City, then roughly along the 35th parallel through Amarillo, Texas, to Albuquerque. But in 1858 Oklahoma was Indian Territory, a trackless wilderness inhabited only by Indians, and Amarillo now stands at what was then the center of the Comanche-Kiowa stronghold.

Indicating that he was present, a correspondent for the *San Francisco Bulletin* reported that there was a great celebration on October 15 when "R. F. Green, guided by John Britton, pulled out of Neosho for Albuquerque, carrying four or five pounds of letters and newspapers." The mail stage was attacked by the Comanches, the men captured, one of them seriously wounded, and the mail destroyed. It was spring before they made their escape, and no

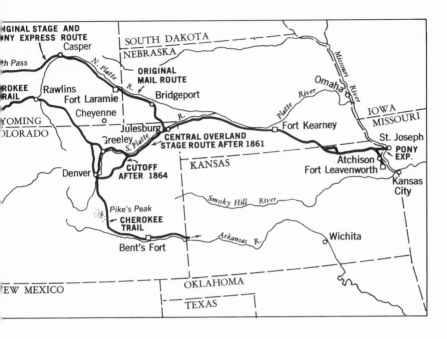

ORIGINAL STAGE AND
PONY EXPRESS ROUTE
Casper
SOUTH DAKOTA
NEBRASKA
South Pass
N. Platte R.
ORIGINAL
MAIL ROUTE
CHEROKEE
TRAIL
Rawlins
Fort Laramie
Bridgeport
Omaha
Missouri River
Platte River
Cheyenne
WYOMING
COLORADO
Julesburg
Greeley
S. Platte
CENTRAL OVERLAND
STAGE ROUTE AFTER 1861
Fort Kearney
IOWA
MISSOURI
St. Joseph
PONY
EXP.
Denver
CUTOFF
AFTER 1864
KANSAS
Atchison
Fort Leavenworth
Kansas
City
Pike's Peak
CHEROKEE
TRAIL
Smoky Hill River
Arkansas R.
Wichita
Bent's Fort
NEW MEXICO
OKLAHOMA
TEXAS

*posed by Southern sympathizers and financially hindered by
a bankrupt holding company.*

record is found of another attempt being made to take mail over
the line.

There is good indication that Postmaster General Brown was
fanatically determined to keep control of California communications in the deep South and that he had little confidence in these
lines or in Butterfield's ability to meet the twenty-five day schedule. Less than a month after the Neosho-Albuquerque contract
was signed, Brown contracted with the Louisiana Tehuantepec
Company for semimonthly mail and passenger service between
New Orleans and San Francisco, via Mexico, on a fifteen-day
schedule. The annual compensation was $286,000, and the contract
specified that steamers be used for crossing the Gulf of Mexico
from New Orleans to Minatitlan, riverboats and stagecoaches for
the 150-mile crossing of the isthmus to Tehuantepec, then steamers
up the Pacific coast.

In the spring of 1857 California had only a semimonthly, thirty-
day mail service via Panama and an insignificant trickle of letters
on muleback via Salt Lake City. A year later the state found itself
with the promise of six mail and passenger lines, not counting the
abortive one between Neosho and Albuquerque—and the United

States Government found itself obligated for an additional annual cost of nearly $1,500,000.

There was bitter criticism of the Postmaster General's prodigality, even by such southern senators as Toombs of Georgia, but there was no doubt that Aaron Brown had the President's backing, and Gwin of California defended him stoutly on the floor of the Senate.

While the wrangling and bickering continued in Congress preparations were going ahead rapidly for providing the service contracted for by the Postmaster General. Preparations had started on the western end of the central overland route early in the spring of 1857. It was then discovered that the $300,000 post road, instead of following the emigrant road—now U.S. Highway 40—to the mouth of the Truckee River canyon, would be turned westward from approximately the present site of Lovelock, Nevada, to reach the California boundary at dry, desolate Honey Lake.

Stagecoaches were by that time running daily to Oroville, eighty miles north of Sacramento, and a passable road had been opened to diggings farther up Feather River. The *Sacramento Union* of May 27 published the following notice: "The President of the California Stage Co. has tendered the free use of a stage coach to any party of men who may wish to make an exploration from Oroville to Honey Lake."

The people of California acted quickly. On June 1 the *Union* reported that enough money had been raised for surveying a wagon road through Placer County to Honey Lake and that A. D. Brown, with a party of seven or eight men, was leaving Oroville in a California Stage Company coach for Honey Lake by way of the Feather River canyon to test its practicability as a stage route.

From Sacramento to Honey Lake, either by way of the Feather River canyon or the proposed road through Placer County, would be approximately 220 miles. Furthermore, if the central overland post road were extended through the Feather River canyon there was considerable possibility that Marysville, rather than Sacramento, would become the transportation center of California. The citizens of Sacramento and El Dorado counties found this quite alarming and decided to do something about it immediately.

When George Chorpenning took the first California mail from Sacramento to Salt Lake City in 1851 he drove his pack mules to the summit of the Sierra Nevada by way of an age-old Indian trail along the north wall of the American River canyon. He descended from the summit to the south end of Lake Bigler (now Lake Tahoe) and followed another old trail eastward across the Carson

Range to the site of present Genoa, Nevada. He then continued to Salt Lake City by way of Carson Valley and the emigrant road along Humboldt River.

In 1855 Howard Egan, the outstanding Mormon desert explorer, struck westward from Utah Lake to the southern tip of the Ruby Mountains, about eighty miles south of present Elko, Nevada. There he veered somewhat to the southwest, crossing the deserts to the Sierra Nevada on the general course now followed by U.S. Highway 50. This route from Salt Lake City to Genoa was fully a third shorter than by way of the California emigrant road, which circled Great Salt Lake on the north. Later the same year Egan rode a mule from Salt Lake City to Sacramento over the new route in ten days, almost unbelievable time.

Jared Crandall, who with Warren Hall operated one of California's first stage lines, had been over the trail followed by Chorpenning from Sacramento to Genoa. He believed that with no great amount of work a wheeled vehicle could be taken over it, and that with an expenditure of not more than $50,000 it could be widened and graded into a good stage road. Even though a railroad line was being built between Sacramento and Placerville, Crandall took over the original Pioneer Stage Line from the California Stage Company. His reason for doing so was that he believed the Egan route, being the most direct, would eventually become the main thoroughfare between California and the East and that a stage line between Genoa and the Placerville railroad terminal would be highly profitable.

Doubtless Crandall discussed his beliefs with a group of influential Sacramento businessmen as soon as it was learned that the central overland post road would probably terminate at Honey Lake. In any event, a committee was quickly formed to promote the construction of what is now U.S. Highway 50 across the Sierra Nevada, and the *Sacramento Union* supported the project with an urgent editorial in its issue of June 2, 1857:

Our citizens, we understand, will be called upon during the week to subscribe towards opening a good stage road to Carson Valley. We hope they will respond promptly and liberally. The vital importance to this city and county of this enterprise is conceded. The advantages to be derived from its completion are too weighty, too numerous and too prominent to need further argument. . . . Now is, therefore, the time for our citizens to be moving towards raising the means to open a first rate roadway for Coaches and wagons over the Sierra Nevada east of this city.

The people of Sacramento wasted no time. A second committee

was formed in El Dorado County, and funds were rapidly subscribed. The *Union* reported that sixteen men, including all the directors of the Sacramento and El Dorado committees, had set out from Placerville on June 10 to inspect the route. On the twelfth it reported, "It is the intention of the Directors to let the contract for improving a portion of the road before they return. . . . Crandall, the proprietor of the stage line between Folsom and Placerville, has made all preparations to put on immediately a semi-weekly or tri-weekly line of four-horse coaches between Placerville and Carson Valley! He has sent on twelve horses and two coaches, and will have the line in full operation within a week or ten days."

Crandall more than lived up to expectations, for on June 15 the *Union* announced, "Mr. Crandall has established a semi-weekly stage line between Placerville and Carson Valley."

Even so, his was not the first stagecoach to cross the Sierra Nevada, for the Oroville party had made it across the range to Honey Lake. The round trip had taken eleven days, but on returning they reported that "a dozen men in one month can make all the improvements necessary for a good immigrant road."

The road, however, was never improved, for in September Sacramento and El Dorado counties each voted $25,000 for improvements to what was then known as the Johnson's Pass road between Placerville and Genoa. When, in the spring of 1858, Postmaster General Brown was awarding California mail contracts over routes as far south as Tehuantepec so as to avoid the "impassable" mountains of the central overland route, Crandall's stagecoaches were regularly making the eighty-mile crossing of the Sierra Nevada twice a week on a one-day schedule.

8

The Butterfield
Overland Line

FROM Concord, New Hampshire, to southern Mexico work was going on at a feverish pace throughout the spring and summer of 1858 to build, equip, stock, and man the new or expanded routes for supplying California and the troops in Utah with mail and passenger transportation. But all the other preparations combined would not equal those being made on the Butterfield line.

When news of the Butterfield contract was released, showing its $600,000-a-year subsidy and 2795-mile route, the newspapers of the North sent up a howl of anguished protest. The *Chicago Tribune* called it "one of the greatest swindles ever perpetrated upon the country by the slave-holders." The *Sacramento Union* blasted it as "a foul wrong; a Panama route by land." New York editors called it a horseshoe or oxbow route avoiding every population center, reported that it lay through impassable savage-infested deserts, and predicted that it would prove too expensive to operate, even with its "scandalous subsidy."

Butterfield and his associates paid no attention to the newspapers. The course of the route and its length were regrettable, but unavoidable under the circumstances. Although the line would be much more expensive to stock and equip than a more direct route, it would have the advantage of being relatively snowless in winter. As to their ability to operate within the subsidy, Butterfield and his group had their own opinions. Their greatest concern was to be so well prepared to operate within a year from the signing of the contract that there would be no danger of defaulting on the twenty-five-day time limit for mail deliveries.

[97]

John Butterfield had been a skillful Yankee reinsman and stage-coach driver in his early youth and became an extremely successful expressman in his early manhood. In 1850 he joined with Henry Wells, William Fargo, and other prominent expressmen to found the American Express Company, which he built into one of the wealthiest firms in the country. Although fifty-six years of age when the mail contract was signed, Butterfield retained all the driving force of his youth and knew the transportation business thoroughly.

The contract was no sooner signed than Butterfield sent representatives to hunt out and employ guides, scouts, and frontiersmen who were friendly with the various Indian tribes along the route and who knew every spring, water hole, stream ford, or mountain pass. At the same time he sent one of his associates, Marcus L. Kinyon (often spelled Kenyon), to San Francisco by sea to engage the most successful stage-line operators available and start construction of the line from that end.

As frontiersmen were being employed and brought in, Butterfield also gathered together the most capable construction and operating superintendents from the four great express companies headed by himself and his associates. No more expert group of men could have been assembled for laying out and constructing a stage line through a wilderness than that which John Butterfield led out of St. Louis in the fall of 1857.

The first 160 miles of the line required no construction or stocking, as passengers and mail would be carried by railroad to Tipton, the railhead about forty miles west of Jefferson City, Missouri. Between Tipton and Fort Smith, Arkansas, the route chosen passed through the cities of Springfield and Fayette, making use of the most direct existing roads where relay posts could be established at towns or settlements approximately fifteen miles apart.

The route between Fort Smith and El Paso that had been agreed upon with the Postmaster General was the trail pioneered by Captain Randolph Marcy in 1849. It had been used by a few parties during the California gold rush, but the loss of life in western Texas was extremely high due to lack of water. At best, it was no more than a set of wheel tracks, and a large portion of it only an indefinite course between rivers, springs, and water holes.

The route laid out by the Butterfield party followed the Marcy Trail from Fort Smith across the southeastern corner of Indian Territory to Sherman, Texas, straight north of Dallas. Almost the entire distance was through the reservation of the Choctaw and Chickasaw Indians, many of whom were prosperous cattle raisers.

Along the way agreements were made for stocking relay posts fifteen to eighteen miles apart at Indian farms or settlements. Arrangements were made for crossing Red River a few miles north of Sherman on a ferry to be installed and operated by Benjamin Franklin Colbert, a Chickasaw Indian and one of the wealthiest men in the region.

From Sherman the Marcy Trail led southwest across the prairies past Fort Belknap on the Brazos River, Big Spring on the Colorado River, and to the Pecos River on the approximate line of present U.S. Highway 80. The latter half of this trail was across Comanche territory, the most arid and dangerous section of the Marcy route, with 132 waterless miles between Big Spring and the Pecos. To avoid this stretch, the Butterfield party laid out a route on the Marcy Trail only as far as Fort Belknap, then followed the cavalry trail to Fort Chadbourne, thirty-two miles southwest of present Abilene. From there they chose a course along the route pioneered by Lieutenant Bryan in 1849, past the headwaters of Concho River and the alkaline Mustang ponds, reaching the Pecos at Horsehead Crossing, the most famous fording place in the Southwest.

Instead of crossing the river and going straight ahead a few miles to intercept the San Antonio-El Paso military road, the Butterfield party laid out a route that followed the *east* side of Pecos River approximately 120 miles upstream (contrary to most published maps of the route). A few miles south of the 32nd parallel the Pecos was forded near the mouth of Delaware Creek. From there the route turned westward along the Texas-New Mexico boundary to El Paso, crossing the Sacramento Mountains at Guadalupe Pass and skirting the southern tip of the Cornudas and Hueco ranges. From Fort Belknap westward, sites for relay stations were chosen only where water and grass were found.

El Paso was then on the Mexican side of the Rio Grande, so the midway station of the mail line was established at the settlement of Franklin, on the Texas side of the river. Between Franklin and Yuma, Arizona, the $200,000 road-building project authorized by Congress was under way. The Butterfield party, however, chose to use only a few miles of it, preferring the original Jack Hays-Mormon Battalion road. This led northward forty-five miles along the east side of the Rio Grande past Fort Fillmore to the little settlement of Doña Ana near present Las Cruces, New Mexico. There it crossed the river at a treacherous ford, intersected the Mormon road at Cooke's Spring, and continued westward across the deserts and mountains to Tucson. This was Apache territory, and Apache Pass through the Chiricahua Mountains was the most dangerous gantlet to be run on the entire line. Due to the danger of Apache raids, only nine relay posts were laid out on the 315-mile stretch between the Rio Grande and Tucson. Beyond Tucson, the mail line was laid out from the western end under the direction of Marcus Kinyon and John Butterfield, Jr.

A time schedule was prepared based upon traveling around the clock at the average rate of four and a half miles per hour, and wherever practicable a way station was laid out at the end of each day's travel. These were to have sleeping and feeding accommodations for passengers, help's quarters, storerooms, blacksmith's and harnessmaker's shops, corrals, an unfailing water supply, and stables large enough to accommodate a score or more of horses or mules and a two-month supply of hay and grain. Each way station was to be placed in charge of an agent who was friendly with the Indians of the vicinity, one if available who spoke their language. He would have from six to a dozen men as

Adobe stage station at Twenty-Two Ranch, Colorado. Most of the relay posts on the desert were constructed of adobe bricks. (Courtesy, State Historical Society of Colorado.)

assistants, hostlers, and guards, depending upon the location and danger of Indian attack.

In populated areas arrangements were made with livery stable owners or farmers for boarding horses and supplying relay service. In uninhabited regions mules were to be used instead of horses. They were not to be stabled but corralled at night or when required for relays. At other times they were to be grazed nearby if grass were available and there was little danger of Indian raids, for the cost of hauling hay and grain to these remote posts would be tremendous. At each isolated relay post plans were made for housing a keeper and from two to six men who would serve as hostlers, guards, and teamsters, depending upon the number of animals to be cared for, the Indian danger, and the distance that feed, and in some cases water, would have to be hauled.

Most of the stations and relay posts on the prairies were to be constructed of sod, and those on the deserts of adobe bricks made on the site by Mexican laborers. Where Indian raids on the stock were to be expected, the corrals were to be surrounded by thick sod or adobe walls six to eight feet high. In Apache territory the buildings were to be constructed of stone whenever it was available.

Although the greater part of the route lay through wild and semiarid territory, it was not particularly difficult to traverse with wheeled vehicles, for it was mostly over open prairies and deserts, with few large rivers or high mountains. Butterfield made no attempt to build an actual road between Fort Smith and El Paso. Roadways were cut into the steep banks of gulches, ravines, creeks, and fordable rivers; the narrower unfordable streams and deep ravines were bridged with logs; and ferries were installed at rivers that were too wide for bridging at reasonable cost. Other obstacles were circumvented, and only enough grading was done to prevent upsets.

While Butterfield was getting construction under way on the eastern portion of the line, Marcus Kinyon was equally busy with preparations on the western end. The *Sacramento Union* of December 22, 1857, reported his arrival at San Francisco by steamer. He at once retained Charles McLaughlin, who owned most of the stage line operating out of San Francisco, as general agent there. As superintendents for manning and stocking the line between San Francisco and Tucson he engaged Warren Hall, of the original firm of Hall & Crandall, and E. G. Stevens, one of the best stage-line men in California.

Kinyon evidently wasted no time, for on January 8 the San Francisco *Alta California* reported: "Two four horse wagons were

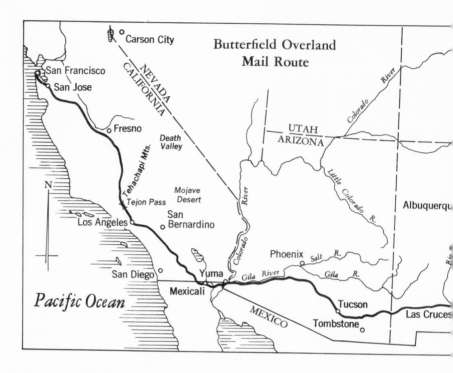

Butterfield Overland
Mail Route

Carson City

San Francisco
San Jose

NEVADA
CALIFORNIA

Fresno
Death
Valley

Tehachapi Mts.

Mojave
Desert

Tejon Pass

San
Bernardino

Los Angeles

N

UTAH
ARIZONA

Little Colorado R.

Colorado River

Albuquerqu

San Diego

Yuma

Mexicali

Gila River

Colorado

Phoenix Salt R.

Gila R.

Pacific Ocean

MEXICO

Tucson

Tombstone

Las Cruces

A victory for the proslavery forces, the Overland Mail Route cut an "oxbow" trail through the southwest. Unlike the

dispatched yesterday by M. S. Kinyon, for the Tejon Pass via the San Jose Valley, designed as a part of the expedition to select the route to be traveled by the line of Mail Stages provided for in the contract with Butterfield & Co. with the Government. Mr. Kinyon, who is a partner in the contract, will remain here a few days and then take the steamer for Los Angeles, where he will join the party under his orders."

The report went on to say that both wagons would cross the Diablo Range to the San Joaquin Valley by way of Pacheco's Pass. They would then separate, one surveying a route to Tejon Pass along the western edge of the valley while the second explored the eastern side.

Two weeks later the *Mariposa Democrat* reported the following from Visalia, then the most southerly settlement in the San Joaquin Valley: "A party to survey a wagon road, over which to carry the United States mail, by the Butterfield contract, stopped at this place on the 17th, and left on the 18th for St. Louis, across

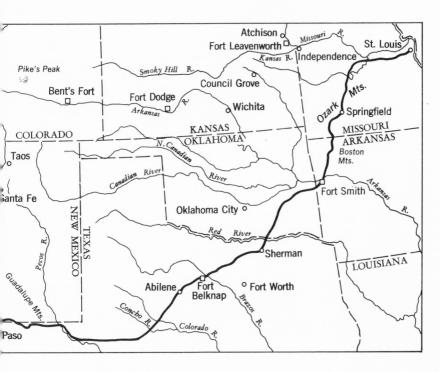

straighter central route, it was almost always passable in winter when snows blocked the trails to the north.

the plains, via Fort Tejon, Los Angeles and Fort Yuma. . . . A son of the contractor, Mr. Butterfield, is with the party."

Neither of the wagon parties, however, appears to have continued on the planned route beyond Tejon Pass. A correspondent for the *San Francisco Call* reported from San Bernardino February 4: "On Saturday evening last, we had an arrival from the vanguard of the overland stage line. Two pioneer wagons belonging to the great Butterfield Stage Company, came here from San Francisco, by way of Tulare Valley, east of the Coast range, through Cajon Pass. They were twenty-four days from your city. On Monday, they pushed on toward Fort Yuma, from whence the route is already known to be practicable. As a matter of course, they are delighted with the route, and when the stage line gets in full blast, your Panama steamers might as well lie up—perhaps."

Cajon Pass is the opening between the San Gabriel and San Bernardino mountains, leading eastward into the Mojave Desert. It is therefore evident that the explorers had a guide from Visalia who led them eastward into the desert from Fort Tejon, over the route that is now California Highway 138, then southeast along the route pioneered by Jedediah Smith in 1826, and over Cajon Pass to San Bernardino, bypassing Los Angeles completely.

From San Bernardino, John Butterfield, Jr., and his party continued southeastward across the Colorado Desert to Fort Yuma, choosing locations for eleven relay stations along the way. They undoubtedly followed the route traveled by most of the forty-niners who came to California by way of the Gila Trail and over which Phineas Banning's freight caravans hauled supplies to Fort Yuma. The line was approximately that which is now U.S. Highway 99 to Mexicali and Mexican Route 2 eastward below the international boundary to the Colorado River. From Fort Yuma Butterfield, Jr., with one of the wagons and most of the men, continued eastward to St. Louis, choosing station locations on their way to Tucson, while Hall and Stevens returned to join Marcus Kinyon.

San Bernardino, then only a few years old, was a town populated mainly by members of the Mormon Battalion who had settled there after finishing out their enlistments at San Diego. To them the route chosen by the road explorers appeared as a godsend, for it was generally believed that a transcontinental railroad, when built, would follow the route of the mail line. Anxious that there be no change in the Butterfield plans, the citizens of San Bernardino at once set about digging wells across the deserts in both directions at locations that had been selected for relay stations.

When news that their city had been bypassed reached the Angelenos they set up a terrible howl. Kinyon, however, refused to change the course already laid out unless the established stage road by way of Santa Barbara and Salinas Valley was decidedly improved or the precipitous grades on the Banning road by way of Tejon Pass were cut down enough so that six horses could pull a heavily loaded coach up them without difficulty. The people of Santa Barbara and San Luis Obispo, eager for the mail line to pass through their cities, went about raising funds for improving the existing stage road, but they were not fast enough. Within hours after Kinyon had set his terms, Phineas Banning and seven other leading citizens of Los Angeles had contributed $3000 toward the cost of cutting down the grades and improving the road across the Tehachapi Mountains by way of Tejon Pass. Among the contributors was Andres Pico, commander of the Mexican force that had soundly whipped Kearny's Army of the West at San Pasqual.

Throughout the summer of 1858 the thunder of blasting powder and the shouts of grading crews echoed through the Tehachapis. The road those determined Angelenos built was hardly comparable to the present six- to eight-lane freeway on which a modern car can easily be driven over the Tehachapis by the same fifty-five-mile route in fifty minutes, but it was then one of the best mountain roads in the West.

With the San Bernardino bypass abandoned, the route selected for the Butterfield stage road from Los Angeles to San Francisco was roughly the same as that of U.S. Highway 99 as far as Visalia. There it took a more westerly course to the tiny settlement of Fresno City (thirty miles west of present Fresno), then followed the west side of the Kings and San Joaquin rivers to Firebaugh's Ferry. Instead of crossing at the ferry, as is generally believed, the Butterfield road continued along the west side of the river to the vicinity of Los Banos, where it turned westward over Pacheco Pass to Gilroy on a toll road built and maintained by Andrew Firebaugh, now approximated by California Highway 152. From Gilroy the route to San Francisco was over the well-traveled El Camino Real through San Jose and along the shore of the bay.

The Tejon Pass crossing of the Tehachapis made the route laid out between San Bernardino and Fort Yuma impractical, so Hall and Stevens laid out another from Los Angeles. To avoid desert travel as much as possible they turned southward from the San Bernardino road at Pomona and followed the route that is now

Escorting the overland mail. (From Nebraska History Magazine, *1948.)*

California Highway 71 through the interior valley east of the Santa Ana Mountains to Aguanga at the end of the range. Circling the base of Mount Palomar, present site of the famous Palomar Observatory, they intercepted the Cooke Wagon Road where it turned westward to San Diego from Warner's Ranch in San Felipe Valley.

Although advertised as the route of the San Antonio-San Diego mail line, the road between Warner's and Fort Yuma had been traveled by vehicles very little since originally opened by the Mormon Battalion. At the south end of San Felipe Valley it threaded a canyon with perpendicular rock walls barely far enough apart to let a wagon through. Beyond the pass the road snaked for twenty miles through rough boulder-strewn canyons, then emerged into Vallecito (Little Valley), a green oasis at the edge of the Colorado Desert. Beyond the valley all signs of the Cooke road were lost in the shifting sands. After crossing what is now Anza Desert State Park in the dry beds of Vallecito and Carrizo creeks, Hall and Stevens laid out a course almost straight to the present site of Mexicali, where they intersected the line to Fort Yuma that had been laid out by Butterfield, Jr. From Carrizo Creek to the Colorado River was ninety miles, without a drop of water to be found during the summer dry season.

Twelve relay posts and way stations were built, supplied, stocked, and manned along the 282-mile section of the line between Fort Yuma and Los Angeles, with tank wagons constantly hauling water to those in the desert. Little trace of the old stage line now remains, but the Vallecito way station with its sod walls and hand-hewn beams, doors, and window frames has been restored. It is thirty-two miles southeast of Julian, and can be reached via the Foster Grade road from California Route 78.

While field crews were building relay posts and stations, digging wells, and bridging unfordable streams, Butterfield and the general superintendents at both ends of the line were assembling and forwarding the provisions, feed, horses, mules, harness, and vehicles necessary for putting the line into operation. Stockton, on the San Joaquin River, could be reached by ocean vessels and was more easily accessible to the line than San Francisco, so Kinyon used it as receiving port for materials shipped from the East.

On August 6, 1858, the *Stockton Republican* reported: "Stages Nos. 3 and 10, of the Overland Stage Company, arrived in town yesterday, and will be dispatched forthwith upon the road. They are large Concord built, spring wagons, capable of carrying fourteen persons comfortably. . . . As the ship in which are fifty of these wagons and two hundred sets of harness has not yet arrived, though out over two hundred days, these coaches were purchased in San Francisco."

Actually, the vehicles, which arrived soon afterward on the overdue vessel, were celerity wagons, mounted on thoroughbraces rather than steel springs. These light wagons had three seats, the backs of which could be turned down to form a bed for night travel. At the outset, celerity wagons were used entirely, except on the San Francisco–San Jose run and that between Tipton and Springfield, Missouri, where Concord stagecoaches were used.

On August 11 the *Republican* reported, "Yesterday morning, six four-horse and two six-horse coaches were despatched by Fisher & Co. out upon the road for use of the Overland Mail Company. This morning, six more four-horse coaches will start, and three hundred California horses. The horses are branded on the hip, O.M.A. detachment of thirty of the employees of the Company started yesterday, and twenty-five more will start today."

Similar reports might have been made from St. Louis, Fort Smith, and Los Angeles, for preparations were being pushed ahead rapidly from both ends of the line. But with nearly fifteen hundred miles of the route lying in an uninhabited wilderness, six months had been required for exploration and layout. The remaining time was too short for completing, supplying, and stocking more than a few of the planned relay posts farthest from sources of supply.

A thousand horses, five hundred mules, eight hundred sets of harness, and approximately five hundred vehicles had been bought at a cost of nearly a million dollars and were being distributed along the line as rapidly as possible. About half the vehicles were celerity wagons, mud wagons, and Concord stagecoaches; the rest were freight, utility, and water wagons. Although there is no exact record, it has been estimated that the line was manned with more than eight hundred employees, each of them chosen for his knowledge of the section in which he worked as well as for his ability. Most of them were rough, tough frontiersmen, for no other men could have performed the tasks demanded by such an undertaking.

Of the nearly 200 way stations and relay posts planned, 139 were completed and stocked during the summer of 1858. California had the greatest number, with fifty between San Francisco and Fort Yuma, the shortest distance between any two being eight miles and the longest twenty-four. The eastern end of the line was equally well prepared, with well-stocked and supplied way stations and relay posts averaging fifteen miles apart on the stretch between Tipton and Fort Belknap. But on the 580-mile stretch between Fort Belknap and El Paso only ten relay posts had been completed, and although feed, provisions, harness, and mules were on the way they had not yet reached some of the posts.

In midsummer Butterfield made an inspection trip over the line, gathered his men at the various way stations, and gave them their final instructions: above all else, passengers and mail must be protected and schedules maintained, and this could be accomplished only by keeping on friendly terms with the Indians along the way. Although drivers and conductors would be armed, they were to use their weapons only when the lives of passengers or safety of the mail were definitely endangered. To avoid the possibility of attacks by highwaymen, no shipments of gold or silver were to be transported under any circumstances. In the event that mules or horses were stolen by Indians, it was the responsibility of the division superintendent to secure their return by peaceful means. Failing in this, he was to report the incident to the nearest U.S. military post, but to take no other action.

Station masters and relay post keepers would be held accountable not only for the safety of passengers and mail, but for the condition and protection of company property and animals in their care. But in case of Indian attack, they were to shoot to kill only if passengers', their help's, or their own lives were endangered. Teams of well-shod and rested horses or mules were to be kept ready for the road at all times and harnessed immediately when, from two miles distant, the conductor of an incoming stage sounded a trumpet call. Ten minutes was the maximum time allowed for a relay stop unless passengers were to be fed, and any keeper would be discharged if a delay was caused by his unreadiness to supply a fresh relay or feed passengers arriving at a mealtime. In the event the driver of an incoming stage was incapacitated for any reason, the keeper was to take his place.

In order for stages to roll swiftly and safely through the darkest night, drivers must know every twist and turn of the road. To make this possible, each driver would have his own route, a section approximately sixty miles long over which, except in extreme emergencies, he would do all the driving in both directions. He would be housed and fed at the way station or relay post at each end of his route, but regardless of rest he must take any incoming coach out within ten minutes after its arrival. Under no circumstances was he to treat his horses or mules with brutality, but was not to spare them at the expense of running behind schedule, and he was not to spare his own life in an effort to protect passengers and mail.

No stage would roll without a conductor seated beside the

driver, and his route would be between way stations about a hundred and twenty miles apart. He would have absolute charge of passengers, mail, and express, guard them with his life if necessary, and be relieved of his responsibility only when he had received a detailed written receipt from the next conductor. If when he reached the end of his route the conductor for the next section was not there and entirely capable of assuming responsibility, he must continue on without sleep or rest until relieved by another conductor or the division superintendent.

The passenger fare between San Francisco and St. Louis or Memphis was set at $200 westbound and $100 eastbound, or ten cents per mile for shorter distances. Each passenger would be allowed forty pounds of baggage without extra charge. He could carry his own food or buy meals at the way stations and certain relay posts for seventy-five cents or a dollar, depending upon the distance provisions had to be hauled.

At each meeting Butterfield's last words to his men were: "Remember, boys, nothing on God's earth must stop the United States mail!"

9

First Overland
Stage Journey

AFTER the Californians' long fight for frequent and rapid transcontinental mail and passenger service, one might have expected them to be jubilant when the first stagecoach pulled away for St. Louis, but it created hardly a ripple in San Francisco. There was a very short article in the *Evening Bulletin* of September 14: "The through mail to Memphis and St. Louis starts from this city at one o'clock to-morrow morning. . . . Preparations have been made, as we are informed, to transport promptly any number of passengers that may offer, or any amount of mail matter."

The same issue carried a longer article regarding the arrival at Placerville on September 13 of "the overland mail coach . . . with two passengers and the U. S. mail which left Salt Lake City Sept. 1st . . . containing St. Louis dates to August 6th, but no news of interest."

The *Daily Alta California* evidently did not think inauguration of the Butterfield service to be newsworthy until after the first stagecoach had rolled out of the city without fanfare and in the middle of the night. On September 15 it ran this short second-page article:

THE SOUTHERN OVERLAND MAIL.—The first mail coach on the Southern Overland Mail route, started this morning at 1 o'clock, for Memphis and St. Louis. Think of that! A semi-weekly coach for these two far distant cities, is now a fixed fact with us, and no longer a coveted project. We can scarcely realize it and yet we find before us the following list of passengers by the first coach . . . L. Aldrich, C. H. Wilkinson, and James

R. Jones, for Springfield, Missouri; Oliver James, for Memphis, Tennessee; Charles Strihle and Samuel Johnson for Fa[l]l R[i]ver and Willet Dunn, for Visalia.

There was no comment as to the amount of mail carried and no mention of Postal Inspector Bailey, who accompanied the first mail to St. Louis. He kept careful notes of the mileage, the condition of roads and stations, the adequacy of stock and equipment, and the efficiency of employees. In his report to the Postmaster General, Bailey wrote that in his opinion the Overland Mail Company had complied with the terms of its contract and that "thus far, the experiment has proved successful," but he noted that the firm had not yet demonstrated its ability to cope with possible Indian trouble.

The eastbound stage was nearly two hundred miles out of San Francisco when, a few minutes before 8:00 A.M. on September 16, a Butterfield utility wagon dashed away from the St. Louis Post Office. It carried the postmaster but only "two diminutive bags of mail," as he had included only letters marked "per overland mail." At the depot the bags were handed to John Butterfield, and the Pacific Railroad's flyer pulled away for Tipton as he swung aboard precisely at eight o'clock. With him went twenty-three-year-old Waterman Ormsby, correspondent for the *New York Herald*, the only through passenger on the first westbound Overland Mail stage. The articles he wrote for his paper provide an excellent description of the earliest transcontinental stage travel and give an unbiased report on the condition of the Butterfield line at the time service was inaugurated.

The wood-burning engines of the mid-1850's were none too dependable, the fireman had trouble keeping up a head of steam, and it was 6:01 in the evening before the flyer reached Tipton. There John Butterfield, Jr. waited with a new, brightly painted Concord stagecoach, with OVERLAND MAIL COMPANY lettered above the doors in gold leaf. In nine minutes John Butterfield, Sr., the publisher of the Fort Smith newspaper, Ormsby, the mail sacks, baggage, and a few express parcels were transferred to the coach. Young Butterfield cracked his whip above the backs of four fast horses, and they pulled away at a smart trot.

The occasion drew a bigger crowd in Tipton than in San Francisco, but the excitement was about equal. Of it Ormsby wrote, "The town contains but a few hundred inhabitants, and they made no demonstration. . . . Not a cheer was raised as the coach drove off, the only adieu being, 'Good bye, John,' addressed to John, Jr., by one of the crowd. Had they have been wild Indians they could not have exhibited less emotion."

Fresh teams were waiting at each relay post, and at times through the night Butterfield, Sr. relieved his son at the reins. The 148-mile drive to Springfield was made in less than twenty hours, putting the mail sixteen and a half hours ahead of the schedule. The Concord coach was not taken beyond Springfield, and Ormsby wrote, "Our stay was just long enough to change from the coach to one of the wagons, such as are used from this point to San Francisco. . . . Each one has three seats, which are arranged so that the backs let down and form one bed, capable of accommodating from four to ten, according to their size and how they lie. I found it a very agreeable bed for one, afterwards. Everything being in readiness, we got started again at four o'clock, having been detained at Springfield three-quarters of an hour. We drove off to the post office and took on a small through mail for San Francisco, and also the postmaster and another citizen, who wished to have it to say that they had ridden in the first coach from Springfield containing the overland mail. It was gratifying to me, as one of the few evidences of interest in the enterprise which we met. One thing struck me as creditable, and that was that the mail bag from Springfield was quite as large as that from St. Louis."

At Springfield, Ormsby evidently became quite enthusiastic because of the amount of time that had been gained on the schedule, and for a few days the trip became for him a race against time. On entering Arkansas he wrote, "We kept travelling all day and night, of course, our way during Friday afternoon and evening being through an extremely dusty, hilly, and stony road . . . over those steep and rugged hills which surround the Ozark range. . . . I jumped out and got water for the horses, kept an eye on the mail bags, walked up the steep hills, and forgot the terrible pain in the back which such incessant riding without sleep occasioned."

At 2:05 on Sunday morning the stage pulled into Fort Smith, twenty-five hours and twenty-five minutes ahead of schedule, and Ormsby wrote, "as we entered the town, though at so unseasonable an hour, we found it in a great state of excitement on account of the arrival of the Memphis mail just fifteen minutes before us. . . . Horns were blown, houses were lit up, and many flocked to the hotel to have a look at the wagons and talk over the exciting topic, and have a peep at the first mail bags. . . . I was the only person in the wagon which left Fort Smith—beside Mr. Fox, the mail agent, and driver. Mr. John Butterfield, the president of the Overland Mail Company, had accompanied us thus far, and . . . had borne the fatiguing journey as well, if not better, than any of the rest. Certainly, if the overland mail does not succeed, it will not be for lack of his arduous personal exertions."

A later passenger called the Butterfield route through Indian Territory "two hundred miles of the worst road God ever built," but Ormsby wrote, "for the first time since our departure from St. Louis I had an opportunity to sleep in the wagon, wrapped up in blankets and stretched on the seats. It took some time to get accustomed to the jolting over the rough road, the rocks, and log bridges, but three days' steady riding without sleep helped me in getting used to it, and I was quite oblivious from the time of crossing the Arkansas . . ."

But Ormsby had been somewhat apprehensive about crossing Indian Territory, and it must have preyed upon his mind, for he wrote, "I awoke but once during the night, having been jolted into a position where my neck felt as if there was a knot in it. They had stopped at a station to change horses, and for the time not a sound could I hear. I had been dreaming of the Comanche Indians, and in the confusion of drowsiness first thought that the driver and mail agent had been murdered, and that I, being covered up in the blankets, had been missed; then I recollected that I had a pistol and thought of feeling for it; but finally I thought I would not stir, for fear the Indians would see me—when I was brought to my senses by a familiar voice saying, 'Git up there, old hoss,' and found it was the driver hitching up a new team."

Ormsby got over his apprehensions when he found the Choctaws friendly. ". . . about sixty-six miles from the river," he wrote, "I met an old Indian who owns seven hundred head of cattle, and a pretty daughter, and is willing to give the half of the one to the white man who will marry the other. Here I gave an Indian boy a paper of tobacco to give me water enough to wash my face, put on a blue flannel shirt, and consider myself pretty well on my way out West."

The Choctaws proved to be excellent relay post keepers, the stock was of fine quality, fresh teams were always harnessed and waiting when the stage pulled in, and every driver was eager to set a time record on his run. Of Sunday night Ormsby reported, "We had taken a splended team of horses at the last station, and had been spinning over rolling prairies at a rapid rate. . . . We now came to a patch of woods through which the road was tortuous and stony. But our driver's ambition to make good time overcame his caution, and away we went, bounding over the stones at a fearful rate. The moon shone brightly, but its light was obstructed by the trees, and the driver had to rely much on his knowledge of the road for a guide. To see the heavy mail wagon whizzing and whirling over the jagged rock, through such a labyrinth, in comparative darkness, and to feel oneself bouncing— now on the hard seat, now against the roof, and now against the side of the wagon—was no joke, I assure you, though I can truthfully say that I rather liked the excitement of the thing. But it was too dangerous to be continued without accident, and soon two heavy thumps and a bound of the wagon that unseated us all, and a crashing sound, denoted that something had broken."

It proved to be nothing more than a broken seat and split wagon tongue, so repairs were quickly made at the next relay post and during the remainder of the night the stage was preceded by a horseback rider carrying a lantern.

For all its bad roads, Indian Territory was crossed at an average speed of better than seven miles per hour, and the stage pulled up to Colbert's Ferry on the Red River at ten minutes before ten on Monday morning, thirty-four hours ahead of schedule. "Mr. Colbert, the owner of the station and of the ferry," Ormsby wrote, "is a half-breed Indian of great sagacity and business tact. He is a young man—not quite thirty, I should judge—and has a white wife—his third. Mr. Colbert evinces some enterprise in carrying the stages of the company across his ferry free of charge, in consideration of the increased travel which it will bring his way. . . . He has a fine farm, and raises considerable corn. . . . At his table I saw sugar, butter, and pastry. . . ." Ormsby was mistaken in thinking Colbert, a full-blooded Chickasaw, to be a half-breed, but correct about his wives.

Upon arriving at the ferry, Ormsby expected the entire trip to be made in twenty days or less, for the first quarter had been traveled in slightly less than four days and two hours. Colbert, however, had not expected the arrival so far ahead of schedule and the horses were all out to pasture, so two hours were lost in reaching Sherman, Texas, the next relay station.

The Texas superintendents had been hard pressed in trying to get their wilderness divisions prepared in so short a time. A rider was sent in advance to have relays ready, and Ormsby noted, "Mr. Bates' part of the road was so poorly stocked with animals, and those he had were so worn out in forwarding stuff for the other parts of the line, that he had to hire an extra team of mules, at short notice, to forward the mail to the next station. . . . Most of the stock consisted of wild mules which had just been broken, and the process had not fitted them very well for carrying the mail with rapidity. . . . [We] had our first opportunity of witnessing the operation of harnessing a wild mule. First he had to be secured with a laretto [lariat, or *la reata*] round his neck, and drawn by main force to a tree or post; then the harness had to be put on piece by piece, care being taken to avoid his teeth and heels. Altogether, I should estimate the time consumed in the process at not less than half an hour to each wild mule. . . . I was much amused with the process, but it seemed a little behind the age for the mail to wait for it, and no doubt when all the company's wild mules are tamed the mail will make better time."

At the next station he wrote, "There was nothing in readiness, the express rider having lost his way, and some detention was experienced in harnessing more wild mules . . . we had the first of a series of rough meals, which lasted for most of the remaining journey. The house was built of rough logs laid together roughly, and the chinks filled in with mud. The house was about twenty feet square, forming one room, and was occupied by two men keeping bachelors' hall, as might well be judged from the condition of things, of which the reader may imagine.

"Our arrival was unexpected, and there was some bustle in getting both breakfast and the team ready. The breakfast was served on the bottom of a candle box, and such as sat down were perched on inverted pails or nature's chair. There were no plates and but four tin cups for the coffee, which was served without milk or sugar. The edible—for there was but one—consisted of a kind of short cake, baked on the coals, each man breaking off his 'chunk.' . . . It tasted good to me, and I can assure you that it would doubtless taste as well to any one coming over the same route at the same rate of speed . . . doubtless it will be [better] when the line gets in running order so as to convey supplies to the stations."

The next morning he reported, "Our mules were exceedingly stubborn and lazy during the night, and required the most constant urging to keep them on a respectable trot. . . . As we left Belknap we crossed the Brazos River, fording it with ease, as the dirty red water was not deeper than an ordinary New York gutter. . . . The fort is not very formidable. The only objects of interest passed on the road were a train of government mules, a Comanche Indian woman riding 'straddle,' and herds of cattle taking care of themselves. This woman, by the way, was the only one of the bloodthirsty Comanche Nation that I had the pleasure of seeing, though terrible tales are told of their deeds of blood in this section of the country. . . .

"Our next stopping place was at Smith's station. . . . No house

[115]

had been built yet, those at the station living in tents. They had nearly finished a fine corral for the stock, making it of brush (as no timber could be had) and filling in the chinks with mud. Our supper consisted of cake cooked in the coals, clear coffee, and some dried beef cooked in Mrs. Smith's best style. We changed horses or mules and swallowed supper in double quick time and were soon on our way again.

"Our next stopping place was at Phantom Hill, a deserted military post, seventy-four miles from Fort Belknap and fifty-six from Chadbourne. . . . After being occupied for some time [it] was destroyed by fire by the soldiers in 1853. . . . Most of the chimneys are still standing. . . . The stable is also a fine stone building, so that, altogether, Phantom Hill is the cheapest and best new station on the route."

Although Phantom Hill station had a fine stone stable, no stock had yet been received for it, so the driver of Ormsby's stage was obliged to go on to the next relay post with his jaded mules. In midafternoon of September 23 the stage pulled into Fort Chadbourne, having lost ten of the thirty-four hours gained on the schedule between Tipton and Colbert's Ferry.

Waiting for the mail in San Francisco. (Courtesy, Old Print Shop.)

At Fort Chadbourne the initial stock of Mexican mules had been received, but they were particularly wild. Several hours were lost in catching a team of them and tying down and harnessing them. Four were at last hitched to the stage wagon, but a start had no sooner been made than, according to Ormsby, "the mules reared, pitched, whirled, wheeled, ran, stood still, and cut up all sorts of capers. The wagon performed so many evolutions that I, in fear of my life, abandoned it and took to my heels, fully confident that I would make more progress in a straight line, with much less risk of breaking my neck. . . . The gyrations continued to considerable length, winding up with tangling all the mules pretty well in the harness, the escape of the leaders, and the complete demolition of the top of the wagon; while those in charge of it lay around loose on the grass, and all were pretty well tired out and disgusted . . ."

Eventually the driver got the wagon back onto its wheels, the mules back into harness, and decided to go on. Ormsby, "finding persuasion of no avail, overcame my strong objections and concluded to go, though if I had had any property I certainly should have made a hasty will . . . but I was bound to go with the mail. Fortunately our course was a clear and straight one, leading across an apparently boundless prairie, with not a tree or shrub to be seen, the parched grass almost glistening in the light of the moon."

The following morning they reached Grape Creek, where a supply of mules had been brought and several men were starting to build a relay station. There was timber along the creek, and they had already built a stout corral of logs, inside which they had pitched their tents for fear of Comanche attacks. To the next relay post, at the head of the Concho River, was fifty-six miles, so a drover was taken along with spare mules for changing teams at intervals along the route.

Since it was necessary to rest and graze the mules wherever grass was found, slow progress was made; Concho River was not reached until the morning of September 25. There was no timber there, and the men were living in tents, but had built a large brush-fenced corral in which a herd of particularly wild mules was enclosed. More than an hour was lost in catching and harnessing four of them to the stage, and again spares were taken along as no relay post had yet been established between the Concho and Pecos rivers.

A few miles beyond the Concho a stop was made at Mustang Spring, "the last water before seventy-five miles of desert," to let the mules drink and fill casks for the crossing. Soon after starting on, the spare mules stampeded and got away from the Mexican drover, and only two could be run down and recovered. With only half a relay, stops had to be made often to rest the jaded mules or to graze them where grass was found. The trail being followed across the Staked Plain between Mustang Springs and Pecos River had been disastrous to the gold-rush parties who took it in the summer of 1849, unaware that no water was to be found. ". . . the bones of cattle and sometimes men," Ormsby wrote, "all told a fearful story of anguish and terrific death from the pangs of thirst. For miles and miles these bones strew the plain—the silent witnesses of the eternal laws of nature, which, in the hope of gain, man hesitates not to brave."

Although there was no suffering by the men in the mail party for lack of water, progress was slowed to less than three miles an hour due to lack of relay stations and fresh mules. Of the thirty-four hours gained on the schedule between Tipton and Colbert's Ferry, all but fifteen minutes had been lost before Horsehead Crossing was reached. There they found the superintendent of the Fort Chadbourne-El Paso division, who had arrived only a few hours earlier with fifteen Mexicans and a herd of mules for stocking the line. Even though the mules were worn down from having just been driven seventy-five miles across the Staked Plain, they were so wild that nearly two hours were lost while four of them were lassoed, thrown, harnessed, and hitched to the celerity wagon. At dawn a start was made up the east side of Pecos River, with a couple of Mexicans driving along a relay herd of eighteen already weary mules, for there were 120 miles to be traveled before fresh animals would be available.

The going was rough. With the top kicked off the celerity wagon during the runaway at Fort Chadbourne, the sun beat directly down on Ormsby's head, and he wrote that it was "by no means pleasant riding in the thorough braced wagon, for the jolting was almost interminable and insufferable [as we] pursued our weary course along the edge of the plain, thumping and bumping at a rate which threatened not to leave a whole bone in my body."

At Emigrant Crossing three Americans and half a dozen Mexicans were found starting to build an adobe station. They had built a corral with high adobe walls, but had neither mules nor feed, and very few provisions. Half the mules that had been driven along from Horsehead Crossing (those nearest exhaustion) were left to stock the relay post, and the mail party continued up the Pecos, "jolting along almost at snail's pace." Before reaching the relay post at the Texas-New Mexico boundary, six of the remaining mules gave out and had to be abandoned.

With fresh mules and only sixty miles to Guadalupe Pass, the next stocked relay post, no spare animals were driven along. The Pecos was forded at the mouth of Delaware Creek and a course set westward toward Guadalupe Peak, which showed clearly in the bright moonlight, towering four thousand feet above the level plain. At daybreak the peak appeared to be only three or four miles away, but the climb to the pass required the whole day, and the exhausted mules were barely able to haul the empty wagon to the summit.

Supper and a fresh team were provided at the head of the pass, and at sunset they set off through the deep, rock-walled canyon leading down to the west. Just before the bottom was reached at twilight the driver pointed out the grave of a Mexican guide who had gone too far in advance of his party and been murdered by Indians. Darkness had settled and Ormsby was feeling more than a bit apprehensive when a spark of light gleamed in the canyon ahead and he heard the sound of voices. Much to his relief, it proved to be the first eastbound stage. Ormsby reported it to be "eight hours ahead of time," though it was actually twenty-two hours and forty-five minutes late, having left San Francisco thirty-one hours ahead of schedule. Only a brief stop was made for exchanging bits of news, and then both parties continued their plodding way across Texas. Doubtless wearied nearly to the point of exhaustion and bitterly disappointed by the loss of time, Ormsby wrote, as the stage approached El Paso more than forty-two hours behind schedule: "Many obstacles have been overcome, and I am sanguine of the ultimate success of the enterprise, however much I may now doubt its efficiency as an expeditious mail or available passenger route."

His dejection was short-lived, for beyond El Paso construction was nearing completion, and the line had been fully stocked from the western end with good-quality, well-broken horses and mules. After leaving El Paso at dawn on September 30, Ormsby wrote, "To my great relief the mules were dispensed with for a while and a good team of California horses substituted, which spun the wagon over the ground at a rate which was quite new to me."

Although a few keepers were still living in tents, the ten relay posts between the Rio Grande and Tucson were stocked with excellent mules. The road was firm and reasonably good, and the mail wagon rolled day and night at better than six miles an hour. On a run of 160 miles through Apache territory only a couple of harmless-appearing Indians had been seen when, at dusk on October 1, the stage pulled into the Stein's Peak station on the New Mexico-Arizona boundary. There it was found that 250 Apaches had besieged the station a few days earlier, demanding a present of twenty sacks of corn. That they had ridden away without further trouble after receiving their present was little comfort to Ormsby, for there was no moon, it was thirty-seven miles to the next station, and ten of those miles were over Apache Pass, where the road wound through a narrow, high-walled canyon, "the most dangerous portion of the Apache country."

The crossing was made without an Indian being seen, and at the western end fresh mules were waiting at the Apache Pass way station. It was another thirty-seven miles to the Dragoon Springs station across a flat, mountain-rimmed alkali desert. The mules were tough and strong, and the crossing was made rapidly and without difficulty. When the station was reached it was learned that two of the builders had been murdered by their Mexican helpers and that a third man had barely escaped with his life.

The next twenty-five miles was over the roughest terrane on the entire Butterfield route, and when the San Pedro Valley (southeast of Tucson) was finally reached Ormsby wrote, "If there is any portion of the route calculated to impress one with the necessity of military protection for the route of this overland mail, it is this very last few hundred miles which I have just described, running through the heart of the Apache country."

The second eastbound mail stage had been passed in the night near Cooke's Spring, just west of the Rio Grande Valley. The third was met twelve miles south of Tucson, "two days ahead of time, but in a decided muss from two balky lead horses tangled in the harness." The trouble had evidently been the driver's fault. The westbound reinsman straightened the team out, and then turned back to drive the seventy-five miles to Dragoon Springs without rest. The westbound stage went on after a short delay and reached Tucson at nine-thirty on the evening of October 2, having made up ten hours and forty minutes of the time lost in crossing Texas.

Because of deep sand and extreme summer heat, the 380-mile stretch of deserts between Tucson and Vallecito Station at the foothills of the California mountains was rated to be the slowest portion of the entire Butterfield route. The first eastbound stage had lost nearly forty hours in making the crossing, but Warren Hall, who had stocked the line west of Tucson, was determined that there should be no recurrence. He himself had brought the third eastbound mail through in record time, and was waiting to take the first westbound sacks to Los Angeles. He had left orders to have fresh six-horse teams ready at all relay posts where deep sand was to be encountered, and personally did a large part of the driving. Instead of falling behind, he made up nine hours and twenty minutes, bringing the mail into Los Angeles on the morning of October 7, only twenty-two hours and forty minutes behind schedule.

In preparing the schedule, twenty-three and a half hours had been cut from the twenty-five-day maximum demanded by the mail contract. This was an allowance for breakdowns, accidents, or unforeseeable delays, and made the scheduled running time from St. Louis to San Francisco twenty-four days and thirty minutes.

With the mail only twenty-two hours and forty minutes behind schedule at Los Angeles, there was little danger of its not reaching San Francisco well within the twenty-five-day time limit, for even though two mountain ranges had to be crossed the road was good, there were thirty-three relay posts along the 462-mile route, and they were stocked with the best horses on the Butterfield line. But there was a natural rivalry between the drivers on the two main divisions of the line, and the western reinsmen were determined to make up every minute of the time lost east of El Paso.

Between Los Angeles and Fort Tejon at the summit of the Tehachapi Mountains there was a rise of more than four thousand feet, but fresh six-horse teams were ready at relay posts spaced from eight to twelve miles apart. The eighty-mile climb was made in eighteen hours, and Fort Tejon reached at 3:40 on the morning of October 8, but the mail was still more than twenty hours behind schedule. The next driver picked the speed up to better than six and a half miles an hour—down the northern rampart of the mountains through rugged Grapevine Canyon, across Kern River on Gordon's flatboat ferry, and along the foothills of the Sierra Nevadas to Visalia—making the 132-mile run in twenty hours.

Although it was nearly midnight, the entire population of Visalia, "about five hundred," came running to celebrate the arrival of the first Butterfield mail from the East. Lacking fireworks, they placed one anvil atop another with gunpowder between and exploded it. Ormsby wrote, "The reports were quite as heavy as those of an eight-pounder. This was the first evidence of any enthusiasm along the route, since we left Fort Smith, and the rousing cheers they gave us as we drove off at 11:50 on Friday, the 8th of October, ought to be remembered in the history of the town . . ."

With the mail still more than twelve hours behind schedule, the driver out of Visalia increased the pace, making the eighty-four miles to Firebaugh's Ferry—"over the barren plain, with no wood except upon the banks of the creeks, and no settlements except the stations"—by eleven-thirty Saturday morning, thus cutting the time behind schedule in half.

The driver out of Firebaugh's was an expert reinsman, the road was good, teams of fast horses were waiting at each relay post, and Marcus Kinyon's brother "Tote" had joined the party as mail agent. The forty-two miles to the foothills of the Diablo mountain range were driven in three hours and thirty-seven minutes, the last eighteen of them at better than fourteen miles an hour. Ormsby was so amazed by the speed that he evidently forgot he was still in the United States, for he wrote, "To run stage horses at such a rate of speed would . . . be considered rather dangerous work in the states, but here stock is cheaper, and if it does not last so long they buy more and keep the coaches moving along right smart."

He was not only amazed but appalled by the run through Pacheco Pass. "Our road led immediately on the brink of many a precipice," he wrote. "There are also many abrupt curves in the road, winding around the sides of steep hills, on the edges of the ravines; many steep roads directly up and down the hills; and many rocks near the road, leaving just sufficient room for an experienced driver to take his team through without striking. Most drivers would have been content to drive slowly over this spot— a distance of twelve miles and every foot of it requiring the most skillful management of the team to prevent the certain destruction of all in the coach. But our Jehu was in a hurry with the 'first States' mail' and he was bound to put us through in good time."

Ormsby, who had been invited to ride beside the driver, protested when he "whipped up his horses just as we started down a steep hill. I expected to see him put down the brakes with all his might but he merely rested his foot on them, saying, 'It's best to keep the wheels rolling, or they'll slide'; so he did keep the wheels rolling, and the whole coach slid down the steepest hills at the rate of fifteen—yes, twenty—miles an hour, now turning an abrupt curve with a whip and crack and 'round the corner, Sally,' scattering the loose stones, just grazing the rocks, sending rattling echoes far away among the hills and ravines . . . and nearly taking away the breath of all." The twelve miles were driven in an hour and five minutes, and the twenty miles to Gilroy in two hours flat. After a short stop for supper and a fresh team, the thirty-mile drive through the Santa Clara Valley was made at a brisk trot. An hour after midnight Tote Kinyon blew a blast on the trumpet as the first westbound mail stage rolled into San Jose. At that hour the streets were deserted, and no one was aroused except the station keeper and hostlers. There the mail and express packages were transferred from the celerity wagon to a Concord coach, the driver cracked his whip, and the horses sprang away on the San Francisco road.

Waterman Ormsby's description of the arrival is one of the best among stagecoaching chronicles:

It was just after sunrise that the city of San Francisco hove in sight over the hills, and never did the night traveller approach a distant light, or the lonely mariner descry a sail, with more joy than did I the city of San Francisco on the morning of Sunday, October 10. . . . Soon we struck the pavements, and, with a whip, crack, and bound, shot through the streets to our destination, to the great consternation of everything in the way and the no little surprise of everybody. Swiftly we whirled up one street and down another, and round the corners, until finally we drew up at the stage office in front of the Plaza, our driver giving a shrill blast of his horn and a flourish of triumph for the arrival of the first overland mail in San Francisco from St. Louis. But our work was not yet done. The mails must be delivered, and in a jiffy we were at the post office door, blowing the horn, howling and shouting for somebody to come and take the overland mail.

I thought nobody was ever going to come—the minutes seemed days— but the delay made it even time, and as the man took the mail bags from the coach, at half-past seven A.M. . . . it was just twenty-three days, twenty-three hours and a half from the time that John Butterfield, the president of the company, took the bags as the cars moved from St. Louis at 8 A.M. on Thursday, 16th of September, 1858.

Ormsby went on to write that he had been "the sole passenger and the only one who had ever made the trip across the plains in less than fifty days." In this last he was mistaken, for by that time the passage was being regularly made over the central route in thirty-eight days or less.

Although the San Franciscans had paid little attention to the departure of the first mail over the Butterfield line, they held a mass meeting to celebrate the first arrival. The *Bulletin* exulted: "To-day for the first time, we experienced an inward consciousness that our state is practically independent of the steamship monopoly." Colonel J. B. Crocker, chairman of the celebration committee, went even further. "In my opinion," he orated, "one of the greatest blessings that could befall California would be to discontinue entirely and at once all communication by steamer between San Francisco and New York."

Ormsby was a little less enthusiastic about the superiority of stage to steamer travel, but was more diplomatic than most young newspaper correspondents. When asked to comment on his enjoyment of the journey, he simply said, "Had I not just come out over the route, I would be perfectly willing to go back."

A later passenger expressed it more bluntly: "I know what Hell is like. I've just had twenty-four days of it."

The eastbound mail had fallen fifty-eight hours behind schedule when it reached Colbert's Ferry, only thirty-eight of them could be made up, and the mail reached St. Louis just three hours and twenty-five minutes inside the twenty-five-day limit.

John Butterfield met the stage at Fort Smith, and from Tipton he telegraphed news of the mail's arrival to his friend President Buchanan. The President replied, "I congratulate you upon the result. It is a glorious triumph for civilization and the Union. Settlements will soon follow the course of the road, and the East and West will be bound together by a chain of living Americans which can never be broken."

A chain which would never be broken had been forged to bind California to the Union, but it was the central, not the Butterfield, route. Settlements along the greater portion of that long-abandoned road are still few and far between.

10

An Unbeatable Adversary

FROM the time the Hockaday and Chorpenning mail contracts were awarded on a combined time schedule of forty-two days, sentiment in Congress had mounted steadily over the inequality between them and the Butterfield contract, both as to required time and the amount of subsidy. It was well understood by the legislators that the cost of operating a long-distance mail-stage line through uninhabited territory was far less affected by the frequency of trips than by the speed, for the faster the service the shorter the relays must be, proportionately increasing labor costs and investment in stations, stock, and equipment. In early June 1858 friends of the central route introduced a joint resolution in Congress, not only authorizing but directing the Postmaster General to increase the speed required for service between Independence and Placerville to thirty days, with a pro rata increase in the subsidies.

The resolution passed the House of Representatives by a large majority and, although met by stiff opposition from the South, it passed the Senate, but was vetoed by President Buchanan. He said his reason for the veto was that the Postmaster General already had discretionary power to order the improvement if it were desirable. The Washington correspondent for the *San Francisco Bulletin* reported: "It is said that the President refused to sign the bill because the projected route was likely to demonstrate the feasibility of a Central Railroad to the Pacific. . . . It is quite evident that in this, as in other matters, the President is guided by the filibuster faction who will support no other but the extreme Southern route." Others were blunt in saying that Buchanan's action was taken to eliminate competition for his friend Butterfield.

To somewhat allay the outraged supporters of the resolution,

Postmaster General Brown shortened the central overland mail route by authorizing St. Joseph instead of Independence as the eastern terminus. He also increased the service between Salt Lake City and Placerville from semimonthly to weekly and reduced the time limit from twenty days to sixteen. This automatically raised the compensation under the terms of Chorpenning's contract to $130,000 per annum and put the service between St. Joseph and Placerville on a weekly schedule, with a time limit of thirty-eight days for each one-way trip and a total annual compensation of $320,000.

As soon as the contract was improved enough to warrant the construction and stocking of relay stations, Chorpenning ordered Concord stagecoaches and commisssioned A. D. Rightmire, the leading horse and mule dealer in Sacramento, to stock his line with the best mules available. He also engaged Howard Egan—probably taking him into partnership—to act as general superintendent and lay out a stage line over the Egan Trail between Salt Lake City and Genoa, marking the route from water to water across the deserts and selecting sites for relay stations.

On June 25, 1858, the *Sacramento Union* reported, "Mr. Rightmire will leave town on Saturday (to-morrow) morning, with five others in company, and a stock of sixty head of team mules and a Concord coach, to establish stations on the line and stock same. . . . The coaches for the same are coming overland. . . . The mules [are] the finest that have ever been dispatched from this city . . ."

With the President having vetoed the bill for speeding up mail service on the central route, Hockaday and Chorpenning set about to prove its superiority over that of the Butterfield route. On July 20 the *Sacramento Union* exulted:

THE FIRST OVERLAND MAIL FROM ST. JOSEPH, on the Missouri river, to Placerville, arrived at the latter place at 11 o'clock P.M., July 19th. . . . Mr. William Lindsey, who came with the mail . . . is confident that the trip from Salt Lake can be made within eight days in a short time. He says on the arrival of his team at Placerville, the citizens had formed in two lines, and welcomed it with repeated cheers. The houses were illuminated, and the usual refreshments indulged in. A WORTHY CELEBRATION. The arrival of an Overland Mail in twenty-nine days from St. Joseph to Sacramento, is an event which ought to be celebrated by public rejoicing.

At the end of July the *Union* again exulted. "There is now a continuous line of stations more than one-half the distance to Salt Lake."

For some time before service was started on the Butterfield line, a considerable passenger traffic was evidently being carried by Chorpenning and Hockaday over the central route, which might well account for the lack of enthusiasm encountered by Waterman Ormsby. On September 22, after announcing arrival at Placerville of the St. Joseph mail, the *Union* reported, "Huntington, in charge of the Overland Mail, met the different mail parties on the route—all well and getting along finely. On the 13th, sixteen miles above Gravelly Ford, Huntington met the mail coach and thirteen passengers. This party were all well."

On September 24, more than two weeks before Ormsby's arrival in San Francisco, the *Sacramento Union* editorialized:

We learn that Senator Broderick, accompanied by Charles G. Hooker, of this city, and Wm L. Dudley, of Mokelumne Hill, will leave Placerville on Saturday, the 2nd day of October, for an overland journey to St. Louis. This trip will give Mr. Broderick an excellent opportunity to become acquainted with the requirements of the mail route, and the facilities for establishing telegraphic and railroad communication with the East. Experience of this character is very much needed by our legislators, and as this will be the first instance of a California representative in our National Councils proceeding to Washington overland, we hope the example will not be disregarded by others.

On October 2, the same newspaper reported, "SENATOR BRODERICK came up from San Francisco in the river steamer Queen City on Thursday night. . . . The overland party of which he is one, will start to-morrow *via* Placerville, on their eastern journey. It is expected the trip will be made inside of thirty days."

As additional relay stations were completed and stocked across Texas, New Mexico, and Arizona, Butterfield seldom failed to get his stages through inside of the twenty-five-day requirement and often beat that time by a full day, occasionally by two. But on the central route John Hockaday and George Chorpenning were unwittingly racing to their own destruction by cutting a week or more from their thirty-eight-day schedule. Worse still, they rashly offered to cut the time to twenty days, the year around, and furnish triweekly service for a compensation equal to that for which Butterfield was providing twenty-five-day semiweekly service.

The southern faction in Washington pooh-poohed the offer, predicting that as soon as winter set in it would be impossible to maintain even a thirty-eight-day schedule, regardless of compensation, because of deep snow in the mountains. Hockaday and Chorpenning countered by saying that they wanted only a fair chance to prove the year-round superiority of the central route. They pointed out that under their present compensation they could afford only to maintain relay stations at intervals of fifty to seventy miles, but that with $600,000 annually they could install mountain stations with snow plows at intervals of eight to ten miles and keep the road open at all times.

In the latter part of October service was to be inaugurated on the steamship mail line between New Orleans and San Francisco via Tehuantepec. The Louisiana Tehuantepec Company had put fast steamers on the Gulf of Mexico and the Pacific, and a fast stage line across the isthmus. The firm boasted that it would get mail from New York or St. Louis to San Francisco several days faster than it could be carried over the Butterfield line, entirely ignoring the central route as being unworthy of mention.

George Chorpenning thought he saw in this an opportunity to prove the year-round superiority of the central route. In early December the President would send his annual message to Congress, and advance copies would be rushed to leading newspapers throughout the nation. Without actually issuing a challenge, Chorpenning proposed that copies of the President's message be delivered simultaneously to representatives of the three lines at St. Louis to be carried to San Francisco over the various routes in the fastest possible time and by whatever means the contractor chose. Since the central route would doubtless be snowbound in December, Butterfield and the Louisiana Tehuantepec Company welcomed the proposal and agreed to make the test of speed.

Arrangements were made in Washington for three sealed packets containing the President's message to be sent by special courier to St. Louis at least a day before it was scheduled for reading to Congress. It was also arranged that the courier be notified by telegram from Washington the moment reading of the message was begun. It was agreed that he would then turn over a packet containing the message to a representative of each of the three routes simultaneously and that the race would start immediately regardless of weather conditions.

Butterfield spared no expense in stationing relays of fast saddle horses at intervals of no more than fifteen miles along the entire route from Tipton to San Francisco. Chorpenning and Hockaday, although their funds were limited, spent $8000 in setting up temporary relay posts, stocking them with fast horses, and chartering a steamer to rush their representative up the Missouri from St. Louis to St. Joseph as soon as the President's message was turned over to him. To insure the greatest possible speed over his part of the line, Chorpenning engaged Jared Crandall, who had recently sold his Pioneer Stage Line, to stock and superintend the western portion, while Howard Egan made preparations from the Salt Lake end.

By December 5 the courier from Washington and a representative from each of the three competing routes had arrived at St. Louis. On the morning of the sixth they eagerly awaited the telegram that would signal the start of the great race. At the Pacific Railroad depot a special engine stood with a full head of steam, ready to speed the Butterfield agent to Tipton. At the wharf lay two fast river steamers, one to rush the Louisiana Tehuantepec Company's representative down the Mississippi to New Orleans, the other to hurry the Hockaday-Chorpenning man up the Missouri to St. Joseph. When, at last, the telegram came it was evident that something was amiss. The courier from Washington had only two packets—one for the Butterfield agent, and one for the Tehuantepec representative.

While the Hockaday-Chorpenning man stood in bewilderment, his two competitors raced away from the starting line. In the packet carried by the Butterfield agent was a copy of the President's message for the San Francisco *Alta California*, and with it a note of explanation by that newspaper's Washington correspondent:

Washington, December 3d, 1858.

The President's Message and the Annual Report of the several Secretaries, leave this afternoon for St. Louis in charge of a special messenger, from which point they are to be dispatched by an overland express to San Francisco via El Paso. This letter goes in the same package, together with an extra package of documents for the *Alta*. The contractors over the Salt Lake route had made arrangements, at a cost of eight thousand dollars to carry the message by express on their line, but the President has refused up to this hour to let them have it, although urged to do so by several members of Congress whose constituents are immediately interested in this route. Should Mr. Buchanan persist to the last in this refusal, the Hon. Mr. Craig of Mo. will come out in a card to-morrow denouncing the President for his partiality in the matter and charge upon him a determination to foster the southern route at the expense of the Salt Lake City Route. These documents are not yet ready for transportation but all hands are pulling to have them ready for the afternoon train. The message will also be left at intervening points in charge of postmasters for delivery. Duplicate copies will also go out by the Steamer from New York on the fifth to avoid the possibility of a failure.

On December 8 the St. Louis correspondent for the *Alta* reported, "The President's Message for California: It was said that three copies had been transmitted from Washington—one for New Orleans, to be sent by the Tehuantepec route; another by the southern overland route, and one via Salt Lake. The latter was not received, however, by the agent here, and I am informed he is still waiting for it . . ."

Another St. Louis reporter wrote: "The management of the Washington part of the business of sending the message was entrusted to A. R. Corbin, a lobby agent in that city, whose services were called into requisition during the process of the engineering of the overland mail bill through Congress. He got the necessary copies. Butterfield saw about getting the fast express put through. Hockaday and Company, the Salt Lake mail contractors, are heavy sufferers by some piece of jugglery. . . . A promise was obtained from Washington that the documents would be forthcoming, and a messenger came down from St. Joseph to St. Louis to await their coming, but strange to say, the President refused them a copy of his message, (so I learn from Washington) and Hockaday's agent instead of getting a fair start with Pardee, (Butterfield's express agent) is still in this city with no prospects of obtaining the document until it appears in our city papers."

It even appeared that the elements had joined forces with the enemies of the central overland route. The Butterfield and Tehuantepec agents had no sooner raced away to the south than the worst storm in a decade swept across the Midwest, the Great Plains, the Rockies, and Sierra Nevadas. On December 9 one St. Louis newspaper reported, "Everything is frozen as tight as a drum, the river falling, with large masses of floating ice being carried down by the current. It is reported that the navigation of the Upper Mississippi and the Missouri is closed for the season."

As predicted, the central-route representative was unable to secure a copy of the President's message until it was published in the St. Louis newspapers. It was December 14 before he could get it up the ice-clogged Missouri to St. Joseph, and by that time the Butterfield riders had a head start of more than a week.

With all the cards seemingly stacked against them and a blizzard raging the entire length of their line, it would have been only reasonable for the mail contractors on the central route to withdraw from the race. By doing so they might have saved themselves from ruin, but neither John Hockaday nor George Chorpenning was a quitter, and the treatment they had received at the President's hands made them more than ever determined to prove the superiority of the central route, regardless of the weather conditions.

Within an hour after the steamer carrying the message docked at St. Joseph a rider, who had been ferried across the Missouri, galloped away to the west and disappeared into the storm. The blizzard was still raging when another rider emerged from it at Salt Lake City, and the correspondent there for the *San Francisco Bulletin* reported:

We were most agreeably disappointed on the evening of Christmas, by the arrival of the Express with the President's Message, through in eleven days from St. Joseph, Missouri, to this city. In consequence of the severe and almost incessant storms which have prevailed for the past five weeks, we had abandoned all hope of receiving the Message by express, and least of all in so short a time. As it was, the expressman was compelled to walk 20 miles through the snow on one occasion, and he was one whole day coming over the Big Mountain into the city, a distance of some 28 miles, in consequence of the trail made by the mail trains becoming filled up with drifted snow to the depth of some eight feet. The Message was immediately forwarded on to California by the contractors on the mail route from this city to Placerville, and they confidently expected to have it reach San Francisco within four days after its departure from here. If they succeed . . . the whole transit across the Plains will be effected in fifteen days; and this in the dead of winter, in a season unparalleled in the number and severity of its storms since the settlement of this country!

I learn from letters received by the express that the Butterfield Overland mail route received the President's Message at least two days in advance of this route, in consequence of the deception (by the Washington courier) who, we are informed by letters from disinterested gentlemen in St. Louis, was bribed by the agents of the Butterfield route thus to act.

The *San Francisco Bulletin* published its correspondent's report of bribery, but obviously did so with tongue in cheek, for evidence to the contrary was all too clear. Californians generally, as well as the mail contractors on the central route, did not believe that John Butterfield would stoop to anything of the sort, but laid the fault squarely at Buchanan's door.

Lot Huntington, Chorpenning's rider out of Salt Lake City, was still floundering through deeply drifted snow in western Utah when, on December 26, Butterfield's man raced into San Francisco with the packet containing the President's message. On December 28 a steamer arrived with the packet sent via the Tehuantepec route. But it was not until New Year's Day that an exhausted rider galloped his tired pony into Placerville, bringing the copy of the *St. Louis Republican* that contained Buchanan's message.

Not only the race had been lost, but John Hockaday and George Chorpenning had sealed their own doom, for the feat they had accomplished was quite unappreciated by the Administration in Washington. Their riders had proved the unquestionable superiority of the central route over any other, for under the worst weather conditions ever encountered on the American frontier they had made the run from St. Joseph in seventeen days and twelve hours, cutting the time required to bring the message over the

Butterfield route by two full days, and that via the Tehuantepec route by twice that margin.

In the session of Congress following the race, an almost continuous battle over mail service was waged between the North and South and between the Senate and House of Representatives. With indignation at the President's action running high, northern forces in the Senate were able to push through a resolution for reducing service on the Butterfield route to weekly trips, and another for increasing service on the entire central route to weekly trips on a twenty-five-day schedule. The southerners, under the guise of an economy program, attempted to amend the annual Postal Routes bill by increasing the postage rate on letters from three cents per ounce to five, abolishing the franking privilege of congressmen, and substituting "star bids" on mail contracts. The latter term originated from a custom in the Post Office Department of stamping a star on files that pertained to contracts having no requirement as to the method by which mail must be carried, whereas the Butterfield, Hockaday, and Chorpenning contracts required the use of four-horse (or mule) vehicles appropriate for passenger transportation.

The amendments failed to pass when introduced, but had nevertheless been tacked onto the bill before it was reported out of the South-controlled Committee on Post Offices and Post Roads with a "do pass" recommendation. Under the impression that the "star bid" amendment would apply equally to all mail contracts, the northern forces put up a less spirited fight, and after considerable debate the bill was passed with only slight changes in the amendments recommended by the committee.

Again the southern forces had outmaneuvered the northerners, for it was later discovered that Postmaster General Brown—whether or not under instruction from the President—had omitted from the Butterfield contract the standard clause reserving the right to decrease service and compensation.

The amended bill found a hostile reception when it reached the House and was not taken up for consideration until the final day of the session, when it was defeated. In the meantime the annual Post Office Appropriation bill was passed by the House with no unusual provisions and went on to the Senate for consideration. After long debate, Senator Yulee of Florida and his adherents were successful in attaching to it their amendments for raising the postage rate on letters and abolishing franking privileges.

When the amended Post Office Appropriation bill was returned to the House, Congressman Grow objected to its being considered.

His grounds were that the amendment for increasing postage was in effect a bill for raising revenue, and that the Senate had no right to originate a revenue bill. March 3, 1859 the House passed a resolution to send the amended measure back to the Senate without consideration, as section thirteen was in the nature of a revenue bill.

The Senate and House wrangled back and forth over who could originate what until nearly the end of the session. Then in an effort to save the Post Office Appropriation bill, a conference committee was hurriedly appointed. It compromised on a measure essentially the same as the original House bill. This passed the House, but failed in the Senate during the last hour of the session. When Congress adjourned without having passed an appropriation bill, the Post Office Department was left without authority even to expend its own income from mail revenues. Its only means of saving its employees and contractors from ruin was to issue statements of indebtedness, but these could seldom be converted into cash without considerable discount. Even so, President Buchanan refused to convene a special session of Congress. To further complicate matters, Postmaster General Brown died on March 8.

As successor to Aaron Brown, Buchanan appointed Judge Joseph Holt of Kentucky, a former commissioner of patents who was fanatically opposed to the policy of fostering and improving public transportation or stimulating westward emigration through mail subsidies. From the time of his appointment he made his position

A government train en route to Utah. (Courtesy, Nebraska State Historical Society.)

clear by stating unequivocally, "The transportation and delivery of mail with the utmost dispatch and security are the true and only missions of this department; in accomplishing this, it discharges its whole duty to the country . . ."

Still unrepealed, though outmoded and disregarded since the Mexican War, was a law passed by Congress in 1845 which provided that mail contracts be awarded to the low bidder "tendering sufficient guarantees for faithful performance, without other reference to the mode of such transportation than may be necessary to provide for due celerity, certainty, and security of such transportation." Judge Holt announced that in future only "star bids" in conformity with the 1845 law would be considered. Furthermore, he insisted that the Post Office Department should be a self-supporting business, that states and communities were entitled only to such mail service as could be provided by the revenues derived therefrom, and that any route failing to meet its own costs should be curtailed or discontinued.

Because of the omitted clause that made Butterfield's contract unique, the Overland Mail Company was safe from Postmaster General Holt's retrenchment drive, and no more efficient man than he could have been found to clear its path. During the spring and summer of 1859, while Congress was not in session, Holt slashed through Butterfield's California competition like a reaper with a sharp scythe. Service on the San Antonio-San Diego line was cut from weekly to semimonthly, with a reduction of $76,000 in compensation. The Tehuantepec, Neosho-Albuquerque, and Kansas City-Stockton routes were discontinued. The contract for steamship mail via Panama was allowed to expire in September, and the compensation was cut approximately in half by making a contract with a competitor for semimonthly service. On the central route both Hockaday's and Chorpenning's contracts were cut from weekly to semimonthly service, with a reduction in compensation of $115,000—enough to bankrupt the contractors or drive them out of business.

Holt made similar reductions of service and compensation on countless routes throughout the sparsely populated West. Thousands of protests poured into the Post Office Department, and when the complainants were rebuffed they appealed to their representatives in Congress. Representative Washburne, of Illinois, reported, "In my district the service has been literally slaughtered. Every cabin which dots the prairies has felt the effects of this action of the Post Office Department."

At the first session of the 36th Congress an irate House of Representatives incorporated the following provision in the Post Office Appropriation bill: "The Postmaster-general is hereby directed to restore the inland service on all routes under contract on the 4th of March, 1859, unless the same have expired by their own limitation; and where the service has been actually performed by the contractor, notwithstanding such discontinuance, the Postmaster-general shall pay the contractors, as if no change had been ordered."

The Senate was, however, firmly under control of the South-dominated administration in the White House. When, on May 26, 1860, the provision came up for debate, a letter from Postmaster General Holt was read in which he justified his action, and Senator Yulee of Florida argued, "If Congress does not sustain the action of the Department now, we must bid farewell for the future to any attempt at reform by the administration in the Department."

California's Senator Gwin, although a strong Administration supporter on most legislation, retorted, "You begrudge the expense of transporting our letters to and from the Pacific Coast. . . . You knew these plains and mountains, covered with perpetual snows, existed when you so eagerly sought possessions on the Pacific Coast. After you got these possessions did you not intend to communicate with them for postal, military, commercial, and social purposes? Did you not intend to make us one people, part and parcel of you? Did the statesmen who shaped that policy count the cost of conveying letters to these distant possessions when they risked war and engaged in war to get them at the cost of tens of millions?"

Gwin was not alone in condemning the action of the Postmaster General. The debate was hot and acrimonious, but when the Post Office Appropriation bill passed the Senate on June 1, 1860, it had been stripped of the provision requiring the Postmaster General to restore the curtailed service. The House refused to concur, and since the Senate insisted upon deleting the entire provision a conference committee was appointed.

No agreement could be reached by the first committee, so it was dismissed and another appointed. When no agreement could be reached by the second committee after three days of conference and debate, the House passed an amendment to its original provision, withdrawing demand for restoration of service on the Neosho-Albuquerque and Kansas City-Stockton routes, since both of them had been clearly useless from the beginning. The Senate, however, stood stubbornly behind its demand that the whole restoration provision be stricken from the bill. On June 25, after four different conference committees had been unable to make any progress toward an agreement, the House of Representatives withdrew from its position in order to avert the catastrophe that almost certainly would have resulted from a second failure of Congress to pass a post office appropriation bill.

The mail contractor suffering the greatest injury from the cutting back of its contract was Hockaday & Company (or Hockaday and Liggett, as the firm had become known). To improve service over their line they had borrowed heavily and invested in excess of $390,000 in stock, equipment, and station facilities. The $130,000 per annum to which their compensation was reduced would not cover ordinary operating expenses, making it impossible for them to meet their obligations for borrowed money. The firm's resources had been strained by the necessity of discounting statements of indebtedness issued by the Post Office Department, and the additional reduction of $60,000 in its annual income forced it into insolvency. The Washington correspondent of the *San Francisco Bulletin* reported, "It is really pitiable to contemplate the financial ruin which the order of curtailment in this case has occasioned to the parties. . . . Hockaday's mental faculties have been seriously affected by his pecuniary misfortunes and Liggett's fortune is lost."

Congress passed a bill awarding Hockaday and Liggett $40,000 as partial relief for the damages suffered because of Holt's curtailment, but when the bill reached the White House Buchanan vetoed it. The case was so flagrantly unfair that Congress passed a similar bill the following year. That time the President allowed it to become a law, but without his signature.

11

Stagecoach Moguls in the Making

A NEW ERA in stagecoaching was ushered in by a combination of circumstances arising in 1858–59: the stationing of troops in Utah, the inability of the army to transport supplies and provisions long distances over uninhabited regions, Postmaster General Holt's curtailment of mail service on the central route, the discovery of gold in what is now downtown Denver, and the finding of an enormous silver deposit in the Washoe Hills of western Utah Territory, now Nevada.

As a stagecoach route the Santa Fe Trail was of little importance, but it had a tremendous effect upon stagecoaching in the West, for it gave men who were to become giants of the industry their start. Foremost among them was Ben Holladay.

Ben Holladay ran away from his parents' farm home in Kentucky in 1836, migrated to the western Missouri frontier, and found a job clerking in a trading post at Weston, across the Missouri River from Fort Leavenworth, Kansas. At the age of seventeen he was hired as a civilian courier by Brigadier General Alexander Doniphan of the Missouri state militia when the Mormons were being driven from that state in 1838. Doniphan refused point-blank to carry out an order to execute Joseph Smith, founder of the Mormon religion, and saved the lives of many other Mormons by secretly notifying Brigham Young of impending attacks by frontier mobs. Ben Holladay, acting as Doniphan's personal courier, carried the messages and won Young's everlasting friendship.

After the Mormons had been driven out of Missouri, young

Holladay returned to his clerking job at Weston, but soon afterward started a trading post of his own there. His principal customers were soldiers from Fort Leavenworth and his principal item of merchandise was frontier whiskey. Before he reached the age of twenty-one he had proved himself to be an astute, farsighted, shrewd, and unscrupulous businessman with indomitable courage, irresistible drive, and ruthless determination.

During the Mexican War, Doniphan, serving as colonel of Missouri Volunteers, marched over the Santa Fe Trail in 1846 as part of the Army of the West and was left in command at Santa Fe when General Kearny moved on to California. Quite possibly because of their earlier connection, Ben Holladay was permitted to operate as sutler to the troops, and there is little doubt that a large part of the merchandise sold from his sutler's wagons was frontier whiskey, for his rate of profit is reported to have been about 200 per cent. By the end of the war he had amassed what was then considered a fortune. He increased the size of his operations at Weston and prospered.

Holladay was quick to recognize the opportunity for profit presented by the Mormon migration to Utah and the California gold rush. He reasoned that the mining camps would be in need of beef, flour, and other provisions and that the Mormons must have an abundance of these since they were excellent farmers and had been in Utah two years. He also reasoned that because of Brigham Young's friendship the Mormons would do business with him, although not with other "Gentiles," and that they must be in need of wagons, firearms, blankets, clothing, utensils, and other surplus war materials that were being offered for sale at Fort Leavenworth at only a fraction of what they had cost the Government. He formed a partnership with Theodore Warner, bought goods costing $70,000—mostly army surplus—loaded them on fifty wagons, and set out for Salt Lake City early in 1849.

Holladay had reasoned well. Brigham Young welcomed him not only as a trader but a friend, bought the entire caravan—merchandise, wagons, and all—and paid for it in beef cattle at six dollars a head and flour at one dollar per hundredweight. Holladay took the plunder on to California, where he sold most of the cattle at six cents a pound and the flour at twenty dollars per hundredweight. The profit was enormous. The next year he operated individually, doubled the size of his caravan—and the profit.

On Kearny's 1846 march from Fort Leavenworth to Santa Fe he transported his supplies and provisions in wagon trains driven by civilian teamsters and bullwhackers under the direction of army officers. By that time frontier merchants in the Santa Fe trade had transported untold thousands of tons over the trail with relatively little loss of livestock or merchandise. But in making the Raton Pass crossing Kearny lost the greater part of his mules and oxen and was obliged to abandon huge quantities of supplies because of his officers' ignorance of freighting through wilderness regions. During 1847 the losses incurred in the army's attempt to supply troops in New Mexico were equally great, and in the spring of 1848 the War Department instructed the quartermaster at Fort Leavenworth to contract for the hauling with civilian freighters.

In May of that year a contract was made with James Brown, an Independence, Missouri, freighter, to haul upwards of a hundred tons of freight from Fort Leavenworth to Santa Fe at $235 per ton. Although army freight caravans had sustained heavy losses because of Indian attacks and the stampeding of stock, Brown encountered no Indian trouble, and made his delivery in good condition well within the allotted time. His service was so satisfactory that the War Department adopted the civilian-contract system for all freight transportation across uninhabited regions.

In the spring of 1849 Brown formed a partnership with William H. Russell of Lexington, Missouri, and on April 30 the firm of Brown & Russell signed a contract with the War Department to transport supplies from Fort Leavenworth to Santa Fe at $9.98 per hundred pounds.

William Russell, then thirty-seven years of age, was an incorrigible "wheeler and dealer." Although his formal education was slight, his appearance, speech, and bearing were those of a cultured gentleman. He had a brilliant mind in many respects and considerable personal charm, and was animated by infinite confidence in his own judgment and ability. He was, however, extremely impulsive, improvident as a grasshopper, sanguine beyond all reason, and actuated in his business dealings by wishful desire rather than considered reasoning. The former characteristics made him promoter pre-eminent on the western frontier, enabling him to make friends among high-ranking Government officials in Washington and wealthy financiers throughout the East, to acquire monopolistic Government contracts, and to float enormous loans. The latter characteristics made him an extremely dangerous business associate.

In the early 1820's Russell's mother and stepfather had emigrated from Vermont to Liberty, Missouri, the most westerly settlement on the frontier. At the age of eighteen William went to work as clerk for a frontier merchant who was in the Santa Fe trade and had general merchandise stores at Liberty, Lexington, and the newly established settlement of Independence. Lexington was then the fourth-largest town in Missouri and the chief trading center on the frontier. In 1837 young Russell, with William Waddell and several others, organized the Lexington First Addition Company. The next year he quit his job, formed a partnership with two local men, and opened a general merchandise store under the name of Allen, Russell & Company. It was the first of many partnerships William Russell was to organize and, like most of its successors, ended in failure.

In the early 1840's, undoubtedly with borrowed money, Russell formed the partnership of Bullard & Russell to open a second general store in Lexington; became a partner in the already established firm of Waddell, Ramsey & Company; bought sixty town lots in Lexington, three thousand acres of Missouri land from the U.S. Government, and controlling interest in the Lexington First Addition Company; and built himself a twenty-room mansion. In 1847 Bullard & Russell went into the Santa Fe trade, joining with a Westport merchant to ship a caravan of general merchandise from Westport Landing, now Kansas City. It has been claimed that this was the first merchant train of private goods ever loaded out of Westport Landing, although this is doubtful. The partners shipped another caravan in 1848, and in 1849 Russell went into partnership with James Brown to transport military supplies.

The venture was successful, and in 1850 John S. Jones was taken into the partnership of Brown, Russell & Company. The firm was awarded a contract by the War Department to transport three hundred tons of supplies from Fort Leavenworth to Santa Fe at $286.67 per ton.

Russell's part in the operation must have been purely promotional and Jones's part purely financial, for the two men were much alike; in *Empire on Wheels* Raymond W. and Mary Lund Settle describe Russell as follows: "An aristocrat by nature, he never took on a single characteristic of the frontiersman. He never wore buckskin or homespun, his clothes were always carefully tailored, he never 'roughed it,' never hunted or fished, never drove an ox team, and avoided sweat, hardship, and toil with his hands."

Although the rate per ton in the 1850 contract was high, the undertaking was risky. The supplies would not be ready for loading until mid-September, when bad weather might be expected, and the investment would be great, for 135 wagons and more than 1600 oxen would be required to handle so much weight in a single shipment.

It was early October before the two-and-a-half-mile-long wagon train pulled away from Fort Leavenworth. On the road James Brown divided it into two caravans, taking personal charge of the advance train with John Jones's brother Charles as his assistant. The weather remained fair and the lead caravan made excellent time; by Thanksgiving it was rounding the end of the Sangre de Cristo Mountains, within about fifty miles of Santa Fe. There it was caught in a severe blizzard and completely snowbound. As soon as the storm let up enough for a horse to get through, Brown rode ahead to report to the commandant of the garrison and request permission to lay over until the weather cleared. He had no sooner reached Santa Fe than he was stricken with typhoid fever, of which he died on December 5.

Doubtless Charles Jones had been a capable assistant to Brown, but he was insufficiently experienced for such an emergency. He finally managed to get the wagons to Santa Fe, but was obliged to incur debts of $14,000 for feed and the replacement of oxen that died under the yoke. Fortunately, the second section of the caravan had made slower time and had followed the Arkansas River to Bent's Fort and wintered there. In a memorial asking relief from Congress, Russell claimed that the firm of Brown, Russell & Company had lost $39,800 on the shipment.

In 1851 the surviving partners, under the name of Jones & Russell, continued in the military-freighting business, probably with Charles Jones acting as operations manager. By that time the Government had established several forts in Kansas and New Mexico for control of the Indians, and the firm was awarded contracts for freighting to five of them from Fort Leavenworth. It is quite probable that without Brown to manage the hauling operations the business was unprofitable, for the freighting firm of Jones & Russell discontinued business on completion of its 1851 contracts and Russell became closely associated with William Waddell.

The close association between Russell and Waddell is strange indeed, for they were completely opposite by nature. Whereas Russell was quick-thinking, dynamic, impulsive, sanguinary, wildly extravagant, and a compulsive gambler who was nothing short of reckless in business ventures, Waddell was phlegmatic, stoical, inclined to sulk if displeased, a cautious penny-pincher, and unable to reach a decision without ponderous deliberation. It can only be assumed that each inwardly recognized his own failings and admired the other as a counterbalance to his own one-sided nature, for although they wrangled almost continuously they stood by each other loyally when the chips were down.

Waddell, five years older than Russell, was well established as a merchant and landowner in Lexington, operating as both a wholesaler and retailer of general merchandise, produce, hemp, and grain. He and Russell had been among the founders of the Lexington First Addition Company, the Lexington Mutual Fire and Marine Insurance Company, and the Lexington Female Collegiate Institute. They were partners in Waddell, Ramsay & Company; each owned considerable farmland and numerous town lots and each built himself a twenty-room mansion. In 1852 they formed the general merchandising firm of Waddell & Russell.

In 1853 Waddell & Russell contracted to haul military freight, and sent wagon trains to Fort Riley, Kansas, and Fort Union, New Mexico, probably under the management of R. W. Durham. In any event, when they were unsuccessful bidders in 1854 they sent Durham to California with their surplus oxen and a trainload of general merchandise. The venture was evidently unsuccessful, for Durham lost 20 per cent of the oxen in crossing the plains and mountains. That fall Russell conceived an idea that was to have a tremendous effect upon transportation and stagecoaching in the trans-Mississippi West for the next decade and a half. His plan was for the firm of Waddell & Russell to form a partnership with Alexander Majors—a highly successful freighting contractor of Westport, Missouri—and to secure a monopoly on all freighting for the War Department in the West.

The Majors family had migrated to western Missouri from Kentucky in 1819, when Alexander was five years of age. He grew to manhood as a farmer, was unusually adept at handling livestock, married early, and had a large family. Most of his children were daughters, however, and in those days a frontier farmer with a large family was hard pressed to make a living unless he had sons to help with the work. Alexander Majors had a knack for making friends with Indians, so to help out the family finances in the summer of 1846 he loaded a wagon with cheap but colorful merchandise at Independence and drove to the Pottawatomie Indian Reservation in Kansas Territory on a trading expedition.

The venture was successful, and it is probable that Majors would have gone into the Santa Fe trade if he had had sufficient capital. Lacking it, he freighted goods over the trail for other merchants. At first he did his own driving, and was so successful that within two years he owned ten prairie schooners and 130 oxen. In 1850 he made a net profit of $13,000, and then turned to freighting for the War Department. By 1854 he was the foremost Government freighter west of the Missouri, and it was probably he who shut

Waddell & Russell out that year by underbidding them, thus giving Russell the idea for his monopoly scheme. In any case, Majors was awarded contracts that year requiring 100 wagons, 1200 oxen, and 120 men.

When he first began spreading out in the freighting business, Majors was ridiculed by other contractors because he would not hire a bullwhacker unless the man signed a pledge to treat animals in his care with kindness, use no profanity, stay sober at all times, and behave like a gentleman while in his employ. Although Majors was a sincerely religious man, he was not a zealot; he simply believed that men willing to sign the pledge would be more reliable and trustworthy than others, and he knew from experience that animals treated with kindness would move more freight than those that were abused.

For a man whose firm had been an unsuccessful bidder for any army freighting in 1854 to anticipate a monopoly on that business in 1855 is quite amazing unless, as seems somewhat more than possible in view of later developments, William Russell already had a silent partner inside the War Department. It is equally amazing that Alexander Majors, who dominated army freighting in 1854 and was in excellent financial condition, should have entered into the proposed partnership unless, as seems likely, Russell was able to convince him that the firm of Waddell & Russell already had control of the monopoly. If such were the case, Majors had little choice but to enter into the partnership or get out of the military-freighting business.

Whatever the circumstances, a two-year partnership agreement, effective January 1, 1855, was signed by Alexander Majors, William Russell, and William Waddell on December 28, 1854. It provided that the capital of the firm be $60,000, one-third contributed by each partner, and that it engage in "buying and selling of goods wares and merchandize and also in a general trading in stock wagons teams and other things used in the outfitting of persons teams or trains across the plains or elsewhere and also in freighting goods or freight for Government or others . . ."

There was evidently little or no contribution of cash toward the capital of the new firm, for the Waddell & Russell stores were taken in as was, presumably, a considerable part of Majors' freighting stock and equipment. There was an agreement among the partners that the business in Lexington should continue to operate under the name of Waddell & Russell but that business in Jackson County would be conducted under the name of Majors & Russell.

Whether or not it had been prearranged before the formation

of the new partnership, a two-year contract between the War Department and the firm of Majors & Russell was signed on March 27, 1855, giving that firm a monopoly on the transportation of all military supplies west of the Missouri River. Probably due to the blizzard loss suffered by Brown & Russell in the fall of 1850, a stipulation was made in the monopoly agreement that whereas the freight rate per hundred miles of haul for loadings made prior to June 1 of both years would vary from $1.14 to $2.20 per hundredweight (according to bulkiness of the materials), the rate for loadings made thereafter would be proportionately higher, depending upon the lateness of the season and the risk involved.

There is little doubt that Russell negotiated the contract alone and was the firm's sole contact with the War Department in Washington, for there was apparently a clear-cut division in the functions of the three partners. Russell spent most of his time in the East cultivating friendship with Government officials and securing freighting assignments from the Quartermaster General's office in Washington, negotiating loans in New York, Boston, and Philadelphia to finance the enormous investment required, and promoting various and sundry projects with other partners or associates. Waddell sat on the lid at headquarters, worrying, sulking, and quarreling with Russell by mail about the impulsive and reckless risks to which Russell committed the firm without prior consultation with his partners. Majors, the only one of the three who was a practical freighter, devoted his entire efforts to supervising the actual freighting operations; he spent the greater part of his time out on the trails with the wagon trains, and was evidently kept in the dark by his partners concerning numerous phases of the business.

As soon as the freighting contract had been signed the firm set about building warehouses, bunkhouses, stables, corrals, offices, blacksmith and wagon shops, a lumberyard, a meat packing plant for supplying their trains, and a general store at Leavenworth, at that time a little squatters' settlement on the Delaware Indian Reservation a mile or two from the fort. There Majors gathered the best wagon-train masters and ox buyers to be found on the frontier and seventeen hundred bullwhackers, muleskinners, herders, freight handlers, checkers, and roustabouts, all willing to sign the required pledge. Rush orders were sent to New England for wagons by the boatload, for acres of canvas, and for wagon tops, oxbows, harness, chains, fittings, and other freighting equipment. Buyers were sent to scour Missouri and Iowa for the strongest yokes of young oxen and the stoutest spans of mules to be found. By May the firm was ready for operation. The advertisements announcing its opening carried two different names, "Majors, Russell & Company" and "Russell, Majors & Waddell," although the latter was almost invariably used thereafter.

During the early spring of 1855 riverboats delivered at the Fort Leavenworth piers an endless stream of military supplies for Santa Fe, Fort Kearney, and the ever-increasing number of frontier forts being established in the uninhabited wilderness between the Missouri River and California. In May twenty heavily loaded Russell, Majors & Waddell wagon trains pulled out onto the trails. Each train operated under the supervision of a well-qualified train master, was accompanied by an agent authorized to act for the firm, and consisted of 26 white-topped wagons, approximately 375 oxen and mules, and 40 to 50 men.

While Waddell was organizing the headquarters offices at Leavenworth and Majors was assembling, stocking, outfitting, and manning the wagon trains, Russell must have been equally busy raising the necessary financing in the East. Bills for wagons, harness, and other equipment were probably settled with drafts payable at the end of the freighting season, and cash loans were probably secured by liens against freighting charges which would become due from the War Department as deliveries were completed.

Even so, the financing must have required extraordinary promotional ability, for there is little doubt that the investment for that first year's operation was in excess of $500,000, a tremendous amount to be secured in loans and credit by a partnership with a capital of only $60,000. Each wagon train, together with supplies and provisions for a hauling season, represented an investment of approximately $20,000, and the payroll for seventeen hundred employees must have been very close to $100,000 per month.

But William Russell was an extraordinary man. He not only managed to secure the necessary financing for the freighting operations, but organized subsidiary partnerships for the firm—quite probably without consulting his partners—and promoted other enterprises which were in no way connected with the firm of Russell, Majors & Waddell. In 1855 alone he organized the Leavenworth Fire and Marine Insurance Company, invested heavily in Leavenworth real estate, joined in the organization and promotion of three other township companies, was prominent among the promoters of the Leavenworth, Pawnee & Western Railroad, and formed a partnership with Luther R. Smoot of Washington, D.C., to open a bank under the name of Smoot, Russell & Co.

All these promotions and investments were, of course, made

with borrowed money, and Russell had so many irons in the fire that he apparently was never able to keep track of them all. It is also evident that in numerous instances there was no clear-cut distinction between the loans and investments he made for the firm of Russell, Majors & Waddell and those he made as an individual or member of unrelated partnerships.

With a monopoly on the military-freighting business, the Government establishing more forts on the western frontier, Waddell keeping a tight-fisted watch on expenses at Leavenworth, and Majors supervising operations in the field, the firm prospered handsomely during 1855 and 1856. Although no accounting records are available, when Alexander Majors wrote his memoirs thirty-five years later he estimated the firm's profit for those two years to have totaled $300,000.

An excellent idea of the magnitude attained by the firm is given in Horace Greeley's writing of his trip across the continent in 1858. "Russell, Majors and Waddell's transportation establishment is the great future of Leavenworth. Such acres of wagons! such pyramids of extra axletrees! such herds of oxen! such regiments of drivers and other employes! No one who does not see can realize how vast a business this is, nor how immense are its outlays as well as its income. I presume this great firm has at this hour two millions of dollars invested in stock, mainly oxen, mules and wagons. (They last year employed six thousand teamsters, and worked 45,000 oxen)."

Greeley's presumption regarding the investment was certainly too high and there is little doubt that Majors' estimate of the profits was much exaggerated. In fact, considering Russell's free-wheeling methods of financing and making commitments for the firm, it is doubtful that even Waddell could have determined the profits with any degree of accuracy. In one respect Greeley was unquestionably right: the outlays were immense. Interest alone must have amounted to more than $100,000 annually, for the firm's loans and debts were nearly equal to its investment, and little if any money for such a venture could be borrowed at less than 10 per cent. Furthermore, although the hauling season was short, considerable help had to be employed the year around, wagons and equipment overhauled between seasons, and great herds of livestock wintered through. Nevertheless, instead of reducing its indebtedness as profits were made, the firm continued to expand its investments. Among other investments in 1856, it bought ten thousand acres of Kansas farmland at a cost of more than $80,000. One of Russell's outside ventures for that year—along with a group of his Lexington friends

—was the building of a large river steamboat christened the *William H. Russell*.

In February 1857 a contract was signed with the War Department, under the name of Majors & Russell, giving the firm a one-year monopoly on the transportation of not more than five million pounds of military freight at rates similar to those in the former contract. It provided that advance notice of desired deliveries be given the contractor, the length of notice to be in proportion to the size of the shipment.

Loadings were made in early May and some twenty half-mile-long wagon trains pulled off across the prairies, bound for the various frontier forts of the West and Southwest. As was his custom, Alexander Majors probably went with them believing they constituted the entire year's hauling, but affairs then taking shape in Washington would more than double the 1857 tonnage.

Ever since the early 1830's the Mormons, a close-knit, aloof, and industrious people, had been hated and persecuted by other frontier

A Concord mail coach of the El Paso Stage Company. This coach is reported to have been used on the San Antonio–San Diego line. (Courtesy, State Historical Society of Colorado.)

settlers; not primarily because of their religion, but for their prosperity and fear that they would take over the political power of the state if not of the nation. They were driven from Ohio to Missouri to Illinois where Joseph Smith, founder and leader of the sect, was arrested on trumped-up charges of treason, then murdered by a mob at the Carthage jail. Others were murdered from ambush, much of the Mormon livestock killed wantonly, crops destroyed, and houses burned.

In hope of isolating themselves from persecutors, the Mormons abandoned their Illinois homes in 1846 and migrated, with incredible suffering, to Salt Lake Basin—then in Mexican territory—a region so arid that it was generally believed to be habitable only by the most primitive Indians. The first Mormon emigrants reached Great Salt Lake in July 1847, planted seed in the desert, and dug irrigation ditches to bring water from the mountains. Within two years Salt Lake City had become a thriving metropolis surrounded by hundreds of well-stocked, prosperous farms. But in the meantime the Mexican territory west of the Rocky Mountains had been ceded to the United States, gold had been discovered in California, and in the summer of 1849 a horde of gold-crazed fortune seekers rushed westward through the Mormon's new Zion.

The Mormons resented the invasion by these "Gentiles," old animosities were revived, and clashes with travelers crossing Utah became progressively more frequent and violent. After their adoption of polygamy in 1852, the Mormons were considered by a vast majority of self-righteous Easterners as a sect of immoral degenerates bent upon establishing a kingdom that would cut off California and its great wealth from the rest of the nation. On the other hand, the Gentiles were looked upon by the Mormons as a rabble of persecuting bigots bent upon the total destruction of the Latter-Day Saints. The situation worsened appreciably in 1853 when eight members of a United States Government surveying party were killed by Indians in Utah. The Mormons had no connection whatsoever with the massacre, but Easterners refused to believe it and insisted that federal courts be established in Utah for the trial of all criminal charges.

In 1855 three federal judges were appointed for Utah, and three worse appointees could hardly have been found. Two of the jurists were apostate Mormons who made no secret of their hatred for the sect, and the third man, W. W. Drummond, was an equally prejudiced political toady. Upon their arrival in Utah the three federal judges were shunned by the Mormons, who continued to try all cases, both civil and criminal, in courts established by the territorial legislature. Raging with frustration and anger, the judges returned to Washington in the spring of 1857, where Drummond testified before the 35th Congress that Brigham Young was a ruthless dictator who employed a band of "destroying angels," that federal officials were constantly insulted, some had been killed, and countless Government records destroyed.

The charges were too absurd to be believed under ordinary circumstances, but sentiment against the polygamous Mormons was then at fever pitch in the East and President Buchanan piously declared, "This is the first rebellion which has existed in our territories and humanity itself requires that we should put it down in such a manner that it shall be the last." On May 26, 1857 he ordered that a force of twenty-five hundred soldiers be assembled and marched against the rebellious Mormons of Utah.

Alexander Majors and the Russell, Majors & Waddell wagon trains had been on the trails a month or more when a representative of the quartermaster's department called upon Russell, told him that troops were being sent to Utah in July, and served notice that the firm would be required to send along sufficient wagons to transport three million pounds of military freight.

In a statement made four years later Russell claimed that he had protested, saying that the notice was too short, that it was too late in the season, that the cost of equipping and stocking wagon trains for a single shipment of three million pounds would be ruinous to the firm, and that he agreed to the undertaking only with the understanding that the Government would not allow the firm to suffer a loss because of it.

Whether the statement was true or an invention by Russell to support his claim for damages has never been proved. In either event, although no such undertaking was covered by the terms of the monopoly-freighting contract, Russell committed the firm to do the desired hauling. He failed, however, to obtain a written agreement or stipulation of any kind from the War Department, even though the requirement was increased to more than four and a half million pounds. His oversight may well have been caused by his anxiety to close a side deal with the Quartermaster General, for he contracted in the name of Waddell & Russell to supply the Utah expeditionary force two thousand beef cattle.

To haul four and a half million pounds of freight required the purchase of more than a thousand additional wagons and fifteen thousand oxen, together with supplies and provisions, and the employment of twenty-five hundred additional men. Orders were rushed away for wagons and equipment, buyers were sent to scour the country for oxen, and agents combed the frontier for train masters, bullwhackers, herders, and roustabouts. To get the required number of oxen the buyers had to strip Missouri and Iowa farms and pay 25 per cent or more above the usual market price. To get enough men for the undertaking agents had to employ the scum of the frontier, and at wages 50 per cent above those paid for top-grade men that spring.

Under such circumstances, the cost of outfitting the wagon trains necessary for hauling the single shipment must have been well in excess of a million dollars. Although at the rates specified in the firm's contract the total freight charges would amount to little more than half the investment, Russell raised the necessary finances by discounting notes secured by liens against the expected receipts.

During July twenty-five hundred infantrymen, a company of mounted dragoons, and an artillery battery were assembled at Fort Leavenworth. A year later Horace Greeley wrote of this makeshift army: "Detained in Kansas to give effect to Governor Walker's electioneering quackeries, it was at length sent on its way at a season too late to allow it to reach Salt Lake before winter. No commander was sent with it; General Harney was announced as its chief, but has not even yet joined it. It was thus despatched on a long and difficult expedition, in detachments, without a chief, without orders, without any clear idea of its object or destination."

When the little army set out from Fort Leavenworth it was accompanied by the Waddell & Russell beef herd of two thousand cattle, and forty-one Russell, Majors & Waddell wagon trains in charge of James Rupe, with Russell's nephew, Charles Morehead, acting as his assistant. Winter was setting in by the time the expedition "of separate, straggling detachments, none of which was ordered to protect the supply train," reached South Pass. Due to the army's disorganized march, the freight trains were strung out over nearly fifty miles of trail.

When word that the army was on its way to Utah reached Brigham Young he proclaimed martial law in the Territory, forbade United States troops to enter, and called up the Mormon militia of about five thousand men to enforce his dictum.

In early October the Army of Utah with its strung-out freight trains reached southwestern Wyoming and the Mormons came out to stop it, not by battle, but by destroying the supply trains. The militiamen were ordered to stampede the livestock, destroy fords, and burn loaded wagons and all grass along the line of march, but to take no lives. On the night of October 4 the Mormons surrounded three straggling provision trains, drove away the oxen, and burned the wagons, which were loaded with enough flour, bacon, ham, and sugar to have lasted the troops three months.

In an effort to save the rest, the trains were ordered into close formation interspersed by companies of soldiers. It was also decided to change the line of march, turn northwest into Idaho, and approach Salt Lake through the Bear River Valley, where it was believed that the grass had not been burned. With the tight formation there was insufficient forage for the oxen even in areas where the grass had not been burned; each day they became weaker from starvation, and progress was slowed to a crawl.

In late October Colonel A. S. Johnston, who had been given command of the Utah force, ordered that the trains turn back to a valley thirty miles north of Bridger's old fort, where there was reported to be good grazing. On arrival many of the oxen were completely broken down, but all were turned out to graze. During the night a band of Mormon raiders swooped down from the mountains, stampeded the cattle, and drove away nine hundred of the strongest among them.

On November 6 a heavy snow fell, burying what little grass had not been burned, and at night the Mormon raiders swooped down and stampeded the oxen again, and drove away five hundred more. The next morning Colonel Johnston began a march toward Fort Bridger, recently evacuated by the Mormons, but during the following night the temperature dropped below zero and more than half the remaining oxen froze to death. The thirty-mile trek required ten days, and when Fort Bridger was reached only three hundred of the Russell, Majors & Waddell oxen were still alive, all the others having died under the yoke. Before evacuating the fort the Mormons had burned all the buildings, leaving only the high stone walls surrounding the quadrangle. The remaining R.M.&W. wagons were stripped of lumber and canvas to build storage space for what provisions and supplies had been brought through.

Meanwhile, news of Brigham Young's proclamation forbidding U.S. troops to enter Utah had reached Washington, and on January 11, 1858, the War Department announced that three thousand reinforcement troops would soon be dispatched from Fort Leavenworth. On January 16, before news of the disaster to the wagon trains had reached the East, the partners signed another two-year contract with the War Department, continuing their monopoly on military freighting west of the Missouri River.

The new contract was made in the name of Russell, Majors & Waddell at greatly increased rates, and contained safeguards to protect the firm in the event of extraordinarily large shipments which would require investment in additional wagon trains. For the first five million pounds the rate per ton per hundred miles of haul varied from thirty-six dollars to ninety dollars, depending upon bulk. For the second five million pounds the rate was to be 25 per cent higher, with an additional step-up of 35 per cent for all weight in excess of ten million pounds and a maximum of thirty million pounds of freight the firm could be required to haul in a single season.

Two weeks or more after the new contract had been signed Rupe and Morehead arrived in Leavenworth with news of the disaster and signed receipts for the goods that had been delivered. Russell telegraphed for them to come to Washington at once. Upon their arrival he presented freighting bills and a statement of losses to the Quartermaster General's office, but was told that the War Department had no money. When preparing its budget for the 1857–58 fiscal year it had not anticipated sending troops to Utah and had already greatly overdrawn its appropriation.

There is no doubt that the news threw Russell into a panic. He had stretched the firm's credit to the absolute limit in outfitting the now nonexistent Utah wagon trains, and unless they were replaced before the start of another hauling season Russell, Majors & Waddell could not retain a monopoly on military freighting in the West, regardless of contract. Furthermore, the firm might be forced into bankruptcy if a substantial portion of the notes already outstanding were not paid before it became known in financial circles that the War Department was currently unable to meet its obligations.

In desperation Russell proposed to Secretary of War John Buchanan Floyd that he be allowed to draw acceptances on the War Department in anticipation of the revenue which would accrue to the firm from its military-freight hauling during the 1858 season. He promised that the acceptances would never be permitted to reach maturity and so would never be presented to the Government for payment; they would simply be used as collateral security for temporary loans which the firm would pay off with the first funds received from the War Department. Amazingly, the Secretary not only agreed to the extremely irregular procedure but used the influence of his position in the President's cabinet to assist Russell in making enormous loans. Even so, Russell was obliged to allow very high discounts because of the firm's overextended financial condition and the War Department's failure to meet its 1857 obligations when due.

In order for the War Department to meet its outstanding obligations a deficiency bill was introduced in Congress in the spring of 1858. It resulted in a wrangle that was embarrassing to the Buchanan Administration and injurious to the reputation of Russell, Majors & Waddell. Many congressmen believed that the Mormons were being persecuted. In both House and Senate the Administration was fiercely attacked for having sent troops to Utah, and resolutions were passed in both chambers requiring Secretary Floyd to produce all contracts in connection with the expedition. The high-rate monopoly freighting contract drew scathing criticism; the suspicion of graft was clearly evident, and Russell, Majors & Waddell were held up to public contempt as gouging contractors of doubtful honesty. The deficiency bill was passed, however, providing funds to pay the firm for its previous year's hauling, but Congress failed to authorize payment of the company's half-million-dollar claim for extraordinary losses.

Majors had apparently had enough of the monopoly. The army's freighting requirements in the spring of 1858 were greater than ever before, and the cost of outfitting enough wagon trains to handle it all would have been staggering. It is also probable that, with the adverse publicity given the firm by the debates in Congress William Russell was unable to raise sufficient financing for such vast outfitting. In any case, Majors made subcontracts with eighteen independent freighters to haul forty-eight trainloads of military freight at rates approximately equal to those in the monopoly contract, in each case stipulating that the independent contractor was to be paid immediately upon receipt by Russell, Majors & Waddell of funds for the goods he had hauled.

As a sideline in the winter of 1857–58, Russell formed a partnership with Waddell and their friend A. B. Miller to undertake a venture as sutler to the U.S. Army in Utah. Using Russell, Majors & Waddell credit, he bought enough sutler type of merchandise in the East to fill a wagon train and had it shipped to Leavenworth by boat. In the spring of 1858 the new firm outfitted a wagon train and sent Miller to take the merchandise to Utah and open sutler stores at the various army camps being established there. By fall the partnership owed the firm of Russell, Majors & Waddell $200,-000 which it was unable to pay. Like most of Russell's sideline projects, this one went broke, and Majors—who would have had no part in the profits if any had been made—was stuck with a third of the loss.

That, however, was simply a foretaste of the staggering losses to which the firm of Russell, Majors & Waddell was soon to be subjected through William Russell's sideline venture into the stagecoaching business.

12

Pike's Peak or Bust

In the late summer of 1858 the "Pike's Peak" gold rush was set off by a man who came into a bank at Leavenworth with a goosequill full of gold dust which he said he had panned from Cherry Creek where it flowed into the South Platte River at the foot of the Rocky Mountains—now downtown Denver.

Russell was in Leavenworth when the gold rush was touched off and was called upon by General William Larimer, who was organizing a prospecting party and wanted advice on transportation to Pike's Peak, as the entire eastern rampart of the Colorado Rockies was generally known, although it was then a part of western Kansas. Probably because Russell had dabbled to a considerable extent in such promotions, Larimer mentioned that he planned to organize a township as soon as he reached the diggings. Both men being extremely visionary and oversanguine, they evidently expected the stampede to Pike's Peak to exceed the California gold rush of '49 and had visions of present Denver springing into being almost overnight. Before the conversation ended Larimer had promised Russell a share in the township he proposed to organize and they had discussed the establishment of a stagecoach line from Leavenworth.

General Larimer went through with his plans, and on November 22, 1858, organized the Denver City Town Company, naming William Russell as one of the original shareholders. At that time Russell was in Chicago on his way to Washington and he wrote Waddell that "Pike's Peak will rage next year and no mistake. . . . I am for sending a cargo of supplies out there."

While in Washington, Russell met John S. Jones, who, in 1850, had been a partner in the freighting firm of Brown, Russell & Com-

pany. Both being impractical, oversanguine promoters and speculators, it is hardly surprising that they were carried away with
enthusiasm about the discovery of gold in the Rockies. Early in
February 1859 they organized the Leavenworth & Pike's Peak
Express Company. The firm was a joint-stock company in which
forty shares of stock at $5000 each were subscribed. William Rus-
sell was elected president, his eldest son, John, was named secretary,
and John S. Jones was appointed general manager. Among the stock
subscribers were Luther R. Smoot, Russell's banking partner in the
firm of Smoot, Russell & Co., and Benjamin F. Ficklin, who had
been a member of the U.S. wagon-road surveying party on the
central route.

Russell is reported to have paid into the new firm $20,000—
borrowed money, of course—and Jones is believed to have paid in
an equal amount. There is, however, no record to show that John
Russell, Luther Smoot, Ben Ficklin, or the other subscribers paid
for stock issued in their names.

Although Russell had not consulted Majors or Waddell before
organizing the Leavenworth & Pike's Peak Express Company, it is
evident that he expected them to subscribe liberally to the stock.
It is also evident that Russell raised his share of the investment on
Russell, Majors & Waddell credit, for Waddell wrote him several
scorching letters censuring him for having involved his freighting-
firm associates in the scheme, accusing him of reckless speculation,
and refusing point-blank to have anything to do with the undertaking.

In his memoirs, Majors told of Russell's trying to persuade him
to invest in the venture. "I told them," he wrote, "that I could not
consent to do so, for it would be impossible to make such a venture,
at such an early period of the development of the country, a paying
proposition, and urgently advised them to let the enterprise alone."

Ben Ficklin may have had some slight stagecoaching experience,
but if so he was the only one in the new firm with any knowledge
whatsoever of the business. Neither this, lack of capital, the fact
that very little gold had been discovered at "Pike's Peak," or warnings against the venture by Majors and Waddell deterred Russell
and Jones a particle. Using Russell, Majors & Waddell credit by
implication if not by direct statement, they ordered fifty-two Concord stagecoaches—many more than were in use on the entire
Butterfield line—at a cost in excess of $100,000. With probably
double that amount, borrowed for ninety days, they sent buyers
into Kentucky for eight hundred of the finest mules to be found.

By early March 1859 Independence, St. Joseph, and Leavenworth were thronged with gold rushers stampeding for the "Pike's Peak diggin's." The more sensible of them took the safe and well-traveled Overland Trail to Julesburg, then followed the South Platte River upstream to Denver. The distance by this route, however, was nearly 750 miles from Leavenworth, whereas it was only 550 in a straight line, or about 600 by way of the Smoky Hill Trail. The latter followed the Kaw River and its tributary, the Smoky Hill, almost due west from Kansas City to the present site of Kit Carson, Colorado, then northwest along Big Sandy Creek to its right-angled bend, westward to reach Cherry Creek about twenty miles above its confluence with the South Platte, and along its right bank to Denver. The latter portion of the route is now roughly followed by three highways: U.S. 40 from the Kansas boundary to Limon, Colorado; state route 86 westward to Elizabeth; and state route 83 from Parker to Denver.

The Smoky Hill route was considered dangerous by frontiersmen, as the western two-thirds of it was through a semiarid region where most of the streams flowed only in wet seasons and both grass and game were scarce. But in their eagerness to reach the diggings before all the claims had been staked, the more improvident, reckless, and greedy among the gold rushers ignored the old-timers' warnings and flocked westward along the Smoky Hill.

William Russell and John Jones were as eager to get their stage line into operation before competition sprang up as the improvident gold rushers were to reach the diggings before all the claims were staked. And in their usual slapdash fashion, they decided to pioneer a new route on a straight line between Leavenworth and Denver. In early March, Jones opened a lavish office in Leavenworth and engaged Colonel William Preston to explore the shortest possible stage route to Denver and to mark locations for way stations not more than twenty-five miles apart.

In the meantime Russell was making a swing through the East, holding press conferences in the larger cities and announcing that, beginning on April 10, the Leavenworth & Pike's Peak Express Company would run two Concord stagecoaches each way daily over the most direct route between Leavenworth and Denver. The fare would be $125, including excellent meals and sleeping accommodations en route, and the firm guaranteed that each trip would be made in ten days or less.

With a couple of wagons and an exploration party Colonel Preston set out on March 15, but did very little exploring until he reached what is now the northwestern corner of Kansas. For the first 135 miles he followed the well-established military road between Fort Leavenworth and Fort Riley, its entire length thronged with gold rushers, and then continued westward a few miles to the little settlement of Junction City, where the Republican and Smoky Hill rivers joined to form the Kaw.

Colonel Preston was far more practical than either Russell or Jones, and there is little doubt that he had a copy of the map prepared by Frémont of the route over which Kit Carson guided him from Independence to South Pass in the spring of 1842. Instead of continuing straight westward or following the Smoky Hill toward the southwest, Preston laid his course almost exactly over Frémont's route for the next 250 miles, striking northwest to the Solomon River, following its left bank to Limestone Creek, then crossing the high, rolling divides separated by Prairie Dog, Sappa, and Beaver creeks to reach the Republican River at the present site of Benkelman, Nebraska, twenty-five miles east of the point where Colorado, Kansas, and Nebraska now meet.

Frémont had continued to the northwest up Frenchman Creek. Due westward in the direction of Denver lay 150 miles of waterless buffalo range. To avoid crossing this arid region Preston followed the Republican River to its source, 120 miles to the southwest, and then crossed a low divide to reach Big Sandy Creek near the present site of Hugo, Colorado. There the colonel's exploration ended, for he intersected the Smoky Hill Trail and followed it to Denver.

Along the way he had piled up rocks or buffalo bones at intervals varying from twenty to thirty miles, marking locations for twenty-six way stations. Each of them was situated where, except in very dry seasons, there would be a dependable water supply and reasonably good grazing. But to achieve this Colonel Preston had been obliged to deviate far from the straight line contemplated by Russell and Jones. The odometer measurement of the route was 687 miles, nearly a hundred more than the distance over the Smoky Hill route, and only about sixty less than by way of the well-established central overland route where there was an abundance of water and grass all the way.

Probably while still in Washington, Russell and Jones had laid out elaborate plans for their stagecoach line. As quickly as possible, permanent station buildings were to be constructed of logs, adobe, or sod. In the meantime passengers and employees would be housed in tents and the stock kept in corrals. Each station would be manned with two hostlers, four drivers, and a keeper who had a wife and family. In addition to cooking for the employees, the wife would serve meals to passengers and provide for their lodging.

Each station would be stocked with twelve or more stage mules, and four or more horses for general utility use. The latter might be grazed near the station if there were little danger of Indian raids, but to keep the stage mules in top condition for fast travel they were to be hay-and-grain fed, and held in corrals or stables when not on the road.

President Russell and General Manager Jones were convinced that the straight-line route they had envisioned would at once become the main thoroughfare between the Missouri River and "Pike's Peak" for the horde of gold rushers having their own transportation. They were also convinced that huge profits could be made by selling provisions, supplies, and clothing to the expected horde at gold-rush prices, so decided to open a general store at each way station. To supply the stores with goods and the stations with hay, grain, and provisions, an ox train of twenty-five wagons would set out from Leavenworth every ten days.

Colonel Preston had no sooner pulled away from Leavenworth on his exploration trip than John Jones began hiring employees to man the line and buying great quantities of oxen, wagons, horses, building materials, tents, equipment, supplies, provisions, hay, and grain. Beverly D. Williams, one of the ten subscribers to stock in the firm, was appointed superintendent of the line, and on March 28 the first wagon train, loaded with building materials and supplies, left Leavenworth. Four days later the second train pulled out, loaded with tents, provisions, and the first hundred employees for constructing and manning the line. Among them were station-keepers and their families, guards, carpenters, blacksmiths, and harnessmakers.

Train after train followed as materials, feed, provisions, and merchandise for the stores arrived on riverboats and were loaded onto wagons. Accompanying each train went the newly hired hostlers and stage drivers, taking a herd of horses and mules for stocking stations. Other drivers, with the pick of the mules, awaited arrival of the coaches and harness that had been ordered "rush" from Concord.

Although service had been advertised to start on April 10, it was the seventeenth before the coaches and harness arrived. The handsome coaches with their red bodies and yellow running gears, and the lavish manner in which the line was being equipped, must have made a deep impression on the people of Leavenworth. Forty years later Frank A. Root, who in 1859 was a young postal clerk at Leavenworth, wrote in his book, *The Overland Stage to California*: "The line was equipped with over fifty Concord coaches, built by the Abbot-Downing Company, of Concord, N.H., the most popular and substantial vehicles of the kind made. They were brought up Missouri river by steamboat and were unloaded on the levee. . . . It cost a vast fortune to open up and stock the new route. The Company spent something near a quarter of a million dollars in their preliminaries, equipment, and in completing arrangements before turning a wheel. . . . The Expense of operating the line was approximately $1000 a day."

On the morning of April 18 two of the new coaches pulled up in front of the Leavenworth & Pike's Peak Express office in the Planter's Hotel. Each of them was drawn by four of the best mules to be found in Missouri, decked out in shiny new Concord harness, and driven by a frontier teamster turned jehu. The street was soon thronged with curious townspeople and envious gold rushers, most of the latter lacking either transportation of their own or the price of stage fare. Prominent in the crowd was General Manager John S. Jones, radiating pride, receiving congratulations, and giving last-minute instructions to Superintendent Beverly Williams, the drivers, and Dr. John Fox, a subscriber to stock in the firm who had been appointed general agent at Denver. To shouting and cheering, the coaches pulled away for the Rockies at a smart trot. In the leading

Stagecoaching in the mountains. (From Harper's Weekly, August 30, 1870.)

coach rode Williams, Dr. Fox, and four passengers. In the second there were only four passengers, among them Libeus Barney from Bennington, Vermont.

Barney, evidently well educated, was one of the relatively few Pike's Peak gold rushers with enough ready cash to make the trip by rail, steamer, and stagecoach. Attracted by the publicity with which Russell was flooding the East, he left New York by train on March 28, reached St. Louis on the thirty-first, took a steamer up the Missouri, and arrived at Leavenworth on April 5. His letters, published in the *Bennington Banner,* have been reprinted and preserved in the Western History Department of the Denver Public Library. They give a vivid description of gold-rush Leavenworth and the only eyewitness account of the first trip over the Leavenworth & Pike's Peak Express Company's luxury stagecoach line. Following are excerpts from the reprinted letters.

Finding we were in advance of the coaches intended for Russell's line, they not having arrived from the manufactory, we were under the disagreeable necessity of awaiting their arrival, which occurred not till the 17th. . . . The emigration is really a godsend to this five-year-old town. . . . "Pike's Peak Line," the shortest, cheapest and most reliable route, the Pike's Peak almost everything, greets you upon either hand, and Leavenworth is realizing glorious profits out of the general excitement.

This being the terminus for laying in supplies, everything in the way of provisions and implements for digging, find ready sale at a handsome advance. Thousands are leaving here daily and in every variety of way the mind can conjecture. Now a party with guns, pistols and picks, their blankets thrown over their shoulders, and with provisions scarcely sufficient to last a week, off they start for the mines, a journey, under the most favorable circumstances, that cannot be performed short of three weeks.

Here another party, with hand-carts loaded down with all the necessaries for a comfortable journey . . . burden enough for a yoke of oxen —and in high spirits they depart. And still again a company of 8 or 10 appear with six yoke of oxen and a monster wagon attached, loaded to excess with the necessaries and a keg or two of luxuries, and off they move. Occasionally some get discouraged after arriving here . . . and make good their retreat ere it is too late; and some have not the wherewith to return . . . having been drained completely dry by those despicable human landsharks that dog their steps from place to place, while they have a "red" to call their own.

April 18th—Everything being in readiness, the mules were hitched to the conveyances, and as soon as the passengers were aboard the hybrids were cracked up and away we went. Our load consisted of four passengers, a small quantity of quicksilver, a few gold scales, and the mail. We reached the first station, 65 miles from Leavenworth, at 11 o'clock in the evening, and put up with a half-breed Indian, couched to rest upon the floor of our host's wigwam, and slept as sweet as if lulled by siren songs and rocked by angel hands.

April 19th—After a hurried breakfast at 6 this morning, we started on our journey, and passed thousands wearily tugging themselves and burdens towards the all-attractive "Peak." Passed Fort Riley at 6, and arrived at Junction City about 8, a place of twenty very poor houses and a poorer hotel, kept by a German. There is a paper printed here, about six months old, and boasts of six subscribers, and exchanges with all the world. The settlement derives its name from the Republican and Smoky Hill forming a junction at this place. We put up here for the night and found better entertainment than outside appearances indicated.

April 20th—Started at half-past 5 this morning, at 1 o'clock dined in a tent, for we had now passed all the houses on the route until we arrived at Denver City. Late in the evening we overtook another station—took a cold cut and struck our lodgings. Another and myself secured a coach for our couch, and pleasantly dreamed the night away.

April 21st—This morning we started at the first gray of twilight, and making every exertion compatible with our means, we succeeded in advancing fifty miles today and . . . got to bunk at 10 o'clock.

April 22nd—We left the station at an early hour, being forced to move or freeze, and amid an avalanche of snow-flakes and a hurricane of wind gusts, which roughly visited us in intermitting squalls during most of the day. Made but twenty-five miles today.

April 23d—Last night was too cold to rest comfortably and we were glad to start at an early hour. Snow ankle deep and atmosphere cold as zero. Saw today the first herd of buffalos, made a halt and went in pursuit of them but all to no purpose. Wolves, buffalos and antelopes have been round about us in abundance the entire day. Camped at 12 and rested well.

April 24th—Left the station at 9 this morning, road bad, made but twenty miles advance today, striking our tent at 5 P.M.

April 25th—Today made two stations and encamped at dusk.

April 26th—Made but one station today, fired at several antelope but missed them.

April 27th—Advanced but one station today and arrived in camp half starved.

April 28th—But twenty-five miles advance made today, and most of us nearly sick. No wood or water for 15 miles either way from this encampment, and found it difficult to keep warm through the night.

[This entry indicates that on the first trip a shortcut to the Republican River was made from the Frémont Trail just south of the Kansas-Nebraska line, and that the encampment of April 28 was made about fifteen miles east of present St. Francis, Kansas.]

April 29th—Cold and foggy. Breakfasted on bean soup, bread and mo-

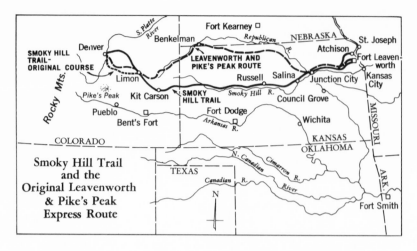

*While the gold rush boomed in Colorado, fast stagecoaches
ran semi-weekly between Leavenworth and Denver.*

lasses and poor coffee, the passengers started on foot and ahead of the
coaches, and have walked the greater part of the day. The country, most
of the way through which we have traveled, is rolling prairie destitute
of even shrubbery save along the margin of the small creeks where are
found a few stunted trees and smaller brush, and so monotonous in regularity is everything appertainly to the country, that the eye feels the loss
of Green Mountain scenery and the never ceasing variety of Vermont
landscape. We encamped at six and were visited by twelve Indians, asking for sugar, coffee, corn and doubly anxious for a little whiskey, and
although refused they appeared perfectly friendly, and left in the utmost
good nature.

April 30th—We were en route this morning at an early hour, and advanced fifty miles during the day over sand knolls destitute of grass and
shrub-wood and water; but our ride was somewhat relieved of its tire-
some monotony by firing now and then at an antelope, a wolf, or a
rabbit. [This stretch was along the valley of the Republican River in
what is now eastern Colorado, where the stream bed is usually dry except after an occasional spring cloudburst.]

May 1st—Last night the rain poured in torrents the livelong night, and
the wind upset our coach and spilled us out, and ere we could right it
for shelter again, we were drenched to the very skin. . . . Today, as yesterday, our route has laid over sand hills, unwooded and unwatered. Our
mules gave out this afternoon and we were compelled to walk the last
12 miles to the station, where we arrived at 8 o'clock. [The vicinity of
present Hugo, Colorado.] Here we found about fifty emigrants who
came *via* Smoky Hill route, and they were indeed objects of compassion.

Some of them started with horses, some with mules, and some with oxen, but the most of them now were without either. Their teams having been deprived of food and water, perished, and their wagons were burned to cook with. Many were sick and sought shelter from the frosty nights beneath their few remaining wagons. One of the lady emigrants here became a mother. Her child lived but a few hours, was buried upon the margin of a convenient brook, which from this circumstance, has taken the name of Infant Creek.

May 2d—Left station 22 this morning at 5 o'clock and reached the next at half-past 1—18 miles distant—should have traveled farther, but the advance train that was surveying the route was but fifteen miles ahead. . . .

May 3d—Moved at 5 this morning. Mules a little more antic. Have found water occasionally during the day. Arrived in camp at 3 o'clock and while dinner was preparing, three of our company went and killed an antelope, and while returning with our game stirred up a nest of rattlesnakes and succeeded in diminishing their number by six, the longest measuring seven feet. Had today the first view of Pike's Peak about one hundred miles in the blue distance. Looked like an immense thunder cloud ere it puts on its rain-threatening livery. . . .

May 4th—Advance train ten miles ahead. Left camp at 7 A.M. Killed several rattlesnakes this forenoon for pastime. . . . Reached the station at 5. An Indian brought into camp this evening a man he had picked up the day before in an almost dying state. The man gave the following account of himself: "Two brothers of mine, myself and five others left Whiteside County, Ill., the latter part of February last for Pike's Peak. Leaving Kansas City, Mo., the first of March with a pony for packing our provisions, we pushed on for the Eldorado. After being out for a few days the pony, for want of food and drink, became exhausted and died. We were then compelled to carry our own grub, which we continued to do until it was all consumed, then we had no resource left but the scanty game our guns could supply. Soon, however, this failed, for our ammunition became exhausted.

"Four of our company now started ahead to find, if possible, a settlement. A Mr. Roach and my brothers were left behind, being already too weak for pioneers. By and by the strength of Roach failed him and starvation looked us all full in the face. We killed our dog one day and devoured him; next day Roach died of starvation, and upon his corpse we subsisted till it was consumed to the very marrow in its bones. My eldest brother, conscious he could last but a little longer implored us to feed upon him as soon as he should die, and travel as fast as possible while he lasted. . . . He died and we devoured him. Next, my younger brother died, and was eaten by me. . . ."

When the Indian found him he lay upon his back, nearly blind and too weak to get a drink of water from the creek but a few yards distant. In the morning the conductor and I went with him and the Indian, and found the remains of the younger brother as he related. The bones, which were perfectly fleshless, lay in a little bough house. . . . We buried the skeleton remains, the flesh of which had preserved a brother from starvation, and left the wolf to howl his funeral dirge. . . . Their names were Rule, Charles, Alexander and George, if I remember rightly. They have a father and mother living in Illinois. This story is dreadful, even at second hand, but to hear the wild and almost distracted brother relate it was heartrending in the extreme.

May 5th—Left camp this morning at 7; made slow progress; each one buried in the contemplation of his own thoughts. We traveled but eighteen miles today. Distance from Denver City, by Yankee guess-work, about fifty miles. Encamped at 6. . . .

May 6th—Hitched on our team at 6 and started off. . . . Indians cease to excite even *my* curiosity. They are constantly following us,—begging for tobacco, powder, caps, lead, blankets, sugar, coffee, etc. Encamped at sunset on the banks of Ciawah Creek. [Here Barney is mistaken. Kiowa Creek had been passed the previous day, and the encampment of May 6 was in the vicinity of present Parker, on Cherry Creek.]

May 7th—Left station 26 just after sunrise. Denver City twenty miles distant, and Pike's Peak looming up grandly, and its white surface brilliantly sparkling in the sunlight. Gave the mules a taste of the "long oats" [whip], and, at 4 P.M., found ourselves, safe and sound, in the place of gold and golgotha, and more, in my opinion, of the skull than the lucre. This marvelous city contains about 150 log cabins, some with roofs, and more without. One hotel, 40 by 200 [feet], built of logs and covered with canvas. Here I am stopping at the moderate price of $3 per day. Business is wholly stagnant; money,—coin, I mean,—scarce, and gold dust scarcer. Hundreds leave daily for their homes; hundreds turn back before they arrive here, and none have any confidence in the "diggins."

I have had three days' experience in gold digging. . . . Near as I can judge, having no means of measuring or weighing, I secured about the sixteenth part of a new cent's worth of the genuine article. Yesterday had a conversation with the correspondent of the New York *Tribune*. He has been here some four weeks, and says, so far as he can ascertain by observation and inquiry, he pronounces it the most prodigious humbug of this or any other age, and shall so report in his next article to the *Tribune*. Reports come in thick and fast of the suffering and starvation of the Smoky Hill emigrants. I have conversed with a number of men who tell me they have lived for two weeks on no other sustenance but prickly pears; and others tell of living for days on a dead ox found by the road-side in an advanced stage of decomposition, and without water for two or three days in succession. They also report passing uncovered dead men and women strung along the route, the air stenched with their putrifying bodies; others starving without the faintest hope of succor. . . .

13

Silent Partners in High Places

Probably before the first L.&P.P. stagecoach pulled out of Leavenworth, and certainly before it reached Denver, William Russell was negotiating a deal to extend the line to Salt Lake City. He was, of course, unaware that the great Pike's Peak gold discovery had been pronounced a prodigious humbug and that the Salt Lake mail was required by contract to be carried via the North Platte route, and he was heedless of the fact that he had already obligated the Leavenworth & Pike's Peak Express Company for many times over what it could possibly pay when its ninety-day notes fell due.

When Postmaster General Holt cut Hockaday & Liggett's mail contract to semimonthly service—effective July 1, 1859—at a reduction of $60,000 per annum, the firm was faced with a situation under which it could not meet its obligations and would be driven to the wall. Less conceited and impulsive men than John S. Jones and William Russell would have realized that if as successful a mail contractor and stage-line operator as John Hockaday could not make ends meet on the reduced compensation there was not the slightest possibility that they, completely inexperienced, could do so. Furthermore, only wildly impulsive gamblers would have paid—or promised to pay—a bonus for the reduced contract.

Nevertheless, on May 11, 1859, just four days after the first L.&P.P. stagecoach reached Denver, Jones & Russell contracted to pay Hockaday & Liggett a bonus of $50,000 for the unexpired year and a half of the St. Joseph-Salt Lake City mail contract, to buy all the firm's stock, equipment, relay posts, feed, and supplies at a price to be fixed by appraisal, and to pay for it in four installments spread over one year from May 15, 1859.

Stretching their credit—and indirectly that of Russell, Majors & Waddell—almost to the breaking point, Jones and Russell sent one wagon train loaded with general merchandise and another of groceries to Denver in the spring of 1859 and opened a huge store in a log building at Blake and F streets. Not to be outdone, Majors and Waddell formed a partnership with Robert Bradford, a relative of Waddell's, sent a wagon train of merchandise to Denver, and opened a competing store under the name of R. B. Bradford & Company. Probably the merchandise for both ventures was supplied at cost by the firm of Russell, Majors & Waddell.

It is apparent that by this time the affairs of the original firm and the supposedly independent partnerships entered into by Majors, Waddell, and particularly Russell had become so intertwined that any clear-cut separation of assets and liabilities would have been impossible. It is also apparent that the original partnership was hopelessly insolvent, drained by Russell's reckless plunging, losses sustained by satellite partnerships established on the firm's credit, the 1857 loss of wagons and oxen in Utah for which Congress had never authorized compensation, and the enormous expense of interest and discount under Russell's slapdash financing methods—to say nothing of the graft that he was doubtlessly paying to silent partners in Washington.

There is little doubt that in buying the Hockaday & Liggett mail contract Jones & Russell had expected to make a considerable saving by carrying the Salt Lake mail between Leavenworth and Denver on their regular stagecoach runs at no additional expense. The Post Office Department, however, insisted that the mail be carried over the route specified in the contract. This made it necessary, at tremendous expense, to abandon the newly established route and move the line to the Overland Trail along the North Platte, with a 210-mile branch operating between Denver and what is now the very northeastern corner of Colorado.

The last stagecoach to travel over the short-cut route arrived in Denver on June 7, carrying two of the most famous journalists in the United States. One of them was Albert D. Richardson, correspondent for the *Boston Journal*, and the other was Horace Greeley, editor of the *New York Tribune*. Both were "dead-headed" (given free transportation) in hope that they would reciprocate by writing articles for their papers that glowed with praise for the Leavenworth & Pike's Peak Express Company and its owners. There was no dearth of articles in the *New York Tribune*, but they were something less than glowing with praise for William Russell and his associates.

Early in 1859 the War Department had advertised for bids to furnish flour for the troops in Utah. Among the bidders was a Mormon firm in Salt Lake City, bidding to supply flour from wheat raised and ground in Utah. This bid, although far the lowest, was thrown aside and a contract awarded to millers in St. Louis for 843,000 pounds of superfine Missouri flour at seven dollars per hundredweight. In March, Russell was notified by Quartermaster General Jesup in Washington that the flour was to be transported to Camp Floyd (about forty miles south of Salt Lake City) and other Utah military posts as soon as the hauling season opened in May, at the freight rate of $22.50 per hundredweight.

Shortly thereafter, Russell was in New York and met his friend Ben Holladay, who, although cursed by many as unscrupulous and dishonest, was trusted by the Mormons and had become fabulously wealthy through his dealings between them and the "Gentiles." It is almost certain that Holladay either knew or suspected that Russell had silent partners in Washington, for he pointed out the enormous profit to be realized if Russell could obtain consent from Secretary of War John B. Floyd to permit acceptance of the St. Louis flour at Leavenworth but delivery to the Utah army camps of flour produced in the Salt Lake area, with no reduction in the freight rate. He also pointed out that the St. Louis flour would bring upwards of forty dollars per hundredweight in Denver.

Without consulting his partners in the freighting firm, Russell agreed to the undertaking and to a partnership with Holladay in the venture if he would handle the Utah end of the deal. Secretary Floyd agreed readily to the fraudulent scheme, leaving little room for doubt that there was collusion of long standing between himself and William Russell.

All through the spring of 1859 Russell was busy as a bird dog with the launching of the Leavenworth & Pike's Peak Express Company and buying out Hockaday & Liggett. Waddell was frantically occupied in holding the strings of an often-empty purse at Leavenworth and bombarding Russell with blistering letters for being a "reckless gambler." Majors was at work from dawn till dark in getting the endless streams of freight wagons loaded and away to army forts and posts throughout the West. In Utah Ben Holladay was equally busy, making a fat side profit on his newfound and gullible partner. He had bought 843,000 pounds of Utah flour—reportedly at seven dollars per hundredweight—to replace that from the St. Louis mills. What he actually paid the Mormons for their flour remained a secret, but it was no secret that in prior years he had paid them as little as one dollar per hundredweight.

Apparently a second highly profitable scheme had been hatched while Russell was securing Secretary Floyd's consent to the flour deal. Soon after Holladay arrived in Salt Lake City the assistant quartermaster general at Camp Floyd received orders from Washington to sell at auction about two-thirds of the mules, harness, and wagons on hand. These were not surplus, but would be needed in order to move or withdraw the troops, and advance notice of the auction was so short as to eliminate buyers from the East or West. The mules had cost the government $175 each, and were being pastured at no expense when not in use. Early in July the auction was held and Ben Holladay was on hand to bid on 782 mules at an average price of $75 each, wagons that had cost $130 at about $20 each, and harness at a fraction of its cost. The freighting firm had evidently not been cut in on these juicy melons, for in payment of his purchases Holladay wrote a draft upon William Russell personally.

In the meantime Jones & Russell had been transferring the L.&P.P. stage line to the North Platte route and combining it with the line to Salt Lake City, while Horace Greeley had spent three weeks junketing around newly discovered gold strikes in the mountains west of Denver and writing enthusiastic articles for his paper.

On June 27 Greeley resumed his overland journey toward California riding as a dead-head passenger on an L.&P.P. stagecoach, and arrived in Salt Lake City at the time of the Camp Floyd auction. With a great editor's keen sense for rooting out sensational news, he headed for Camp Floyd, unearthed the flour deal, and wrote the following:

By a little dexterous management at Washington . . . they had no difficulty in . . . making a clear profit of one hundred and seventy thousand dollars on the contract, without risking a dollar, or lifting a finger.

Again, pursuant to a recent order from Washington, the Assistant Quartermaster-General here is now selling by auction some two thousand mules—about two-thirds of all the government owns in this territory. . . . Nobody here has recommended the sale of these mules; . . . the army can never move without purchasing an equal number; and they can neither be bought here nor brought here for two hundred thousand dollars more than these animals are now fetching. *Somebody's* interest is subserved by this sale; but it is certainly not that of the army nor of the people. . . . Who issues such orders as this, and for whose benefit?

The army would cost less almost anywhere else, and could not any-

Blake Street, Denver, Colorado, in 1866. (Courtesy, Old Print Shop.)

where be less useful. A suspicion that it is kept here to answer private pecuniary ends is widely entertained. It is known that vast sums have been made out of its transportation by favored contractors. . . . There have recently been received here thirty thousand bushels of corn from the states at a net cost, including transportation, of three hundred and forty thousand dollars, or over eleven dollars per bushel. No requisition was ever made for this corn, which could have been bought here, delivered, for two dollars per bushel, or sixty thousand dollars in all. The dead loss to the treasury on this corn is two hundred and eighty thousand dollars, even supposing that the service required it at all. *Somebody* makes a good thing of wagoning this corn from the Missouri at over ten dollars a bushel. Who believes that said somebody has not influential and thrifty connections inside of the War Department? I will not pursue this exposition; Congress may.

Greeley's scathing articles were not only featured in the *New York Tribune* but picked up and republished by newspapers throughout the East. They dealt a staggering blow to the freighting firm's reputation and its already badly strained credit, but William Russell had apparently conceived the notion of outstripping John Butterfield as the stagecoaching king of the West and was not to be stopped by adverse publicity or lack of credit. Using War Department acceptances signed personally by Secretary Floyd as security, he borrowed tens of thousands of dollars on ninety-day notes and invested the money in fixed assets. Additional stock and equipment were bought for the St. Joseph to Salt Lake City stage line, permanent stations were built at intervals of sixteen to forty-three miles apart, and a completely new line built from Denver to Julesburg at the northeast corner of present Colorado.

The coveted and dearly bought Salt Lake City mail contract proved to be a distinct liability rather than an asset. The weekly volume of westbound mail ranged from twelve to seventeen sacks, most of them weighing upwards of a hundred pounds apiece and filled with printed matter from the War Department or franked government documents being sent by politicians in Washington to constituents in the West. Until the contract was cut to semimonthly service on July 1 the weight was no great problem, for there was little passenger traffic between Julesburg and Salt Lake City. Mail bags for which there was no room in the back boot or under the driver's seat were carried inside the coach, and the time schedule could easily be maintained by using six- instead of four-mule teams. But if carried only twice a month a single coach could not handle the volume, even if passengers were eliminated entirely.

To operate a single stage over the line weekly cost very little more than to operate it semimonthly, since in either case an equal number of mules and employees had to be maintained at relay posts and way stations. The cost was considerably increased, how-ever, if the mail were doubled up, for two coaches were then required, making it necessary to double the number of mules and drivers that had to be maintained at all times. Furthermore, the eastbound mail was very small, and the eastbound passenger traffic even smaller. If two coaches were used to carry the westbound mail, one of them had to return empty.

To relieve the situation, the Leavenworth & Pike's Peak Express Company offered to continue providing weekly mail service be-tween St. Joseph and Salt Lake City even though the compensa-tion had been reduced by $60,000. Much though weekly mail service was desired by the Mormons and military forces in Utah, Postmaster General Holt refused to permit it under any circum-stances, and so instructed the postmasters at Salt Lake City and St. Joseph. The refusal may have been for some perverse reason of his own, but it seems more probable that it was at the instruc-tion of the President, determined to protect his friend Butterfield from competition for the overland passenger business to and from California.

Undaunted by the refusal, Russell continued borrowing large sums of money—using War Department acceptances signed by Sec-retary Floyd as security—and pouring it into the Leavenworth &

Pike's Peak Express Company. New relay posts and way stations were established on the line between Denver and Leavenworth until the distance between them averaged barely more than twelve miles, and at each of them a relay of fresh grain-fed mules was kept ready for the road day and night. Twenty-five of the larger stations, in charge of married keepers and their wives, were "home" stations for drivers and were equipped to provide excellent meals and lodging for passengers. There was no denying that the service on the L.&P.P. line—at least between Leavenworth and Denver—was far superior to that on the Butterfield line.

Nor was the quality of the service unappreciated. On August 13 the Denver *Rocky Mountain News* published an article by one of its readers who had just returned from a trip East: "A tribute of praise is due the Leavenworth and Pike's Peak Express Company for the very superior accommodations they offer to travelers over their route.

"On our recent journey from the States, we found their stations along the South Platte fitted up in the best style possible. Several new stations have also been made below the crossing, in addition to the old Salt Lake mail company's stations. Houses have been erected, wells dug, and the conveniences of life are rapidly being gathered around points along a distance of hundreds of miles, where two months ago there was not a fixed habitation. Passengers by this line get their regular meals, on a table and smoking hot."

Another passenger was even more enthusiastic about the L.&P.P. meals, writing that they put "many an Eastern brag house in the shade."

Terming the Pike's Peak gold discovery a humbug was well justified by the small amount of dust washed from the sand of Cherry Creek. But on the day before the first L.&P.P. stagecoach arrived at Denver, John Gregory discovered a rich deposit of gold-bearing quartz at the present site of Central City, Colorado. The news spread rapidly, prospectors swarmed through the mountains in every direction, and other important discoveries were made. Reports of these discoveries sent to the *New York Tribune* by Horace Greeley revived the flagging gold rush from the East, and the business of the L.&P.P. Express Company boomed. Fast stagecoaches were run semiweekly between Leavenworth and Denver, every seat occupied by a passenger, the rear boot crammed with express packages and excess baggage at seventy-five cents per pound, and the front boot stuffed with sacks of letters at twenty-five cents each and newspapers at a dime apiece. The eastbound coaches carried fewer passengers and far less mail, but every one

Horace Greeley, a famous passenger on the Leavenworth & Pike's Peak Express Line, reported the Central City gold discovery in his paper, the New York Tribune.

of them carried gold shipments to eastern banks, probably at an express rate of 10 per cent. A stagecoach line was established between Denver and Golden, and was doing capacity business.

All in all, William Russell's prospects appeared to be fabulous, and there was little indication that Horace Greeley's accusations of graft and dishonesty had done him and his Utah partner any lasting harm. Although Russell had never been west of Leavenworth, articles appearing in California newspapers left no doubt that he had formed an alliance with Ben Holladay, not only to milk the Government with the aid of a silent partner in the War Department but to corner the California beef market, and that they were already planning to acquire the Chorpenning mail contract and monopolize all transportation on the central overland route.

Under dates of August 1 and 3, 1859, the Salt Lake City correspondent for the *San Francisco Bulletin* reported:

The great sale of Government property, has just closed. It has been, without doubt, the largest Government sale that has taken place since the Mexican war, 2,500 mules, besides wagons, harness, etc., having been sold. The original cost to Government was not less than $500,000. The mules sold very low. . . . Holladay and Russell bought over 800, selecting the largest and finest ones only. I understand that they intend driving them to your State *via* Simpson's new route. They are undoubtedly the finest lot of mules ever brought together. . . . Holladay and Russell have also purchased about 4,000 head of cattle for the California market, and are negotiating for all to arrive in time to send forward this year. By this means they monopolize the cattle trade, and will have entire control of the market, so far as American beef is concerned, the ensuing year. Their entire investment in flour, mules, cattle, horses, wagons and outfitting amount to nearly $600,000; and knowing ones say that their profits will exceed $300,000. . . . Questions are being asked now as to the integrity of certain of our military officials. . . ."

From an article regarding the Simpson (or Egan) route which appeared in the *California Farmer* before the end of August, it is evident that the number of army mules bought by Holladay and Russell was considerably in excess of eight hundred and that they sent more than four thousand cattle to California, and there is an implication that at least a part of the cattle may have been involved in the Camp Floyd auction.

After reporting that Ben Holladay had just come through from Salt Lake City to Sacramento in less than six days, the article continued, "This was an enterprise of Holladay to test the route. . . . It should be understood that Holladay had chartered a coach for himself, clerk and servant, so as to have control of the same the entire route, that he could make a fair and impartial trial. . . . The Stage Co. continues to run a weekly line without pay. . . . Holladay and Russell have now en route over this new road twenty-five hundred head of cattle and one thousand mules, in charge of Egan. . . . Egan, of whom we have just spoken, conducted the first drove (of one thousand head of cattle) over this route, for Holladay and Russell from Camp Floyd without the loss of a single head. This road is *the* road for stock men. Holladay and Russell sent one thousand head of cattle, also in charge of an efficient man (Sublette) over the old Northern route which occupied thirty-two days losing twenty-eight oxen and two mules."

There is no positive proof that Secretary Floyd was a silent partner in William Russell's dealings with the War Department; there is, however, strong indication of it in the following excerpts from letters written by Russell to Waddell between the spring of 1858 and the summer of 1859 (in the Waddell Collection of Huntington Library, at San Marino, California).

"I am really astonished and mortified at your conclusions with regard to the results of my visit to Washington . . . Knowing as I do that my course . . . secured to us all the advantages we have enjoyed the past two years. And that what I have secured in outside things, which I well know would have been lost, had I not pursued the course I did, and which has amounted to largely more than I have expended or given away, not only so[;] through the influence brought to bear in this way we have obtained much work and many favors that otherwise would have been cut off. l will only refer to one. How could we have gotten along without Gov't accept [acceptances]? . . . I have already obtained from the Department $125,000.00 that no other living man could have carried, and I think I will be able to get half as much more out of matters that you are not dreaming of. . . . Secretary of War and Quartermaster General are strong friend in the matter as also all the clerks and assistant quartermasters in this Department. . . ."

Another excerpt from a letter Russell wrote to Waddell indicates clearly that the shady business was being kept a secret from Alexander Majors: "Mr. Majors starts tonight. You must not say a word to him about what I wrote you yesterday. All will go right. You need have no fear. Secretary of War has promised us all we want, tho he cannot change the contract."

Furthermore, if the profits from the Camp Floyd auction and the fraudulent flour deal were anywhere near as great as they were believed to have been, it is obvious that Russell was having to split with someone other than Ben Holladay, for he was desperately short of money in the fall of 1859.

To make matters worse, suspicion of collusion and graft in the War Department was sufficiently strong in Congress that the Buchanan Administration was put under severe pressure, and Russell had good reason to fear that the Russell, Majors & Waddell monopoly on military freighting in the West might not be renewed. His fear was evidently shared by his partners in the freighting firm, for it was decided to sell thirty-five hundred of the best oxen from the Utah wagon trains. They were to be pastured through the winter in Ruby Valley, 150 miles west of Camp Floyd, and then driven on to California for sale in early spring when the ox market should be at its peak.

Although the L.&P.P. stagecoaches between Leavenworth and Denver had been running with near-capacity loads during the summer, the receipts had fallen far short of enough to pay the extravagant operating expenses, to say nothing of the interest on borrowed capital. As the ninety-day notes with which the company had originally been financed fell due Russell met them with new loans made on Russell, Majors & Waddell credit—probably secured by War Department acceptances signed by Secretary Floyd.

The Salt Lake City line had proved a near catastrophe from the outset. John S. Jones had decided to act personally as route superintendent when the operation was first taken over from Hockaday & Liggett. Like Russell, he was a promoter, not an operator, and the line soon got out of hand. Beverly D. Williams, the stock sub-scriber who had been acting as general superintendent at Denver, was next appointed. Although a good and honest man, he was inexperienced in the stagecoaching business. The appointment was a mistake. By fall all semblance of control had been lost, the ex-penses were exorbitant, mules and feed were disappearing from the stations in large quantities, and the condition of the line was com-pletely chaotic.

From the time the Leavenworth & Pike's Peak Express Company was first conceived, John Jones and William Russell had anticipated that it would be awarded a lucrative contract for carrying the Denver mail, but Congress had been apathetic about passing an appropriation bill. By October 1859 even Russell had to concede that there was little hope of securing a mail contract during the current year. Furthermore, two competing stage lines had been established between Denver and Golden, fares had to be cut sharply, and the line was no longer profitable. Early snows in the mountains had curtailed mining operations for the winter, many miners returned to their homes in the East, and the population of Denver dropped to no more than three thousand. There was not enough passenger and express business between that point and Leavenworth to justify running more than one stage a week, the receipts from which would pay only a small fraction of the tre-mendous operating expenses of the company. By late October payrolls had fallen $10,000 in arrears, stations were running out of feed, the firm owed more than $525,000, and Russell was unable to make additional loans. He could only admit to Majors and Waddell that the L.&P.P. Express Company was hopelessly bank-rupt, and appeal to them for help.

Majors and Waddell found themselves in the position of men who had a bear by the tail and didn't dare let go. In his memoirs Alexander Majors wrote that the firm of Russell, Majors & Wad-dell took over the bankrupt Leavenworth & Pike's Peak Express Company and paid its debts to save Russell from ruin. This was a considerable understatement. Not only did the L.&P.P. Express Company owe Russell, Majors & Waddell the $190,000 shown by its books, but the financial affairs of the two firms were so inex-tricably entwined, and the credit of the freighting company so overextended, that if the former were allowed to go into bank-ruptcy it would certainly drag the latter down with it.

On October 28, 1859, Russell, Majors & Waddell entered into a contract to take over all of the assets and liabilities of the Leaven-worth & Pike's Peak Express Company, with the provision that a new company be formed for the purpose of transporting freight, passengers, and United States mail. Russell's domination over Majors and Waddell must have been tremendous. The capital stock of the proposed new firm was fixed at $200,000, divided into forty shares, and allocated as follows: Alexander Majors, 2; William Waddell, 2; William Russell, 30; his son John, 2; and John S. Jones, 4. William Russell was elected president, his son secretary, and Jones superintendent. As a means of attracting new capital into the proposed firm, Russell was given power of attorney and proxies for the purpose of acquiring additional associates through stock sales.

It is probable that Russell, if not Majors and Waddell, knew at the time of the meeting that a large part of the future military-freighting business had been lost, for the news had already reached California. On the previous day the *San Francisco Bulletin* had reported, "Russell, Majors & Co., have lost the Utah and Oregon Army transportation contract. It has been given to Irving & Co. . . . Irving & Co.'s bids were 36 cents per mile less than those of the late contractors. It is said the bids of Childs & Scott will take the two contracts for New Mexico . . ."

With the meeting over, Russell returned to the East, supposedly to raise capital for the embryonic firm by selling at $5000 each most of the thirty shares that had been allotted to him, to stave off creditors to whom more than a million dollars was owed and to get an act passed by Congress authorizing payment of the half-million-dollar claim he had presented for the firm's 1857 losses due to the Mormon War.

As was his custom, Russell entirely disregarded the agreement made with his partners; he took Jerome B. Simpson into the enterprise without any cash investment and set about preparing the articles for a corporation to be chartered under the extremely liberal laws of Kansas Territory. That he had let his imagination and enthusiasm run wild was clearly evident in the name he chose for the new corporation: Central Overland California & Pike's Peak Express Company. The capital stock, which could be increased at any time by a two-thirds vote of the stockholders, was to be $500,000, divided into shares of $100 each. The proposed articles not only gave the corporation the right to operate transportation lines "by land or water for the conveyance of persons, mail, or property in Kansas or beyond its limits," but to explore for minerals, operate mines and assay offices, carry on banking, and write fire, marine, and life insurance policies. In two respects, however, Russell did carry out the provisions of the agreement made with his partners on October 28: he named himself president of

Bandits holding up the Montana coach. (From Beyond the
Mines, *Albert D. Richardson.)*

the new firm, and his son John secretary. On November 22 he
wrote Waddell from New York, for the first time revealing the
corporate name he had chosen, and saying that "if we can manage
Dec." he had no fear of inability to stave off the creditors.

Ben Ficklin replaced Beverly Williams as superintendent of the
Salt Lake City line at the time the L.&P.P. was taken over by the
freighting firm, and had since been rooting out thieves with the
help of "Jack" Slade. Slade, a rough, tough, hard-drinking frontiersman who had been bullwhacker, Indian fighter, and stage
driver, was one of Hockaday & Liggett's division superintendents
at the time the line was acquired. Julesburg, where the Oregon
Trail crossed the South Platte, was named for "Old Jules" Beni, a
somewhat famous mountainman of shady reputation and equally
shady cronies who had founded the tiny settlement by establishing
a trading post there. Beverly Williams, being honest, presumed
everyone else to be the same, so hired Old Jules as stationkeeper
at Julesburg and several of his cronies as keepers at nearby relay
posts. By the time Ficklin was appointed they had just about

stripped their portion of the line of anything they could use or trade to Indians.

Ben Ficklin began his clean-up campaign by assigning Jack Slade to headquarters at Julesburg and instructing him to fire Old Jules. Slade, a powerful man, not only fired the old trader but bullied him into returning considerable of the stolen property. To get even, Jules ambushed Slade and peppered him with a blast from a double-barreled shotgun, but the range was a bit long and Slade's wounds, although severe, were not fatal. Ficklin was aboard the next stagecoach to come over the line, accompanied by a few stalwart assistants whom he had gathered for dealing with thieves. They dragged Jules out of his trading post, strung him up by the neck, and drove on as soon as he stopped kicking. But the tough old rascal wasn't quite done for. One of his gang cut him down and revived him, probably with some of his own trade whiskey, before his heart had completely stopped beating. With his cronies Jules went into hiding in the foothills of the Rockies where, in spite of Ficklin's clean-up crew, they continued their raids on the stage line.

As soon as Slade had recovered enough from his wounds to get around, he asked to be transferred to the division where Jules and his gang were raiding. Keeping under cover, he rode the line night and day until he found the gang's hideout. A few days later he and the clean-up crew surprised the thieves, and a stiff battle was fought in the corral where stolen horses and mules were being held. The gang was routed and Jules was seriously wounded. Here Slade committed the first of the many infamous acts that would make him the terror of any frontier settlement in which his shadow was cast. He tied the helpless old man up to a corral post, cut off his ears and nailed them to the fence, and then riddled his body with bullets. As a warning to anyone else who might consider waylaying him, Slade is said to have worn one of Jules's ears as a charm on his watch chain.

Whether or not this is true, his act of barbarity discouraged further raids by white men on any division of the line where he was assigned as superintendent. Before the end of the year Ficklin had fully regained control of the operation, and although the line was far from profitable it was no longer a catastrophic drag on the firm.

Meanwhile William Russell had been in the East, paying off threatening creditors by raising additional loans at ruinous discounts and dreaming up one of the most fabulous undertakings ever carried out in the United States. Although the Central Overland California & Pike's Peak Express Company had not yet been chartered, he telegraphed his son John at Leavenworth on January 27, 1860, "Have determined to establish a Pony Express to Sacramento, California, commencing 3rd of April. Time ten days." Young Russell released the announcement to the newspapers, and again Majors and Waddell found themselves with an unwanted bear by the tail.

14

Pony Express and the Bond Scandal

A GREAT DEAL has been written about the Pony Express, giving numerous conflicting accounts as to the origin of the idea and the purpose of its undertaking. In his memoirs, Alexander Majors gives the following account:

During the winter of 1859 Russell became acquainted with Senator Gwin of California, who told him that all his attempts to get a "thoroughfare opened" over the central route had failed because "his fellow senators raised the question of the impassability of the mountains on such a route during the winter months." He asked Russell if his company could be induced to start a pony express to test the practicability of establishing on that route a daily line of communication the year around. Majors says that he and Waddell refused to take part in the scheme as it could not possibly make expenses, but that Russell "strenuously insisted we should stand by him, as he had committed himself to Senator Gwin before leaving Washington . . . that as soon as we demonstrated the feasibility of such a scheme he [Senator Gwin] would use all his influence with Congress to get a subsidy. . . . After listening to all Mr. Russell had to say upon the subject, we concluded to sustain him in the undertaking . . ."

Another account of the idea's origin is that in 1854 Senator Gwin made an overland journey from California to Washington, D.C., and that during the trip he discussed the matter of a fast pony express with Ben Ficklin, the general superintendent of Russell, Majors and Waddell. This is obviously straight fiction. In 1854 the Russell, Majors and Waddell partnership had not yet been formed, and Ben Ficklin was never employed by· the firm until it took over the bankrupt L.&P.P. Express Company in October 1859. However, in an 1860 speech at Stockton, California, Gwin claimed credit for the Pony Express, saying that it had been "fostered and nurtured" by his labor. But in his memoirs he wrote that it was Ficklin "who originated the scheme and carried it into operation." The latter might well be due to Ficklin's having superintended the stocking of the pony line and inaugurating the service. As to the former, it would hardly be amazing if a politician were to claim credit for something pleasing to his constituents even though he had done no fostering and nurturing.

Still another version is that in the early winter of 1859 A. B. Miller, who as a partner in the firm of Miller, Russell & Company had opened a sutler's store at Camp Floyd, was discussing the overland mail with John Scudder. Both were good horsemen, and after figuring distances they wrote to Russell at Washington that they would undertake to deliver letter mail between St. Joseph and Sacramento in twelve days. When he wrote back for more information they told him their plan was to station relays of fast horses and lightweight riders along the stage routes, and Miller offered to make a run to test the feasibility of the plan. The only reason to doubt this version is that the feasibility had already been proved, and under the worst imaginable weather conditions, when the Hockaday and Chorpenning riders carried the St. Louis newspaper containing President Buchanan's message over the same route in December 1858.

Actually, the idea of a pony express was far from novel. In the thirteenth century Genghis Khan had established relays of fast horses and light riders throughout the larger part of the then known world for the rapid carrying of messages. And as recently as 1832 a pony express had been in operation between New York City and Washington, D.C. There is good evidence that Russell was considering the establishment of a pony express between the Missouri River and California as early as February 1858. At that time his nephew, Charles Morehead, Jr., and James Rupe were in Washington, having been called there by Russell upon their return from Utah with news that several wagon trains and most of the oxen had been lost due to the Mormon War. In his *Narrative* Morehead later wrote: "With Secretary Floyd the question of the feasibility of a pony express across the continent was presented by Mr. Russell, and fully discussed. Captain Rupe's views were called for, and he expressed the opinion that it was entirely practicable at all seasons on this route, all the way to California."

This has a more authentic ring than the other versions since

Morehead seeks no part of the credit for himself. It also shows that Russell was interested in a California mail contract for some time before the establishment of service on the Butterfield line. This interest certainly accounts for the purchase of the Hockaday & Liggett line, and probably for Ben Holladay's chartering a private stagecoach for testing the Chorpenning route in August 1859.

Although the semiweekly mail service over the Butterfield line was thoroughly dependable, there had been increasing dissatisfaction with it in California. The complaints were not against the Butterfield firm but about the waste of time caused by the "oxbow" route. The *San Francisco Bulletin* editorialized: "The energy and enterprise which have brought us the mails overland from St. Louis to San Francisco in from 18 to 24 days, if expended upon as short and available route as can be found, would give us the mails regularly in sixteen days. It was a stupid blunder if nothing worse, on the part of the Administration, which compelled the contractors to take the circuitous route . . ."

Throughout 1859 there had been growing demand that the state be provided with daily mail service over the central route, and the demand was fanned to an insistent clamor when Postmaster General Holt cut the service over that route to twice a month. After Horace Greeley's trip over the route he advocated in the *New York Tribune* that daily mail service be established on it at once; other influential eastern newspapers also supported the recommendation, and many congressmen were reported to have "simultaneously fallen into the idea." It was generally believed that the House, controlled by northern Republicans, would support legislation for such service but that it would be impossible to get an appropriation bill passed by the Senate without the efforts of a strong Administration Democrat.

There is little doubt that when Russell chose the name Central Overland California & Pike's Peak Express Company, he already had focused his ambitions upon securing a contract for daily California mail service over the central route at an annual subsidy of not less than a million dollars. The logical man for him to approach in furthering his ambition would certainly have been Senator Gwin, a strong Administration Democrat whose popularity in California was at a low ebb. Also, in view of Russell's writing to Waddell that what he had "expended or given away" in Washington had "secured to us all the advantages we have enjoyed," it would seem logical for him to offer Gwin compensation for pushing through the Senate a million-dollar central-route mail appropriation. That year—1860—was an election year, so what better compensation could have been offered the senator than credit for "fostering and nurturing" ten-day mail service between California and the East? If, as Morehead wrote, Russell had been contemplating a California pony express as early as February 1858, it seems probable that it was he, not Gwin, who made the original proposal.

As for Alexander Majors' account, he undoubtedly reported the matter as he understood it, but correspondence between Russell and Waddell clearly shows that he was not always informed regarding the financial manipulations of the firm. Available records indicate that he devoted almost his entire time to the actual transportation of freight, a large part of it on the road with his men, and usually left the financial affairs of the firm to his partners.

In any event, Russell came to Leavenworth immediately after wiring his son, obtained agreement for inaugurating the Pony Express from Majors and Waddell, and presented to the Kansas Territorial Legislature articles for chartering the Central Overland California & Pike's Peak Express Company. Although constantly urged by Russell, the legislature refused to approve the proposed corporation until February 20, probably because of the charter's extremely lenient provisions. It may be that Russell's final urging was of a pecuniary nature, for Waddell later accused him of "buying the charter."

Without waiting for the corporation to be chartered, Russell advertised in the *Leavenworth Daily Times* on February 10 for "two hundred grey mares, from four to seven years old, not to exceed fifteen hands high, well broke to saddle, and warranted sound, with black hoofs, and suitable for running the overland Pony Express." Similar ads were run in Salt Lake City and Sacramento, and workmen were hurried away with wagon trains of materials for building a line of relay stations between the two cities at intervals of ten to fifteen miles. Other workmen were sent out with trains from Leavenworth and Denver, and when they had finished their work 153 way stations and relay posts stood along the 1966-mile route between St. Joseph and Sacramento.

Meanwhile rush orders were sent for saddles and mochillas (leather saddle covers with locked pockets for carrying mail), five hundred swift horses were bought, and two hundred additional stationkeepers and hostlers were hired, as were eighty frontier-toughened young riders, none of them under eighteen years of age or weighing over 120 pounds. To get the best riders in the West, $150 a month and keep was offered, five times what they could earn elsewhere.

It is probable that the Central Overland California & Pike's Peak

Express Company had no sooner been chartered than news reached Leavenworth of a staggering financial blow that had been dealt the parent company. When, in the late summer of 1859, the R.M.&W. wagon trains had been unloaded at Camp Floyd, the firm's Utah agent selected thirty-five hundred of the best oxen for spring sale in California. He sent them, in charge of Jackson Cooper, to be pastured through the winter in Ruby Valley, about a hundred miles south of present Elko, Nevada. Cooper set out on September 20, but during the previous two months Howard Egan had driven forty-five hundred beef cattle and mules to California over this route for Holladay & Russell, with the result that forage was very scarce. Cooper was obliged to travel slowly, as the oxen weakened on the scant grazing, and was still three days' travel from Ruby Valley when he was caught in a severe blizzard. When at last he reached the valley noted for its mild winter climate, at the foot of the Ruby Mountains, he found thirty inches of snow on the ground and drifts of twice that depth. Throughout the rest of the year the cold was severe, the winds strong, and snowdrifts so deep that the starving oxen could not be moved to sheltered canyons where there was a little grass to be found. By Christmas half of them were dead, and only two hundred were alive by the time spring came.

This loss alone was estimated at more than $150,000, and additional heavy losses were being sustained by partnerships founded with Russell, Majors & Waddell goods or credit—such as Miller, Russell & Company; R. B. Bradford & Company; Smoot, Russell & Company, etc.

Besides the headquarters at Leavenworth, Russell had offices opened for the C.O.C.&P.P. and the Pony Express at Washington, New York, Chicago, St. Louis, St. Joseph, Salt Lake City, and San Francisco. Additional coaches, mules, and employees were put on the line, weekly stagecoach service inaugurated to Salt Lake City and triweekly service to Denver, and the running time reduced. For the Pony Express alone, more than $75,000 had been spent on stocking and equipping the line before the first riders set off from opposite ends of the line on April 3, 1860. Russell was on hand at St. Joseph to receive an ovation from Mayor Jeff Thompson and the enthusiastic crowd gathered for the great event, and then hurried back to Washington to stave off creditors and lobby for the coveted mail contract.

On April 11 the firm of Russell, Majors & Waddell was awarded military-freighting contracts for New Mexico posts only, and only then by underbidding Childs & Scott. Majors at once moved the headquarters of the firm's freighting operations to Kansas City, and the Leavenworth facilities were virtually abandoned. This move was probably influenced by his having an outfitting store there, as well as 500 wagons and 2140 mules which were used in freighting between Kansas City and Denver. These were personally owned by Majors, and had no connection with the Russell, Majors & Waddell partnership in any way.

On May 11 the C.O.C.&.P.P. Express Company acquired a monopoly on mail service over the central route. When the route had been cut from weekly to semimonthly service the previous July, George Chorpenning's compensation under his Salt Lake City-Placerville contract was reduced from $130,000 to $75,000 per annum. At the time Ben Holladay chartered a private stagecoach to make a time check of the line, Chorpenning was in Washington trying to raise cash on Post Office Department statements of indebtedness which he, like all other mail contractors, was obliged to accept for his services after Congress failed to pass the Post Office Appropriation bill. He had since been unable to meet expenses but was still maintaining the service well within the required time when, without prior notice, Postmaster General Holt annulled his contract on May 11—five weeks after inauguration of the Pony Express—alleging failure to render satisfactory service. Whether or not the annulment of Chorpenning's contract was due to Russell's activities in Washington, on the same day Russell was awarded a "star" contract for semimonthly service over the same route at $33,000 per annum.

Under a star contract the mail could be carried by any means providing "celerity, certainty, and security," but it was far too heavy to be carried by the Pony Express, and $33,000 a year would cover no more than a quarter of the cost of carrying it by stagecoach. Apparently, however, Russell had not only set his ambition upon securing a million-dollar mail contract, but on taking the California overland passenger business away from the Butterfield line. Borrowing every dollar he could get, at any price demanded and secured by any collateral he could lay hands on, he stocked the Salt Lake City-Placerville line with fast mules, equipped it with Concord coaches, and inaugurated through passenger service between St. Joseph and Sacramento.

Although the C.O.C.&P.P. Express Company was losing money at the rate of more than a thousand dollars a day and creditors were pressing William Russell from every side, he was at the height of his optimism during the spring of 1860. The Pony Express —running right on schedule—was being acclaimed throughout the

"Welcome Pony Express," a painting by A. O. Dinsdale.
(Courtesy, Wells Fargo Bank History Room.)

world as the greatest accomplishment of the age, and his stage line
was carrying more than its share of the California overland passenger business. Furthermore, Senator Hale of New Hampshire had
introduced a California mail bill proposing triweekly service over
the central route for one year at a remuneration not to exceed
$600,000, and daily service thereafter at a compensation not to
exceed $800,000.

On June 13 Russell wrote Waddell, "I am in treaty for tri-weekly
mail at $600,000.00 which have hope of closing today. And although
it will pay very handsome it is not as good as we wanted. It will
however lay the foundation for a mail which will give us
$1,200,000.00." There is little reason to believe that he was "in
treaty" concerning Hale's bill, but good indication that he was
soon afterward a party to a treaty for a much larger fish.

It was generally believed that Hale's bill would have passed
the Senate if Gwin had supported it, but he found himself in an
awkward position. Hale was a Republican. If his bill went through,
his party would get credit from the Californians for their greatly
improved mail service—a bad situation for a not-too-popular
Democratic senator seeking re-election. Gwin introduced a substi-

tute bill that had little possibility of passage but that would effectively block Hale's.

In commenting on the action, the Washington correspondent for the *San Francisco Bulletin* wrote, "Mr. Gwin was persuaded by the Administration to contribute to the defeat of Hale's bill with the most positive assurance that after the adjournment of Congress the Department would immediately put up the service via Salt Lake. . . . This, you see, would accomplish two ends: 1st, it would prevent the Republicans from getting any credit from the legislation . . . and 2nd, it would secure Mr. Gwin the sole credit of having obtained the service via the Central route, and thus secure him needed capital to aid in his re-election."

The correspondent apparently had an inside source of information or else he was a keen analyst of political maneuvering. Russell made a proposal to the Post Office Department, offering to carry the entire California mail between St. Joseph and Folsom on a twenty-five-day-or-less schedule for a compensation of $900,000 annually, the service to be triweekly during the first year, and six times a week thereafter at no increase in compensation. Then on June 22 he again wrote to Waddell, "Do not think any mail service will pass. . . . Will lay still until Congress adjourns, which will be tomorrow or Monday, then get to work for the contract. . . . We will certainly get a good thing."

The next act in the drama took place a few days later, after Congress had adjourned without passing legislation for the renewal of steamship mail service to California. Senator Gwin urged President Buchanan to have the $900,000 per annum central route mail contract proposed by Russell awarded to the firm of Russell, Majors & Waddell, but Buchanan failed to act and Gwin wrote testily, reminding him that in a conversation they had held with the Postmaster General, he had been induced to believe that if Congress took no action and public necessity required, Buchanan himself would authorize a mail contract over the central route. Gwin then made the flat statement that the necessity had arisen.

Either the President disagreed regarding the necessity having arisen or he was still disposed to protect the interests of his friend Butterfield by withholding assistance to a competitor on the central route. In any case, he took no action. Gwin returned to California to campaign for re-election on the claim that he had fostered the Pony Express, and Russell hurried to New York in a frantic search for money. He was confident that the contract would soon be awarded, but the delay was distressing, for the C.O.C.&P.P. was faced with huge unforeseen expenses.

Silver had been discovered in the eastern foothills of the Sierras, only a few miles north of the Genoa station on the stage and Pony Express line. These hills were the homeland of the Washoe Indians, but stampeding prospectors from California swarmed over them in droves, killing Indians who tried to defend their homes and driving the rest of the tribe into the desert. In retaliation the Washoes had ravaged the stage line more than halfway to Salt Lake, burning stations, killing several keepers, stealing the horses and mules, and forcing both the Pony Express and stage service to a standstill. Even though Congress had failed to pass a subsidy bill for the Pony Express, Russell was determined to allow no avoidable interruption in the service before the $900,000 contract had been secured. He had ordered that the ravaged section of the line be rebuilt and restocked with all possible speed, and by hook or crook he must raise at least $75,000 to pay the cost.

Without the expected mail contract to use as security, and with his and his associates' credit already stretched to the absolute limit, Russell was unable to borrow a dollar in New York, so he returned to Washington. There he chanced upon an amazing benefactor, a man willing to let him have bonds worth $150,000 to be used as security for loans.

By the end of June the destroyed section of line had been rebuilt and the ponies, now on a semiweekly ten-day schedule, were racing letter mail across the deserts, mountains, and prairies at five dollars per half ounce. Through stagecoaches were running regularly between St. Joseph and Sacramento, although they carried mail only semimonthly. No action had yet been taken by the Post Office Department on the proposed $900,000 contract, all the bonds supplied by Russell's generous benefactor had been hypothecated for loans, both the C.O.C.&P.P. Express Company and Russell, Majors & Waddell were desperately in need of money, and the situation was rapidly worsening.

Military shipments to New Mexico were customarily made in late April, so when a freighting contract for approximately five million pounds was awarded to the firm on April 11 Alexander Majors made all haste to ready wagon trains for the hauling. He established headquarters at Kansas City, hired crews, and had great herds of oxen brought in; before the end of April he had 837 wagons overhauled and ready to roll. But it was late July before the New Mexico military supplies began arriving by riverboat from the East. As a result, the firm was obliged to board and pay one thousand men and feed ten thousand oxen through more than three months of idleness. Not only would the year's freighting operations result in a tremendous loss, but it would be late fall before the deliveries were made and bills could be presented for payment. Anticipating the income at midsummer, Russell had borrowed upwards of half a million dollars on notes payable in August and September. Most of these loans were secured by acceptances drawn against the War Department and endorsed by Secretary Floyd.

To further complicate matters, even though the Pony Express was being acclaimed a glorious success and the C.O.C.&P.P. was carrying more than its share of transcontinental passengers, the operating expenses on the California line were more than double the income. Notes fell due and were protested for nonpayment, past-due feed and supply bills mounted, payrolls fell behind, and employees began saying the firm's initials stood for Clean Out of Cash & Poor Pay. The only bright spot in the whole Russell-dominated domain was the Denver branch of the stage line.

From the time the L.&P.P. Express Company was founded, Russell had been lobbying in Washington for a lucrative mail contract for service between Leavenworth and Denver, but no action had been taken by either Congress or the Post Office Department. In the spring of 1860 he discontinued lobbying, for the Denver branch of the C.O.C.&P.P. was doing better on its private mail business than it could expect to do on a Government contract. Every week it was carrying fully five thousand letters at twenty-five cents each, and bales of newspapers at a dime apiece. In addition, it was taking in nearly $6000 per month from the Hinckley Express Company for carrying its boxes to and from St. Joseph, the income from transporting gold was equally great, and the triweekly coaches were loaded to capacity with passengers paying $100 each.

On August 29 the Post Office Department administered a blow from which Russell and his associates were never able to recover. It awarded to the Western Stage Company, operating between Omaha and Fort Kearney, a contract for weekly mail service to Denver. In mid-September the firm extended its line to Denver and initiated passenger as well as U.S. Mail service, shattering the C.O.C.&P.P. monopoly. The Hinckley Express Company at once entered into an agreement with Western for establishing an express messenger service over its line for the transportation of gold and other valuables. Few people would pay the C.O.C.&P.P. twenty-five cents for carrying a letter that could be sent by U.S. Mail for a few pennies, and many travelers preferred the shorter route to Omaha over the longer one to St. Joseph.

The first eastbound coach over the Western Stage Company's line left Denver on September 20 carrying mail and treasure express on which the C.O.C.&P.P. would have collected fees of at least $3500 if its monopoly had not been broken. Its one profitable operation had suddenly been turned into a money-losing liability. Worse still, the Post Office Department had awarded a contract for trimonthly steamship mail service to California via Panama. For that year all hope had to be abandoned for securing the coveted $900,000 central-route contract or of obtaining any subsidy for operating the fabulously expensive Pony Express service.

It is doubtful that any other man capable of raising the finances and putting into operation such an undertaking as the Pony Express would have continued that operation under the circumstances, but William Russell was adamant in his determination. Some historians of the Pony Express attribute his action to patriotism, writing that he considered war inevitable and feared that California would swing to the cause of the South unless kept in close and rapid communication with the North. This might have been true, but it hardly squares with his action in other matters, and he is not known to have made any statement as to his reason. It seems more likely that he had set his ambition doggedly upon securing a million-dollar mail contract, and that, as in all his other promotions, he was determined to attain his goal by any means available, regardless of how injurious his action might be to his associates and creditors.

Apparently all of Russell's business decisions were actuated by wishful desire and oversanguine expectation instead of reasoned judgment. The campaign for the November presidential election was in full swing; there was a four-way split in the Democratic party, and it was believed that a number of southern states would secede from the Union if Lincoln were elected. Rather than being moved by patriotism, Russell very probably anticipated a Republican victory, with secessions in the South and the abandonment of the Butterfield line, and believed that if he could stave off creditors and keep the ponies running until the new Administration took office in March it would reward him with an extremely lucrative mail contract in appreciation. Whatever his thinking may have been, he called upon his Washington benefactor in September, borrowed additional bonds worth $300,000, used them as collateral to secure cash loans, and poured most of the money into the Pony Express and C.O.C.&P.P. with no more effect than if it had been water poured into a prairie dog's hole.

Alexander Majors was under no such delusions as Russell, and of the three partners he alone appears to have been uncompromisingly honest. In all probability he returned from supervising the New Mexico freighting operations in mid-October, for at that time he faced squarely up to the fact that the firm of Russell, Majors & Waddell, together with all its entangled satellites, was insolvent, and that as a partner in that firm he was responsible for its debts. It is also apparent that he had very little knowledge of the extent to which the firm was in debt. On October 17 and 19 he gave deeds of trust covering 125 town lots, his Missouri and Kansas farms consisting of 2600 acres, and all the livestock and equipment on them, for the benefit of his, Russell, Majors & Waddell's, and the Central Overland California & Pike's Peak Express Company's creditors, stating the total liabilities to be $75,540.74.

Waddell was, to say the least, more cautious in disposing of his assets. In *Empire on Wheels* the Settles write: "Waddell family tradition says that Mrs. Waddell, because of distrust of Russell, had previously caused him to set aside $100,000 in her name." Alexander Majors was more specific as to the source of the funds. He stated publicly that Waddell had taken $50,000 from the firm of Russell, Majors & Waddell and appropriated it to the benefit of his children. There is no record of Waddell's having denied the accusation. Also, the records of Lafayette County, Missouri, show that he executed a deed of trust on his palatial Springfield home to his son John for the sum of one dollar and an agreement to pay an $8000 debt.

A Central Overland California & Pike's Peak Express Company coach. (From Vol. 4 of Pageant of America, *Kier.)*

A few weeks after Majors' futile contribution toward relieving its insolvency, Russell plunged the firm into irretrievable ruin. Desperate for money with which to stave off creditors and keep the Pony Express and C.O.C.&P.P. in operation, he again called upon his Washington benefactor and persuaded the man to let him have enough more bonds to bring the total up to $870,000. The man was Goddard Bailey, whose father-in-law was a cousin to Secretary of War Floyd, and the bonds were embezzled from the Indian Trust Fund in the Department of the Interior.

Russell had discovered Bailey by chance. When unable to secure loans in New York following the adjournment of Congress, he had taken a train back to Washington in company with Luke Lea, a friend of Luther Smoot's. On the way Russell told of the late military shipments to New Mexico putting his firm in a tight money position, and asked if Lea knew anyone in Washington from whom he could make a loan. Lea replied that he did not, but that he knew a clerk named Bailey in the Department of the Interior who, "though as poor as anybody," was related to the Secretary of War. He suggested that Bailey might be able to induce Secretary Floyd to make an advance payment on the freight bills before the goods reached destination. Russell then admitted that Floyd had already endorsed unauthorized acceptances drawn against the War Department for more than the New Mexico freight charges would amount to, and that they had long since been used as security for loans which would fall due within a few days. He asked Lea to see Bailey as soon as possible and inform him that Floyd would be ruined if the loans could not be met when due, the notes protested, and the acceptances presented to the United States Treasury for payment.

Lea did as requested, and the next day Bailey removed from the Indian Trust Fund in the vaults of the Interior Department negotiable bonds in the amount of $150,000. That afternoon he took them to Russell's room and exchanged them for an equal amount in Russell, Majors & Waddell unsecured notes. His only other requirement was a promise from Russell that the bonds would be returned intact before March 4, 1861, when, if elected, the Republican administration would take office. Difficult though it is to believe, Russell afterward made a written statement that he accepted the bonds only because he believed Bailey "had a perfect right to control them," and that he would have had nothing to do with the transaction if he had suspected them of being misappropriated.

He made no such statement regarding the additional bonds, to the value of $720,000, which he induced Bailey to turn over to him during the next few months, but wrote as an excuse for his action, "In the distress of my difficulties, I was in no condition, and, as I have said before, I had no time to weigh the responsibility, on the one hand of wrecking our firm, discrediting the War Department, and permitting the hypothecated bonds to be sold beyond my reach, against that on the other hand of accepting more bonds with which to protect those that I had already used. . . . I determined upon the latter alternative."

There had been a Republican victory at the polls, with Lincoln elected President, before Bailey turned the last batch of stolen bonds over to Russell. Soon thereafter he became frightened and wrote a confession of the whole affair to Jacob Thompson, Secretary of the Interior. President Buchanan was apprised of the thefts on December 22, warrants were issued for the arrest of Russell and Bailey on the twenty-third, and they were jailed on the twenty-fourth. On the same day the House of Representatives appointed a committee to investigate the entire matter, and hearings were begun on December 27.

The committee apparently believed that Secretary Floyd had personally been receiving large graft payments from Russell, and questioned the man suspected of being the payoff go-between. To every question bearing on the subject he availed himself of the provisions of the Fifth Amendment to the Constitution and replied, "I decline to answer."

Russell, under arrest for a criminal offense, could not be compelled to appear and testify before the congressional committee, but did so voluntarily. He admitted receiving the stolen bonds, but when asked, "Did you ever, directly or indirectly, pay any person any consideration, or make any person a present, for services rendered to you connected with the War Department?," he declined to answer.

There is nothing to indicate that Secretary Floyd knew of the bond transactions until Bailey told him of it two days before the matter was reported to Buchanan. In the congressional investigation there was no conclusive evidence that he had received payments from Russell, but refusals to testify left so little doubt of it that, at the President's request, he resigned from the Cabinet on December 29.

On December 31 Russell made the first move in a series that might be construed to indicate that he had fallen almost completely under the domination of Ben Holladay, who was at that time in the East.

Among a multitude of others, Russell was indebted to James N. Simpson of New York, vice-president of the C.O.C.&P.P. Express Company. On the last day of 1860 Russell, out of jail on bond, had a deed of trust on four thousand acres of Missouri land drawn up to cover a debt in the amount of $61,850, plus a penal bond of $100,000 for nonpayment of the obligation. Supposedly it was intended for Simpson to be the beneficiary and Ben Holladay the trustee, but the draftsman was said to have erred inadvertently and reversed the position of the names, making Holladay the beneficiary. The deed of trust was signed by all three parties concerned, and it is claimed that none of them noticed the error until it was called to Simpson's attention by his Missouri attorney. There is reason to doubt that the switching of names was inadvertent, for it would have been a very simple matter to correct the error by rewriting the instrument, but this was never done. Eventually Simpson sued and won a judgment, but by that time most of the land had been sold to innocent purchasers and no recovery was ever made.

Historians disagree as to the probability that Majors and Waddell, or either of them, knew of Russell's involvement with Floyd and Bailey prior to his arrest and the publication of news concerning testimony before the congressional committee. The best indication would seem to be the actions of each man before the close of the investigation.

On January 25 and 26 Alexander Majors filed with the Recorder of Deeds of Jackson County, Missouri, assignments of everything due him or that he owned—including even the furnishings of his home—for the benefit of his creditors and those of the Russell, Majors & Waddell partnership or its affiliates, leaving himself penniless. With these assignments he apparently washed his hands of both Russell and Waddell, for no record has been found to indicate that he ever again saw or was in contact with either of them.

During the last week in January Waddell, through five deeds of trust, divested himself of such assets as he had not already sequestered by putting them into the name of his wife or children, but continued to operate the C.O.C.&P.P. and the Pony Express from the firm's Leavenworth offices.

On January 29 Russell, Floyd, and Bailey were indicted by a District of Columbia grand jury. When Russell's case came up in criminal court his attorney pleaded that since he had already been examined on the same subject by the congressional committee he should be allowed to go free. On this technicality the court quashed the indictment and freed him from prosecution for his part in the embezzlement. His attorney—a former Lexington, Missouri, pastor—wrote Waddell a long letter exonerating Russell and laying all the blame for the embezzlement on Floyd. "It is firmly believed," he wrote, "that Floyd sent Bailey to Mr. Russell in the first instance. . . . It is further believed that Bailey acted under a promise of a pardon and the course of the prosecution sustains this view of the case. . . . In a word if it were possible to drag to light the doings of the administration the evidence would be as clear as noonday that the President and his pliant Cabinet ministers have deliberately spread their meshes to entangle and victimize Mr. Russell."

Russell's friends, of course, did everything possible to spread the propaganda, and it was widely enough believed that H. H. Bancroft, the great historian of the West, wrote in his *Chronicles of the Builders* that Russell "fell into difficulty, if indeed, it were not a trap set for him by the friends of the Southern Route." Russell made almost every other excuse for himself, but there is no record of his ever mentioning that he was in any way entrapped.

The prosecution of the culprits—or lack of it—might, however, leave an impression that the Buchanan Administration and the District of Columbia courts were rather anxious to give an ill-smelling affair a quick and unpretentious burial. Floyd had moved his family to Virginia when he resigned as Secretary of War. When indicted by the District of Columbia grand jury he returned to Washington, posted bail, and demanded trial. The United States Attorney, however, entered a *nolle prosequi* on the grounds that there was insufficient proof to sustain the charge of malversation in office.

Bailey, released from jail on $5000 bail, was arraigned in the District of Columbia Criminal Court on a charge of larceny, abstracting bonds, and conspiracy to cheat the United States Government. He entered a not-guilty plea, and no other action was taken in the case for a year and a half. In July 1862 Congress passed a bill to reimburse the Indian Trust Fund from the Treasury for the value of the stolen bonds, and in September of that year Bailey was called up for trial. He failed to appear, so his $5000 bail was declared forfeited, and following the Civil War the case was dropped.

Russell had no sooner been freed from prosecution than he executed a second deed of trust covering the same property as the Simpson-Holladay deed of December 31. Ben Holladay was again named beneficiary, but this time there was no claim that it was due to an inadvertent error on the part of the draftsman. One chronicler writes that the trust deed was executed in "an effort to protect Holladay for money advanced to Russell, Majors & Waddell and the Central Overland California & Pike's Peak Express Company." Another refers to "certain records" showing that it was May 1862 before Russell, Majors & Waddell had begun to borrow money from Holladay.

On the same day—January 30, 1861—Russell made a third deed of trust, this one for the benefit of certain individuals and concerns, most of them in Lexington, to whom he admitted debts of $46,664.05. Ironically, and typical of Russell's irresponsible business methods, the land placed in trust by this instrument had been included in both deeds of trust naming Ben Holladay as beneficiary.

15

Wells Fargo in the Driver's Seat

WITH all his involvement and disgrace, Russell never gave up expectation of securing a million-dollar mail contract. On December 20, 1860, South Carolina seceded from the Union, to be followed by five other southern states during January, and by Texas on February 1. The secession of Texas, giving the South full control of the Butterfield route, made it imperative that California be kept in communication with the Union by daily mail and passenger service via the central route. On February 2 a bill was taken up in the Senate which provided for such service at $800,000 per annum. But Senator Gwin contended that a responsible contractor could not be obtained at less than a million dollars, and Senator Hale argued for immediate discontinuance of service over the southern route. On the eleventh Russell wrote to Waddell at Leavenworth, "Have great faith in getting mail contract all right."

The bill for mail service via the central route was again considered by the Senate on February 18 and 23, with Gwin holding out for daily stagecoach service at $1,000,000 or triweekly stagecoach and pony express service at $800,000. The Committee on Post Offices and Post Roads recommended that the two contractors consolidate and operate over the central route, and that the southern route be abandoned. On February 26 the bill as originally proposed passed the Senate, but with the understanding that it would be altered and improved by amendments to the annual Post Office Appropriation bill.

The bill had no sooner passed than word reached Washington

that the Butterfield line through Texas had been devastated—stations and relay posts burned, vehicles destroyed, and provisions, horses, and mules stolen. Immediate action had to be taken, so the Post Office Appropriation bill was taken up in the Senate on February 27. An amendment was offered providing that the Butterfield operations be transferred to the central route, increased to daily service, and a semiweekly pony express service maintained until the completion of the overland telegraph, at a compensation of $1,150,000 annually.

Gwin opposed transferring the Butterfield operations to the central route and giving that firm the contract outright. He proposed that the annual compensation be reduced to not more than $1,000,000 and the presently operating contractors on the central route be permitted to bid for it, saying that it was unfair for the men who had been running the Pony Express at their own expense to be "put off to give place to the Butterfield people."

The justice of Gwin's proposal was not questioned, but Congress could not put itself in the position of awarding a million-dollar mail contract to a firm headed by a man involved in the most flagrant scandal to have rocked Washington in a decade. It did, however, provide a loophole.

On March 2 the Post Office Appropriation bill was enacted into law, directing the Postmaster General to discontinue service on the Butterfield route on or before July 1, 1861, and to modify the Butterfield contract in the following manner:

The contractors on said route shall be required to transport the entire letter mail six times a week on the Central route, said letter mail to be carried through in twenty day's time, eight months in the year, and in twenty-three days the remaining four months of the year, from some point on the Missouri River connected with the East, to Placerville, California, and also to deliver the entire mails tri-weekly to Denver City, and Great Salt Lake City; said contractors shall be required to carry the residue of all the mail matter in a period not exceeding thirty-five days, with the privilege of sending the latter semi-monthly from New York to San Francisco in twenty-five days by sea, and the public documents in thirty-five days. They shall also be required, during the continuance of their contract, or until the completion of the overland telegraph, to run a pony express semi-weekly at a schedule time of ten days eight months and twelve days four months, carrying for the Government free of charge, five pounds of mail matter with the liberty of charging the public for transportation of letters by said express not to exceed one dollar per half ounce. For the above service said contractors shall receive the sum of one million dollars per annum; the contract for such service to be thus modified before the 25th day of March next, and expire July 1, 1864.

[198]

The act further provided that the Butterfield firm be paid two months' compensation as liquidated damages, and receive full pay under the modified contract for the time required to move its operations to the central route. No provision was made for the C.O.C.&P.P. Express Company, but the contractor was granted permission to subcontract for service over any portion of the route desired, which was tantamount to a provision. The Butterfield firm was not prospering and would be hard pressed to stock and equip the entire central route after its Texas losses; it almost would be obliged to subcontract to the current operators of the line.

If John Butterfield was in any way responsible for failure of the Overland Mail Company to prosper, it was in his original agreement to operate over the circuitous southern route insisted upon by Postmaster General Aaron Brown. No other stage line was ever so well organized and operated under such adverse conditions as the Overland Mail Company under Butterfield's management. He inspired loyalty and pride of accomplishment in his men, from division superintendents to Mexican hostlers; and, although stock was occasionally stolen, his policies for dealing with the Indians avoided any serious trouble. As a result, the mail very seldom failed to go through well inside the twenty-five-day limit, regardless of weather. Before the end of the first winter all the way stations and relay posts had been completed and stocked, the Butterfield stages were running with almost the regularity of a railroad schedule, and most of the trips were being made in twenty-four days or less.

The firm's first big difficulty came when Congress failed to pass a Post Office Appropriation bill in March 1859. On March 20, the Washington correspondent for the *Sacramento Union* wrote: "Already the mail contractors are here endeavoring to settle with the Government. Some of them have been carrying the mails for a long time and have not received a cent. Butterfield & Co., the Overland mail contractors, are among the sufferers. On the first of next month the Government will owe them nearly $300,000. Unless they are paid a portion of it, they cannot go any longer on credit, and will give up their contract, alleging that the Department has broken its stipulations. An effort will be made to settle with Butterfield & Co. in some manner. From the statement of the Department it appears that the deficiency is over a million dollars more than the amount estimated by Governor [Postmaster General] Brown!"

The threat to discontinue operations was undoubtedly made to put pressure on Congress, but no settlement was made with the firm and there was no break in the service. As for the statement

A Wells, Fargo & Company express box. (Courtesy, American History Room, New York Public Library.)

"they cannot go any longer on credit," there was no other mail contractor so capable of operating indefinitely on credit as the Overland Mail Company. It was owned by executives of the wealthiest express companies in the United States—if not directly by the companies—and through William Fargo was very closely allied with Wells, Fargo & Company, the biggest express and banking firm in the West. While other mail contractors were obliged to convert the Post Office Department statements of indebtedness received for their services into cash by allowing ruinously large discounts, it is reported that Wells, Fargo & Company made advances to the Overland Mail Company equal to the amounts owed it by the Government. It is not to be supposed, however, that these advances were made without the high interest rates then customary in the West.

Safely over the first hurdle, Butterfield bent every effort to improve the service on the line. By the spring of 1860 the Overland Mail stages were carrying more California mail than the steamship line, and the passenger service had increased to about $200,000 a year, but still the line was barely able to meet operating expenses in spite of its $50,000-per-month subsidy. The route was entirely too long for the size of the subsidy, the stations and relay posts through Texas, New Mexico, and Arizona were extremely expensive to supply, the loss of horses and mules to Indians was excessive, and travel through the southern wilderness was too arduous to attract cross-country passengers. Almost the entire passenger income was from short hauls at the line ends, between San Francisco and Los Angeles or Tipton and Fort Smith. The frequency of trips made little difference in operating costs, since stock and equipment had to be kept in readiness for the road at all times. It became evident that for the original investment to be recovered by the expiration of the contract, the subsidy would have to be increased to at least a million dollars a year, but for that sum the firm would be able to maintain daily service.

This was the dilemma in which John Butterfield found himself when in the early spring of 1860 William Russell put the Pony Express into operation on the central route. Butterfield realized immediately that it was a bid to Congress for a daily mail contract over that route, and that unless the southern route matched the service even his friendship with the President might not be enough to secure the needed subsidy increase. He determined to stock the line with swift horses and start pony express service immediately, but the directors of the firm, aware of the tremendous expense and probable loss involved, refused to approve the undertaking. Butterfield felt so strongly about the matter that he resigned the presidency and retired from the firm. He was replaced as president by William Dinsmore, an executive of Adams Express Company.

Under Dinsmore's management the Indian policies established by John Butterfield were not maintained. The strict discipline and efficiency he had demanded were allowed to be relaxed, the morale of the organization fell off badly, and operating losses rose in proportion.

Trouble with the Comanches and Apaches developed during the summer of 1860. Ten drivers were killed and hundreds of horses and mules were stolen. The frontier cavalry posts proved of little help, and one of their officers caused immense harm. While the line was still being constructed, Wallace, the keeper of the Apache Pass station, had won the friendship of Cochise, the great Apache chief. In October 1860 Cochise was visiting Wallace when Lieutenant George Bascom, just graduated from West Point, rode into the station yard with a company of cavalry from Fort Buchanan. He had Cochise seized and tried unsuccessfully to hold him as hostage for the return of some cattle claimed to have been stolen from a nearby ranch. Suspecting Wallace of treachery, the Apaches went on the warpath against the stage line. Wallace and four other men were killed, the Butterfield line through Apache territory was stripped of stock, and service was brought to a standstill for weeks. It had barely been restored when Confederate raiders devastated the line through Texas.

On March 12, 1861, the Overland Mail Company accepted the modifications to its contract stipulated by the act of March 2 and agreed to move its operations to the central route as quickly as possible. On March 16 the firm entered into contracts with the Central Overland California & Pike's Peak Express Company and the Western Stage Company. The contract with the latter provided payment of $20,000 per year to the end of Western's Denver mail contract for the discontinuance of all operations west of Fort Kearney, thus clearing the entire central route of competing mail or passenger service.

The contract with the C.O.C.&P.P. Express Company was much more complicated, and shows clearly that the Overland Mail Company was firmly in the driver's seat. The distance between St. Joseph and Placerville over the central route was at that time 1920 miles, approximately 65 per cent of it east of the Salt Lake City and 35 per cent west. The contract provided that the subcontractor operate and pay all expenses on the portion of the route east of Salt Lake City, including the Pony Express, for the residue of $470,000 per annum (47 per cent of the total remuneration) after deduction of half the cost of shipping by sea such nonletter mail as the prime contractor might decide upon.

Receipts from through passenger and express business between Missouri River points and California, and all Pony Express receipts, were to be divided equally. The subcontractor was to pay $14,000 per annum on the Western Stage Company contract, and turn over to the prime contractor 30 per cent of all receipts from express and passenger business east of Salt Lake City. The Overland Mail Company reserved the right to make an exclusive contract with Wells, Fargo & Company for all express business originating or terminating west of Salt Lake City, the receipts from which were to be divided equally.

A general superintendent appointed by the Overland Mail Company, whose salary and expenses would be shared equally, was to have charge of the entire line, but with no authority to interfere in the management of the subcontractor's division. The contract was signed by Russell and Dinsmore, and Russell gave a bond in the amount of $100,000 for performance by the C.O.C.&P.P. Express Company. The bond was signed by Ben Holladay.

There is no point concerning stagecoaching in the West upon

which historians have differed more widely than the relationship between the Overland Mail Company, the Pioneer Stage Line, and Wells, Fargo & Company at the time the mail service was transferred from the southern to the central route. The confusion appears to be attributable to the destruction of Wells, Fargo & Company's records in the San Francisco earthquake and fire of 1906 and to historians having relied upon recollections or correspondence of old-timers who had been in the employ of one or another of the firms—often in capacities which would give them little or no knowledge of company ownership.

On the other hand, David Street was paymaster of the C.O.C.&P.P. Express Company and the Holladay Overland Mail and Express Company during their entire existence and continued as paymaster for Wells, Fargo & Company's stage-line operations until the completion of the transcontinental railroad, so he was probably more conversant than other employees with changes in ownership. In reply to an inquiry, he wrote Frank Root in 1901: "The Overland Mail Company passed into possession of Wells, Fargo & Co. some time before they bought Holladay out; they acquired it in about the same way Holladay did the C.O.C.&P.P. Express Company—by advancing money, or loans; first commenced

"Stagecoach Arriving at Mother Lode," a painting by Louis Macouillard. (Courtesy, Wells Fargo Bank History Room.)

Overland Mail Company advertisement of 1858.

as advances on quarterly mail payments and ended in mortgages and foreclosures." This would indicate that the advances were made during 1859 and '60 when the Post Office Department was unable to meet payments on mail contracts. If so, it seems likely that control of the Overland Mail Company passed to Wells, Fargo & Company at that time.

On the contrary, Waddell F. Smith, a descendant of William Waddell, has published a monograph in which he states that during its history as an express company in California Wells, Fargo & Company "never at any time operated a stage line in the entire state of California." Although there has been wide disagreement among historians, no other writer on the subject is found to agree with Mr. Smith, and he cites no authority for his statement.

Louis McLane, son of the first president of the Baltimore & Ohio Railroad, was a devoted horseman and a stagecoaching enthusiast as well as being an astute banking and transportation executive. In October 1855 he was appointed agent (general manager) in charge of all Wells, Fargo & Company's California operations, and remained in that position until the building of the transcontinental railroad.

In 1860 the Pioneer Stage Line was bought in Louis McLane's name from Jared Crandall's successor. To some historians it has seemed quite probable that Wells, Fargo & Company, rather than Louis McLane, was the actual purchaser even though, in 1864, the president of Wells, Fargo & Company announced from his New York office that the firm had bought Louis McLane's Pioneer Stage Line. Dr. W. Turrentine Jackson has recently conducted research that proves beyond doubt both the original ownership and date of sale; the General Cash Book from Wells, Fargo & Company's New York office has been discovered and shows that on December 15, 1864, the firm officially bought the Pioneer Stage Line from Louis McLane for $175,000.

No conclusive evidence has ever been discovered to prove that Wells, Fargo & Company had acquired outright ownership of the Overland Mail Company and the Pioneer Stage Line on or before July 1, 1861, the date on which the overland mail contract was transferred to the central route. If, however, all three operations were not actually under the same ownership at that time, the connection between them was extremely close, and they were very definitely under a single management, that of Louis McLane.

As to the time that control or ownership of the Overland Mail Company was acquired by Wells, Fargo & Company, it is significant to note that for nearly a year before the overland mail was moved to the central route announcements of schedule changes on the Butterfield line were signed "Louis McLane, Agent Overland Mail Co." Also, on April 30, 1860, the *San Francisco Bulletin* reported, "It is understood here that the Overland Mail contract is now under the control of Wells, Fargo & Co." Furthermore, the Minute Book of the Overland Mail Company, recently discovered in New York, shows that as early as 1858 the three largest stockholders in the firm, except for John Butterfield, were directors of Wells, Fargo & Company. There seems little doubt that Wells, Fargo & Company's control of the Overland Mail Company was absolute by July 1, 1861, even though it may not have had outright ownership.

Because of the bond scandal, Russell was probably forced to relinquish the presidency of the C.O.C.&P.P. Express Company in order to secure the subcontract from the Overland Mail Company. Also, the trust deeds executed the previous December 31 and January 30 indicate that he had entered into a secret agreement to turn the remnants of his empire over to his friend, Ben Holladay. In any case, Holladay was present in New York when the subcontract was executed, for he signed the performance bond as guarantor. A few weeks later a meeting of the C.O.C.&P.P. Express Company's stockholders was held at Leavenworth, Russell resigned, and Ben Holladay's cousin, Bela M. Hughes, was elected president.

16

Big Ben Holladay
Makes a Grab

BY THE CLOSE OF 1860 rich gold deposits had been discovered along
the entire length of Clear Creek. Golden, Central City, Black
Hawk, Idaho Springs, and Empire City had become populous towns,
and Denver a thriving metropolis. On February 28, 1861, Colorado
Territory was established from portions of Nebraska, Kansas, New
Mexico, and Utah. When, two weeks later, Congress required re-
moval of the overland mail to the central route, the Coloradoans
insisted that the main line pass through Denver and continue westward to Salt Lake City by way of Clear Creek Canyon.

The terms of the amended contract provided that Denver be
furnished triweekly mail service, but the nearest station on the
main line was Julesburg, two hundred miles down the South Platte.
To operate a branch line would entail sixty thousand miles of travel
a year and the cost of maintaining a dozen relay posts. But if a
direct route could be opened between Denver and Salt Lake City
it would save all that and should be at least two hundred miles
shorter than the established route through South Pass. Moving the
line, however, would require considerable investment, as eight hundred miles of stations would have to be abandoned and others built
along the new route.

Soon after Russell negotiated the subcontract for operating the
line east of Salt Lake City, John S. Jones went to Colorado to investigate the feasibility of altering the route to pass through Denver. He found that fifty miles west of the city Clear Creek Canyon

was blocked off by the Continental Divide, rising in a solid wall to an altitude of more than twelve thousand feet, and old-timers told him that the shortest way around the bulwark was by way of the Cherokee Trail.

The Cherokee Indians were one of the Five Civilized Tribes, with a written language and a government similar to that of the United States. Before being deported to Indian Territory in 1838 many of them had gained gold-mining experience in Georgia. In the early spring of 1849 fourteen Cherokee miners joined the gold rush to California in company with about a hundred white settlers from Arkansas. With their provisions in forty wagons, they followed the Arkansas River westward to the Rockies. At Pueblo they met a party of trappers (among them Richard Owens, who had been in the Frémont expedition that Kit Carson guided to California in 1845), and were told that it was impossible to take wagons over Frémont's route—now approximated by U.S. Highway 50.

The argonauts then separated into two groups, one trading their wagons for pack mules and employing Owens to guide them over Frémont's route. The other group, including nine Cherokees, employed a half-breed Osage among the trappers to guide them by the shortest route over which they could take their wagons. He led them northward 175 miles along the foothills, over a route now closely paralleled by U.S. Highway 87—up Fountain Creek to its source, down Cherry Creek to present Denver, and along the South Platte to the vicinity of present Greeley. There he made a fording and guided the wagon party up the Cache La Poudre River to the Laramie plains, around the northern end of the Medicine Bow range, across the Continental Divide at Bridger's Pass, and westward to intersect the Overland Trail near Bridger's Fort.

This route had been used by Indians for centuries and known to American beaver trappers since 1825, when William Ashley took the first wheeled vehicle to cross the Rockies over part of it. The Cherokees wrote home, and the next year others took the same route to California, except that they made a shortcut from Cherry Creek to the Cache La Poudre and in doing so discovered gold in a branch of Clear Creek. Their route became known as the Cherokee Trail, and is now followed rather closely by U.S. Highway 287 between Denver and Laramie and Interstate 80 on to Fort Bridger.

Routing the main line of the C.O.C.&P.P. via Denver and the Cherokee Trail would reduce operating expenses substantially, but the company had no money with which to open a new route, and had fallen so far behind with its payrolls that the employees were writing on waybills going to the Leavenworth office,

> *On or about the first of May*
> *The boys would like to have their pay;*
> *If not paid by that day,*
> *The stock along the road may stray.*

To avoid admitting that the firm was in tight financial circumstances, John Jones offered to reroute the main line of both the mail coaches and the Pony Express through Denver if the Coloradoans would bridge the North Platte and Green rivers and build relay stations no farther than fifteen miles apart along the Cherokee Trail. They showed little interest in a stage line that would not run through the mining towns along Clear Creek, but the *Rocky Mountain News* was enthusiastic for Jones's proposal, and on April 18 appealed to its reluctant readers:

There are but two alternatives. One to give him satisfactory assurance that the stations will be supplied hence by way of the Cherokee Trail; the other to permit the line to remain where it now is. By the former we will receive a daily mail, in 4½ to 5 days from the Missouri River, and in ten days from California, a daily Pony Express each way, the great bulk of the overland travel and trade, and the telegraph line before next winter, and eventually the great Inter-ocean Railway. By the latter we lose all except perhaps the Railway, and will receive but a triweekly mail, a branch telegraph line, provided we give the stock subscription asked by the Telegraph Company. Certainly our business men and property owners cannot long hesitate in making their choice.

A week after the article appeared in the Denver paper Bela Hughes was elected president of the C.O.C.&P.P. Express Company and, according to Frank A. Root, "assumed the sole management of it," although Russell, Jones, and Waddell remained directors of the firm. Although the Coloradoans still refused to finance building a stage line unless it ran through the Clear Creek mining towns, Hughes decided to move the operations to the Cherokee Trail if Jim Bridger, the famous frontiersman of the Rockies, believed it practicable as a stagecoach route. By the next Pony Express rider he sent a message asking Bridger to meet him in Denver as soon as possible. Without waiting for a reply, he set out for Colorado, taking with him the deposed president of the company.

This was Russell's first trip west of the Missouri, and must have been a great joy to him after his disgrace in the East and being obliged to step down from the presidency of his company. The Coloradoans had no interest whatsoever in the bond scandal, but they did have sincere admiration for the man who had given them mail and stagecoach service from the beginning without Government subsidy. The editor of the *Rocky Mountain News* wrote, "The people of Pike's Peak will extend him a warmer welcome than to any other man who has ever visited us."

Still determined to have the overland mail line run through their towns, the miners along Clear Creek raised funds and engaged Captain E. L. Berthoud, who had been construction engineer on the Panama Isthmus Railroad, to lead an expedition in search of a pass through the Snowy Range of the Rockies. Captain Berthoud gathered an exploration party at Empire City on May 6, the day on which Hughes and Russell arrived in Denver. Two days later Jim Bridger arrived at Denver with two other mountain men, Emory and Goodell. They confirmed the report that the Cherokee Trail was a feasible stagecoach route, and that by its use the distance from St. Joseph to Salt Lake City via Denver would be only slightly longer than via South Pass. Bridger believed, however, that a feasible stagecoaching route a hundred miles shorter could be opened between Denver and Salt Lake City if a pass across the Snowy Range could be found at the head of Clear Creek Canyon. Hughes therefore decided to postpone moving the line to the Cherokee Trail and sent the mountain men to join Berthoud's exploration party. After spending a few days in Denver, he returned to Leavenworth, leaving Russell to enjoy his popularity in Colorado.

Bridger, Emory, and Goodell joined Berthoud and five other explorers on May 10. The next day they climbed the range at a point about two miles northeast of the highest fork of Clear Creek, but were unable to reach the summit. On the twelfth Bridger and Emory followed the south branch of the creek, searching for a side canyon that led to the summit. Berthoud took the remainder of the party up the right-hand branch, climbed northward from a point near the headwaters, and discovered the 11,330-foot pass that has ever since borne his name. Several days were spent in searching out the most gradual line of ascent to the pass and blazing a pack trail up the mountainside that is now the approximate course of U.S. Highway 40. The party then followed Frazier River (which they called Moses Creek) down the western slope to its junction with the Colorado River and continued down that stream to the present site of Hot Sulphur Springs. The explorers then returned to Golden, where a grand ball had been given to honor Russell and Colorado's newly appointed first governor, William Gilpin.

The Coloradoans joyfully celebrated the news that a pass through the Snowy Range had been discovered which, at no great expense, could be made passable by wheeled vehicles. And as was his nature, William Russell was more carried away by his enthusiasm than anyone else. He at once set off for Empire City, inspected the trail Berthoud had blazed and, although he had no experience in such matters, declared it entirely feasible for a stagecoach road. He was so positive that it would immediately become the great transcontinental thoroughfare, and his credit was still good enough in Colorado, that he bought several mining claims along Clear Creek and numerous town lots in Idaho Springs. He then rushed back to Denver and made the stagecoach trip to Leavenworth in three days and twenty-one hours, by far the fastest the route had ever been traveled by a vehicle. A meeting of the board of directors was held at once, and Russell's enthusiasm was so contagious that a resolution was passed to "dispatch Major Bridger and E. L. Berthoud immediately to review, locate, and mark out this proposed new road from Denver to Great Salt Lake City."

Stage stop in Rifle, Colorado. (Courtesy, State Historical Society of Colorado.)

The age-old Indian trails through the mountainous region between the Snowy Range of the Rockies and Great Salt Lake were as familiar to Jim Bridger as the highways of his area are to the modern motorist. Furthermore, by far the greater portion of our national highways west of the Great Plains follow courses that were originally animal and Indian trails. From Golden to within twenty miles of the Colorado-Utah line, U.S. 40 is almost identical to the "proposed new road" laid out and marked by Bridger and Berthoud.

From the Colorado line Route 40 bears northwest, crosses Green River at Jensen, Utah, and circles the northern end of Asphalt Ridge at Vernal. There it swings southwest to cross the Uinta River at Fort Duchesne. Instead of bearing northwest around Asphalt Ridge, Bridger and Berthoud continued a few miles southwest to White River, followed it to the Green, crossed near the mouth of the Uinta River, and marked a course up its valley to Fort Duchesne. The route which is now Highway 40 between Fort Duchesne and Heber, Utah, had been in use by beaver trappers since the 1820's. But whereas Highway 40 now continues northward from Heber to cross the summit of the Wasatch Mountains due east of Salt Lake City, Bridger laid out the proposed stage road along a far less rugged course—down Provo River to Utah Lake, and on the line that is now U.S. Highway 50 to Salt Lake City.

Berthoud reported to Hughes that "beyond a shadow of doubt a good wagon road of easy, practicable grade" could be quickly constructed over the route at a cost of not more than $100,000. With Denver on the main line and the over-all distance between St. Joseph and Salt Lake City reduced by more than a hundred miles, use of the proposed route would save more each year in operating expenses than its total cost. Its exploration, however, was of no value to the C.O.C.&P.P. Express Company, for it was as "clean out of cash and poor pay" under Bela Hughes's management as it had been under William Russell's regime, and had been obliged to start daily service over the old South Pass route on July 1.

On July 5 a special meeting of the board of directors of the C.O.C.&P.P. Express Company was called, at which five of the seven directors were present. At this meeting Bela Hughes was authorized to execute in favor of Ben Holladay a deed of trust covering all the company's property of every kind, although the amount owed Holladay—if any at that time—was an extremely small percentage of the firm's total indebtedness. Probably to avoid word of the irregular action reaching other creditors, the trust deed was not recorded for more than four months.

Historians rather generally agree that Holladay made loans and advances of approximately $200,000 to the C.O.C.&P.P. Express Company but disagree as to whether they were made before or after the execution of the deed of trust. A letter Holladay wrote twenty years later indicates very clearly that he made no loans to the firm and accepted none of its drafts until the chattel mortgage and deed of trust had been executed in his favor.

Whatever the situation may have been, on November 22, 1861, Bela Hughes, as president of the C.O.C.&P.P. Express Company, and William Russell's son John, as secretary of the firm, gave Ben Holladay a bond in the amount of $400,000 and a mortgage upon the entire company. The instruments were for a term of three years, during which Holladay agreed to advance money as required on condition that the total of past and future loans should not exceed $300,000. On the same day Hughes, on behalf of the company, executed a deed of trust to Theodore F. Warner (Holladay's partner in his first trading venture with the Mormons) and Robert L. Pease, naming Ben Holladay as beneficiary.

Inasmuch as Bela Hughes was Ben Holladay's cousin and had been rather obviously planted in his position, it might be suspected that he was somewhat under Holladay's influence, if not his direct orders. Nevertheless, barely two weeks after the three-year mortgage had been executed, and before making any further loans or advances to the firm, Holladay declared its $400,000 bond forfeited because of failure in performance. He then called upon the trustees to take possession of the property and operate it for his benefit and to advertise a date on which the assets would be sold. Warner refused to act in the matter, but Pease—a long-time Holladay employee—took possession as trustee on December 6, 1861, and published notice that a sale of the assets would be held in Atchison on December 31.

As soon as the notice was published, other creditors obtained an injunction to stop the sale, but a local judge dissolved it within a few weeks, and on February 15, 1862, the sale was again advertised, this time to take place at the Massasoit House in Atchison on March 7. Creditors evidently secured a second injunction, which was also quickly dissolved, for the sale was not held until March 21, 1862. With few except curious bystanders present, the trustee sold the entire assets of the Central Overland California & Pike's Peak Express Company at public auction to the sole bidder, Ben Holladay, for $100,000.

After the withdrawal of Alexander Majors and William Waddell, the board of directors of the C.O.C.&P.P. Express Company fell under the control of William Russell and a few of his cronies, although the actual control doubtless rested with Ben Holladay after the election of Bela Hughes. Webster Samuels and Alexander Street, however, remained independent and uncontrolled. Immediately after the sale they insisted that the board take legal action to have it set aside, but the other five members refused.

Samuels and Street then brought suit in the United States Circuit Court, Kansas Territory, on grounds that the sale was illegal. The court found in their favor, ruling that the sale had been made without authority and in violation of trust. Holladay, however, ignored the decision, and the United States Marshal for Kansas Territory failed to enforce it. Samuels again brought suit before the same court, and won the same decision, but again the U.S. Marshal failed to enforce the order. So the matter dragged on for several years, until both cases were dismissed when the marshal reported that he could find no representative of the company in his district upon whom he could serve a summons.

If money changed hands under the table it was never proved, but the U.S. Marshal for Kansas Territory and the judge who dissolved the injunctions were only two of the many public officials whose actions or lack of action were unduly beneficial to big Ben Holladay. Wars have a degrading effect upon the moral fiber of a people and their public officials, and the Civil War was no exception. Following the war, graft and privilege are said to have been rampant throughout the Federal Government, with the Post Office Department in the forefront.

"Straw" bidding was one of the devices used for defrauding the Government with the connivance of highly placed postal officials. Under the law, the Postmaster General was required to advertise for bids before awarding a new mail contract or renewing an old one and make the award to the lowest bidder who could post a satisfactory performance bond. In straw bidding, an unscrupulous contractor had a few accomplices enter bids low enough to discourage honest competition while he entered a bid that was far above the value of the service to be performed. After bidding on the contract had been closed, the accomplices withdrew their "straw" bids, and the Postmaster General was then technically within the law when he awarded the contract to the lowest remaining bidder. At the peak of the straw-bidding fraud, a congressional investigation established that by use of the system the compensation on the twenty-six routes examined had been increased from

$65,216 to $530,319, and that some of the lines averaged no more than three letters per week.

What part, if any, Ben Holladay took in such fraudulent schemes can only be conjectured from the actions that certain Government officials and army officers took, or refrained from taking, in the course of their dealings with him. There is no doubt that he was one of the most dominant and forceful characters of his time, and, like all such men, he was worshiped by his admirers but feared and hated by everyone else who had contact with him. So complete, in fact, was his domination of admirers that his biographers, almost without exception, have sought to omit his rascalities or excuse them as being justified by the circumstances under which he was obliged to operate.

The most revealing of all the vast amount of material published regarding Ben Holladay is a letter from his friend and attorney, John Doniphan, to the St. Joseph *Catholic Tribune*, which appeared in its issue of June 22, 1895.

After a few comments regarding the town of Weston, Doniphan wrote, "But my chief object in writing this is to do justice to Benjamin Holladay's memory. He had his home in Weston from 1839 to 1859, and was a character of whom the city of Weston may well be proud. . . .

"In February, 1849, he and Theodore F. Warner, one of God's noblemen, formed a partnership to trade to Salt Lake. The goods were bought on Warner's credit; the wagons and oxen were mostly furnished by Holladay. They made a good deal of money by that enterprise, and Ben. Holladay never mistreated Warner in any respect. I was the attorney for both of them ten years, and for Warner twenty. . . .

"I read letters from Holladay to Warner in 1867 from Salem, Ore., recalling the kindness of Warner, offering him sympathy and assistance, proposing if he would come to Oregon to join him in building the Oregon & California railroad and manage the finances, out of which he expected to realize $3,000,000, that he should have a large amount of the profits. This road proved to be Holladay's Waterloo. He opened a hotel at Salem, possessed himself of a majority of the legislature, elected his own senator, expecting to succeed to the position himself, bought ships, obtained a land grant from the legislature of thousands of acres of the best lands; he issued millions in bonds and sold them in Europe; his ships sent there failed to procure immigrants as expected; his railroad bonds ripened coupons before the lands would sell or before the immigrants arrived, and he undertook to pay the interest as it matured out of his private fortune. Sherman's bill had passed in 1869 to pay all Government debts in gold, and Holladay was paying thirty per cent. to satisfy the greed of the bondholders. It broke him. . . .

"It is due to the truth of history to correct the impression which wrongs both of these old and time-honored citizens of Weston. I regard Ben. Holladay as one of nature's gifted children. Had he been on the same theater, he was capable of playing the role of Napoleon, as I think he resembled him in many characteristics. He believed results justified means, and he trusted in his star too far. Haughty and dictatorial, he was the most companionable of men, and would always cheerfully undergo more than his share of the discomforts or personal sacrifices. Anxious to get the best of every bargain, he would often turn it, with all the profits, to some friend or deserving man."

Whether, as charged by their detractors, William Russell and Ben Holladay were thieves and scoundrels, who with the wicked prize itself bought out the law, or whether, as their admirers vehemently insisted, their acts were justified by circumstances and the necessity of dealing with corrupt Government officials, there is little doubt that these two men did as much as any other pair of their time to speed the westward expansion of the United States.

17

Roughshod Master
and Crew

NOT LONG after the outbreak of the Civil War, sympathizers with
the Confederate cause burned numerous buildings in St. Joseph,
including the Pony Express office. The St. Joseph & Atchison Railroad, however, had by that time been completed as far as Winthrop,
Missouri, directly across the river from Atchison, Kansas. In September 1861, six or seven weeks before the discontinuance of the
Pony Express, the Post Office Department issued an order making
Atchison the eastern terminus for the overland mail line. Thereafter, until the building of the transcontinental railroad, all the
overland mail passed through the Atchison post office, where in
1861–62 Frank A. Root was assistant postmaster. In 1863 he was
employed by Ben Holladay as an express messenger and was soon
after appointed mail agent at the Latham, Colorado, way station.
Nearly forty years later he wrote of his experiences in *The Overland Stage to California*, the only eyewitness account of stagecoaching in the West during the Civil War period.

The pony line was operated semiweekly, and each trip brought about
350 letters. In those last few weeks every pony express letter was mailed
at the Atchison post-office, and I thus became quite familiar with them
from handling and postmarking each letter. . . . The letters, many of
which were written on tissue paper, were very light, for it cost something in those days, even after the "pony" rates were reduced to one
dollar per half-ounce, to indulge in California correspondence. . . . Some
of the letters were rather bulky, and I have postmarked those that had
affixed to them as many as twenty-five one dollar "pony" stamps.

In going overland, a stage-coach left Atchison, the eastern starting-point, every morning at eight o'clock, shortly after the arrival of the mail by train on the St. Joseph & Atchison railroad from the East. The mail came over the Missouri river on the steam ferry-boat *Ida* and was taken direct to the postoffice, where it remained until loaded on the stage, and was then carried across the plains to California, six times a week. No mail arrived from the East on Monday morning, the coach that left Atchison that morning was in charge of a messenger, and was called a "messenger coach."

The messenger coach was loaded with express packages of various kinds, besides a strong iron box that two persons could handle, containing the treasure and the most valuable of the smaller packages. On the regular Concords the safe was carried in the front boot, under the driver's box. Whenever there happened to be an extra-big run of express packages (enough to comfortably fill the stage), no passengers were taken on that trip; but it was a very rare occurrence if the express coach left Atchison without at least one or more, and often it carried as many as half a dozen passengers, either for Denver, Salt Lake, or on through to the western terminus.

The charges on express matter other than gold dust, coin, or currency, between Atchison and Denver, was at the uniform rate of one dollar per pound. More express matter was carried to Denver, Central City and Black Hawk in 1863 than to all other points combined on the main stage line.

The number of mail pouches carried west on the stage-coach six times a week ran about as follows: San Francisco, two; Sacramento, one to two; Virginia City and Carson, Nev., one each; Salt Lake, one to two; Denver, two. In addition, there was a way pouch which was opened at the few [post] offices along the route—Daniel's Ranch, Valley City, Fort Kearney, Cottonwood Springs, Fremont's Orchard, Latham, and Fort Bridger.

During the summer and fall of 1861 Bela Hughes considerably expanded the C.O.C.&P.P. Express Company's stagecoaching and express operations in Colorado. In addition to serving Golden, Central City, Black Hawk, and the Clear Creek towns, he extended lines southward through the mountains to Breckenridge, Fairplay, Tarryall, Buckskin Joe, and the mining towns along the Arkansas and Blue rivers. But the venture was unprofitable, for other stage and express firms were organized; they crowded into the field and began cutting rates. By March 1862 seven companies were operating between Denver and Central City, and the fare had been cut from ten dollars to six dollars.

Among the seven was the Pike's Peak Express Company, founded by John Kehler, sheriff of the county in which Denver was situated and son of Father J. H. Kehler, Colorado's most colorful pioneer minister. Father Kehler came to Denver in midwinter 1860, when crime and ruffianism were at their height. He arrived with his family in an ox wagon from Shepardstown, Virginia, where he had been the pastor of a conventional Episcopal parish. On the evening of his arrival he delivered a lecture entitled "Great Men of the Age" under the auspices of Denver's first library, the Denver and Auraria Reading Room. Six days later he organized the town's first Episcopal congregation, then he founded St. John's Church in the Wilderness, now St. John's Cathedral. As deputy sheriff under his son, John, he led more than a score of murderers to the scaffold, administering spiritual consolation as they waited for the hangman to trip the drop platform. Of the first twelve burial services he conducted, two of the deceased had been executed for murder, five had been shot by antagonists, one had committed suicide, one expired in delirium tremens, and the other three died of natural causes.

Ben Holladay took possession of the C.O.C.&P.P. Express Company in Atchison on March 21, 1862, and immediately set about killing off his competition. The running time for stagecoaches to Denver was then six days, so he must have sent orders for the reduction of Colorado stagecoach fares and express rates on the first stage to leave Atchison after he gained control of the line. In any case, before the end of the month the C.O.C.&P.P. had cut the passenger fare between Denver and Central City from six dollars to two dollars and had made corresponding reductions in the express rates.

Then, according to the *Rocky Mountain News*, he put into operation between Golden and Denver "a double-decked omnibus commodious and comfortable enough to accommodate 18 to 20 passengers, and two daily coaches of standard (9-passenger) type." Soon afterward he extended the same sort of service, using standard Concord stagecoaches, to Buckskin Joe, Montgomery, Hamilton, and other towns in the southern mining area. It was not long until the pressure had driven all the other operators out of business, most of them selling their horses and equipment to Holladay for less than their worth.

On August 11, 1862, the Central City *Tri-Weekly Miners' Register* complained that Holladay had gained control of Colorado transportation to such an extent that he had been able to double passenger fares and express charges from what they were when he acquired the C.O.C.&P.P. Express Company, and that he had cut schedules "to the point where every coach is fully loaded."

By 1862 Kansas had been sparsely settled for a hundred miles westward from St. Joseph. Denver was a populous city, flanked for sixty miles to the west by twoscore thriving gold-rush towns. Salt Lake City could compare favorably with the capital of many an eastern seaboard state, and for fifty miles or more along the foothills of the Wasatch Mountains prosperous Mormon farms lay shoulder to shoulder. The Nevada Territory had been established, millions in silver were being mined from the Washoe hills, Carson City and Virginia City were fairly bursting at the seams, and the road that Jared Crandall had pioneered across the Sierra Nevada had become one of the busiest thoroughfares in the United States.

But between these islands of population lay three six-hundred-mile stretches of wilderness and mountains roamed by buffalo, antelope, wild horse herds, and lobo wolves. They were inhabited only by Indians, a score or two of frontier rancher-traders along the course of the Overland Trail, the keepers of the stage-line relay posts, and woefully inadequate garrisons of soldiers at Fort Kearney, Fort Laramie, Bridger's Fort, and Fort Churchill in western Nevada.

To man these isolated relay posts and to keep stagecoaches rolling over the road day and night through rain, sleet, blizzards, scorching heat, or subzero cold required men as rugged and rough as the wilderness that was their adversary. It is hardly surprising that many of the C.O.C.&P.P. employees found a hero in Ben Holladay —admired the dominating manner in which he snatched the floundering company away from its other creditors, the fact that he virtually thumbed his nose at the court that ruled the snatch illegal, and the ruthless way he killed off his Colorado competition. One of his men, Nat Stein, wrote *The Driver's Song*, heard by nearly every passenger who rode a Holladay stagecoach across the prairies:

> *You ask me for our leader, I'll soon inform you then;*
> *It's Holladay they call him, and often only Ben;*
> *If you can read the papers, it's easy work to scan;*
> *He beats the world at staging now, or any other man.*

Nor is it surprising that more than a few of the drivers copied the example set by their hero, hogging the right-of-way, cursing emigrants who failed to pull off the road at a distant blast from the stage horn, or, if the man cursed back, sideswiping his wagon and wrecking a wheel with the ironbound hub of a speeding Concord coach.

Cursing emigrants and freighters, forcing them off the road, smashing a few wagon wheels, and being insolent to complaining passengers was as far as most of the drivers went in emulating

*Virginia City, Montana, a gold-mining town at the end of a
stagecoach line. (From* Harper's Weekly, *December 1860.)*

their hero, but Jack Slade far exceeded him in ruthlessness and
brutality. Ellis Lucia writes in *The Saga of Ben Holladay* that "Big
Ben couldn't be everywhere at once, though he often tried, spread-
eagle fashion. He extended his rule in other ways, by picking his
first lieutenants with calculating care. They were strong counter-
parts of himself, little Holladays only a shade less in stature than
their boss and equally as fearless. The Overland came above all
else, and they helped extend the Holladay shadow. . . . Best of
them all, in Ben's opinion, was burly, bullnecked Joseph Alfred
'Jack' Slade. . . . Slade was cut from the same tough, coarse cloth
as Holladay himself, which was why Ben took to him."

As a superintendent under Ben Ficklin, Slade had been satisfied with killing off thieves along his section of the line, but after Holladay took over the company Jack Slade seemed obsessed with determination to inspire fear in anyone failing to knuckle under to him.

A heavy drinker, he surrounded himself with a following of the toughest men on his section of the line and took delight in terrorizing frontier settlements when drunk, shooting up towns and sending the settlers scurrying for cover. His most famous killings, however, were committed in cold blood when he was perfectly sober. It was said that he would take offense if a saloonkeeper refused to serve him further drinks when he was becoming drunk and quarrelsome or if a stranger made some comment he thought to be less than complimentary. If sufficiently angered, he would torture his victim for a few days by being particularly affable, like a cat playing with a mouse, and then calmly point a Colt's navy revolver between the man's eyes, pull the trigger, and walk away as he lay dying.

Laporte, Colorado, with no more than a dozen cabins but "no less than half a dozen places where liquor was dispensed at all hours of the day and night," was Slade's favorite hangout. In writing the history of the town some time later, a correspondent of the *Rocky Mountain News* recalled, "The Indians were not the only source of annoyance in the early days. The Overland Stage Company's employees were in many cases more carefully guarded against. They were a drunken, carousing set in the main, and absolutely careless of the rights or feelings of settlers. . . . In his commonest transactions with others, Slade always kept his hand laid back in a light, easy fashion on the handle of his revolver. One of his most facetious tricks was to cock a revolver in a stranger's face and walk him into the nearest saloon to set up drinks to a crowd."

Slade's reputation as a cold-blooded killer was known from coast to coast as early as 1861. At that time Mark Twain's brother Orion was appointed Secretary of Nevada Territory, and Mark got the job of being secretary to the Secretary. Their trip from St. Joseph to Carson City during July and August 1861 is one of the most famous stagecoach journeys in American history, for Twain vividly described many of its incidents in his 1871 book, *Roughing It.* One of the most amusing tales in the book is of his meeting with Slade, and one of the most vivid is his description of a Pony Express rider:

We had a consuming desire, from the beginning, to see a pony-rider, but somehow or other all that passed us and all that met us managed to streak by in the night, and so we heard only a whiz and a hail, and the swift phantom of the desert was gone before we could get our heads out of the windows. But now we were expecting one along every moment, and would see him in broad daylight. Presently the driver exclaims:

"HERE HE COMES!"

Every neck is stretched further, and every eye strained wider. Away across the endless dead level of the prairie a black speck appears against the sky, and it is plain that it moves. Well, I should think so! In a second or two it becomes a horse and rider, rising and falling, rising and falling —sweeping toward us nearer and nearer—growing more and more distinct, more and more sharply defined—nearer and still nearer, and the flutter of the hoofs comes faintly to the ear—another instant a whoop and a hurrah from our upper deck, a wave of the rider's hand, but no reply, and man and horse burst past our excited faces, and go swinging away like a belated fragment of a storm!

. . . . .

Even before we got to Overland City [Julesburg], we had begun to hear about Slade and his "division" (for he was a "division agent") on the Overland; and from the hour we had left Overland City we had heard drivers and conductors talk about only three things—"Californy," the Nevada silver-mines, and this desperado Slade. And a deal the most of the talk was about Slade. . . .

In due time we rattled up to a stage-station, and sat down to breakfast with a half-savage, half-civilized company of armed and bearded mountaineers, ranchmen and station employees. The most gentlemanly-appearing, quiet, and affable officer we had yet found along the road in the Overland Company's service was the person who sat at the head of the table, at my elbow. Never youth stared and shivered as I did when I heard them call him SLADE!

Here was romance, and I sitting face to face with it!—looking upon it—touching it—hobnobbing with it, as it were! Here, right by my side, was the actual ogre who, in fights and brawls and various ways, *had taken the lives of twenty-six human beings,* or all men lied about him! I suppose I was the proudest stripling that ever traveled to see strange lands and wonderful people. He was so friendly and so gentle-spoken that I warmed to him in spite of his awful history. . . .

The coffee ran out. At least it was reduced to one tin cupful, and Slade was about to take it when he saw that my cup was empty. He politely offered to fill it, but although I wanted it, I politely declined. I was afraid he had not killed anybody that morning, and might be needing diversion. But still with firm politeness he insisted on filling my cup, and said I had traveled all night and better deserved it than he—and while he talked he placidly poured the fluid, to the last drop. I thanked him and drank it, but it gave me no comfort, for I could not feel sure that he would not be sorry, presently, that he had given it away, and proceed to kill me to distract his thoughts from the loss. But nothing of the kind occurred. We left him with only twenty-six dead people to account for, and I felt a tranquil satisfaction in the thought that in so judiciously taking care of No. 1 at that breakfast-table I had pleasantly escaped being No. 27.

In another episode Twain tells of a boy who had ridden the Overland Stage to California and had "gushing admiration of Mr. H." The boy, however, knew little of biblical history, and upon hearing the story of Moses leading the Children of Israel to the Promised Land, he exclaimed, *"Forty years? Only three hundred miles?* Humph! Ben Holladay would have fetched them through in thirty-six hours!"

Although Holladay improved service materially on the line eastward from Denver as soon as he took over the company, stagecoach service between Denver and Salt Lake City came to a complete standstill in the spring of 1862, owing to a combination of weather and Indian trouble. The winter of 1861–62 was severe in the Rockies. One blizzard followed closely after another, and passes were drifted deep with snow. In the high mountains stagecoaches were replaced with light sleighs, and following each new fall of snow loose stock was driven through the passes in an effort to keep them open. Even so, to get the sleighs through, Government printed material and newspapers had to be left at way stations, and only the letter mail taken through. By the end of January the San Francisco *Alta California* reported that it had been a week since mail of any kind had been received overland from the east.

By the time Ben Holladay took the line over on March 21, stations all the way from the eastern foothills of the Rockies to Bridger's Fort in the Green River valley were piled high with mail sacks. When the snow began to melt in late March rivers overflowed their banks and the roads through the mountain valleys became quagmires in which coach wheels sank to the hubs. Arrangements were then made for all Government printed matter and newspaper mail between California and the East to be carried via Panama by the Pacific Mail Steamship Company. By April, Indian trouble along the line had made it necessary to send all California mail by sea.

When white men first penetrated the unknown region between the Mississippi and the Pacific they found the Indians, for the most part, friendly. Although there were a few battles between Indians and the American mountain men who stripped their streams of beaver, there was nothing that could be termed an Indian war. Throughout the westward migration to the Pacific Coast that took place between 1836 and the California gold rush, the Indians along the Overland Trail were friendly to the whites. They often stole livestock unless it was closely guarded, and committed other minor depredations, but killings by Indians were almost unknown. There is little doubt that in the westward migration during that entire period there were more white lives saved than taken by Indians. But abuses suffered at the hands of Kearny's Army of the West and the gold-crazed forty-niners, together with seeing untold thousands of buffalo killed for their tongues alone by American hunters, aroused bitter resentment in the plains Indians toward all white men.

Following the depredations of the Comanches, Kiowas, Cheyennes, and Arapahoes along the Santa Fe Trail in 1847, the Government had held the Indians in check by establishing forts and cavalry posts at infrequent points on the principal migration and mail routes throughout the West. But at the outbreak of the Civil War many of the soldiers left their posts to join the Army of the Confederacy, while those who remained were transferred east to strengthen the Union ranks. The Colorado troops were sent to New Mexico, where they were needed to turn back Sibley's rebel force. The forts and cavalry posts along the central route were no sooner abandoned than the Indians began to exhibit their resentment toward the encroaching whites.

In March 1862 General Halleck was ordered by the War Department to send troops for the protection of the overland mail route, and on April 4 the *Rocky Mountain News* announced that Brigadier General James Craig had been placed in command of these troops. Also in early April the Third Regiment of California Volunteers, under command of Colonel Connor, was ordered to Utah to garrison forts and protect the mail route. The War Department had delayed too long. By April 4 the Bannock Indians had gone on the warpath and had attacked the stage line, burned several stations between Fort Bridger and the present site of Casper, Wyoming, driven off sixty horses and mules, destroyed mail and coaches, and killed several men. The best-authenticated of these attacks was made on two stagecoaches that set out from Atchison on April 2, 1862. They were surrounded by mounted Indians on April 17, at a point on Sweetwater River that was midway between Rawlins and Lander, Wyoming, on what is now U.S. Highway 287. Among the nine men in the party was T. S. Boardman, whose report of the attack was published on May 26 in the San Francisco *Alta California*:

We drove to the top of a slight elevation to the left of the road; the other coach was driven up along side, distant about ten feet; mules badly frightened; one of them was shot through the mouth, and the bullets whistling rapidly among them, it was thought best to let them go. They were accordingly cut loose and were soon drove up a canon to the southwest of the road, by some ten or twelve Indians. Everything that could afford protection, mail sacks, blankets, buffalo robes, etc., were thrown out of the coaches and from the front boots, and were placed upon the north and south sides between the coaches, against the wheels and along the east side of us, behind which we barricaded ourselves. James Brown who was standing by the hind wheel of one of the coaches, then received a shot in the left side of the face. . . . Lem Flowers (Division Agent) was then struck in the hip. . . . Phil Rogers received two arrows in the right shoulder. . . . James Anderson was shot through the left leg, and William Reed through the small of the back.

The bullets pattered like hail upon the sacks that protected us. We returned the fire with the rifle and our revolvers whenever we got sight of any of the foe, reserving most of our revolver shots for their charges. They charged upon us twice, but the volleys that we poured upon them repelled them. About four o'clock P.M. they withdrew in parties of two and threes. . . . We soon determined to get away if we could, with the wounded to the next station.

After a fatiguing walk of eight miles we reached the station at Three Crossings. Where we found the station keeper, wife and three children, and the men employed by the Company, who informed us that Indians—probably the same band—had stolen all the mules and eight head of cattle the night before.

For four days they remained forted up in the Three Crossings station, nursing the wounded and awaiting an attack by the Indians. When none was made, they yoked a span of cows to a light wagon, loaded the wounded and children aboard, and set out on a trek of nearly two hundred miles to Fort Bridger, which they reached safely on May 2.

The transcontinental telegraph line, following the Overland Mail route, had been completed in October 1861, and during its building along the Sweetwater River linemen worked out a trick for keeping the Indians from molesting the wires. The men would get two groups of curious Indians a mile or so apart, then transmit messages back and forth between them for a few minutes. One man at each end of the line tapped out the messages in Morse code while another held a wire in each hand and repeated the message aloud, leading the Indians to believe that the sound was being transmitted to the wire through his hands. An Indian at each end of the line was then allowed to hold the wire and at the first word spoken by either of them a jolt of electricity was sent over the line that nearly knocked the holders off their feet. Few lessons of this kind were required to teach the Bannocks that touching telegraph wires was bad medicine for Indians. As a result, they did not break the wire in their attack on the mail stations, but knowing that news of their depredations could be flashed over the line, they struck quickly and withdrew to their stronghold in southeastern Idaho.

When Ben Holladay took over the C.O.C.&P.P. Express Company he appointed his morose, hard-drinking brother Joe as general agent of the line west of Denver, with headquarters at Salt Lake City. Also stationed there were F. Cook, assistant treasurer of the company; H. B. Rowe, superintendent of the Utah division; and E. R. Rurple, the local agent. Word of attacks on the stage stations had no sooner been telegraphed to Salt Lake City than Joe Holladay appealed to the acting governor of Utah Territory, Frank Fuller, for adequate military protection of the line. The acting governor had no jurisdiction over the Mormon militia, but he rushed off a telegram to Secretary of War Stanton, signed by himself, his surveyor general, Joe Holladay, Cook, Rowe, and Rurple. The telegram implied that the Indians had destroyed the mail line to a greater extent than was actually the case and that their purpose was to stop the overland mail. Secretary Stanton was petitioned to have mounted soldiers raised immediately by the superintendent of Indian affairs, and to have them required to serve until the arrival of an adequate force of United States troops.

Brigham Young, although still a friend to Ben Holladay, was not taken in by the histrionics. On April 14, three days before the attack on the stagecoaches reported by Boardman, he telegraphed the territory's Washington representative that, as far as he knew, the Indians were quiet but that the Mormon militia could control all the Indians in Utah and would protect the overland mail if asked to do so by Federal authorities. The representative evidently transmitted the message to the White House, for at President Lincoln's request General Thomas telegraphed Young on April 28, asking him to raise and equip a company of cavalry for ninety days' service to protect the telegraph line and overland mail stages. Without waiting for the request, however, Young had sent twenty militiamen under Colonel Burton to guard a party, including Senator Hooper, which went east from Salt Lake City in late April.

On May 16 Burton telegraphed from Deer Creek station (near present Glenrock, Wyoming) that no Indians had been seen but that all livestock along the Sweetwater River had been stolen or abandoned. He reported that he found twenty-six locked sacks of mail cut open and scattered over the ground at Ice Springs, and ten more at Three Crossings. Senator Hooper, however, reported

An Indian attack at the North Platte crossing.

that only sixteen sacks of mail had been destroyed, and that he believed renegade white men to have led the Indians in their attacks, as several were said to have spoken English, and one German.

Ben Holladay's biographer, J. V. Frederick, writes, "Some of the Mormons were southern sympathizers, and they were also suspected as the cause of some uprisings. The Snakes and Bannocks led in the depredations on the Holladay property. . . . In April Sioux, Cheyennes, Arapahoes, and Utes were reported to have stolen about 160 head of livestock on the Holladay line at Split Rock, Dry Sandy, Rocky Ridge, and Red Butte."

No other source has been found to suggest that Mormons were in any way involved in the affair. It is possible that the Sioux may have attacked the line at these locations, as some of them were in Sioux territory. But it is very improbable that Cheyennes, Arapahoes, or Utes had any part in attacks so far from their homelands. The report of 160 head of stock being stolen must have been prepared strictly for claim purposes, as there is little probability that there was more than a quarter of that amount at all four little relay posts combined. In describing the line at the peak of its operations, Frank Root wrote, "There were from eight to twelve animals kept at each station."

As requested by the President, Brigham Young outfitted a force of seventy-two mounted militiamen and seventeen officers for the protection of the mail line. They served for a period of ninety days, but saw little action. On May 15 eighty men of the Eleventh Ohio Volunteer Cavalry passed Fort Laramie on their way to the devastated section of the line, and another company of Ohioans had passed Fort Kearney.

At about the same time Ben Holladay came west from New York City, stopped at Denver to confer with Governor Evans, and went on to Salt Lake City. By June 15 service had been restored on the mail line, but it was reported that in May alone fifty-three thousand letters and tons of newspapers had been stolen or destroyed by Indians. Few westerners believed that white renegades had led the Indians in attacks upon the stage stations, but they were not at all convinced that some of Ben Holladay's employees had not been playing Indian. They pointed out that the attacks were very conveniently made at stations stacked to the rafters with mail that had accumulated during the winter blizzards and spring floods, and that it seemed strange for Indians who could not read to steal mail.

In July Holladay moved the stage line from the route along the North Platte and Sweetwater rivers to the Cherokee Trail. Root writes that the change was made "on the recommendation of Colonel Chivington, commanding the district of Colorado, and by the consent of the post-office department." Dr. LeRoy Hafen is more specific: "The Indian disturbances during the preceding April and May upon the northern course was the excuse given the Post Office Department for transferring the line. . . . The chief reason, perhaps, for changing the route was to shorten it. Such a change had been seriously considered the year before . . ."

On August 14 the Colorado legislature, then in its second session, passed a special Private Act granting Holladay's "Overland Stage Line" the right to build bridges and operate ferries on the Cherokee Trail within the State of Colorado and to collect tolls for their use. On September 11 the *Rocky Mountain News* published the following letter received from Ben Holladay under date of September 3, 1862.

Permit me, through your columns, to return my thanks for the liberal charter granted to the Overland Stage Line by the Legislature of Colorado, and also for the generous support extended to the line by the citizens. In view of these facts, I have instructed my agents to change the route from its present course, to one bearing via Denver to Laporte, so that hereafter you will have the great through mails passing directly through your city. I am happy to announce that the new route to Salt Lake City realizes the most favorable expectations and is already in such fine running order that I was enabled to make the trip from Salt Lake City to Latham in four days.

BEN HOLLADAY,
Prop'r Overland Stage Co.

The Central Overland California & Pike's Peak Express name had become inappropriate with the discontinuance of operations beyond Salt Lake City and the establishment of Colorado Territory. It is said that Ben Holladay was envious of the Overland Mail name, and he apparently chose one as much like it as possible. Thereafter he used no other name for his lines until incorporating the business in 1866.

No one can say whether Holladay actually intended, when writing his letter of September 3, to change the main line of the mail route to pass through Denver or whether, as was his wont, he wrote what he thought to be best for his business, but avoided any direct promise by saying he had instructed his agents to make the change. In any case, the main line was not rerouted through Denver until more than two years later.

The original stage route to Salt Lake City had never followed the North Platte all the way to the Sweetwater and South Pass. From the present site of North Platte, Nebraska, it had continued along the right (southeast) bank of the South Platte about a hundred miles to old Julesburg, at the mouth of Lodgepole Creek. There it crossed the river at a reasonably shallow ford, followed the creek westward about forty miles, and then turned northward across Thirty-Mile Ridge to the North Platte, roughly the course that is now followed by U.S. Highway 385 between Julesburg, Colorado, and Bridgeport, Nebraska. When Hockaday & Liggett was bought out by the Leavenworth and Pike's Peak Express Company the line was extended two hundred miles along the right bank of the South Platte to Denver. This section then became a branch line when the overland mail contract was transferred from the Butterfield line to the central route.

About sixty miles north from Denver the South Platte makes a right-angle turn to the east. There, opposite the mouth of Cache La Poudre River a few miles east of present Greeley, stood the Latham way station. Approximately thirty-six miles up the Cache La Poudre was the little frontier settlement of Laporte on the Cherokee Trail, but to reach it by way of Denver the distance was 136 miles. When the mail stages were moved to the Cherokee Trail route, Holladay made the branch along the South Platte from old Julesburg to Latham the main line of the route, but instead of continuing it on to Denver in accordance with his letter to the *Rocky Mountain News,* he turned it across the South Platte at Latham, up the Cache La Poudre Valley to Laporte, and onward to Fort Bridger over the Cherokee Trail. Denver continued to be served triweekly by a branch line along the right-hand bank of the South Platte. When the change was made, Jack Slade was made superintendent of the division between Latham and newly established Fort Halleck, midway between the present Wyoming cities of Laramie and Rawlins. He gave his wife's maiden name, Virginia Dale, to the third relay post north of Laporte, the last in Colorado.

After the change to the new route there were no more Indian attacks on the mail line during the remainder of 1862, but the mail service was still irregular between Latham and Salt Lake City. In late August, Indian trouble erupted in Minnesota, and was believed to have been instigated by agents of the Confederacy. There was fear in Washington that a general Indian war throughout the West might be touched off. In anticipation of this the Post Office Department suspended overland service for three weeks and had all the mail between California and the East sent by ocean steamers. When service was again resumed on the line, newspapers and "Pub Docs," as the stage-line employees called Government mail, were often cached at way stations if a coach was heavily loaded with passengers and express.

Creek bottoms and mountain valleys turned into quagmires when the fall rains came, but the drivers discovered an expeditious method of road building. Frank Root wrote, "Occasionally the drivers . . . would get stalled going through a bad slough, and be unable to move. In that case they were obliged to take out sack after sack of the Pub Docs., open the bags, and pile the massive books from the Government printing office in the slough, and, by building a solid foundation with them, were thus enabled to pull the coach out of the mire."

The *San Francisco Bulletin* accused Holladay of keeping up appearances by getting mail addressed to newspapers through in fairly regular time so that subscribers would believe that it was not the mail service that was delinquent but rather that their friends in the East were delinquent about writing.

The failure of service on the line was almost entirely east of Salt Lake City, and there were demands in California for a congressional investigation, but it is apparent that Ben Holladay already had a friend in court. The Postmaster General stated in his annual report of December 1862 that service on the Overland line had not been satisfactory during the year, but that he believed it would soon be made so. He pointed out that new mineral deposits were being discovered in the regions through which the route passed, and concluded, "As an agency in developing these resources for the government the mail line is indispensable, and every needful protection and support should be given to the Company, and some allowance made for failures in the beginning undertaking."

18

Rise of the Stagecoach King

DURING the winter of 1862–63 the Ohio Volunteer Cavalry guarded the telegraph line along the abandoned stage route as far west as South Pass. Beyond that point it was considered to be in Utah district and under the protection of the California Volunteers commanded by Colonel Connor. On November 24, 1862, the Bannocks attacked the telegraph station at Pacific Springs, killed one linesman, stole all the horses, and made their getaway to southern Idaho. There, in January 1863, Colonel Connor assembled his entire force, severely defeated an equal force of Bannocks and Shoshones in the Battle of Bear River, and forestalled any further depredations by them on either the telegraph or stage line.

The Goshutes of western Utah were "Digger Indians," considered cowardly and generally peaceable, but when they discovered that all the soldiers had been withdrawn from their area they went on the warpath. Before the coming of the Mormons they had lived in holes like coyotes and subsisted on roots, grasshoppers, lizards, and desert rats. Their only weapons were primitive bows, clubs, and stones, and hiding was their only means of defense. But they had stolen horses and firearms from Camp Floyd during its occupation by U.S. troops and from travelers on the Egan Trail to California. In early March 1863 they attacked Eight Mile relay station, near the Utah-Nevada boundary, killing the keeper and crew, and then lay in wait for the eastbound stage. From generations of practice, they concealed themselves so skillfully that the stage was within twenty-five yards of the station buildings before Hank

Harper, the driver, realized that he was running into an ambush.

Fortunately, Harper's team on that relay was made up of six fast California mustangs. The instant he sensed an ambush he swung the team off the road, lashed the whip above their backs, and yippeeed for them to turn on the speed. But he had sensed the danger too late. Indians with muskets or bows sprang from behind every greasewood bush, and a hail of lead and arrows raked the coach. At the first volley, Harper and a passenger riding on the seat beside him were seriously injured and fell into the mail boot. Although mortally wounded, Harper held onto the reins and called for Judge Mott to come and take them.

Judge Mott, well along in his sixties, was Nevada's newly elected delegate to Congress and was on his way to Washington. He was no reinsman, but he and Hank Harper were made of the sort of stuff it took to settle Nevada, and each had confidence in the other. The horses were racing in panic across the greasewood-dotted desert; the coach was reeling and pitching. Amid a storm of bullets and arrows from a band of shrieking Indians racing their ponies in pursuit, the judge crawled out through a coach window, dragged himself hand over hand up to the seat, took the reins from the dying driver's hands, and braced his boots against the footboard. Miraculously, he gained control of the frightened team, made an eight-mile dash for Deep Creek station, outran the Indians on their half-starved mounts, and brought the stagecoach with its cargo of mail and frightened tenderfeet in safely. Hank Harper had given him advice as long as he could speak, but was dead when the coach pulled up at the station. The wounded passenger survived, and the mail went through without interruption.

Until the Goshutes were brought back under control in mid-summer, a detail of cavalrymen accompanied each stagecoach through eastern Nevada and western Utah, but the protection was not always effective. In May a coach was fired upon from ambush near Eight Mile station. The driver was killed outright, but Major Egan, who was riding with him, took the reins and brought the passengers and mail through safely. The attack was made from among rocks, and the Goshutes were so clever at hiding that the cavalrymen were unable to discover them. In June a mail coach was attacked, supposedly by Indians, as it approached Salt Lake City from the west. The driver and messenger were killed and scalped, and the mail destroyed.

On July 8 the Goshutes set a predawn ambush at Canyon Station in western Utah. They waited in hiding until the unsuspecting keeper and his four men had stacked their guns outside and gone to breakfast in a dugout. Apparently the Indians then raised a war cry and massacred the men as they rushed out to reach their firearms. Only four of them were scalped. The fifth was bald, but had a luxuriant growth of whiskers, so the Indians lifted his chin lock as a trophy.

The Canyon massacre ended the Goshute trouble, but later in July a band of Colorado Utes went on a rampage. From the time horses were first acquired by North American Indians, horse thievery among the various tribes on the Great Plains had been an honorable occupation. Long before the Louisiana Purchase they had developed horse stealing into a highly skilled art, and could see no reason except fear of reprisal for not practicing it against the white man—particularly when his horses were eating grass that belonged to the Indians' buffaloes.

In the early spring of 1863 a band of Utes came to Fort Halleck begging for tobacco, sugar, coffee, and other provisions. The generosity of their white brothers, however, proved negligible, so the Utes helped themselves to a few mules from the stage-line relay posts on the Laramie plains. A small company of soldiers was sent out to overtake the thieves, punish them, and get the stock back, but the Indians had no difficulty in making a getaway into the mountains with their plunder. From this adventure they learned that mule meat was as good to eat as horse meat, much easier to come by than venison, and that the few poorly equipped soldiers at Fort Halleck were capable of little in the way of retaliation. As spring advanced the Utes increased their raids on the stage-line stock. Each time, a company of soldiers sallied out to retrieve the stock, but was unsuccessful, and the Utes became increasingly contemptuous of the white man's might.

On July 5 the Utes attacked the Cooper's Creek relay station, about twenty-five miles northwest of present Laramie, Wyoming, and ran off all the mules. Seemingly as a show of contempt for the soldiers, they then attacked Medicine Bow station, less than twenty miles from Fort Halleck. There they not only stole all the stock, but all the firearms, ammunition, and provisions, and then stripped the keeper and his crew. When news of the attacks reached Denver an expedition against the Indians was quickly organized, and six companies of the First Colorado Volunteer Cavalry set out for the Laramie plains under command of Major Wynkoop, accompanied by sixty wagons loaded with two months' supplies, rations, and ammunition. About thirty miles beyond Fort Halleck they found the Utes forted up behind log breastworks on a wooded hillside. A rather sharp battle was fought in which one soldier was killed and four wounded. After putting up a gallant but losing fight throughout the day, the Utes retreated and scattered. The number of their dead was variously estimated at anywhere from twenty to sixty.

That spring several chiefs representing the Arapahoes, Apaches, Cheyennes, and Utes had been taken on a visit to Washington to impress them with the power of the United States Government. Among them was Ouray, the great chief of the Utes, and he alone seems to have been sufficiently impressed. Not long after Ouray's return to Colorado, Governor Evans, accompanied by Lincoln's private secretary, John Nicolay, met with the Utes at Conejos, on the upper Rio Grande. There, due to Ouray's influence, the Utes entered into a peace treaty under which they agreed to move onto a reservation in the Gunnison River area. Shortly before that, Governor Doty of Utah and General Connor had made a peace treaty with the Indians on the western side of the Rockies.

On the other hand, the crafty representatives of the plains Indian tribes who had gone to Washington were not at all impressed by the military might of the United States. Instead, since most of them were warriors by profession and training, they were quick to observe that the war was going badly for the Union and that its entire military strength was needed in the battle lines, and they reasoned that few if any troops would be sent west to punish raiding Indians. The more brilliant of the chiefs, such as Mangas Coloradas of the Apaches and Red Cloud of the Sioux, believed that by concerted action the Indians could drive the white men completely out of the West.

Governor Evans was kept informed of the Indians' actions and attitudes by Elbridge Gerry, a highly intelligent frontiersman married to an Indian woman, and grandson of the Elbridge Gerry who was a signer of the Declaration of Independence. The governor repeatedly notified authorities in Washington that the plains Indians had acquired many firearms and large quantities of ammunition since the outbreak of the Civil War, and that a general uprising was being planned.

The unimpressed visitors to Washington had been correct in their surmise. Lincoln and the War Department were at that time hard pressed to hold the Confederate forces in check, and no forces could be spared for a campaign against Indians in the West who had committed no serious depredations. Evans was instructed to meet with leaders of the recalcitrant tribes, distribute presents, and try to negotiate peace treaties. With Elbridge Gerry as a go-between, he tried to arrange peace parleys with the Sioux,

Cheyennes, and Arapahoes in September, but the Indians were either insolent or indifferent, and no amount of bribing with presents would induce them to attend the proposed meetings. Nevertheless, during the remainder of 1863 there was no further Indian looting along the Overland Mail line.

Although the Indians along the stage line were not on the warpath during the fall of 1863, the officers at Fort Halleck still had their troubles, for the fort had become Jack Slade's favorite hangout. From the time Ben Holladay took over the stage line, Slade had been going from bad to worse, swaggering, drinking, intimidating all with whom he came in contact, and killing wantonly. He was immune from such law as there was in Colorado, for he was outside the jurisdiction of the army, and because he was the fastest gunman on the frontier, no sheriff dared attempt his arrest. He stayed drunk most of the time, beat up drivers and station keepers who displeased him, was time and again involved in brutal brawls or senseless killings, and took delight in treating the officers at Fort Halleck with insolence.

Ben Holladay certainly knew of Slade's escapades, for it is said that he often paid damages for property destroyed in the bully's drunken brawls, so it can only be assumed that he believed the notorious killer a handy man to have around in case of trouble. But in 1863 Slade went so far that even Ben Holladay could not protect him. In a drunken spree at Fort Halleck he entertained himself by shooting up the commissary, and the commandant telegraphed Holladay in no uncertain terms to get Slade out of his employ at once.

It has been reported that Holladay had to come from New York to do the firing himself, and that he was obliged to do it at the point of a Colt .45. Slade hung around Colorado for a few months, drinking, brawling, cursing Holladay and the stage line, and killing at will, and he was suspected of taking part in a $60,000 Government-payroll robbery. Soon afterward he drifted to Virginia City, Montana, where gold had recently been discovered and the toughest outlaws on the continent were congregating. For a while he continued adding to his fame, but in due time a vigilante committee was formed and Slade was among those strung up. He died a coward, whimpering and begging for mercy as he was dragged to the improvised scaffold. His wife had a coffin made with a leakproof zinc lining and, after Slade's body had been ensconced, very appropriately filled it with alcohol. She kept her perpetually pickled husband under her bed until spring, then took the coffin to Salt Lake City in a freight wagon and had him buried in the old Mormon cemetery.

When Holladay fired Slade he replaced him as superintendent on the division west of Latham with twenty-four-year-old Robert Spotswood, as completely opposite from Slade as a man could possibly be. He was a grandson of Sir Alexander Spotswood, the first colonial governor of Virginia, and had attended the University of Missouri for two years. In 1858, at the age of eighteen, he had gone to Leavenworth and taken a job as a bullwhacker hauling freight to Camp Floyd, Utah. By 1860 he had bought mule teams and wagons of his own. During the next two years he made a trading trip to Fort Kearney and hauled three consignments of freight from Atchison to Denver and one to Salt Lake City. In the fall of 1861 he sold his outfit and returned to Leavenworth. He was waiting on the pier for a boat to take him for enlistment in the Union Army when Bela Hughes sent a boy to call him back, as he needed a trustworthy express messenger on the Denver stagecoach. Bob took the job, and six months later Ben Holladay appointed him superintendent on the branch line between Denver and Julesburg.

Bob Spotswood did more for stagecoaching in Colorado and more to improve service on the eastern division of the Overland Stage Line than any other man. He was a natural leader of men, quiet but forceful, who would put up with no ruffians on his division and no brutality to teams, and was one of the finest judges of horses in the West. Following the lead set by Jim Birch on the San Antonio-San Diego line, Butterfield, Hockaday, Chorpenning, and Russell had all used mules exclusively on uninhabited, wilderness, and desert sections of their lines, the theory being that horses could not endure the extremes of weather, scarcity of feed and water, or the punishment of long runs day after day over rugged terrain. Spotswood was convinced that the theory was invalid as far as the central route was concerned. Furthermore, mules in general were stubborn, slow, and lazy. Very soon after being appointed superintendent he began replacing all but the very best and fastest mules on his division with high-grade stage horses, each team matched and balanced as carefully as the wheels of a Concord coach.

Mules, however, were superior to horses in deep sand, so Bob Spotswood matched the best on the division into teams and used them on sandy stretches along the South Platte. Two of the teams became famous: the Spike team and the Benham mules. Between Junction Station (now Fort Morgan) and Fremont's Orchard lay sixteen miles of deep sand, and Frank Root wrote that there was "not a drop of water nor a tree or a shrub for the entire distance." A heavily loaded stagecoach could be pulled over this stretch of road at no faster pace than a walk, and only the Spike team was able to stand up to the grueling task day after day. It was made up of five big brown mules, all the same size, and they were called the spike team because of being hitched in two spans with a single mule in front. The Benham mules, used on the run into and out of Denver, were perfectly matched, had the characteristics of horses, and were the fastest team on the entire Overland Stage Line in getting a heavily loaded stagecoach over sandy road.

Ben Holladay was a showman and gambler in everything he did. In eulogizing him, Frank Root wrote, "Few men in the country, at the time, accumulated wealth more rapidly; but he spent his money freely and was quite lavish with it, squandering vast sums when he was making it so easily. After he had accumulated a snug fortune he went to New York to live. He built one of the most magnificent residences a few miles out, on the Hudson, and called his place Ophir Farm. Subsequently, after he was awarded several fat mail contracts, he built an elegant mansion in Washington. . . . His house contained superb furniture and fittings; a large classical library of handsomely bound volumes, with fine oil paintings by celebrated masters in Europe and America; also a number of elegant bronzes and marble statuary. . . . While holding so many important Government contracts, Mr. Holladay resided, during the sessions of Congress, in Washington, for he had vast interests at stake in the great West and he often needed important congressional legislation."

It was Holladay's custom to make two trips a year over the line, and his equipage was evidently as luxurious as his mansions, for one of his biographers wrote, "Holladay made frequent trips over the line in his private coach, said to have cost several thousand dollars. This special de luxe model had cushioned seats and was mounted on spiral springs, so even his wife, who was not strong, could make the journey without too much discomfort. The interior was equipped with expensive side curtains, beautiful lamps with silver cases, and a writing table. On tour it was followed closely by another coach carrying a cook and servants, as well as supplies of necessities and luxuries for the trip, such as special mattresses, brandy, and cigars. Each coach was drawn by six horses, and the whole gave an impression of importance in keeping with the position of a stagecoach king."

What the biographer failed to mention was that Ben Holladay was brutally ruthless with animals and demanded that each trip be made at breakneck speed without regard for the number of horses and mules killed or ruined in the process. When in Salt Lake City in 1862 he made a large wager that on his return to Atchison he would cut several hours from the fastest time ever made on wheels, including a round trip between Julesburg and Denver. Bob Spotswood, who had by that time replaced practically all the mules on the branch line with horses, drove Holladay from Denver to Julesburg, then a distance of 225 miles, in seventeen and a half hours without killing or breaking down a single animal.

Holladay was so impressed by the performance that, except for a few extremely sandy or rough stretches, he had mules replaced by horses on the entire line. The Pioneer Stage Line had never used mules, and by the end of 1863 Wells, Fargo & Company had replaced all those on the line between Virginia City and Salt Lake. Without the change to horses it is extremely doubtful that overland stagecoaching would ever have been surrounded with the dash and glamour that cling to it even today, and certainly the time for a transcontinental journey could never have been reduced to seventeen days.

The matched teams that Bob Spotswood put on the Overland Stage Line became famous throughout the United States, and for more than half a century lived clearly in the memory of Coloradoans who had seen and known them. There was a matchless team of six snow-white albinos on the Georgetown branch and a team of midnight blacks on the Central City run, and the "catfish" team of dappled grays set an all-time record by making the fifteen-

Post office notice about the proper care of horses and mules. (Courtesy, Western History Department, Denver Public Library.)

STAGE HORSES AND MULES

The U. S. postal regulations contain this clause:

"57. The horses or mules used for carrying the mails must be suitable for the work and properly cared for. The cruel treatment of an animal while in the performance of service will be considered cause for imposing a fine on the contractor or requiring the dismissal of the driver."

Any passenger or other person who sees stage animals sore, lame, poor, overworked, beaten or in any way abused or neglected should notify

POST OFFICE DEPARTMENT, Washington, D. C., or

The State Bureau of Child and Animal Protection,

N. B. Destruction of these notices is a criminal offense, punishable by fine and imprisonment.

State House,   DENVER, COLO.

mile uphill run from Denver to Golden in fifty-five minutes flat.

In 1937 James Harvey of the Colorado Historical Society interviewed Alonzo H. Allen of Longmont, who as a boy had moved with his parents to Colorado Territory in 1863. After more than seventy years, the stagecoaches with their matched teams lived as vividly in his mind as if they had stopped at his mother's "stagehouse" but yesterday:

At the time of our arrival, the settlement in this locality was known as Burlington, located just south of the St. Vrain River, at the south edge of the present city of Longmont. The town of Burlington consisted mostly of one general store, operated by J. K. Manners. It was located on the west side of our present highway. The trail or stage road followed pretty much the course of our present highway, and came on north from Burlington through the prairie along what is now Longmont's main street. . . .

In 1864 Bob Spotswood, superintendent of the Overland Stage Company, contracted with my mother to operate a "stagehouse" or hotel for the accommodation of passengers upon the stages, the drivers, barn men, and others connected with the company. . . . For regular meals to stage coach passengers mother was paid $1.50. Maybe that sounds a little steep, but when you consider that flour cost $25.00 per hundred sack . . . you can see that there was some expense to serving meals. The average meal would consist of a big bowl of good soup as a starter; the main course, served family style, having plenty of meat—usually beef, buffalo, antelope, or deer; vegetables, such as potatoes, squash, and beans cooked with plenty of salt pork; light bread; fruit, usually apples dried on strings; home-made pastries; coffee, or tea.

The Overland coaches were pulled by six horses, all matched in size and color—blacks, bays, grays, sorrels, and one of our coaches was pulled by a six of creams with white tails. They ranged in size from 1,250 pounds for the wheelers to 1,100 for swings and 1,000 for leaders. Every horse had his own genuine Concord [James R. Hill & Co.] harness and Concord collar, and every harness was cleaned with castile soap suds before it was hung up directly behind the horse to which it belonged. Bob Spotswood, making regular trips on the coaches or with team and buckboard, with the shoers and veterinarian, would travel from station to station and inspect every horse.

In a somewhat earlier interview, Dr. T. A. Hughes, son of Bela Hughes, said, "The stage horses, rather heavier than the saddle stock, and similarly well-bred and well-cared for were able to outdistance the Indian ponies, even with the handicap of a loaded stage. Colonel Spotswood, division superintendent, who bought these horses, must have had an extraordinary eye for a good horse to

[240]

have been so wonderfully successful in his selection of stage stock."
("Colonel" was an honorary title of respect often accorded to
venerated stagecoach operators of the old West.)

By 1863 there were numerous "stagehouses" being operated by
settlers along the Overland Stage Line between Atchison and
Denver, but few of the frontier women served such meals as Alonzo
Allen's mother put before the passengers. William Russell, an impractical idealist, had tried to attract passengers to his line by
providing them in the midst of the wilderness with the comforts
of life which he himself enjoyed. The excellence of meals at his
"home" stations had won him high praise in the Denver and Leavenworth newspapers, but it is doubtful that they attracted a single
additional passenger, and the tremendous expense of manning and
maintaining these hostelries cost his firm's unfortunate creditors
untold thousands of dollars.

Ben Holladay was no idealist. Furthermore, he had absolutely no
interest in either the comfort or praise of his passengers. To him
they were simply a source of profit; to be acquired by killing off
competition and gouged for all the traffic would bear when obliged
to ride his stagecoaches. As for hostelries, he considered them
folderol and foolishness. Home stations at intervals of fifty to sixty
miles were necessary for lodging and feeding drivers at the ends
of their runs, for keeping a few spare horses, and for making meals
available to passengers, but nothing further.

Except for the Mormons and pockets of population attracted by
the discovery of gold or silver, the westward expansion of the
United States followed lines of transportation and communication.
When the Pony Express was inaugurated the only non-Indian habi-
tations between Fort Kearney and Denver were C.O.C.&P.P. way
stations and relay posts. By the summer of 1863 ranches had been
established at fairly frequent intervals the entire length of the rich
North and South Platte valleys.

Practically all these early ranchers settled along the stage line
on the south side of the Platte and put up their buildings at or
very near a station or relay post. This was not only done as a
means of defense against Indian attacks, but to have a nearby market, as thousands of tons of hay and bushels of grain were needed
each year to feed the stage-line horses, while great quantities of
meat and other ranch products were required for feeding crews
and passengers. Then too, during eight months of the year thousands of emigrants moved westward along the Overland Trail, and
hundreds of wagon trains creaked by, hauling freight to Denver,

the Colorado boom towns, and Salt Lake City. Almost invariably, they made their night camps at a stage station and often traded with the rancher for feed and provisions.

In many cases Ben Holladay's superintendents made arrangements with the ranchers, as Bob Spotswood had with Alonzo Allen's mother, to operate "stagehouses" at the home stations and to board not only the stage-line crew but its horses. These arrangements were extremely valuable to Ben Holladay for they not only saved wages but cut down the tremendous cost of hauling feed and provisions great distances, and decidedly reduced his risk of loss by Indian attacks.

At its height old Julesburg, being a junction and division point, boasted nearly a dozen buildings, all constructed during Russell's extravagant operation of the line and built of logs hauled more than a hundred miles by ox teams. They included the stage station, telegraph office, warehouse, stable, blacksmith's shop, a general store, and a billiard saloon which "dispensed at all hours of the day and night the vilest of liquor at two bits a glass." For a hundred miles east of Denver the stations were built of rough-sawed lumber hauled down from the mountains in 1859, but all the others west of Fort Kearney were either of sod or sun-dried adobe bricks. Although Mark Twain's description in *Roughing It* is certainly exaggerated, there were doubtlessly numerous stations where, before the coming of the ranchers and their wives, the exaggeration would have been slight:

The station buildings were long, low huts, made of sundried mud-colored bricks, laid up without mortar. The roofs which had no slant to them worth speaking of, were thatched and sodded or covered with a thick layer of earth, and from this sprung a pretty rank growth of weeds and grass. The buildings consisted of barns, stable-room for twelve or fifteen horses, and a hut for an eating-room for passengers. This latter had bunks in it for the station keeper and a hostler or two. . . . In place of a window there was a square hole about large enough for a man to crawl through, but this had no glass in it. There was no flooring, but the ground was packed hard. There was no stove but the fireplace served all needful purposes. There were no shelves, no cupboards, no closets. In a corner stood an open sack of flour, and nestling against its base were a couple of black and venerable tin coffee pots, a tin teapot, a little bag of salt, and a side of bacon. . . . The table was a greasy board on stilts, and the tablecloth and napkins had not come—and they were not looking for them, either.

Judging from such names as "Dirty Woman Ranch," there must have been some equally squalid stagehouses after the coming of the settlers, but passengers on Ben Holladay's Overland Stage Line gained nothing by complaining. They could pay the price and eat what was set before them or go hungry. Even the drivers learned better than to complain at certain stations. The *Rocky Mountain News* carried a story of one of the boys who made that mistake. After giving him a thorough tongue-lashing, the "lady of the house" wound up her diatribe by telling him, "I've been married three times, am the mother of thirteen children, and have had two ribs broke and lost one eye, but I can just whip any damn driver on the Holladay line!"

With all Ben Holladay's insolence and abuse of the public, and although he was ruthless with any employee whom he believed to be shiftless, cowardly, or disloyal, he was quick to commend a job well done and treated those who worked for him with no trace of the master-to-servant condescension customary to wealthy employers of that period. If a man had performed beyond the call of duty, Ben was quite apt, on his next trip over the line, to present him with an initialed gold watch. Or if a keeper's wife had particularly pleased him with a meal, he would slap a twenty-dollar gold piece onto the table and boom, "By God, Hatty, that was a Jim-dandy feed! Keep the change. Understand?"

But the thing that probably endeared Ben Holladay to his help more than anything else—particularly to those who had been on the line when it was known as the Clean Out of Cash and Poor Pay—was that they never had to wait a single day for their pay when it was due. As was then the custom for employees who were furnished board and lodging, pay day was four times a year. As regularly as the seasons changed, David Street made his round, counting out each man's wages in gold pieces and settling accounts with the ranchers along the line. Because of the mail contract, Holladay issued a written rule that any employee who drank on the job would be discharged and fined three months' wages. None was ever fined, although Frank Root tells us that "nearly all were so fond of an occasional 'eye opener' that it was unnecessary ever to give them a second invitation to 'take a smile.' "

The women along the stage line were fully as hard working as their husbands, and had less opportunity for social life of any kind. But on the first Saturday night after payday there was always a dance at one or more of the home stations on each division. These were the big social events of the year, and no frontier woman missed one if she could possibly get there. Even with a blizzard blowing, some of them are known to have wrapped their children in blankets with hot rocks at their feet, packed them in a wagon bed filled with hay, driven fifty miles to a pay-day dance, danced all night, and driven home the next day.

The movies, television, and western fiction have surrounded stagecoach travel in the West with an aura of romance and glamour, but if those who rode Ben Holladay's stagecoaches and wrote of it are to be believed, there was nothing romantic or glamorous about it. In *From the Atlantic to the Pacific, Overland*, published in 1866, Demas Barnes wrote:

The condition of one man's running stages to make money, while another seeks to ride for pleasure, are not in harmony to produce comfort. Coaches will be overloaded . . . passengers will get sick, a gentleman of gallantry will hold the baby, children will cry . . . passengers will get angry, the drivers will swear, the sensitive will shrink . . . and the dirt [is] almost unendurable. . . . Stop over nights? No you wouldn't! To sleep on the sand floor of a one-story sod house or adobe hut, without a chance to wash, with miserable food, uncongenial companionship, loss of a seat in a coach until one comes empty, etc., won't work. A through ticket and fifteen inches of seat, with a fat man on one side, a poor widow on the other, a baby on your lap, a bandbox over your head, and three or four persons immediately in front, leaning against your knees, makes the picture, as well as your sleeping place for the trip. . . . I have just finished six days and nights of this thing; and I am free to say, until I forget a great many things now very visible to me, I shall not undertake it again.

Stagecoach travel has had few more loyal supporters than Frank Root, but even he wrote, "Being jostled about when the road was rough, it would be anything but pleasant for nine crowded passengers, inside a coach, riding six days and nights between the Missouri and Denver. It occasionally happened that there would be a fat woman among the passengers, perhaps weighing 250 pounds. It was a great relief, however, for such people, at the end of each ten or twelve miles, to get out and exercise two or three minutes while the horses were being changed at the station."

In summer the coach was constantly surrounded by a cloud of dust raised by the horses' hoofs, and in crossing the prairies the heat inside a stagecoach often rose to above a hundred and ten degrees. After an hour's ride on a dry, hot day, passengers looked like soft-coal miners coming off shift. From head to foot they were covered with grime, their faces streaked with rivulets of mud from trickling sweat or tears from dust-inflamed eyes.

To break the monotony of an overland journey, the passengers often sang hymns, recounted their own experiences, or bored their fellow travelers with recitals of their misfortunes. As day wore on toward evening nerves became frazzled, tempers flared, children cried, and the everlasting dust and jolting seemed intolerable. There was no such thing as a night's sleep. When darkness fell the passengers dozed in their places or, if there was room, curled up in a seat corner like a dog on a rug. But many a time in the dead of night a wheel would drop into a chuck hole, the coach lurch forward on the thoroughbraces, and all the dozing passengers be tumbled into a heap on the floor. If the night were particularly hot and the coach crowded, the younger men would bed down on the top, tying themselves with rope to the baggage railing to keep from being thrown off.

In winter, windblown snow seeped in around the curtains to cover the floor, the seats, and the passengers. Night temperatures were sometimes below zero. Passengers wrapped themselves in buffalo robes and huddled tightly together to conserve as much body heat as possible. Half frozen, they crawled out at relay posts to stir their blood into circulation by stamping their feet and thrashing their arms. Then—with a cup of hot coffee for the women and children, if any—a swig from the keeper's jug for the men, a fresh team, and maybe a few hot rocks from the fireplace wrapped in gunny sacks—they were off for the next relay post, two to four hours farther down the line.

In spring, when a sudden thaw turned the black gumbo soil of the North Platte valley into a morass of hub-deep sticky mud, six stout horses had all they could do to drag an empty Concord coach through the worst stretches. The passengers—men, women, and children, young and old—had to get out and slog through the mire, often a mile or more, until solid ground was reached. But when the weather was mild and the road firm there was no finer stretch of stage road in the world than the four hundred miles along the valleys of the North and South Platte rivers, and few stagecoach journeys were more enjoyable.

Between Fort Kearney and mile-high Denver there is a rise of more than four thousand feet, but it is so gradual as to be imperceptible. The only really rough going was at O'Fallon's Bluffs, a dozen miles or so east of present Ogallala, Nebraska, but on the opposite side of the river. For a few rods the winding road pitched downward through the bluffs at an angle of nearly forty-five degrees. Locking the wheels held a heavy stagecoach back so little that, to keep from being run over, the horses had to make the descent at an all-out gallop, while the coach rocked and rolled like a ship in a storm. At the time the main line of the mail route was moved to the Cherokee Trail a safe detour road was opened around the south side of the bluffs, but it increased the distance by several miles. Thereafter the Devil's Drive cutoff was seldom used unless an annoyed driver with a light load and a few belts of frontier whiskey aboard had a particularly obnoxious tenderfoot whom he wanted to give a worthwhile fright.

When the Leavenworth and Pike's Peak stages first started running over the Platte Valley route, great buffalo herds in western Nebraska often delayed a coach for hours and the howling of prairie wolves at night made shivers run up and down the passengers' backs. As traffic over the trail increased with the Colorado gold rush, fewer and fewer buffalo grazed in the valleys of the North and South Platte. Although they were no rarity along the stage line, by the close of 1862 the great herds seldom came farther north than the valley of the Republican River, along the Kansas-Nebraska boundary.

Even without the buffalo, the Platte valleys were a sportsman's paradise. The rich bottomlands, waist high in grass, were dotted with herds of antelope; geese, ducks, and sandhill cranes abounded along the streams; and on the rolling hills that skirted the valleys there were countless thousands of prairie chickens, grouse, and sage hens. Today the Rockies, less than ten miles away, are often obscured from Denver by a brown pall of smog, but in stagecoaching days the atmosphere in Colorado was crystal clear. Pike's Peak was visible for more than a hundred miles, and from fifty miles away the Rockies looked as if they were just beyond the next row of hills.

19

"May the Lord Have Mercy upon Them"

IN 1862 gold was discovered in the Boise Basin of Idaho and at Bannack in southwestern Montana. Early in 1863 a rich strike was made at Alder Gulch, sixty miles east of Bannack, and Virginia City sprang into being almost overnight. Within a week A. J. Oliver & Company began running stage wagons between the new boom town and Bannack, from where a pony express was being run weekly to Fort Bridger, carrying half-ounce letters at fifty cents apiece. Soon afterward Oliver stocked the four-hundred-mile trail from Virginia City to Salt Lake City with mules, stage wagons, and a few old coaches and then established triweekly service, carrying passengers at $150 apiece and letters at a dollar each. At about the same time two competing stage lines, one operated by Peabody and the other by Caldwell, went into operation over the same trail between Bannack and Salt Lake City.

In the meantime gold had been discovered at a dozen or more localities in Idaho. By the summer of 1863 ten thousand gold rushers were camped in the Boise Basin, Idaho City had been founded and had boomed to a population of six thousand, and nearby Placerville had grown to five thousand. Since early spring there had been a veritable stampede westward from the Missouri. Ben Holladay doubled the stage fare and the express and excess baggage rates, and put on extra coaches, but Root said that "it was impossible for the stage line to carry one-fourth of the big rush." Colin B. Goodykoontz, in *Colorado as Seen by a Home Missionary, 1863–68*, wrote that seats on coaches leaving Atchison for Salt Lake City were booked a week or more in advance, and that a man with a reservation on a stagecoach ready to pull away could sell his seat and ticket for a premium of from forty to fifty dollars.

Passengers for Salt Lake City were given preference over those for Denver, and every coach carried as many as could be seated: nine inside, one on the seat with the driver and express messenger, and three on the roof seat behind them. Then, unless the load was already as heavy as a six-horse team could pull and keep reasonably up to schedule, sacks of mail were packed between the legs of passengers inside the coach. Letters, reports, and books of the time—with the exception of Root's *The Overland Stage to California*—indicate clearly that on the Holladay stagecoaches express and passengers were given priority over nonrevenue baggage and the United States mail. Mrs. Walter Taft wrote that it sometimes took two weeks for a traveler's baggage to arrive after he had completed his journey. Demas Barnes wrote, after the line had been rerouted through Denver, "I have seen the stages pass through here loaded with passengers and not carry a pound of mail, while perhaps two weeks' mail, or more, lay heaped in the office."

Traveling packed into a stagecoach with sacks of mail must have been anything but enjoyable, for the Overland Trail was crowded with gold rushers driving their own vehicles and freighters hauling supplies and provisions to Idaho and Montana mining camps, Colorado boom towns, Denver, and Salt Lake City. Root reports that along the Platte River "hundreds of wagons, some drawn by six yoke of cattle, passed over the road daily" and that "in hot weather the dust encountered was almost intolerable." With the coming of winter there were fewer freighters and gold rushers on the road, but as the snow deepened coaches had to be loaded less heavily, it was impossible to maintain schedules during storms, and the mails went through irregularly.

In January 1864 a resolution was introduced in the Senate for an inquiry into the failures of the overland mail during the preceding two months, but the Postmaster General rallied to the contractors' defense. In his annual report he stated, "The service on this route has been performed during the past year with commendable regularity and efficiency, and no accident, Indian hostility, or other casualty has occurred to prevent or retard the safe and prompt transmission of mails and passengers, the trips being, with rare exceptions, accomplished within the schedule time."

In its edition of February 2 the *San Francisco Bulletin* also rushed to the defense of the mail contractors, evidently in fear that the mail contract might be canceled. "An overland daily mail has always been a favorite of the California public," it declared, and "when it fails during a month or two of the winter to serve us as handsomely as it always does in summer, it does so from no fault of those who undertake to maintain it. . . . It would be a misfortune indeed if, for any cause save and except the completion of long sections of the railway between the Missouri and the Pacific we should be deprived of this method of getting to and from the Atlantic States in person or by correspondence."

It was not until the middle of June, however, that the same newspaper reported all the winter's accumulation of stranded mail to have been brought through and the service back on a regular daily schedule. By that time Ben Holladay had a whole panful of other fish frying over a hot fire, and from then on the California mail was relegated to the position of a necessary nuisance.

Both the stage lines operating between Salt Lake City and Bannack were making huge profits, and Oliver & Company's Virginia City line was one of the richest gold strikes in the Idaho-Montana district. Larry Barsness wrote of it in *Gold Camp*, "Ten people crammed into a Concord coach, as they frequently were, were worth $1500 to Oliver three times a week going and three times a week coming, a most profitable venture. The beauty of the enterprise was that the trip would have been profitable without passengers: northbound, the boot was full of letters for Virginia City forwarded from Utah at one dollar each, and, southbound, letters for home carried to Utah at the same price."

Ben Holladay was not a man to sit back and watch another reap the rich harvest from a field of endeavor into which he had set his own plow, and by early spring in 1864 it became apparent that he had done some valuable fence building in Washington. In March reports reached Salt Lake City that Holladay had secured two contracts for mail service out of that city—one to Virginia City, Montana, the other to Walla Walla, Washington, via Boise, Idaho— and that he was planning to put stagecoaches on both routes and begin passenger and express service by the first of July.

The reports were no idle rumors. Holladay had secured a two-year contract at $156,000 per year for triweekly mail service, beginning on July 1, 1864, between Salt Lake City and Walla Walla, which was soon thereafter extended to The Dalles, Oregon, and the annual compensation increased to $186,000. The second was a four-year contract, at $13.271 annually, for carrying the mail triweekly to Bannack and Virginia City from Fort Hall, the point on the Overland Trail (a few miles north of present Pocatello, Idaho) where mail coaches from Salt Lake City to Boise would turn westward along Snake River.

There was at that time no mail or passenger service between Salt

Lake City and Boise, but in 1863 a triweekly service, similar to that of Oliver & Company's on the Virginia City line, had been started between The Dalles and Boise. Then, early in 1864, a competing stage line, with widely separated relay stations, was put onto the Overland Trail between Walla Walla and Boise by George F. Thomas and Company. At about the same time a third firm, Hailey and Ish, put a line into operation between Umatilla Landing on the Columbia River and Boise. They bought their first stagecoach, a secondhand Concord, at Shasta, California. It was driven over the California-Oregon stage road to Portland, shipped to The Dalles on a Columbia River steamer, then driven on to Umatilla, the entire trip taking fifty-nine days.

On March 21 Holladay sent an agent, Nat Stein, to Salt Lake City to hire help and supervise the construction of relay posts on the new lines. At about the same time he assigned Bob Spotswood to buy upwards of three hundred horses and mules, thirty passenger vehicles, ten freight wagons for hauling feed and supplies, harness and all the other equipment necessary for putting stage lines into operation; to get it to Salt Lake City; and to have the line to Virginia City in operation on July 1.

The trail from Salt Lake City to Virginia City was over approximately the same route as present U.S. Highway 91. The 180 miles of road between the Mormon capital and Fort Hall had been a main emigrant thoroughfare for twenty years, and although far from being a boulevard it was a well-improved road for those times. But the only road for the remaining 225 miles was a skein of often widely separated pack trails and wagon tracks following Snake River upstream to its sharp eastward bend above Idaho Falls, on northward across the arid Snake River plains to Signal Peak, over the Continental Divide by way of a wheel-shattering pass, and down to the headwaters of the Missouri in newly established Montana Territory. The only passenger vehicles durable enough for service over such a road were Concord coaches and mud wagons, but to have put new coaches on the line would have been reckless extravagance—and Ben Holladay was not given to extravagance in the operation of his stage lines.

Spotswood was obliged to scour the river ports in Kansas and western Missouri to find the necessary vehicles, equipment, mules, horses, and drivers who could handle a six-horse team on rough roads. When, on the way back he and his men reached Julesburg, a telegram had just been received reporting that Cherry Creek was in flood, the Denver city hall and the *Rocky Mountain News* offices had been swept away, and the South Platte was rising rapidly.

To avoid the flood, Spotswood forded the river at once and continued westward along the abandoned stage line through South Pass. At Poison Springs the little caravan was attacked by a strong band of Indians, well supplied with muskets and ammunition. A sharp skirmish was fought in which two of Spotswood's men and several horses and mules were killed, but the rest of the stock was kept from stampeding and the Indians withdrew with their dead when they found themselves getting the worst of the battle. Delayed by the attack and the necessity for caution, Spotswood was unable to reach Salt Lake City until June 20. But he had the line stocked in time, and the first Holladay stage pulled away for Bannack and Virginia City on July 1, 1864.

It is probable that the entire effort was put into readying the Bannack-Virginia City route, where there was the greatest amount of passenger and express business to be had, and over which Caldwell, Peabody, and Oliver & Company were operating. In any event, the line to the northwest was not put into operation until August 11, and Holladay's stages ran no farther than Boise, for he had made a subcontract with George F. Thomas and Company to carry the mail triweekly between Boise and Walla Walla, and on to The Dalles when the route was extended.

Even though service was not started until August 11, the Postmaster General's annual report showed that Holladay was paid $39,000 for carrying the mail on this route until September 30, the date on which it was extended to The Dalles and the compensation increased to $186,000 annually—an overpayment of nearly $18,000.

With the Virginia City line already in operation triweekly between Salt Lake City and Fort Hall, and with the Thomas and Company subcontract, Holladay was obliged to construct, stock, and equip only the 265-mile portion of the route that lay between Fort Hall and Boise. The reported time schedule for the entire route was sixteen days and eight hours: equal to less than sixty miles per day, or about half the speed maintained between Atchison and Sacramento. With so slow a schedule, infrequent relays of fresh teams were needed, so it is extremely improbable that more than five stations were established between Fort Hall and Boise. In that case, the $18,000 overpayment by the Post Office Department was unquestionably sufficient to cover Holladay's entire investment in the $186,000-per-year mail route. One might suspect that there had been some "straw" bidding in connection with Holladay's securing these two contracts, but there is no proof of such manipulation.

Mail service had barely been started on the route to The Dalles when Ben Holladay set about killing off his competition on the Montana line. On September 1 he reduced the fare between Salt Lake City and either Virginia City or Bannack from $150 to $25 and put on enough extra coaches and mud wagons to handle all the passenger and express business; within three months he had driven his poorly equipped competition off the road. By that time gold had been discovered in Last Chance Gulch, about a hundred miles north of Virginia City, and Helena had become a populous gold-rush city.

As soon as Oliver had been run off the Salt Lake City route he went east, bought new stagecoaches, and was back in Virginia City with them early the following May. With the best horses he could buy locally, he established daily passenger, mail, and express service between Virginia City and Helena. Probably in hope of avoiding competition from Holladay, he made the 125-mile run in the amazingly fast time of fourteen hours and set his rates low: fifteen dollars for passengers one way, or twenty-five for round trips, twenty-five cents for letters, two dollars for extra suitcases, and five dollars for trunks. Not long thereafter, the Post Office Department decided to establish a mail route between the two cities. Oliver and Company made the mistake of being the low bidder, and was awarded the contract.

Ben Holladay let Oliver operate through the winter, when the going over the mountain roads was so rugged that his new coaches were badly damaged and he was obliged to double his rates in order to meet expenses. But with the arrival of spring "The Napoleon of the West," as Ben Holladay had sarcastically been dubbed by the local newspapers, moved in a string of brand-new seventeen-passenger Concord coaches and several of his fastest six-horse teams from the main line. In the manner that had won him his Napoleonic title, he cut the passenger fare between Virginia City and Helena to $2.50, made no charge for excess baggage, carried express at the same rates that freighters were charging for flour, and reduced the running time to ten hours. Within two months Oliver was again driven off the road, obliged to assign his mail contract, and put his worse-for-wear coaches onto feeder lines to outlying mining camps.

With a monopoly on stage-line operations in Montana, Holladay put the squeeze on everyone obliged to travel or ship express or valuables by any faster conveyance than a plodding wagon train. He had no sooner driven Oliver and Company off the Virginia City-Helena road than he doubled the running time, replaced the new Concord coaches with any sort of vehicle that would carry a

Receipt for letter and packages shipped on Ben Holladay's Overland Stage Line. (Courtesy, Western History Department, Denver Public Library.)

load, and raised the one-way fare to $37.50. Larry Barsness wrote, "There was of course no rebate of fare to passengers who had paid for first-class travel and had to put up with any conveyance Holladay chose to thrust upon them. Nor did Holladay ever rebate any fare to the passengers who were fool enough to pay out good money to ride the coach from Salt Lake City to Virginia City in the spring, and who found that they also had to push, or at least get out in the boggiest part of the road and wade through gumbo so that the vehicle could move. These mud-bedaubed trips were so common they became a wry joke among the b'hoys who called them, 'walking to Virginia City on the coach . . .'"

The greater part of the gold from the Montana mines was shipped to the East by Holladay coaches. No report of the rate for carrying gold between Montana and the Missouri River has been found, but the *Rocky Mountain News* reported that in a single day the Holladay Express office there had shipped $68,000 in gold to Atchison at the rate of 1½ per cent. As the distance from Helena to Atchison was nearly three times as great, it is to be presumed that the express rate on gold was also triple that from Denver.

One traveler wrote to the editor of the *Montana Post* after a

[253]

trip on which six passengers, the driver, and a full load of express and baggage were all piled into a seatless "hack," making it necessary over the rough road for the passengers to "lock hands and hang across the load saddle bag fashion. . . . If the earnestness and deep sincerity with which the maledictions are uttered could insure their taking effect, I would not stand in Ben Holladay's shoes for *two* mail contracts."

Ben Holladay was not in the least disturbed by the maledictions being heaped upon him by his passengers, shippers, or anyone else. Apparently his sole interest was in wringing every possible nickel from the United States Government and those unfortunate enough to be dependent upon stage service in the territory he had staked out for his own. And he was eminently successful at it, for Frank Root, who was doubtless in a position to know, wrote, "Receipts from passenger and express business were very large, often being from $150,000 to $200,000 per month. At one time fare from Atchison to Placerville was $600; to Helena, Mont., $525; extra baggage 75 cents to $1.50 per pound. . . . The advance in rates of fare from time to time appeared to make very little difference in the extent of the passenger traffic. Still there was an occasional party whose time was not limited who would buy a team and go across by private conveyance, being on the road at least three weeks between the Missouri river and Denver, rather than pay what he considered an extortionate price for passage. Nearly every business man, however, whose time was money to him took passage on the stage, no matter what the fare might be."

Nor were exorbitant fares and baggage rates the only way in which travelers on Holladay's lines were gouged. It is reported that meals on the twenty-day trip between Atchison and Helena cost $200, and were often inedible, while between Denver and Atchison the charge for meals was greater than the passenger fare charged by the railroads a few years later. Passengers were required to carry their own blankets, and anyone stopping for rest along the way was charged two dollars for space to lie on the dirt floor of a relay station. In *Missouri-Montana Highways*, H. A. Trexler tells of a bishop's wife who was obliged to pay an excess baggage charge of $195 on her trunk.

Although the express and passenger business from the Idaho gold-rush towns was nowhere near so great as that from Montana, it was highly lucrative and Holladay made an effort to maintain regular service. Denver and San Francisco newspapers, however, complained bitterly that he was doing so at the expense of mail service to their cities. Inasmuch as the Overland Mail Company's contract would expire the following June, one might have expected Holladay to be worried by such complaints in the public press about the manner in which he was fulfilling his subcontract on the portion of the route east of Salt Lake City. But Ben Holladay was not in the least concerned.

The expiring million-dollar contract stipulated twenty-day service between the Missouri River terminal of the line and San Francisco during eight months of each year, and twenty-three-day service during the remaining four months. In the summer of 1863 Holladay was already negotiating with the Post Office Department for the new contract, but on a sharply reduced time schedule with a corresponding increase in compensation. In a dramatic piece of showmanship to demonstrate the speed with which his organization was capable of carrying the California mail, Holladay had fast teams spotted at frequent intervals along the Overland route between Salt Lake City and Folsom, as well as on his own section. Then, in his private coach, he made the run of nearly two thousand miles from Folsom to Atchison in twelve days and two hours. There is no record of how many horses Holladay killed or ruined in his spectacular demonstration, but Albert D. Richardson, correspondent for the *Boston Journal*, estimated that "it cost him 20,000 dollars in wear and tear of stock and vehicles."

The Postmaster General was sufficiently impressed by the demonstration that in October 1863 he invited bids at sharply reduced time on a new four-year contract or contracts, beginning on July 1, 1864. The successful bidder for the eastern section was to furnish eleven-day service between Atchison or St. Joseph and Salt Lake City from April 1 to December 1 and fourteen-day service for the remaining four months of the year, and to supply Denver with daily mail service from the nearest main-line station. The time schedule on the western section was set at five days from April through November and six days for the other four months. Also, the successful bidder was required to furnish Virginia City, Nevada, with daily mail service. A successful bidder for the entire route was to meet the provisions stipulated for both sections.

There is little doubt that Postmaster General Blair expected Ben Holladay and the Overland Mail Company, or Wells, Fargo & Company, to be the bidders for a new contract, but Holladay withheld his bid until the Post Office Department had published its fifth invitation in the spring of 1864.

When the winter of 1863–64 set in, mail was again stacked up at way stations along the Holladay section of the line, as had been the case during the two preceding winters. It was well known in Washington that the fifty or more tons of newspapers and public documents being mailed annually to the West Coast had been a drag on the Overland service from the time of its transfer to the central route, and it was no secret there that large quantities of this inferior-class mail had been jettisoned en route to lighten loads and fill bog holes. To relieve the situation, Congress passed an act in March 1864 requiring that, after June 30 of that year, all newspaper and document mail between the East and the Pacific Coast be transported by sea.

Soon after passage of the act, complaints about irregularity of first-class mail on the eastern division of the Overland route became so persistent and angry that a congressional investigation was threatened, and Postmaster General Blair sent a special agent to inspect the line and ascertain the cause. He reported that numerous badly needed bridges and ferries were lacking on the section of the line between Atchison and Salt Lake City, resulting in delay of the mail whenever streams were swollen. Nevertheless, the Postmaster General recommended renewing the contract with the existing carriers, and a bill to authorize such a renewal was introduced in the Senate. Its passage was blocked by Senator John Conness of California.

Although the old contract would expire at midnight on June 30 and bids on the new contract had been invited as early as October 1863, the Post Office Department extended the time limit for the acceptance of bids until 3:00 P.M. on June 14, 1864. Ben Holladay, evidently in a maneuver to delay the closing until so late that no other bidder would be able to stock the eastern division of the line and begin service on July 1, withheld his bid until close to the time limit.

When, at the appointed time, the bids were opened, there were several for service between Atchison and Salt Lake City. The lowest was $375,000 per annum, submitted by Joseph Burbank of Falls City, Nebraska, and the highest was Ben Holladay's bid of $385,000. For service over the entire route, the highest bid was $880,000 per annum by the Overland Mail Company, the lowest was $750,000 by John A. Heistand of Pennsylvania, and the next lowest Ben Holladay's bid of $820,000.

Postmaster General Blair awarded a contract at $160,000 per annum for steamship transportation of newspaper and document mail between the Atlantic and Pacific seaboards, with service to begin on June 30, 1864. It was obvious, however, that neither of the low bidders for supplying mail service on the Overland route would be able to stock the line and begin carrying the first class mail on that date. The Postmaster General therefore made arrangements for the Overland Mail Company and Ben Holladay to continue service until the end of September, at the rate of compensation specified in the old contract.

On June 16 an assistant postmaster general mailed a letter to Heistand, informing him that his bid of $750,000 per annum had been accepted, asking him to sign and return the contract at once, and instructing him to be prepared to take over the mail service on the central overland route on October 1. On the same date Heistand telegraphed Postmaster General Blair that conditions had arisen that would prevent him from rendering the service, and that he therefore wished to withdraw his bid. Also on the same date Holladay wrote Blair from New York that inasmuch as Heistand had withdrawn his bid, he (Holladay) was legally entitled to the contract at his own next lowest bid of $820,000 per annum. In the letter he cited acts of Congress that required the Postmaster General to award contracts to the lowest remaining bidder, provided he could furnish satisfactory bond and had not failed on a previous mail contract.

It was the end of the month before the *Rocky Mountain News* received a report of the very evident straw-bidding manipulation from its Washington correspondent. The publisher jumped to the conclusion that the maneuver would succeed, and in his issue of June 30, 1864, voiced the sentiments of the vast majority of westerners dependent upon mail, express, or passenger service on the central overland route: "The probability is that Mr. Heistand was playing stool pigeon for Mr. Holladay. If so, he ought to be histed. At any rate the great western autocrat has unquestionably become the assignee of Mr. Heistand's contract. For four years more Colorado, Utah, and Nevada belong to Ben Holladay for a footstool and may the Lord have mercy upon them."

The newspaper publisher was not alone in suspecting manipulation. The House of Representatives passed a resolution to secure full information from Postmaster General Blair and investigate the bidding and negotiations for the central overland mail contract. The Senate quickly appointed a committee to consider the House resolution, whereupon Blair wrote to one of the committeemen, enclosing Holladay's letter of June 16 and saying that he wished to reserve his own opinion regarding the legal points raised by Holladay until the committee had reached a decision.

To further complicate matters, Heistand wrote to the Postmaster General on June 21, saying that the letter of June 16 had been received, informing him that he had been awarded the contract, and that he was now prepared to post the required bond and furnish the service specified. Ben Holladay then left no doubt that he was either in direct communication with Heistand or being kept closely informed of developments by someone high in the Post Office Department. On June 22 he telegraphed Blair from New York, informing him high handedly that the contract could not legally be awarded to Heistand after his once having withdrawn his bid, and that he himself would carry the United States mail on the central overland route for the ensuing four years at his bid of $820,000 annually.

California's Senator Conness, however, led a fight in Congress to prohibit the Postmaster General from awarding the contract to Holladay. To counteract Conness' opposition, Holladay marshaled every resource at his command. He entertained congressmen lavishly and almost continuously at his sumptuous Washington home

The Overland Trail mud wagon of 1866, shown many years later with a railroad train in the background. (Courtesy, Union Pacific Railroad Museum.)

while his friend General Ingalls and his cousin Bela Hughes carried on a campaign of high-pressure lobbying. For a while Senator Conness was able to maintain his block, but before the middle of July Ben Holladay had outmaneuvered him, and Congress passed a resolution authorizing Postmaster General Blair to contract with the low remaining bidder.

Indications of a liaison between Holladay and Heistand then became even more apparent than ever before. On July 15 Heistand wrote Blair that his guarantors wished to be released, so he was now willing to withdraw his bid. George McLellan, second assistant postmaster general, replied to Heistand that he had been released, and the matter was closed. Before this letter was written, however, Postmaster General Blair had instructed McLellan to offer Holladay a contract at $750,000 per annum for carrying the first-class mail daily between Atchison or St. Joseph and Folsom, California, with daily service to all intermediate post offices on the line, and to Denver by a direct branch from the main line. The proposed contract was for the period from October 1, 1864, to June 30, 1868, and stipulated that as the Pacific Railroad extended its line the mail route would be shortened, with a corresponding reduction in running time and compensation.

Although the Pacific Railroad bill had been passed by Congress more than two years before, no funds were yet available for the construction and no track had been laid, but Holladay flatly refused the proffered contract. Blair then instructed McLellan to offer the same contract to Joseph Burbank, who had originally bid to furnish mail service between Atchison and Salt Lake City for $375,000 annually, as against Holladay's bid of $385,000.

On July 20 McLellan sent Burbank a letter giving full details and offering him the contract, in reply to which Burbank telegraphed on July 29, "The proposition is accepted. I await a reply at White Cloud, Kansas, before preparing for service." Strangely, Blair withheld a reply, and immediately Ben Holladay set about exploiting every incidence of Indian trouble along the Overland route.

Ever since the outbreak of the Civil War, the Sioux in Minnesota had been in a belligerent mood, possibly incited by agents of the Confederacy but more probably by excessive slaughter of buffalo by white hide hunters. The trouble had spread steadily to the southwest, and in April and May 1864 General Robert Mitchell, commander of the Nebraska Military District, held two peace parleys with the Sioux on the Platte River, both of which ended in failure.

Until abused by Kearny's Army of the West on its march to Santa Fe in 1846, the Cheyennes and Arapahoes had always been friendly to the whites. Since then they had intermittently been driven onto the warpath by the westward white migration, the depletion of their best hunting grounds, and broken treaties.

In 1851 the United States Government had promised these tribes a share in a $50,000 annuity if they would accept the area between the Arkansas and Platte rivers as their permanent and exclusive hunting grounds. The Indians accepted the proffered treaty, but the United States Government was unable to control the white buffalo hunters or the horde of gold-rushers stampeding to the Rockies in 1859–60. Furthermore, the Cheyenne-Arapahoe treaty would be an obstacle to the building of a transcontinental railroad along the central route. In 1861 the Government negotiated another treaty with the Cheyennes and Arapahoes under which they were to be transferred to protected hunting grounds south of the Arkansas River. But because of the war the treaty had not been put into effect, and the Indians had progressively become more discontented and belligerent.

Late in April 1864 a hundred-man detachment of the First Colorado Cavalry fought a sharp but indecisive battle with mounted Cheyennes near Fort Larned, Kansas, on the Santa Fe Trail. Soon thereafter Cheyennes and Arapahoes began raiding ranches and stealing horses along the South Platte in northeastern Colorado. They were engaged by a cavalry detachment sent out from Denver and a hundred horses were recovered, but again the battle was indecisive. In May travelers on the Overland Trail were attacked by Indians near present North Platte, Nebraska, two men killed, their wagon burned, and the horses stolen. On the "cutoff" road between Junction Station (now Fort Morgan, Colorado) and Denver, a freighters' camp was attacked, and its horse herd was stampeded and driven away.

The first decisive battle with the Cheyennes was fought in late May by a company of the First Colorado Cavalry under Major Jacob Downing. The engagement took place at Cedar Canyon, 140 miles down the South Platte from Denver. Thirty-eight Indians were killed, their village destroyed, and several hundred ponies captured. Quite possibly in retaliation, on June 11 a band of Indians made a ghastly attack on the Hungate ranch, thirty miles southeast of Denver. Hungate, his wife, and their two children were murdered, scalped, and their bodies horribly mutilated.

At the time of these attacks Colorado Territory was in the throes of a political campaign on the question of applying for statehood, the prostatehood party taking the stand that the Indians had no rights in the territory and should be severely punished for their depredations. On this ticket Governor Evans was a candidate for the United States Senate and Colonel J. M. Chivington—military commandant of Colorado Territory—was a candidate for election to the House of Representatives. The *Rocky Mountain News*, Denver's only daily newspaper, supported both Evans and Chivington and also their stand on Indian rights and treatment. The anti-statehood party was headed by Judge Armour, who had rendered court decisions stating that the Indians still held legal title to Colorado land. Judge Armour and his stand were championed by the *Black Hawk Journal*, and the wrangle between the two papers and parties was acrimonious. Governor Evans, Colonel Chivington, and the *Rocky Mountain News* made the greatest possible capital of every Indian theft or depredation—and Ben Holladay supported them wholeheartedly.

When the mutilated bodies of the Hungate family were discovered and brought to Denver, Governor Evans had them placed on public exhibition, frightening the citizens to the verge of panic, and rumors spread rapidly that the city and all the settlements were to be attacked. The women and children of Denver were crowded into the second story of the Kountze bank building while the men gathered such weapons as they had and stood guard to protect their families from massacre. In a dramatic declaration, the governor ordered all business houses to close at 6:30 P.M. and all able-bodied men to meet for drill at seven o'clock.

The anticipated Indian attack on Denver was, of course, never made, but in mid-July there was further Indian trouble along the South Platte. Two emigrants were killed at Bijou Ranch, and seventeen horses were stolen. The same small band of Indians ran off five horses from the Junction stage station and sixty more from Murray's ranch, a few miles farther down the South Platte. A detachment of cavalry overtook five Indians with the stolen stock the next day, killed all five, and recovered the horses. On July 18 a raid was made near Valley Station, and the *Rocky Mountain News* made the most of it: "The women and children are all leaving for Denver. Dead cattle, full of arrows, are lying in all directions. A general Indian war is anticipated . . ."

On August 9 the same newspaper reported that three wagon trains had been attacked by Indians thirty-five miles east of Fort Kearney, that fourteen men had been killed, women and children taken prisoners, and the wagons robbed and burned. Three men were reported killed near Gilman's ranch, a few miles below the joining of the North and South Platte rivers. The next day another was reported killed near Cottonwood Springs, across the river from present-day North Platte, Nebraska.

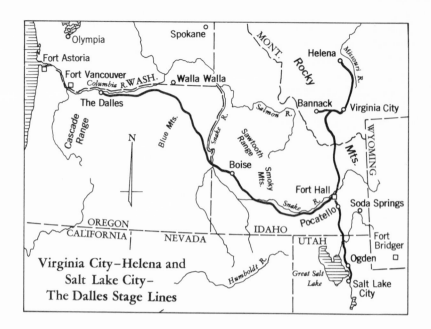

Map labels:
Olympia, Spokane, Helena, Fort Astoria, Fort Vancouver, *Columbia R.* WASH., Walla Walla, MONT., Rocky, *Missouri R.*, The Dalles, Bannack, Virginia City, Cascade Range, Blue Mts., Sawtooth Range, *Salmon R.*, *Snake R.*, WYOMING, Mts., N, Boise, Smoky Mts., Fort Hall, Soda Springs, OREGON, IDAHO, *Snake R.*, Pocatello, Fort Bridger, CALIFORNIA, NEVADA, UTAH, Ogden, *Humboldt R.*, Great Salt Lake, Salt Lake City

**Virginia City–Helena and
Salt Lake City–
The Dalles Stage Lines**

*Ben Holladay established a profitable monopoly on the lines
to the gold mining towns in Montana and to The Dalles.*

On August 11 the *Rocky Mountain News* reported that on the
previous day a band of Cheyennes had raided the valley of Little
Blue River, 170 miles east of Cottonwood Springs, murdering
whites and destroying wagon trains. The same issue quoted a
dispatch from Omaha that the eastbound stagecoach had passed
eleven dead bodies, and that six white men had been killed at
Thirty-two Mile Creek. At Liberty Farm station, keeper Joe
Eubanks was reported to have been killed and scalped, and his
wife and two children carried away by the Indians. The *News*,
however, failed to mention that the raid reported on August 9 as
taking place thirty-five miles east of Fort Kearney, as well as the
one reported to have occurred 170 miles east of Cottonwood
Springs on August 10, and the killings and abduction reported from
Omaha, all concerned a single Cheyenne raid down the valley of
Little Blue River in southeastern Nebraska.

Although it was more than four hundred miles from Denver to
the scene of the Cheyenne atrocities, Governor Evans issued a
proclamation in the *Rocky Mountain News*: "Patriotic citizens of
Colorado:—I again appeal to you to organize for defense of your
homes and families against the merciless savages . . . Any man who

kills a hostile Indian is a patriot; but there are Indians who are friendly and to kill one of these will involve us in greater difficulty . . ." The publisher of the newspaper added his own views: "A few months of active extermination against the red devils will bring quiet and nothing else will."

There is no doubt that during the summer of 1864 there were scattered Indian plunderings at ranches along the stage route through northeastern Colorado and southern Nebraska. There is, however, considerable doubt as to their extent or severity, except for the Cheyenne raid along the Little Blue. Nevertheless, the *Rocky Mountain News* issues of that summer indicate that the stage line and almost the entire valleys of the South and North Platte rivers through Colorado and Nebraska were completely in control of the Indians, and that their depredations were atrocious. On August 24, the *News* reported, "The last eastern mail arrived ten days ago. No more need be expected for some time to come."

Frank A. Root was then mail agent at Latham, Colorado. His book, *The Overland Stage to California*, is generally considered a prime source of information regarding these Indian incursions, but it is apparent that he had little firsthand knowledge, for he wrote:

The *Rocky Mountain News* . . . gave us the telegraphic news quite regularly, and kept us posted for a time, as best it could, concerning the depredations almost daily being commited by Indians along the line down the Platte. . . . Wild rumors of Indian depredations continued to reach us almost daily—sometimes the reports were so thick that they came every few hours—recounting the brutalities being committed by the hostiles down the Platte east of Latham. Some of the stories told almost made the blood run cold.

The arrival daily of east-bound passengers from the Pacific slope and coast continued, until between fifty and seventy-five were at the stationhouse. . . . The mails from California and the West daily accumulated, until there were 109 sacks—weighing two or three tons—and these were piled up to the ceiling around the room for breastworks. . . . The Indians were masters of the situation and virtually held undisputed possession of the line for fully 350 miles. Nearly all the stations were burned, and the torch was applied to the stage company's supply of hay and grain. The red devils likewise burnt a number of coaches, ran off a portion of the stage stock, and, at old Julesburg alone, it is said property to the amount of over $100,000 belonging to the stage proprietor was destroyed by them. . . .

While the critical period lasted, nearly every ranch along the Platte for hundreds of miles was vacated, owing to the horrible butcheries by the Indians. A dozen or more persons were killed and scalped at Plum Creek. Scores of families or ranchmen abandoned their homes and everything they possessed on the plains and, nearly frightened to death, joined those fleeing east for their lives. Everything they had, except what was hastily taken along, was left to the mercy of the infuriated savages, who, after appropriating what they could easily get away with, applied the torch, and what remained was reduced to ashes. Of the stage property destroyed along the Platte at the various other stations, the amount was estimated at the time from $50,000 to $100,000.

Root's book was not published until 1901, and it is evident that either the facts were no longer clear in his mind or that time had exaggerated them in his memory. There were thirty stage stations and relay posts on the 350-mile stretch of the route over which he says the Indians held virtually undisputed possession, and since coaches had been running in both directions daily it is probable that those stations and posts were stocked with at least four hundred stage horses. But in the obviously padded claim which Holladay later made on the Government for all his losses due to Indian depredations between July 1864 and February 1865, he listed only four stations and one stagecoach burned, and only thirty-nine horses stolen or killed.

Plains Indians would often raid an isolated and weakly defended ranch, relay post, or emigrant camp to steal horses. But unless in large bands and on the warpath, they seldom attacked a stagecoach on the trails, for even with a loaded coach stage horses could usually outrun Indian ponies, and men traveling through the West during the 1860's went well armed. Although the Cheyennes returned to their hunting grounds in western Kansas immediately after the raid on Liberty Farm station, and even though there was apparently little damage to other stations along the line, Holladay stopped all service between the Missouri River and Colorado.

He then appealed to the Postmaster General, the War Department, and President Lincoln for military protection of the line, declaring that he could not resume service without it. His timing was strategically perfect. The Civil War was going badly for the Union and troops could not be withdrawn from battlefields to guard the mail line, but a disruption of the overland mail service for a few weeks would make it virtually impossible for any other contractor to stock the line and initiate service by October 1.

If the President and Postmaster General were impressed by Holladay's appeal, Postmaster Moffatt at Denver and Senator Conness were not. On the floor of the Senate, Conness charged vehemently, "These Indian raids are mere fabrication! The braves are being hired by Holladay himself. I am utterly opposed to extending protection to his coaches simply because he is unable to fulfill the terms of his mail contract."

In spite of Governor Evans' proclamation and the manner in which the *Rocky Mountain News* was dramatizing every Indian misdeed, many Coloradoans disagreed with Senator Conness in only one respect: they believed that Holladay was perfectly able to fulfill the terms of his ninety-day mail contract, and that his failure to do so was, in effect, a strike. The antistatehood followers of Judge Armour said bluntly that Holladay was using a few isolated Indian attacks as an excuse for disrupting the mail service in an effort to force the Government in a time of war into awarding him the $820,000-per-annum mail contract he was demanding. How nearly correct they were is indicated by the letter books of postmasters Curtis and Byers at Arapaho City (a town a few miles east of Golden) for the years 1864 and 1865.

These books are preserved in the historical collections of the University of Colorado, and in them there are thirty-seven copies of letters written by Postmaster Curtis to the Postmaster General's office in Washington during the period between February 3 and October 10, 1864. He ordered stamps to the value of more than $6,000 and reported on the affairs of his office, but made no mention of mails being interrupted or endangered because of Indian trouble. In November 1864 William Byers took over the position of postmaster at Arapaho City. The letter books contain copies of twenty-one letters he wrote to the Postmaster General's office at Washington before mentioning, on January 14, 1865, that Indian attacks on the stage route were endangering the mail service.

In any event, Postmaster General Blair was evidently convinced by Holladay's appeal. Mail for the West that had accumulated at Atchison was returned by rail to the East Coast and sent to San Francisco by ship and transport across the Panama Peninsula. Postmaster Moffatt at Denver received orders from Washington to ship all mail for the East to San Francisco, from where it would be shipped by sea to New York. He immediately sent a telegram to the Postmaster General, protesting that there was not sufficient danger to justify interruption of the mail service between Denver and Atchison. On the same day the *Rocky Mountain News* castigated Holladay severely, reporting that he refused to restock the line (although his own damage claim makes it clear that practically no restocking would have been necessary) until the mail contract he demanded had been awarded to him. ". . . we hope," the publishers concluded, "that the contracts may be given to someone to carry the mail with ox-teams if no better can be done. Ben Holladay seems to have obtained such complete control of this western country that he can play with it as he pleases."

Nor was "this western country" the only place where Ben Holladay appeared to be exercising control. Postmaster General Blair completely ignored Moffat's protest and continued to withhold any reply to Joseph Burbank's telegram accepting the contract that had been offered him on July 20.

There is no indication of liaison between Burbank and Holladay, but one might suspect that Ben was being kept closely informed of developments by an influential member of the Post Office Department at Washington. Before the middle of August he suddenly abandoned his demand for the mail contract at his original bid of $820,000 per annum, and telegraphed Blair from New York that he would accept the contract at Heistand's bid: $750,000 per annum with no provision for reduction as the railroad line was extended. McLellan wired back that Postmaster General Blair wished to see Holladay in Washington within the next week for signing of the necessary papers.

Although no records have been found of the maneuvers leading up to such a seemingly inequitable arrangement, it is reported that Holladay was tendered a contract for the entire route at Heistand's bid, but requested that the Overland Mail Company be awarded more than 50 per cent of the $750,000 for carrying the mail 35 per cent of the distance. In any event, two contracts were awarded: one to Holladay at $365,000 per annum for service on the 1255 miles of route east of Salt Lake City, and one in the name of W. B. Dinsmore, president of the Overland Mail Company, for service on the remaining 678 miles at $385,000 per annum.

In the meantime Burbank had sent an agent to Washington to execute the contract which had been offered to him and which he had accepted by telegram. There was no claim by the Post Office Department that the telegram of acceptance had not been received, but when the agent arrived he was told that the matter had been closed and the contract awarded to Holladay and the Overland Mail Company. Burbank then wrote Blair from Falls City, demanding a full explanation of the highly irregular transaction, but was simply informed, as his agent had been, that the matter was closed.

With a four-year contract effective October 1 in his pocket, Ben Holladay was not long in discovering that the Indian menace along the Overland Trail between Atchison and Denver had subsided enough that service might safely be resumed. On September 23 the first stagecoach since mid-August rolled westward from Atchison, and the next day eastbound service was resumed from Denver.

20

Aftermath of Massacre

WHEN IN 1861 William Russell entered into a subcontract for his firm to carry the overland mail between Atchison and Salt Lake City, William Dinsmore had exacted harsh terms, particularly regarding the receipts from express handling. He reserved for the Overland Mail Company the right to make an exclusive contract with Wells, Fargo & Company for all express transportation between the Missouri River and points west of Salt Lake City, and required Russell to agree to an equal division of the revenue from such business, even though most of the express would be carried more than two-thirds of the distance by the C.O.C.&P.P. Express Company. He also required that the Overland Mail Company be paid 30 per cent commission on all passenger and express business done by the C.O.C.&P.P. on its own portion of the line, east of Salt Lake City.

Since the signing of the Dinsmore-Russell agreement, millions of dollars in silver had been mined from the Comstock Lode in western Nevada. Virginia City had become a fabulously wealthy metropolis and express shipments over the central route had increased tenfold, but Ben Holladay had profited very little from it. Until the expiration of the subcontract he, as successor to the C.O.C.&P.P. Express Company, was bound by the terms to which Russell had agreed.

Very few express shipments both originated and terminated on the portion of the line east of Salt Lake City. After dividing the revenue with Wells, Fargo & Company, there was no profit on shipments to or from points farther west. Most of those to or from points east of the Missouri were consigned through either the American or United States express companies, close affiliates of

Wells, Fargo & Company. On these shipments Holladay received a pro rata division of the express charges, based on mileage, but there was little profit left after paying 30 per cent commission to Wells Fargo through its subsidiary, the Overland Mail Company.

The moment the new mail contract of 1864 was signed, Ben Holladay set about to even the score with his powerful adversary. He established his own express business and set rates that were little short of confiscatory for carrying shipments consigned through Wells, Fargo & Company or its eastern affiliates. When all attempts at negotiation failed, the giant express companies threatened dire reprisal, but Holladay was not in the least concerned. He had a stranglehold on rapid transportation between the Missouri River and the West, and the big fellows would either pay his rates or get out of the transcontinental express business.

There was one more score that Ben Holladay determined to settle. Under the terms of the Dinsmore-Russell agreement he had been obliged to pay the Western Stage Company $14,000 per year as compensation for having discontinued operation between Fort Kearney and Denver at the time the overland mail was moved to the central route. Furthermore, he had been required to transport Western Stage Company passengers to destinations beyond Fort Kearney for a pro rata share of the fare from Omaha or Nebraska City, the two Missouri River termini of Western's lines.

At the expiration of the C.O.C.&P.P. subcontract Holladay was no longer obligated, and the Western Stage Company was again free to extend its line westward if it chose to do so. Holladay not only coveted Western's lucrative operation, but recognized it as a threat to his monopoly. With a line already established halfway across Nebraska, there was danger that the firm might join with the disgruntled express companies, extend its line to Salt Lake City, and break both his passenger and express monopolies.

Holladay believed in striking quickly when he had an advantage —and in striking hard. His coaches suddenly stopped accepting passengers from the Western Stage Company's line and left them stranded at Fort Kearney, a squalid frontier outpost with little or no accommodation for travelers. E. F. Hooker, superintendent of the Western Stage Company at Omaha, complained bitterly, and on October 30 Holladay telegraphed him from Salt Lake City: "You will continue to sell through tickets to Denver at one hundred and fifty dollars. I will not discriminate against your passengers. Ben Holladay."

Thereafter, instead of discriminating, Holladay took care that there were no seats available in his westbound coaches when they reached Fort Kearney. The result of his ruthless strategy was to further increase the number of stranded passengers at Fort Kearney and to completely destroy the Western Stage Company's business west of the Missouri River. Shortly thereafter he bought the coveted lines for a small fraction of their actual value.

In September 1862 Holladay had announced to the citizens of Denver through the *Rocky Mountain News* that, in appreciation of the Colorado legislature's granting him a charter to build bridges and collect tolls on the Cherokee Trail, he had instructed his agents to reroute the main course of the Overland Stage Line through their city. The change, which would have lengthened the main line by about a hundred miles, was not made, however, and Denver continued to be served, triweekly at best, by a branch line from Latham.

Holladay's failure to change the route was hardly surprising, for it would have increased operating costs without increasing revenue, and he was no man to spend money for favors already received. But the mail contract of 1864 required that Denver be furnished daily mail service. Furthermore, a good toll road had been built directly across the prairies from present Fort Morgan to Denver, cutting fifteen miles from the distance by way of the stage route and avoiding the deep sand along the South Platte.

A thousand miles of stagecoach operation per month could now be saved by rerouting the main line through Denver and eliminating the branch line from Latham, but Holladay evidently foresaw an opportunity to drive a lucrative bargain, for he refused to make the move when resuming service in September 1864. He not only wanted free passage for his coaches over the cutoff toll road, but for the United States Government to stand the cost of moving the line. Also, he and his cousin, Bela M. Hughes, were organizing a project for opening a toll road by way of Boulder Canyon to connect with the route to Salt Lake City which had been surveyed by Berthoud and Jim Bridger in 1861 and wanted the Colorado legislature to grant them an exclusive right-of-way from Denver to the western boundary of the state. On the other hand, Governor Evans and Colonel Chivington were campaigning on the statehood ticket for election to the United States Senate and House of Representatives. Chivington, as commander of military forces in Colorado, could issue orders obligating the War Department, and Evans' influence on the Colorado legislature was great. Both needed strong support by Denver voters in the oncoming election, however, and one of the surest ways of gaining it would be to get credit for securing passage of the Overland Stage Line through that city.

Whether or not the strategy was prearranged, on October 5, 1864 the *Rocky Mountain News* announced, "On Friday last, Colonel Chivington and Secretary Elbert visited Latham to meet Mr. Holliday [sic] to talk over a proposed change in the Overland mail route. Last night they returned and, we are pleased to learn, with the good news that their efforts were successful. Immediate steps will be taken for the transfer of stock and stations from the Platte route to the Cutoff . . ." Soon thereafter the main line of the Overland was altered to pass over the cutoff, through Denver, and northward over the route that is now U.S. Highway 287 to rejoin the former route at La Porte. On February 10, 1865, the Colorado legislature granted Holladay, Hughes, and their associates the coveted right-of-way, and when Holladay filed with Congress a claim for losses due to Indian depredations he included $50,000 for "cost of removal of line" in November 1864, by order of Colonel Chivington.

From the time of the Hungate massacre, Governor Evans and Colonel Chivington had played up Indian atrocities to the limit in their prostatehood campaign. But long before the coming of white men it had been the plains Indians' custom to make war on their enemies in summer and then make peace with them when winter set in and the warriors' time was needed for hunting. The custom changed only slightly as the whites pushed westward beyond the Missouri and the Indians discovered that they could trade peace treaties for clothing and provisions. A tribe, or subdivision of it, might build up its horse herd by raids on frontier farmers and travelers all summer, or wreak vengeance for wrongs at the hands of the whites by murder and destruction of property. In these raids they seldom failed to take a few white prisoners for trading purposes—preferably women and children. Then, with winter approaching, they would make peace overtures, offering to exchange their prisoners for a winter's supply of food, blankets, and clothing.

Shortly after the Cheyenne attack on the Overland route, three men were killed and a woman captured by Cheyennes on the Santa Fe Trail in southeastern Colorado. A rumor was soon circulated that a concerted Indian attack had been planned to wipe out all Colorado settlements, and Governor Evans issued another proclamation, warning hostile Indians that he condoned their annihilation as enemies of the United States.

The threat of annihilation was evidently disturbing to Black Kettle and other Cheyenne chiefs in southeastern Colorado. Without waiting for the approach of winter, they sent overtures to the governor for a peace treaty and offered to release their white prisoners. In early September an officer from Fort Lyon went with a small detachment of soldiers to a Cheyenne village on the headwaters of Smoky Hill River, where four white prisoners were turned over to him. The chiefs were then escorted to Denver for a peace parley with Governor Evans and Colonel Chivington.

Evans and Chivington were by no means alone in their belief that Indians who were hostile to the white despoilers of their hunting grounds should be annihilated. Major General S. K. Curtis, Chivington's superior officer on the western frontier, believed that no lasting peace could be made with the Cheyennes until they had been soundly punished for their depredations and killings during the summer. Upon hearing of the proposed peace parley he telegraphed an order from Kansas that no peace treaty was to be entered into until the Indians had been made to suffer severely for their crimes.

There is little doubt that Governor Evans and Colonel Chivington exploited General Curtis' telegram to the limit. Authority was obtained from the War Department to raise a force of hundred-day volunteer soldiers for defense against hostile Indians, and the proposed peace parley came to nothing. As winter approached Chivington set out with the volunteers to administer to the Cheyennes of southeastern Colorado the severe punishment recommended by his superior officer. On the night of November 29, 1864, he surprised a winter camp of Cheyennes on Big Sandy Creek, twenty-five miles north of present Lamar. A fresh snow had fallen and most of the warriors were away on a buffalo hunt; the camp was occupied by several hundred old men, women, and children.

Many conflicting reports have been written of the "battle" or "massacre" that followed, and estimates of the number of Indians killed, with practically no casualties among the soldiers, vary from one hundred to six hundred. Many citizens of Denver who for political reasons had been led to believe the Indian menace to be far greater than it actually was were jubilant when news of the "glorious victory" reached the city. There is little question but that Frank Root, who was then postmaster at Latham, expressed the majority feeling of Coloradoans of the time, when thirty-five years later he referred to the attack as the Sand Creek battle and wrote, ". . . the Colorado volunteers, under command of the gallant Colonel Chivington, a noted military leader of pioneer days, surrounded a tribe of hostile savages and almost wiped them from the face of the earth." An investigating commission from Washington, however, took a different view of the matter and branded it an outright massacre of peaceful Indians.

Whether battle or massacre, the "Sand Creek" affair resulted in uniting the Arapahoes and Sioux with the Cheyennes, and precipitated the great Indian uprising of 1865.

Fort Rankin (later renamed Fort Sedgwick) had been built about a mile from old Julesburg, and at the close of 1864 was garrisoned by a company of Iowa Volunteer Cavalry. On the morning of January 7, 1865, the post was surrounded by a band of about a hundred poorly armed Indians. It was not uncommon for Indians to visit frontier forts in winter, begging or demanding food and blankets, nor was it uncommon for them to become troublesome if their demands were refused.

Anticipating no particular difficulty, a part of the garrison sallied out to drive the annoying Indians away, for the westbound stage was due at any minute. Showing just enough insolence and belligerence to arouse the soldiers' anger, and shooting a few arrows in their direction, the Indians withdrew toward the sandhills beyond the edge of the valley, with the unmounted cavalrymen in pursuit. They had followed the Indians some distance from the fort when it became apparent that they were being drawn into an ambush. The Indians were being reinforced from behind every knoll and bush, and the reinforcements were better armed than the soldiers.

Hard pressed by upwards of twelve hundred Cheyenne, Arapaho, and Sioux warriors, the soldiers fought a retreating hand-to-hand battle back toward the fort. Fourteen cavalrymen were killed in the engagement, and annihilation of the entire force might have resulted if those who had remained at the fort had not dragged a howitzer into position and held the Indians at bay with artillery fire.

While the pursuing cavalrymen were being drawn away toward the sandhills, the westbound coach arrived at the Julesburg stage station. The horses were being changed, and the passengers had alighted for breakfast when the battle erupted at the edge of the valley. Stage-line employees, passengers, and a Government paymaster who had arrived on the coach made a run for the fort, abandoning everything except their firearms.

Through trading and raiding, the Indians of the plains had long since acquired muskets, rifles, and pistols. They were thoroughly familiar with the power and range of these weapons, and showed no extraordinary fear of them in the hands of white men, but many Indians believed loud-booming artillery, like thunder and lightning, to be of divine origin, and all of them gave it a wide berth. With a single howitzer the soldiers were able to hold the Indians away from Fort Rankin, but could do nothing for the protection of Julesburg, well beyond howitzer range. Howling and shrieking, the warriors set about plundering the stagecoach, trading post, stage-line station, warehouses, and stables. In the coach the paymaster had abandoned a locked box of "greenbacks," the paper money issued by the U.S. Government during the Civil War. The Indians pried the box open, but on finding that it contained only green paper the warriors flung it into the wind and gleefully watched it scatter like a flock of frightened birds. The mail sacks were also ripped open and their contents sent flying after the greenbacks.

The Indians had apparently made careful plans for their raid on Julesburg. Many extra ponies and plenty of extra travois poles had been brought along, and a camp for the old men, women, and children had been set up at a safe distance down the river. While the braves fought among themselves over trinkets, articles of clothing, ammunition, and other plunder, the squaws came from the camp with strings of ponies dragging travois. These they loaded with goods from the trading post and shelled corn from the stage-line granary. After a day of plunder and fighting among themselves, the Indians withdrew in the direction of a Cheyenne winter camp on the headwaters of the Republican River in southwestern Nebraska.

Not knowing where the Indians had gone or when they might return, the little garrison and those who had taken refuge at Fort Rankin did not dare venture far beyond the range of the howitzer. But on January 10 the Julesburg telegraph operator wired Denver that the bodies of thirteen soldiers and five civilians had been brought to the fort, and that fifty-five Indians had been killed during the raid.

Governor Evans was in Washington at the time, and Acting Governor Elbert telegraphed him, "The Indians are again murdering travelers and burning trains on the plains. . . . We must have five thousand troops to clean out these savages or the people of this territory will be compelled to leave it. . . . The General Government must help us or give up the Territory to the Indians."

Ben Holladay also rushed urgent telegrams to Washington, appealing to the War and Post Office departments for military protection of his stage line, and warning that if his facilities at Julesburg were plundered or destroyed it would be necessary to suspend overland mail service until spring.

As news of the Julesburg attack was flashed along the stage line by telegraph, freighters pulled their wagon trains in at the larger stations or at ranches with substantial buildings to fort up for mutual defense. With the flow of traffic from the East stopped, and with agriculture not yet developed in Colorado, Denver and the mining towns in the mountains were soon desperate for provisions. The price of sugar and bacon leaped to fifty cents a pound, and flour to twenty-seven dollars a sack. To relieve the situation a train of more than a hundred wagons and three hundred heavily armed men was organized at Denver. It set out for the East on January 14 carrying the accumulated mail and accompanied by a military escort with light artillery.

Although they kept out of sight, the Indians were evidently watching the Overland Trail closely. The strongly armed wagon train was allowed to go through unmolested, but the day after it passed American Ranch, fifteen miles southwest of present Sterling, Colorado, the Indians attacked, ran off the stock, and burned the buildings, in the ruins of which the remains of seven bodies were later found. Two other large ranches were attacked, and although the defenders were unable to save their livestock, they held the Indians at bay and saved their own lives.

The only troops stationed along the three hundred miles of stage line between Denver and Cottonwood Springs (now North Platte, Nebraska) were small garrisons at Fort Rankin and Valley Station (now Sterling), both too weak to check the raids in any way. On January 28 the Indians renewed their attack on the South Platte

A Wells Fargo coach attacked by Indians.

Valley en masse. Contemptuous of the garrison at Valley Station, they pitched camp on the north side of the river, crossing on the ice just beyond artillery range, and for six days devastated a stretch of seventy-five miles along the valley. Upwards of a thousand cattle were driven away, every haystack burned, and wagon trains pillaged and destroyed. But the loss of lives was comparatively small, as following the attack on American Ranch most of the white inhabitants and freighters took refuge at the two military posts, where the Indians could be held off by artillery fire.

Nine miles up the valley from Fort Rankin a freighter with several men, more than a hundred oxen, and eight enormous prairie schooners loaded with cases of bottled liquors took refuge at Gillette's ranch when word of the renewed Indian attacks reached him. The Indians, moving camp as they proceeded down the valley —looting, burning, and driving an enormous herd of stolen livestock before them—reached Gillette's ranch on the forenoon of February 1. They burned outlying haystacks and laid siege to the buildings, but Gillette, his ranch hands, and the freighters were able to stand them off until dark. Knowing that they could not keep the Indians from sneaking in and setting fire to the buildings during the night, the defenders made a dash for the river and went down to Fort Rankin on the ice, running from one to another of the willow-covered islands that dotted the shallow stream, and then standing their pursuers off with a round of rifle fire.

After generously sampling the captured bottled goods, the Indians came down the valley en masse on the morning of February 2. Among them there were evidently some who knew how to yoke oxen and hitch them to wagons, but none who knew how to drive an ox team. In the vanguard was the herd of stolen livestock being hazed along erratically by a horde of half-drunk, war-whooping mounted warriors. Seven or eight spans of oxen had been yoked and chained to each wagonload of liquor and then turned into the herd and hazed along with it, leaving wheel tracks that zigzagged crazily across the prairie. Behind came the squaws with long strings of Indian ponies carrying the aged and children and dragging travois loaded with tepee covers, buffalo robes, blankets, clothing, and spoils accumulated in the raids.

Although Julesburg had been forewarned by the refugees from Gillette's ranch, there was little preparation that could be made except to turn the stage horses loose and drive them away to the north, hoping they would scatter and avoid capture. A few days earlier two large trains of freight wagons heavily loaded with flour, sugar, canned goods, hardware, clothing, shoes, bolts of cloth, and other drygoods had pulled off the road there, hoping for protection from the soldiers. But with more than a thousand liquor-crazed Indians on the warpath there was no possibility of protection beyond howitzer range of the post. As the awesome horde came into sight and hearing, stage-line employees, freighters, and other civilians at Julesburg snatched up what firearms and ammunition they could lay their hands on and ran for Fort Rankin.

The Indians gave the fort and its howitzer a wide berth, but swooped down on Julesburg like an enormous flock of buzzards on a deserted battlefield. While the squaws and old folk were left to drive the livestock across the river and set up camp on the north side, a frenzied, howling mob of drunken warriors attacked the wagon trains in an orgy of pillage and destruction. Crates, bales, and cases were smashed open and goods scattered far and wide as liquor-crazed braves fought over articles that caught their fancy.

Grasping the loose end of a bolt of cloth, a shrieking warrior would leap onto his war pony and race away across the prairie, a fifty-yard pennant of bright calico streaming behind him. On one of the wagons there was a crate or two of hens. These were turned loose, and several of the younger braves found great sport in chasing squawking, terrified hens and pinning them to the ground with arrows shot downward from their racing ponies. Others had found sharp axes among the hardware and were having a glorious time chopping down telegraph poles.

While the warriors reveled in their orgy of pillage and destruction, the Indian women were hard at work setting up tepees, sanding a roadway over the river ice so that their unshod ponies could cross without slipping, and dragging the poles cut from the telegraph line into camp. They hauled away on travois hundreds of bushels of corn from the stage-line granary and hundreds of sacks of flour and sugar from the wagon trains, together with countless cases of canned goods, bales of clothing, bolts of cloth, cases of shoes, and all manner of other merchandise.

When all that their ponies could carry or drag away had been plundered, the Indians set fire to the buildings and wagon trains. As darkness settled, their camp, illuminated by the roaring flames, could be seen clearly from Fort Rankin. According to Captain Eugene Ware, who was at the fort, Indians of all three tribes and of all ages—men, women, and children—"were having high jinks with fires made out of telegraph poles, drinking S.T. 1860 X, Plantation, Hostetter Bitters, and all kinds of good stuff which they had found in those wagons."

In their drunken celebration the Indians allowed their campfires to set the dry prairie grass ablaze, and were obliged to scatter and fight fire. They could no longer be seen from the fort, and when daylight dawned they were gone, the entire horde having trekked away to the north with their plunder.

The telegraph line had been destroyed along much of the seventy-five-mile stretch of South Platte Valley that had been ravaged, and for several miles east of Julesburg. As soon as it was discovered that the Indians had withdrawn, the Julesburg telegrapher set out to find the point from which a wire to the east was intact and to send appeals for help. With his telegraph instrument destroyed in the burned office, he was obliged to send dots and dashes by grounding the wire on an axe head driven into the earth, and to receive by putting the end of the wire into his mouth so as to feel the weak shocks on the tip of his tongue.

In this way he got messages through to and from Cottonwood Springs, headquarters for the Eleventh Ohio Volunteer Cavalry in western Nebraska. Colonel W. O. Collins, with as large a force as could be mustered, set out at once to intercept the retreating Indians. By hard riding he was able to cut their line of march in the vicinity of present Sidney, and fought them a delaying battle there on February 6, but was unable to stop their advance or recover any of the stolen property. Two days later he fought them again near present Bridgeport, on the North Platte, but his force was insufficient to more than annoy the combined tribes. They continued their migration to the Powder River Valley in north-eastern Wyoming, where they encamped to spend the remainder of the winter and enjoy the spoils of their raiding.

Although Ben Holladay had threatened to discontinue overland mail service until spring if his facilities at Julesburg were destroyed, the threat was not carried out. Major General G. M. Dodge, then in command of the Kansas-Nebraska Department, telegraphed him to resume service at once and promised that ample military protection would thereafter be provided for mail coaches, travelers, and freighters in the West. On February 3 word reached Denver that Julesburg had been completely devastated, but that the Indians had left the South Platte Valley and were moving northward. Before the day was over five Holladay stagecoaches set out for Atchison carrying a few passengers and nearly six tons of accumulated mail. They were accompanied by twenty other vehicles carrying east-bound travelers and escorted by a troop of forty cavalrymen.

Following the Sand Creek investigation, Chivington had been re-placed by Colonel Moonlight as military commander in Colorado. He quickly recruited a volunteer force of 360 men to guard the road to Julesburg until the arrival of Federal troops, and to repair the telegraph line. The repair was completed by February 13, and the first message to come over the wire was news that two thousand troops were on their way to escort travelers and mail coaches along the Platte.

On February 7 the first westbound coach in nearly a month had set out from Atchison, carrying more than a ton of mail. There had been no Indian attacks east of Fort Kearney, and the Ohio Volunteer Cavalry was patrolling the road between there and Cottonwood Springs. One by one, four coaches that had been stranded between Cottonwood Springs and Julesburg joined the little caravan, which reached Denver soon after the middle of the month. By March 8 the devastated portion of the line had been restocked, and the mail was again being carried on a daily schedule. A month later Robert E. Lee surrendered the Confederate forces at Appomattox Courthouse, and seasoned troops became available for controlling the plains Indians. By early June ten regiments of cavalry, most of them from Sheridan's command, had passed through St. Louis on their way west, and two thousand more were en route from Cincinnati.

All during the Indian raids along the South Platte there had been no interference with the stage line west of Denver and the coaches had operated on regular schedule. But in May trouble broke out along the Cherokee Trail. In early June seven men were killed between Virginia Dale and Green River, one station was burned, eighty-seven stage-line horses and mules were stolen, and the coaches could not get through because of massed bands of hostile Indians who blocked the line west of Fort Halleck.

At that time Schuyler Colfax, Speaker of the House of Representatives, reached Virginia Dale in the course of making a trip to the Pacific Coast. Quite concerned by the situation, he scribbled in pencil the following note—now in the Colorado Historical Society files—to his brother-in-law, Daniel Witter:

> Virginia Dale, 100 miles from Denver,
> a beautiful spot in the mountains.
>
> Sunday 7 A.M. June 4, '65.
>
> Dear Daniel,
>
> We shall lay over here a day or two. We have authenticated reports from the West that two men have been killed at Sage Creek, 15 miles West of the North Platte, and the stock of the Stage Company run off by the Indians as far as Bridger Pass, 33 miles. There are flying but as yet unconfirmed reports that there are 500 to 700 Indians up there.
>
> Mr. Spotswood, the Division Agent on that line has gone out from

Fort Halleck with 35 soldiers to prospect. If we reach Fort Bridger will telegraph you if wire is up. But we may have to drive our train through the disturbed country, laying over at night to feed and rest; and may be a good while on the road. Don't alarm Mother, but if you don't hear from me in a fortnight send her this with my love to all,

Yours very truly,
Schuyler Colfax

Besides being the best stagecoach man in Colorado, Bob Spotswood was highly ingenious and thoroughly acquainted with Indian superstitions and psychology. In a wagon shed which was in clear view of the threatening Indian mob, he mounted two joints of stove pipe on the rear axle of a wagon undercarriage in such a way as to give the appearance of a cannon. He then had the doors of the shed flung open, the "thunder wagon" pulled into full view, and the loading begun. Within moments the hostiles had scattered like leaves in a hurricane, and although there were a dozen more killings along the Cherokee Trail that summer, coaches on Bob Spotswood's division of the stage line were allowed to go through unmolested.

21

Climax and Death Knell

DAVID BUTTERFIELD, unrelated to John Butterfield of stage-line fame, was one of Denver's most successful and best-liked business-men of the early 1860's. Engaged in the wholesale grocery and commission business, Dave Butterfield was known throughout Colorado Territory and in all the river ports along the Missouri. His personality was so magnetic and his power of persuasion so great that many Coloradoans said he could charm a bird out of a tree.

In June 1864 Butterfield moved to Atchison, went into the commission business there, and became agent for the line of Missouri River packets that transported most of the freight between St. Louis and the western frontier. Practically all the freight carried by the packets beyond Kansas City was destined for Denver, Salt Lake City, or the Colorado, Idaho, and Montana mining communities. Whether unloaded at Leavenworth, Atchison, Nebraska City, or Omaha, this freight was hauled westward on the Overland Trail along the Platte River by independent owners of ox-drawn wagons, moving at the rate of ten to twelve miles per day.

The mining communities were booming. More freight was arriving at the river ports than could be handled by the snail-paced caravans, and there was an insistent demand by mine owners and merchants for faster overland transportation. It is not surprising that Dave Butterfield, with his wide acquaintance in the West, his contact through his commission business with wealthy interests in the East, his agency for the river packets, and his flair for organization, should have stepped into the breach. In December 1864 he established a "fast freight line" between Atchison and the West, his drivers using the Overland Trail.

Early in 1865 Butterfield went to New York for the purpose of interesting eastern capital in his freighting business, and he was highly successful. A joint stock company, "Butterfield's Overland Despatch," was formed and stock to the amount of $3,000,000 is reported to have been subscribed, with half of it paid in cash. Among the stockholders were seven wealthy New York capitalists, including George E. Cock, president of the Park Bank. E. P. Bray was elected president of the new firm, W. E. Kitchen treasurer, and D. A. Butterfield was appointed superintendent and general manager. An eastern headquarters office was opened in New York, announcements of the forthcoming service advertised in leading newspapers east of the Mississippi, and an enormous sign was erected near the Astor House depicting a train of white-topped prairie schooners crossing the plains.

The financing taken care of, Butterfield returned to Atchison with several ideas for speeding up freight service between the Missouri River and the Rocky Mountains. The distance between Atchison and Denver by way of the Smoky Hill Trail—approximately the same course as that now followed by transcontinental highway U.S. 40—was nearly seventy-five miles shorter than that by way of the Overland Trail along the North and South Platte rivers. The former route, however, had been abandoned since the height of the Colorado gold rush because so many unprepared easterners had died of thirst and starvation on it during that year of severe drought. Dave Butterfield believed that if water could be found at reasonable intervals through western Kansas and eastern Colorado the freighting time between the Missouri River and Denver could be cut in half by use of the abandoned route, high-grade mules instead of oxen, and relay stations located fifty miles apart through the uninhabited regions.

Leavenworth had suffered a severe loss of business since the abandonment of the Smoky Hill route, so Butterfield had little difficulty in convincing the city council to vote $4,000 toward the cost of a survey which might result in its reopening. Major Isaac Eaton, a retired frontier army officer, was employed to make the survey, and his wagon train was accompanied by Major Pritchard with an escort of 250 soldiers from Fort Riley. After a thorough examination Major Eaton reported that, except for a twenty-one-mile arid stretch between Cheyenne Wells and Big Sandy Creek in eastern Colorado, water had been found along the entire route at distances no greater than five miles apart. He also reported that the Smoky Hill route was far superior to that along the Platte.

[281]

Butterfield set about stocking and equipping the abandoned route at once. He bought twelve hundred fine Missouri mules and two hundred huge prairie schooners; assembled harness, feed, building materials; and constructed bridges and relay stations. He soon became as popular and well liked in Atchison as he had been in Denver. The most influential men of the community became his close friends, and he inspired the wholehearted admiration of his employees. On the evening of June 7 they gathered en masse at his home and presented him with a beautiful gold tablet. On one side a train of freight wagons was engraved, encircled by the words "Butterfield Overland Despatch; established by D. A. Butterfield, Esq., 1865." On the other side was engraved "Presented to D. A. Butterfield by his employees, in token of their estimation of him as a man and an employer."

There seems little doubt that Butterfield's original intention was to transport freight only, for his first advertisement, appearing in the Atchison *Daily Free Press* in the spring of 1865, simply read:

BUTTERFIELD OVERLAND DESPATCH

COLORADO, UTAH, IDAHO, and MONTANA
TERRITORIES.
Principal Office, Atchison, Kan.

NEW YORK OFFICE
No. 1 Vesey Street, Astor House.

Through Bills of Lading Given From
New York, Boston, Philadelphia,
Pittsburg, Chicago, St. Louis,
and Burlington, Iowa.

D. A. BUTTERFIELD, Proprietor,
Atchison, Kans.
A. W. Spalding, Gen'l Ag't, New York

Although only one express company executive is listed among the founders of the Butterfield Overland Despatch Company, Frank Root has stated that the United States, the American, and the Adams express companies were "not the least" among the stockholders of the firm. It seems quite probable that these companies, because of Ben Holladay's refusal to carry their express over his line for a pro rata share of the charges, became investors in the Butterfield firm after its original organization. That is indicated by the following advertisement, which appeared in the Atchison *Daily Free Press* of June 30, 1865:

BUTTERFIELD OVERLAND DESPATCH
To All Points in
Colorado, Utah, New Mexico, Arizona, Idaho and Montana
Territories and the State of Nevada.

Contracts can be made with this Company through their
Agents, to Transport Freight from all of the Eastern
Cities, to all localities in the Territories, the
rate to include Railroad and Overland carriage and
all commissions upon the Missouri River.

The Company owns its own transportation and gives a
through Bill of Lading which protects the shipper
from the extreme East to the Far West.

EXPRESS DEPARTMENT.

About August 1, 1865, the Company will have a line of
Express Coaches running daily between Atchison, Kansas,
and Denver, Colorado; and, about September 1, to
Santa Fe, New Mexico, and, as soon in the spring as
possible, a tri-weekly between Denver and Salt Lake City,
over which merchandise will be carried at fair express rates.

TIME TO DENVER, EIGHT DAYS.

Mark Goods for Cattle and Mule Trains "But'd Ov'd Desp'h."
Mark Goods for Express "B.O.D. Express, Atchison."

The first train of Butterfield freight wagons set out from Atchison on June 24, 1865, loaded with seventy-five tons of freight for Denver and other Colorado points. Thereafter, during the summer and fall of 1865, the business grew with such amazing speed that additional mules and equipment had to be added as rapidly as they could be bought and hundreds of additional employees hired. River packets discharged great quantities of freight on the Atchison levee for transshipment via the Butterfield line, and no train arrived on the St. Joseph & Atchison Railroad without several carloads consigned through the new firm.

On a single day in July nineteen carloads were received by rail, together with a vast amount of packet freight. On July 15 a Butterfield wagon train left Atchison with seventeen great steam boilers for Colorado ore-stamping mills. It was followed by a train for Virginia City, Montana, loaded with 150,000 pounds of mining machinery. Early in August a single train set out for Salt Lake City with 600,000 pounds of general goods consigned to merchants there. Before the end of August these trains and a score of others had moved over the Smoky Hill route without military escort, and with no interference by the Indians.

[283]

As soon as the freighting business was well under way Butterfield set about preparing his line for handling express and passengers. Twenty new stagecoaches—probably not Concords—were bought in Chicago, more than two hundred high-grade stage horses brought from the East, and relay stations were being built along the entire Smoky Hill Trail at intervals of approximately twelve miles. But from an article that appeared in the Atchison *Daily Free Press* in August it is evident that the enterprise had not been hailed in all quarters by enthusiastic approbation:

We must say that we admire Butterfield's pluck. Croakers on the Missouri river, skeptics in Denver and secret vindictive enemies who proposed "to fight the thing to death" have produced no effect upon the master mind of this new and immense overland enterprise. Succeed it will, and such a triumph would warrant any man in fostering a feeling of pride for the work accomplished.

By mid-September the preparations were well along, and the first stagecoach over the Smoky Hill route, with Dave Butterfield a passenger, arrived in Denver on September 23, 1865. It is little wonder that the city went wild with joy. Scarcely more than a year earlier its leading newspaper had lamented, "For four years more Colorado, Utah, and Nevada belong to Ben Holladay for a footstool and may the Lord have mercy upon them."

Several miles from Denver the coach was met by a large delegation of the city's leading citizens, headed by the mayor. The First Colorado mounted band greeted Butterfield with a fanfare of trumpets and a banner inscribed, " 'Westward the course of Empire takes its way.' The energy of our old townsman Col. D. A. Butterfield proves him the Hercules of Express men. Welcome Dave and your Express."

Amid cheering and applause, Butterfield was transferred to the mayor's carriage and sped away to a grand reception and banquet at Denver's finest hotel, the Planter's House. Enthusiastic speeches were made, predicting that Dave Butterfield would soon become the transportation king of the West. For a month or two it appeared that their predictions were well founded.

Branch offices were opened and agents appointed in Boston, Philadelphia, Cincinnati, St. Louis, Chicago, Denver, Salt Lake City, and San Francisco. With a line seventy-five miles shorter than Holladay's, the Butterfield drivers had a distinct time advantage, but the Holladay men were bound not to be beaten. A correspondent for the *Alta California* reported, "The route from Denver to Atchison is now a race course. . . . The time is frequently inside of five days, whereas six days was once thought good time."

Ben Holladay was no man to stand idly by and watch a competitor cut into his monopoly and profits, and Dave Butterfield was not easily intimidated, so a head-to-head battle for the express and passenger business between Atchison and Denver ensued. To draw attention to his line and prove it the fastest, Holladay had himself driven from Denver to Atchison in three days, eleven hours, and fifteen minutes—doubtless at the cost of a hundred or more ruined horses. Next he slashed the fare from $175 to $75, but Butterfield met the price and, unquestionably in retaliation, put competing stages on Holladay's highly profitable route between Denver and Central City. Holladay countered by cutting the fare on that line to a dollar, but again Butterfield met the competition.

From the time of Julesburg's destruction, stagecoaches on the Overland route had been accompanied by an escort of cavalry, but no military protection had been given the Smoky Hill route since the completion of Major Eaton's survey.

Seventeen-Mile House on the Smoky Hill Trail southeast of Denver. (Courtesy, State Historical Society of Colorado.)

[285]

The first attack on a Butterfield stagecoach was made on the night of October 2. Although a shotgun guard was on the box with the driver, thirty war-painted "redskins" struck with such suddenness and ferocity that there was no possibility of defense. But their manner of dealing with their victims left considerable doubt as to the color of the skin under the war paint, and speculation circulated that they might all be on Ben Holladay's payroll. Almost invariably, Indians capturing a stagecoach would kill and scalp all the men in the party. In this case the horses were run off and the coach plundered and burned, but the passengers, driver, and guard were left unharmed to make their way afoot to the next station.

The *Atchison Champion* did no speculating, but made the flat statement that the attackers were not Indians but white men in disguise. The harassment of the line during the remainder of 1865, when the Indians were peaceable along the Overland route, appeared to be somewhat more than coincidental, although nothing definite was ever proved. During November there were numerous attacks all along the Smoky Hill Trail in western Kansas, and the Bluffton relay station was burned and two men killed. Soon afterward, the stagecoach in which General Brewster was traveling with a correspondent and artist for *Harper's Monthly Magazine* was attacked near Smoky Hill Spring. The attackers were unquestionably Indians, but the man who appeared to be their leader was definitely white. As a result of these attacks the Government stationed troops at various points along the Smoky Hill route. The protection, however, was too little and too late to save Butterfield's passenger business. With newspapers and magazines throughout the East playing up the attacks, and with the bad reputation given the Smoky Hill route during the Colorado gold rush, few passengers were willing to risk a trip over the line. Nevertheless, the B.O.D. express business was not seriously affected and was still a definite threat to Ben Holladay's transcontinental monopoly.

The harassment of its stagecoaches and stations was not the greatest injury suffered by Butterfield's Overland Despatch during the fall and early winter of 1865, for at that time the mining industry throughout the West was crippled by the postwar blight. Before the end of the year it became certain that transportation charges could never be collected on thousands of tons of freight already delivered or in transit. To avoid further losses on mining machinery and boilers in transit, great quantities had to be unloaded and left to rust on the prairies. The losses to the Butterfield firm were tremendous, its financial structure was shaken, and a reorganization became necessary. On January 20, 1866, the Council and House of Representatives of Colorado Territory passed an act "To Incorporate the Butterfield Overland Dispatch Company." George E. Cock, president of the Park Bank in New York City, was elected president of the new corporation, and Dave Butterfield was retained as superintendent and general manager.

That the primary purpose of the reorganized firm was to break Ben Holladay's express monopoly seems rather apparent, for after granting the right to construct a road on the Smoky Hill route, the charter continued, "and the said company shall have power further to construct and continue said main wagon road from the said city of Denver westwardly, to the western boundary of the territory of Colorado, in the direction of Salt Lake City, territory of Utah, by the way of any one of the passes in the Rocky Mountains now discovered . . ."

Although not using the name, Ben Holladay had operated under the charter granted to the C.O.C.&P.P. Express Company by the legislature of Kansas Territory. But in the fall of 1865 he filed articles of incorporation with the legislature of Colorado Territory. On February 5, 1866, he and his associates were granted a charter under the name of The Holladay Overland Mail and Express Company. The rights granted the firm were extremely broad, reading, in part, "to establish, maintain and operate any express, stage or passenger or transportation route or routes by land or water, for the conveyance of persons, mail or property of all kinds . . . the said company shall have the power to draw, accept, endorse, guaranty, buy, sell and negotiate drafts and bills of exchange, inland or foreign; to receive coin, money, silver and gold in any form or other, and any kind of valuables on deposit at its offices . . . to buy, sell and dispose of gold or silver coin and bullion, gold dust, money and securities for money, and to do a general exchange and collection business. Said company may change its name whenever the same shall be ordered by the vote of a majority of the board of directors thereof, at a meeting duly convened for that purpose . . ."

Ever since the exploration by Berthoud and Bridger of the route which is now U.S. 40 between Denver and Salt Lake City, Ben Holladay's cousin, Bela Hughes, had been determined to open it as a short-cut toll road. He had invested a large amount of time and money in opening a wagon road on the Berthoud-Bridger route eastward from Salt Lake City to the Continental Divide, but had failed in an effort to construct a usable road over Berthoud Pass. He and Ben Holladay had later secured a charter for the construction of a toll road via Boulder Canyon to connect the uncompleted

Hughes road with Denver, but that project also failed. In February 1866 the Butterfield Overland Dispatch Company announced that it was going to extend its line to Salt Lake City via the Berthoud-Bridger route and invited bids for construction of a stage road across Berthoud Pass. The project was never begun.

The B.O.D. had no sooner established its stage line between Atchison and Denver than the big express companies began putting pressure on Ben Holladay, threatening to open an express line that would close the gap to Salt Lake City unless he agreed to accept a pro rata share of the charges on interline express shipments. He therefore suspected that they were behind the reorganization of the B.O.D. and its plan to extend its line, and clandestinely discovered that no agreement had yet been worked out between them. He

A Wells, Fargo & Company stagecoach. (Courtesy, State Historical Society of Colorado.)

at once instructed David Street, his general superintendent at Denver, to have two well-qualified men who were unknown to any employee of the Butterfield Overland Dispatch ride over the Smoky Hill line as passengers and make a careful appraisal of its physical condition and worth. Street was to meet the men at Atchison on completion of their examination and bring their reports with all speed to Holladay in New York City.

By a strange coincidence, within an hour or two after Street's arrival, Ben Holladay received identical letters from Wells, Fargo & Company, the American Express Company, and the United States Express Company informing him bluntly that unless he agreed to accept a pro rata division of interline express revenues they would stock and equip a line to close the gap in their service between Denver and Salt Lake City. Frank Root writes that Holladay then told Street, "Now, I am going to take the bull by the horns." He is said to have sent his private secretary to the Park Bank with an invitation to George Cock, president of that bank and the Butterfield Overland Dispatch Company, to have lunch with him at his office.

David Street was present at the meeting and afterward reported that Ben Holladay towered above the diminutive bank president by more than a foot, outweighed him by a hundred and fifty pounds, and fairly cowed him with his booming voice and bullying attitude. He later quoted Holladay's opening remarks as follows, "I want to see you about your Despatch line. I know more about your line than you do yourselves. You are out over a million dollars, and that is not the end of the expense or outlay. You can never get your money back; if you don't do something quickly you will be out a whole lot more. But I can get you out of it in better shape than anyone else."

He then made the thoroughly convinced and discouraged president an offer for the assets of the business which was only a small fraction of their actual value, and told him that he would withdraw even that unless it was accepted immediately. George Cock promised to call a meeting of the B.O.D. board of directors immediately and give Holladay an answer by three o'clock that afternoon. When, promptly on the hour, a messenger arrived with an acceptance, Holladay is reported to have turned to his secretary and bellowed, "Answer those express companies and tell them to stock and be damned."

Ben Holladay bought the entire assets of the Butterfield Overland Dispatch Company in March 1866, and with a monopoly on passenger and express transportation between the Missouri River and Salt Lake City securely in his hands again, he set about gouging the public, the big express companies, and the United States Government to the limit.

First-class mail was left behind whenever there was as big a load of express and passengers as could be crammed into a single vehicle, schedules were disregarded, equipment allowed to run down, and passenger fares and express rates raised to the limit the traffic would bear. In spite of the postwar blight on mining, Holladay raised the express rate on gold shipments between Montana or Idaho and Atchison to 5 per cent of the mint value if the shipper was a bank, but 6 per cent to miners or the general public. He raised the passenger fare from Atchison to Salt Lake City, originally $150, to $500.

William Dixon, an Englishman who traveled from Wamego, Kansas (a few miles east of Junction City), to Salt Lake City in the spring of 1866, wrote that the vehicle in which he and his fellow passengers rode was a "frame" wagon with a canvas roof and flapping curtains which failed to protect them from rain. Upon returning to the wagon after a breakfast of pancakes and tea at Junction City, they found it already filled with express and mail sacks. When they protested, the driver replied that on the rough roads the sacks would soon shake down enough to make plenty of room for them. The wagon was drawn by mules, fresh teams were furnished only at intervals of forty to fifty miles, and although Dixon had boarded the stage nearly 150 miles west of Atchison he was obliged to pay the full fare of $500.

The winter of 1865–66 was severe in the Sierra Nevada. After reporting drifts fifteen feet high at the summit on January 8, the San Francisco *Alta California* continued, "Notwithstanding these difficulties the Overland Mail Company's stages arrive and depart with their usual regularity, making the trip from Salt Lake City to Virginia in 120 hours; distance six hundred miles. . . . Unfortunately the Company east of Salt Lake City have lost the continuity, but this is nothing very new for them."

Before many weeks had passed the same newspaper reported that Holladay's service had worsened to the extent that San Francisco was receiving overland mail from east of Salt Lake City no oftener than three times a week. Holladay's mail contract of 1864 stipulated that pay was to be forfeited for failure to make any scheduled trip, for violation of rules on any trip, or for failure to maintain the time schedules specified. Whether or not it was because of his influence within the Post Office Department, Ben Holladay was not penalized a single dollar for his flagrant disregard of the contract terms.

Early in 1866 Holladay presented to Congress a claim of $526,739 for losses he alleged to have sustained because of Indian depredations during the four years ending December 31, 1865. Of this amount, $77,000 was claimed to be the cost of moving the mail line from the South Pass route to the Cherokee Trail "by military order" in 1862. He listed $50,000 as the cost of altering the main line of the route to pass through Denver in 1864 "by order of Colonel Chivington" and $30,000 for "property taken by soldiers." Damage to stations, furniture, corrals, etc., was listed at $78,375, loss of hay and grain $166,059.72, and "horses and mules taken" $111,970, but only $1700 for "stage-coach destroyed and two coaches injured."

Preposterous as the claim obviously was, Ben Holladay had enough influence in Washington that the Senate passed a resolution referring it to the court of claims for settlement. The House, however, refused to concur, and Congress adjourned without taking further action. Although Holladay stormed and raged, the matter was postponed again and again. Then, in 1877, Congress finally offered $100,000 in settlement of all claims, but Holladay refused it angrily. It was not until November 1912 that the claim of Holladay's heirs was finally denied by the court of claims and the case dismissed.

From the time the Butterfield overland mail contract was transferred to the central route in 1861, Wells, Fargo & Company had been developing the transcontinental express business, convinced that the firm controlling express transportation by stagecoach would be awarded an exclusive franchise for its shipment by rail when the transcontinental railroad was eventually built. When, in early 1865, the firm was unable to reach an agreement with Ben Holladay for carrying its transcontinental express shipments between Salt Lake City and Atchison on a reasonable basis, Louis McLane (general manager of both Wells, Fargo & Company and its subsidiary, the Overland Mail Company) had made a trip over the Holladay line. He is reported to have at that time made Holladay an offer for his line that was far in excess of its actual value, fearing that a breach in his firm's control over the transcontinental express business would jeopardize a future exclusive railroad franchise. It is also reported that McLane renewed his offer, at a considerably higher figure, after Holladay caught the big express companies napping on the Butterfield Overland Dispatch deal, but that Holladay ridiculed the offer even though the transcontinental railroad was then being constructed.

Although President Lincoln had signed a bill chartering the Union Pacific Railroad Company on July 1, 1862, Congress had passed legislation to subsidize the builders with enormous land grants, and half a million dollars had been spent for surveys and other preparations, only fifteen miles of track had been laid westward from Omaha by mid-October 1865. On the California end of the line the Central Pacific had not made much more progress, and ahead of its builders lay the seemingly impossible task of blasting nineteen tunnels through solid granite in order to reach the summit of the Sierra Nevada.

But late in 1865 Congress passed an amendatory act to that of 1862, making additional concessions to builders of transcontinental railroads. A few unprincipled stockholders of the Union Pacific Railroad Company, by financial juggling through the infamous Crédit Mobilier of America, raised construction funds. General Grenville Dodge and the Casement brothers were put in charge of the project, and pushed the rails rapidly westward. At about the same time, work was begun on the Kansas Pacific Railroad, 160 miles to the south.

By July 1, 1866, the Union Pacific had reached Columbus, Nebraska, a hundred miles west of Omaha, and the Kansas Pacific had laid rails westward from Kansas City that reached more than halfway to Junction City, Kansas. By the end of August the Union Pacific had reached Fort Kearney, and the Kansas Pacific was within a few miles of Junction City. On August 30 Henry Reed, Ben Holladay's express superintendent on the eastern end of his line, wrote him urging that he put daily express messengers on both these railroads and give the public the best possible service between the Missouri River and Denver. He predicted that if it were not done the big eastern express companies would "engulf the business, and it is not beyond the mental calculation of the meanest brain to state how long it will take to leave this company without an express run."

No record has been found to prove whether or not Holladay took his superintendent's advice, but in view of his other actions to protect his interests there is little doubt that he did.

Although the Union Pacific had laid rails as far west as Fort Kearney, there was still a gap of some thirty-five miles in the line east of Council Bluffs, Iowa. But with the Missouri Pacific having reached Kansas City from St. Louis, there was an unbroken rail connection between the East Coast and Manhattan, Kansas, by August 15, 1866. The eastern terminus of the overland mail route was moved from Atchison to Manhattan on that date by order of the Postmaster General, with instructions that mail for or beyond Denver was to be carried via the Smoky Hill route.

Building the transcontinental railroad. (From Beyond the Mines, *Albert D. Richardson.)*

In the fall of 1866 the gap in the Union Pacific east of Council Bluffs was closed. Most of the transcontinental mail to and from New York City or points farther north was thereafter routed via Chicago and Omaha. Holladay was notified by the Post Office Department that, beginning on November 13, he was to provide daily mail coach service between Fort Kearney and Denver, as well as between Manhattan and Denver, and to continue daily service between Denver and Salt Lake City. At about the same time Postmaster General Randall announced that as rail service was extended farther westward the mail contractor's compensation would be reduced in proportion to the length of his carry. There was only one way in which Ben Holladay could avoid the reduction, but he did avoid it.

Although construction of the transcontinental railroad was being pushed forward rapidly in the Midwest, it had practically come to a halt in California. Early snows fell deep in the high Sierras and blizzard followed blizzard, and although there was still a gigantic task to be accomplished before the summit of the range (less than a hundred miles east of Sacramento) could be reached by rails, little or no progress would be possible before spring.

It is hardly surprising that Louis McLane and his associates in Wells, Fargo & Company should have reached the conclusion that it would be at least ten years before the transcontinental railroad was completed. They certainly knew, however, that train service was being extended farther and farther westward from the Missouri, and that express was being carried on those trains. It is very probable that they, like Henry Reed, believed that unless preventive action was taken immediately the big eastern express companies would "engulf the business, and it is not beyond the mental calculations of the meanest brain to state how long it will take to leave this company without an express run."

In any event, at the approach of winter in the high Sierra Nevada, Louis McLane made Ben Holladay another offer for his stagecoach empire. What the details of the bargaining may have been are unknown, but on November 1, 1866, Wells, Fargo & Company bought the Holladay Overland Mail and Express Company lock, stock, and barrel. For it Holladay received capital stock in Wells, Fargo & Company worth $300,000 and $1,500,000 in cash, plus the market value as of that date for all the hay, grain, and supplies in the warehouses, stables, and stations. Two weeks later Wells, Fargo & Company combined all its stage-line holdings, including the Overland Mail Company and the Pioneer Stage Line, under the charter granted to Ben Holladay on February 5, 1866, by the Territorial Legislature of Colorado.

Wells, Fargo & Company, by purchasing Ben Holladay's holdings, became owners of all the stage lines of any consequence between the Missouri River and California, with the exception of the rapidly shrinking Kansas City-Santa Fe line. Exactly contrary to Ben Holladay's method of operating a monopoly, Louis McLane reduced passenger fares sharply, replaced worn-out equipment, and stocked the entire line with horses as fine as those on Bob Spotswood's division. In the nearly six years that Holladay controlled the line between the Missouri and Salt Lake City, and although he added approximately a thousand miles of line in Idaho and Montana, he is reported to have bought only forty-three new stagecoaches—twenty-nine of them for the purpose of driving competition off the Idaho and Montana lines. To serve only the crews building the Union Pacific Railroad, Wells, Fargo & Company bought thirty nine-passenger Concord coaches, the largest single order ever filled by Abbot, Downing & Company. These thirty beautifully decorated coaches were shipped from Concord to Omaha in April 1868 on a special train of flatcars, one of the most spectacular events of the time.

Under Wells Fargo ownership, stagecoaching in the West reached its ultimate peak of glory, efficiency, and service to the public, but that glory was short-lived.

It was not until November 1867 that the Central Pacific completed its first hundred miles of track and crossed Donner Pass at the summit of the Sierra Nevada. But by that time the Union Pacific had reached Cheyenne, Wyoming, and was starting its ascent of the Continental Divide. In the spring of 1868 the Central Pacific passed Reno and began pushing track out across the Nevada deserts, while the Union Pacific drove its rails across the summit of the Rockies. The building then became an incredible race from both ends of the line. When the Central Pacific enlarged its crew to ten thousand Chinese and a thousand teams, the Union Pacific put on a like number of Irishmen and even more teams.

Breaking through the Wasatch Mountains and out onto the Great Salt Lake plain in the spring of 1869, Jack Casement and his Irishmen set a world's record by laying seven and a half miles of track in a single day. Charlie Crocker and his Chinese were not to be outdone, and allowed the record to stand for only a matter of hours. Rushing eastward across the Bonneville salt flats, where all modern automobile records are set, they unloaded a thousand tons of steel rails by hand and laid an even ten miles of track between dawn and twilight.

On May 10, 1869, the golden spike was driven at Promontory Point, Utah, connecting the rails from east and west. The hammers that drove that spike also struck the death knell of transcontinental stagecoaching, but for another decade or more the stagecoach, the spirited horses that sped it over mountain roads, and the amazingly skillful drivers who handled the reins would still be the backbone of passenger transportation west of the Missouri.

22

*Where There's Gold
the Wheels Still Roll*

UNDOUBTEDLY from the time a man first became capable of mounting a horse and doubling the speed with which he could travel, there has been glamour about the most rapid means of transportation available, but the glamour of the old fades quickly when a new and faster means is discovered. Just as we of the jet age find a long train trip exasperatingly slow, dirty, tedious, and uncomfortable, so Westerners found stagecoach travel after the coming of the railroads. But until nearly the close of the nineteenth century the stagecoach was to remain the chief means of travel throughout the mountainous and sparsely inhabited regions of the West.

Before the Union Pacific and Central Pacific railroads were joined at Promontory Point, the board of directors of Wells, Fargo & Company voted to dispose of all the firm's stagecoach lines. The main line between Sacramento and Atchison was, of course, abandoned, but the existing branch lines and all surplus stagecoaches, horses, harness, and other goods were sold soon after the completion of the railroad. Most of the sales were made to former division superintendents or other employees of the company and to small competing operators, at prices that were about a third of the original cost. The terms of sale were extremely lenient, making it possible for successful operators to pay off their investment from profits, but the sales contracts in every case stipulated that for at least one year the buyer could transport express and treasure chests for no other firm than Wells, Fargo & Company.

The Colorado branch lines were, for the most part, sold to Billy McClelland and Bob Spotswood. McClelland, as a boy, had gone to work in the Denver office of the C.O.C.&P.P. Express Company at the time of its founding. By the time the transcontinental railroad was completed the Kansas Pacific rails were nearing Denver, and much of the surplus stock and equipment from the Smoky Hill line was sold to Barlow & Sanderson, operators of the stage line between Santa Fe and the Kansas Pacific railhead at Kit Carson, Colorado. The surplus Utah assets and the Idaho and Montana branches were sold to Jack Gilmer and Monroe Salisbury, and the stock and equipment from the old Pioneer Stage Line went to various small California operators. McClelland & Spotswood, Barlow & Sanderson, and Gilmer & Salisbury established branch lines that spread out far and wide from the railroads to serve remote communities and mining towns of the mountains, prairies, and deserts. For two decades they were the backbone of north-south passenger, mail, and express transportation throughout the West.

McClelland and Spotswood confined their operations mainly to the mining towns of the Colorado Rockies, their main line being westward from Denver to Morrison (where the famous Red Rocks Park is situated) and over what is now U.S. Highway 285 through Turkey Creek Canyon to Fairplay on the headwaters of South Platte River. From Fairplay branch lines reached out to mining camps and towns all along the eastern rampart of the Continental Divide in central Colorado.

In 1873 the partners established a line of passenger and express coaches between Colorado Springs and Canon City. They later continued it westward across the Continental Divide by way of the route that is now U.S. Highway 50 to Salida, then northward on the road that is now U.S. 24 to Granite and Oro. They established another line between Colorado Springs and South Park, over the route that is now Highway 24. In 1877 silver-bearing carbonates were discovered at Leadville, less than twenty air miles west of Fairplay, but on the opposite side of the Continental Divide and eighty miles away by wagon road. The interest of Colorado miners and businessmen had been almost entirely in gold, and Bob Spotswood was one of the first to realize the tremendous value of the silver discovery. He and his partner at once put a stage line into Leadville from Fairplay, going over breathtaking Weston Pass to save a forty-mile detour through the much lower Trout Creek Pass.

As soon as the fabulous value of the discovery became known there was a tremendous rush of fortune seekers to Leadville, and

The stage from Georgetown to Hot Sulphur Springs at the summit of Berthoud Pass, Colorado, in 1898. (Courtesy, State Historical Society of Colorado.)

the Post Office Department advertised for bids on daily mail service from Denver to the new bonanza. Bob Spotswood made a hurried trip to Washington, secured a four-year mail contract, and stopped in the East to buy stagecoaches and heavy stage-type horses for the project. Soon afterward the Denver and South Park Division of the Union Pacific Railroad began building a narrow-gauge railroad through Platte Canyon, twenty miles south of Denver.

When the tracks reached Pine Grove, near present Tarryall, the rush of mail and passengers became so great that the Post Office Department ordered McClelland & Spotswood to double their service to Leadville. Again Bob Spotswood went East for additional stagecoaches and horses of the proper type. Within a month or two the firm was running five coaches daily between Pine Grove and Leadville, carrying an average of a hundred passengers in addition to mail and express. The precipitous haul across the Continental Divide was forty-one miles, but four relays of fresh horses were provided for each trip and the equipment was kept in tiptop condition. Men who had traveled the world over reported it doubtful that stagecoach service of such excellence had ever been given elsewhere under similar conditions. At first the firm had no competition, and the income from express alone often amounted to a thousand dollars a day.

As the population of Leadville boomed, Barlow & Sanderson established a competing line from Pueblo, running stagecoaches over the routes that are now U.S. Highway 50 to Salida and 24 to Leadville. The demand for transportation was so great, however, that the competition had little if any affect upon McClelland & Spotswood's business. To Bob Spotswood the disturbing development was the speed with which the Denver & Rio Grande Railway was laying track westward from Pueblo through the Royal Gorge of the Arkansas River.

While there was still a year remaining on the mail contract Wall and Witter put a competing line of stagecoaches on the McClelland & Spotswood route between Pine Grove and Leadville. The new competition cut somewhat into the firm's profits, but that was not Spotswood's greatest worry: the population of Leadville had zoomed to nearly 30,000, the postal rate on newspapers had been reduced, and the volume of mail matter the firm was required to carry with no increase in compensation was growing by leaps and bounds. Much to everyone's surprise, McClelland and Spotswood sold out their lucrative Leadville line to their new competitors. The price—including four relay stations, twelve Concord coaches, and a hundred horses—was only $19,000 and an agreement by Wall and Witter to carry the Leadville mail for the remainder of the Mc-Clelland & Spotswood contract. Long before the year was out, the volume of mail on the route had skyrocketed to five thousand pounds daily. Wall and Witter were obliged to put on twelve additional coaches and another hundred horses to handle it, nearly bankrupting the firm.

With the completion of the Rio Grande Railroad and various branches of the Denver & South Park Division of the Union Pacific through the mining areas of the Colorado Rockies, Bob Spotswood and Billy McClelland discontinued their stage lines and sold most of their stock and equipment to the rapidly expanding firm of Barlow & Sanderson. They retired wealthy men, and Bob Spotswood remained one of Colorado's most revered citizens until his death in 1910.

Barlow and Sanderson had been the only successful stage-line operators between Kansas City and Santa Fe, coping with the Indian menace and reducing the running time from a month to thirteen days. As the rails of the Kansas Pacific Railroad were pushed westward at the close of the Civil War, shortening the stage route from railhead to Santa Fe, Barlow & Sanderson established branch lines to Pueblo, Canon City, and Colorado Springs. Barlow remained in the East, handling the financial affairs of the firm and negotiating mail contracts with the Post Office Department, while "Colonel" J. L. Sanderson carried on the operation of the stage lines. As gold and silver were discovered in the Sangre de Cristo and San Juan mountains, Sanderson extended the firm's stage lines throughout south-central Colorado and north-central New Mexico, with through service to Santa Fe.

With fast stagecoaches running between Pueblo and La Junta (railhead for several years on the Santa Fe branch of the Kansas Pacific Railroad), Barlow & Sanderson could cut two days from the time required for Easterners to reach Leadville by way of Denver. Hordes of prospectors and hundreds of tons of mail and express were carried over the La Junta-Pueblo stage line during the 1870's. In February 1879 the firm brought in two hundred additional horses from St. Louis, along with a dozen Abbot-Downing stagecoaches and fifty sets of Hill harness from Concord for its Canon City-Leadville line alone. When in 1880 gold and silver were discovered in the Gunnison River area of Colorado, Barlow & Sanderson extended their lines westward over the route that is now U.S. Highway 50, with branches leading off through the mountains to north and south. At one time the firm had five thousand horses and mules in constant use on stagecoach runs through southern Colorado and northern New Mexico.

As more and more mineral deposits were discovered and new communities established in the remote regions of the western mountains and deserts, Barlow & Sanderson stage lines followed—across Utah, Nevada, into California, and northward to Oregon and Washington—providing mail and passenger service until superseded by a railroad, and then moving on.

Widespread though the Barlow & Sanderson operations became, they were far outstripped during the late 1870's by those of Gilmer & Salisbury. Jack Gilmer, like Bob Spotswood and Colonel Sanderson, was the dominant member of his firm and the partner who handled the actual stagecoaching operations. Also like Bob Spotswood, his entrance into the transportation business had been as a bullwhacker and muleskinner for Russell, Majors & Waddell. He had been one of the first stagecoach drivers on the Leavenworth & Pike's Peak Express line, a division superintendent for Ben Holladay, and manager of the Idaho and Montana branches of the line under Wells, Fargo & Company ownership. He took great pride in saying that he had turned the first wheels on the great overland stage line, and the last.

Wells, Fargo & Company had a tremendous amount of surplus equipment on hand in Utah at the time the golden spike was driven at Promontory Point, including $70,000 worth of Concord coaches in excellent condition. This surplus, together with the Idaho and Montana branches, was sold to Gilmer & Salisbury. Within seven years Jack Gilmer had established prosperous and efficient stage lines throughout the entire mining region of the Northwest. The most famous was the Deadwood line between Cheyenne, Wyoming, and the Black Hills.

To make peace with the warlike Sioux Indians and move them far enough into the wilderness so that they would not be likely to raid the settlements springing up along the central routes of transportation, the United States Government entered into a treaty with the tribe by which the Sioux were given as their exclusive domain forever a vast area in eastern Wyoming and South Dakota. Although United States citizens were forbidden by law to trespass upon lands set aside exclusively as Indian domain, it was impossible for the few soldiers stationed at Indian agencies to control the gold-crazed prospectors who ranged like hunting hounds through every mountain canyon in the West.

The Cripple Creek stage carrying U.S. mail, 1895. (Courtesy, State Historical Society of Colorado.)

Early in the 1870's gold was discovered in the Black Hills of South Dakota, at almost the center of the Sioux domain, but the amounts were not great. Due more to the Sioux's reputation for quick and bloody retaliation than to fear of the troops stationed at the widely scattered agencies, few miners entered the exclusive area until 1875. A rich strike was then made in Deadwood Gulch, and word of it was no sooner out than a full-blown stampede was on, with hundreds of gold rushers arriving on every train that pulled into Cheyenne, the nearest point to Deadwood on the Union Pacific Railroad.

Mail service had been established for several years to the Spotted Tail agency, about fifty miles from the edge of the Black Hills. The mail contract was held and the line operated by Todd Randall, who had a trading post at the agency, but no express or passengers were carried. In December 1875 the Wyoming territorial legislature passed a bill authorizing the establishment of a daily stage line to carry passengers and express between Cheyenne and the Black Hills. But due to fear of Indian attacks, and because no Government contracts could be secured unless the Sioux treaty was repudiated or the Indians relinquished their title to the Black Hills, Cheyenne businessmen were unwilling to gamble money on a stage line. In January 1876, however, Captain W. H. Brown, who was stationed at the Red Cloud agency, and his son-in-law Frank Yates subcontracted for the mail service to Spotted Tail, and on February 3 the Cheyenne newspaper reported that "the first coach of the Cheyenne and Black Hills Stage, Mail and Express line, owned by F. D. Yates & Co., stopped in front of the Inter-Ocean hotel at 7 A.M. to pick up passengers." A few days later "Stuttering" Brown, business scout for Gilmer & Salisbury, arrived in Cheyenne, bought out Yates & Co. (whose total assets, except for the mail subcontract, probably consisted of a single wagon and a few mules), and got a telegram away to the partners in Salt Lake City.

Luke Voorhees, a thoroughly experienced frontiersman and stage-line operator, was immediately sent to Cheyenne to lay out the stage route, hire drivers and station keepers, establish relay posts, and organize the new line. Agents were at the same time sent to St. Louis to buy six hundred well-bred stage horses and mules, an order was rushed off to J. R. Hill & Co. at Concord, New Hampshire, for a hundred sets of stage harness, and Abbot, Downing & Company was telegraphed to build thirty heavy-duty Concord coaches and ship them to Cheyenne "with all haste." To get the line started without delay, a carload of road-toughened horses and what Concord coaches could be spared were shipped by rail from Salt Lake City. Among the coaches were several of the thirty that had been in the famous trainload shipped to Wells, Fargo & Company at Omaha in the spring of 1868—one of them destined for far greater fame.

There was at that time no established road between Cheyenne and the Black Hills. Yates had gone by a roundabout route via the Spotted Tail agency, and only as far as the present site of Custer, South Dakota. The few freighters who had risked Indian attack during the fall of 1875 set a course across the prairies that was almost due north from Cheyenne to Fort Laramie on the North Platte River. Beyond the Platte a few of the freighters veered somewhat to the east; followed Rawhide Creek nearly to its source; crossed a low divide to the headwaters of Old Woman Creek, a tributary of the Cheyenne River; and continued along those streams to the Black Hills. Others set a more direct course from Fort Laramie to the point where Cheyenne River crosses the Wyoming-South Dakota boundary. Like all early wagon routes across the prairies of the West, there was no single road, only a skein of wheel tracks all tending in the same general direction.

The course that Luke Voorhees chose for a stage route and which became the famous Cheyenne-Black Hills Trail was almost identical to that of present U.S. Highway 87 between Cheyenne and Chugwater. There it veered slightly eastward to cross the North Platte at Fort Laramie. Beyond the river the route continued almost due north to the present site of Lusk, Wyoming, and went on to Deadwood over a course that is now closely approximated by U.S. Highway 85 and its eastern branch, 85 Alternate. The stage route, however, was established only as far as Custer City in the spring of 1876.

Six weeks were required to build relay stations and get the horses and mules through from St. Louis and the coaches and harness from Concord. On April 3 the first three Concord coaches rolled out of Cheyenne, with Jack Gilmer himself handling the reins of the first team. Each coach carried from eighteen to twenty passengers—crammed inside or clinging to the top—and the front and back boots were packed tightly with express and baggage.

During the late winter the Indians had begun running off stock and attacking freighters going into the Black Hills along the Cheyenne River or as they made their way through Red Canyon at the southern end of Custer Valley. The convoy of three coaches, loaded with heavily armed men, was not attacked. But on his return trip Luke Voorhees found a pioneer family murdered at Red Canyon. Soon afterward Stuttering Brown was murdered and robbed on the Old Woman branch of the Cheyenne, but there were those who did not believe his attackers to have been Indians.

As more and more gold rushers pushed into the Sioux domain the Indians intensified their attacks. Even the largest and most strongly armed freight caravans were harassed, their night camps raided, and their mules stampeded, with hundreds driven away. Stagecoaches were attacked, drivers killed, and passengers wounded. Three of Gilmer & Salisbury's new stations between Custer City and Fort Laramie were raided, the stock stolen, and the buildings

Buffalo Bill Cody brought back a nostalgic glimpse of stage-coaching days with his Wild West Show. He is shown here in Denver in 1912.

burned. The damage was so great that for a short time service had to be discontinued. The day after regular trips were resumed General George Custer and his entire force of 256 cavalrymen were killed in the Battle of the Little Big Horn.

Following the Custer Massacre, Congress repudiated the Sioux Treaty, the Black Hills were legally opened to settlement and mining, a lucrative mail contract was awarded, troops were stationed along the Cheyenne-Black Hills Trail, and the stage line was extended to Deadwood. Within a few weeks more than a half million dollars' worth of gold was shipped to Cheyenne in Gilmer & Salisbury stagecoaches.

Thugs and desperadoes were attracted to every rich gold discovery like moths to a lamp in the night, and Deadwood drew more than its share. Outlaw bands sprang up by the score, and the stage line, traversing three hundred miles of uninhabited wilderness, was extremely vulnerable to them. Highwaymen could make attacks from hiding at hundreds of points along the line, and the stationing of troops at intervals of fifty miles or more was little deterrent to them. It soon became evident that many crimes for which the Sioux had been blamed were actually committed by white men in disguise. Two men were killed and the mail sacks plundered in an attack north of Fort Laramie. Both men were scalped in Sioux fashion, but only the registered mail was plundered from the sacks.

The stage-line horses were the finest in Wyoming, and were greatly coveted by the Indians. To protect them from raids, the company built corrals that were actually stockades; the walls were heavy posts set close together and deep in the ground, and the split-log gate was hung on ponderous hinges and securely closed with an equally ponderous padlock. In the summer of 1876 one of the larger stations between Fort Laramie and Cheyenne was attacked by a band of war-painted, feathered, shrieking "savages," the keeper and his men penned up in the station by withering gunfire, the corral breached, and a score of fine horses driven away. When the dust had settled and the keeper was able to leave the station, he found that the lock on the corral gate had been opened with a duplicate key.

Shotgun guards, one of them Wyatt Earp, were put on all stagecoaches carrying treasure chests, but still the holdups continued, highwaymen suddenly racing their horses from the mouth of a blind gulch and getting the "drop" on the guards before they could raise their guns. An outlaw gang captured the Canyon Springs relay post, knocked the mud chinking from between the logs in the barn wall, and greeted the next southbound stage with a fusillade of gunfire, killing one guard and severely wounding the other. The driver and passengers were tied up and left to watch as the bandits broke open the chest and made off with its $27,000 treasure.

When the next large shipment of gold was ready to leave Deadwood, Jack Gilmer put Fred Hopkins and "Quick-Shot" Davis on the box with the driver, armed himself with a double-barreled shotgun loaded with buckshot, and strapped himself onto the platform of the rear boot. Hopkins and Davis were well known as the best shots in Wyoming, and no one doubted Jack Gilmer's courage or determination. The coach went through to Cheyenne without a bit of trouble.

Soon after Gilmer & Salisbury opened their line to Deadwood, the Western Stage Company established a competing line from Sidney, Nebraska, but its coaches were virtually driven off the road by highwaymen. Gilmer & Salisbury bought the line to relieve congestion on their Cheyenne-Black Hills route, and had a coach known as The Iron Clad fitted up for carrying gold over their new line. The interior was lined with bullet-proof steel plates, with two portholes in each door and a chilled-steel safe was bolted to the floor. Three or four of the best riflemen in the West rode inside, with two others on the box with the driver, making The Iron Clad as nearly bandit-proof as possible. More than a quarter million dollars' worth of gold was occasionally taken through from Deadwood to Sidney in a single shipment.

Banditry and murder in the Black Hills region had reached an all-time high for the American West at the time of the Canyon Springs holdup. As had been the case in other frontier mining communities where law enforcement officers were unable to control the outlaws—or were in "cahoots" with them—the miners in the Black Hills formed vigilante committees and took law enforcement into their own hands. Three of the men who took part in the Canyon Springs killing and robbery were run down, captured, and hanged, and a board was erected over their common grave with a warning to others of their kind:

> Here lies the body of Allen, Curry and Hall.
> Like other thieves they had their rise, decline
>   and fall;
> On yon pine tree they hung till dead,
> And here they found a lonely bed.
> We're bound to stop this business, or hang you to
>   a man,
> For we've hemp and hands enough in town to swing
>   the whole damn clan.

*The Wells Fargo overland stage now in the Wells Fargo Bank
History Room in San Francisco. It weighed 2,500 pounds and
seated nine passengers inside.*

After a few more vigilante hangings, and the discouragement to
highwaymen provided by The Iron Clad, the outlaws scattered
and the Gilmer & Salisbury coaches went through unmolested. By
1880 the firm had become "one of the most powerful corporations
in the West." Their stagecoaching operations far exceeded those
of Ben Holladay when at the peak of his power and passed the mark
set by Wells, Fargo & Company before the completion of the
transcontinental railroad. At the firm's climax its stagecoaches ran
daily over more than five thousand miles of line connecting centers
of population throughout the sparsely settled region from the
Canadian boundary to the deserts of southern Utah, and from the
Great Plains to the Sierra Nevada and Cascade mountains.

One of the Concord coaches originally shipped to Wells, Fargo & Company at Omaha in 1868 was kept in constant use on the Cheyenne-Black Hills route until the arrival of the railroad. After being fitted out with a chilled-steel treasure chest that was bolted to the floor, it was attacked innumerable times by highwaymen and fairly riddled with bullet holes. The first driver to be shot from its box was John Slaughter, son of the marshal at Cheyenne.

Although it may be legend, there is a report in Wyoming that Martha Canary, known throughout the West as Calamity Jane, was riding on the box when the next driver was killed. She is said to have snatched the reins from his lifeless hands, whipped up the horses while the guards fought a running gun battle with the mounted highwaymen, and brought the coach, passengers, and mail safely into the next station.

When Buffalo Bill Cody returned from scouting for the U.S. Army following the Custer Massacre, he rode to Cheyenne in the already famous coach. But when the railroad reached Deadwood and the stage line was discontinued, the badly battered old coach was abandoned on the prairie.

Cody, who had recently organized his Buffalo Bill's Wild West Show, heard that the old coach had been abandoned, had it brought to the railroad, shipped to Abbot, Downing & Company at Concord, and completely overhauled. As the Deadwood Mail Coach he used it in his shows and parades throughout the United States and Europe. The Prince of Wales rode in it in London and it was examined and admired by the President of France, the King of Spain, the Emperor of Germany, and Pope Leo XIII. It is now preserved in the Smithsonian Institution in Washington, D.C.

23

Twilight of
the Golden Era

ALTHOUGH highwaymen had been driven from the wilds of eastern Wyoming and western South Dakota by 1880, the most amazing stage robber in the history of the West was still plying his trade with bewildering success in California. Railroads already served the major cities, all the sandbars along the rivers and creeks had long since been stripped of gold dust, most of the mines had been worked out, and many of the thriving gold-rush cities of the 1850's and '60's were becoming ghost towns. The great stagecoach lines had been broken up and their equipment worn out or scattered far and wide among the small owners who still operated between the railroad lines and the remote towns in the mountains carrying Wells Fargo express boxes and a few passengers.

On a bright July morning in 1875 John Shine set out from Sonora on his regular stage run to Copperopolis and Milton. At his feet the Wells Fargo express box bounced and rattled, its $300 contents too light to hold it steady. One of John's five well-dressed passengers was a lady and two of the men were evidently gold-dust buyers, for they were armed and carried carpetbags.

Shine kept his four horses at a smart trot until he reached the Stanislaus River. There he made a short stop at "Grandma" Rolleri's inn for breakfast, crossed the river on Reynold's ferry, and relaxed comfortably on the high seat as his team made the long, slow climb up Funk's Hill. John had driven that route for twenty years, and as he neared the top of the hill he was thinking back to the long-gone days when there were mining camps all along the Stanislaus and Funk's Hill was known as Robbers' Roost. Suddenly a tall, gaunt figure, covered from shoulders to heels by a white linen duster and with a flour sack pulled down over his head, slipped from behind a boulder at the roadside. The ghostlike figure crouched in front of the rearing lead team, aimed a double-barrel shotgun steadily at Shine's head, and demanded in a deep voice, "Throw down the box!"

From inside the coach one of the passengers shouted, "Drive on!" But John didn't drive. The shotgun was being held too steadily, and the deep voice boomed, "Keep your eyes on the passengers, boys, and be ready with both barrels! If one of them dares to shoot, give them a solid volley!"

As Shine glanced nervously along the roadside he could have sworn he saw ten or twelve shotguns poked out through the bushes. He wasted no time in tossing down the Wells Fargo box and calling to his passengers, "He's got a gang with him. If you want to live, don't monkey with your guns!"

As the Wells Fargo box hit the ground the highwayman stood up, looking to be well over six feet tall. Still covering Shine with the shotgun, he came back toward the coach with quick, springy steps and demanded, "Throw down the mail sacks!"

"They're in the back boot," Shine told him. The woman passenger panicked and tossed her purse out the coach window to the deep-voiced bandit.

He picked the purse up, bowed courteously, and passed it back, saying, "Madam, I do not wish your money. In that respect I honor only the good office of Wells Fargo."

Unhurriedly he took the mail sacks from the boot and called into the bushes at the roadside, "That will be all, boys!" Then he told Shine jovially, "Hurry along now, my friend, and good luck to you."

Jim Hume, chief of Wells Fargo's detective force, reasoned that the highwayman must be well educated, intelligent, and young. The amount lost was not great, but if such a man were heading a newly organized large band of stage robbers it might well be costly to the company. Hume posted a sizable reward for apprehension of any member of the gang and hurried to the scene of the holdup. By getting there quickly, he felt sure he could pick up the trail of so large a gang. If not, he could certainly run down the leader, for with most of the mines closed few strangers came into the Mother Lode country. A tall, slender young man who spoke excellent English in a deep voice would be spotted immediately.

When Jim Hume reached Funk's Hill he found a dozen or so sticks poked through the bushes in such a way as to look like shotguns, the Wells Fargo box lying at the roadside with the lock battered off, a rusty axe beside the box, and two empty mail sacks slit open in the form of a T. He searched every inch of the surrounding area without finding a footprint or any place where a getaway horse had been tied. No one in the nearby towns had seen a tall, deep-voiced stranger in several months.

Five months passed without Hume's turning up a clue of any kind. Then a coach was held up between San Juan and Marysville, a hundred miles north of Funk's Hill. Sticks poked through the bushes to simulate shotguns, a rusty axe lying beside the smashed Wells Fargo box, and mail bags slashed in the form of a T left no doubt as to whom the highwayman had been. After another five months an identical holdup was made on the Yreka-Roseburg stagecoach, more than two hundred miles still farther north. Again Jim Hume rushed to the scene of the holdup as soon as news of it had been telegraphed to San Francisco, but as in the previous cases he could find no tracks, no clues, and no one who had seen a tall, deep-voiced stranger. The next strike of the ghostlike highwayman, identical in every respect to those of the past two years, was made in August 1877 on a coach in the coastal hills about a hundred miles north of San Francisco.

For a year Jim Hume and his men kept up a fruitless search for any clues regarding a tall, well-educated young stranger with a deep, resonant voice. Then, in the Feather River canyon of the Sierras, the phantom highwayman made two strikes in quick succession. This time he left a jeering clue on a waybill in one of the smashed-open Wells Fargo boxes, each line in a different style of handwriting:

> Here I lay me down to sleep
> To wait the coming morrow,
> Perhaps success, perhaps defeat,
> And everlasting sorrow.
>
> I've labored long and hard for bread,
> For honor and for riches,
> But on my corns too long you've tred,
> You fine-haired sons of bitches.
>
> Let come what will, I'll try it on,
> My condition can't be worse;
> And if there's money in that box
> 'Tis munny in my purse.

> Black Bart, the Po8

Two months later Black Bart, the "poet," struck twice more in rapid-fire succession, this time near Ukiah on the opposite side of the state. Following each holdup, newspapers all over California demanded that the "bloodthirsty criminal" be captured and hanged. Mothers kept their children indoors, and travelers went armed to the teeth, but Black Bart had never yet hurt anyone, and his only robberies had been of mail bags and Wells Fargo boxes.

At each new outburst from the newspapers local sheriffs were driven into a show of action and Wells, Fargo & Company was driven nearly to distraction. But there was little that any of them could do, for although Black Bart's flour sack and linen duster had become famous, no one had the slightest notion as to what the man who wore them looked like, and no one had ever been able to pick up his trail.

Mendocino County, in which Ukiah is situated, lies along the coast midway between San Francisco Bay and the Oregon boundary, and its low but rugged mountains are covered by dense redwood forests. In 1878 there were a few lumbering towns along the coast and a few frontier farms in the valleys of the Russian and Eel rivers, but the mountains to the east of the rivers were inhabited only by Indians. With the exception of the Apaches, these Indians were the finest trackers in the world. They needed no footprints to follow, but read a trail unerringly by every broken twig, turned stone, or bit of matted grass.

Immediately after Black Bart's Ukiah holdups the sheriff of Mendocino County went to the mountains and brought back several of the best Indian trackers. They quickly picked up the trail that no white man was able to see, followed it for sixty miles, and then lost it completely. But in three days they learned more about Black Bart than white men had been able to learn in three years. They reported back to the sheriff that the man they had trailed was an expert woodsman and mountaineer, knew the country thoroughly, could slip through dense forests as tracklessly as a fox, was a tireless walker, and did no hunting or cooking but lived on crackers and sugar, which, together with a sawed-off shotgun dismounted at the breech, he carried rolled in a single blanket. He was not over five feet eight inches tall, weighed no more than 140 pounds, and had covered sixty miles afoot over extremely rugged country in three days, holding a course almost due north.

With something, little though it was, to go on, Hume sent his entire detective force into the area where Bart's trail had been lost. Everyone, white or Indian, living within fifty miles was questioned, but the only stranger anyone had seen was a traveling preacher who had stopped for a meal at the McCreary's farmhouse in the Eel River valley. To let no possible clue escape him, Jim Hume went to talk with Mrs. McCreary. She became indignant when he suggested that the stranger might have been Black Bart in disguise. Although the gentleman hadn't actually said he was a preacher, she said she knew it from his intellectual conversation and because his hands were slender and "genteel" like a preacher's. It was ridiculous, she said, to try to make out that the man was the stage robber the Indians had trailed. He couldn't have walked more than five miles in a whole day's time, as he was an elderly gentleman, and poor, with bad feet. His hair, mustache, and a little tuft of beard on his chin were snow-white, his coat and derby hat were shabby, his shoes were old and had been slit to ease his bunions.

Was there anything else she had noticed about the stranger? Well, he was about two inches taller than she, and stood up as straight as a ramrod. His eyes were blue and sort of piercing, but kindly, and he'd laughed and joked as he ate. No, she didn't exactly remember anything he'd said, but she had noticed that two of his front teeth were missing. Yes, his voice was rather deep, but it was gentle. Why of course he was carrying a bedroll; anyone traveling afoot on the frontier had to, but it was only a single blanket and the roll was too small to hold a shotgun. It wasn't more than two feet long. No, she hadn't noticed which way the gentleman went when he left, probably toward the road that ran north and south through the valley.

There seemed little possibility that the man who had stopped at Mrs. McCreary's house could be the phantom highwayman, but his deep voice and bedroll were the nearest thing to a clue that had yet shown up, and his joking tied in with the doggerel left in the smashed Wells Fargo box after the Feather River holdup. Jim Hume wrote out every detail of his conversation with Mrs. Mc-Creary and filed it away in his San Francisco office.

During the next two years Black Bart made seven holdups, all identical with those in the past, although he left no more poetry in the smashed boxes. Immediately after each strike Jim Hume moved his entire detective force into the area and combed it thoroughly, but no trail could be picked up and no one was found who had seen a suspicious-appearing stranger with a deep voice.

At last Hume believed he saw a pattern emerging. Black Bart had held up two stages in 1875, one in '77, four in '78, three in '79, and four in 1880—in reverse ratio to the value of gold being carried in Wells Fargo boxes from year to year. Between most of the hold-ups Bart had leapfrogged a hundred miles or more across the northern third of California, but in three cases he had made a pair of holdups in quick succession and in the same area. The amount of loot had been no more than $500 in any of his single holdups, and when he made them in pairs the amount taken in the first one was very small. It seemed apparent that Black Bart held up stages only when he needed money to live on, and he had taken no more than enough to support a single man.

It would have been much cheaper for Wells Fargo to let Bart continue robbing express boxes than to spend thousands of dollars in an attempt to catch him, but the firm had a policy of running down and punishing highwaymen who robbed their express boxes, regardless of cost or the amount lost. Hume continued to move his men wherever Bart struck and to question everyone within fifty miles. Following a stage holdup near Redding, he found a rancher in the Trinity Mountains who said that a stranger had stopped at his cabin a few days before and asked for breakfast. He said the gentleman was elderly, with a big white mustache, a little tuft of gray chin whiskers, bright blue eyes, a deep but kindly voice, and two front teeth missing. He was on foot, wore a rather shabby over-coat and derby hat, and carried nothing but a small bedroll.

Hume was now convinced that the old gentleman was the phantom highwayman, and that his absolute naturalness was what made him almost impossible to run down. His only unusual traits appeared to be his ability to get away from the scene of a holdup without leaving tracks and to cover great distances rapidly through rugged mountains—and his courage at his age to be a highwayman.

From what he had learned, the detective made another deduction: the description of the man, together with his leapfrogging and his robbing a second stagecoach almost immediately if the first yielded little or no plunder, indicated that he lived in a large city—probably San Francisco, that he made a trip to some distant town when he needed money, held up a stagecoach, or two if necessary, and returned to live as a respected citizen until the money had been spent on a modest living. But such a deduction seemed to be of little value, for identifying such a man in a big city would be like singling out of a swarm the hornet that had stung you. Mustaches and small tufts of chin whiskers were popular, and in San Francisco there were hundreds of elderly gentlemen with such adornments and a missing tooth or two.

During 1881 and '82 Bart held up nine stagecoaches, eight of them without a hitch, but the ninth nearly ended in disaster. Horses had always before reared and come to a stop when he slipped from behind a boulder and crouched in front of them, but this time

*Black Bart, last of the colorful highwaymen of the West.
(Courtesy, Wells Fargo Bank History Room.)*

the frightened leaders swerved aside and raced past, knocking Bart sprawling. As the wildly rocking stagecoach lurched away George Hackett, the driver, snatched up his shotgun, turned on the high seat, and fired. Unhurt by the fall, Bart had scrambled to his feet and was making a dash for the bushes along the roadside when Hackett's near miss ripped off his flour sack and the high-crowned derby that made him look more than six feet tall when masked. Hackett, with a frightened team to handle, got only a glimpse of the unmasked highwayman, but said he could swear that the man had gray hair and a big white mustache.

Bart's narrow escape did not appear to have either frightened or discouraged him. Two months later he robbed the stage running between Redding and Yreka, struck twice near Cloverdale in the early spring of 1883, and in June held up the Ione stage near Jackson, 150 miles farther south.

It is said that criminals always return to the scene of their first crime. If so, Black Bart was no exception.

An hour before dawn on November 3, 1883, Reason McConnell drove his four-horse stagecoach out of Tuttletown with no passengers but the most valuable cargo he had carried in many a month. On this trip the Wells Fargo agent at Sonora had insisted that the steel treasure box be bolted solidly to the floor inside the coach, and in it there was now $4200 in gold amalgam, $550 in gold coin, and dust worth $65.

Reason kept the team at a smart trot, for although highwaymen were now about as scarce in California as albino crows Black Bart was still at large, and that loaded treasure box couldn't be turned over to the agent at Copperopolis any too soon. Shortly after daylight he pulled his blowing horses to a stop at Grandma Rolleri's little inn at Reynold's Ferry and left her nineteen-year-old son Jimmy to watch them while he had a bite of breakfast.

As Jimmy waited he decided to ride over to Copperopolis with Reason. There was a herd of fat deer on Funk's Hill, and maybe he could get a shot at one of them. McConnell was more than glad to have the company, and as they crossed the ferry Jimmy told him that he'd drop off at the foot of Funk's Hill, circle through the brush to try for a shot at a deer, and meet him on the far side. When the team slowed to a walk on a sharp curve at the foot of the hill Jimmy jumped down, slipped four cartridges into the chamber of his rifle, and, silent as an Indian, glided away among the scrub oaks.

The plodding horses were within a hundred yards of the hilltop when McConnell heard a sound in the brush at the roadside, turned his head toward it, and found himself looking down the twin bar-

rels of a sawed-off shotgun. At the far end of them, bright blue
eyes shone through peepholes in a flour sack, and a deep voice
asked, "Who was that man—the one who got off down below?"

Reason McConnell believed he caught a note of unsureness in
the voice, and an idea came quickly into his mind. "That wasn't
no man," he answered, "but a boy from the inn at the ferry. He
rode out to fetch in some cattle down yonder that had strayed."

It was evident that Bart believed him, and equally evident that
he knew the Wells Fargo treasure box was bolted to the floor of
the coach. Instead of ordering Reason to throw down the box, he
demanded, "Throw down your gun and get down. Unhook your
horses and drive them over the hilltop! Be quick about it!"

McConnell stalled as much as he dared, to give Jimmy time to
get around the hillside. As he drove the team toward the summit he
heard heavy pounding behind him, proof that Bart was having no
easy time in trying to break open the bolted-down steel treasure
box.

Reason had barely driven out of sight of the coach when he
saw Jimmy coming toward him through the bushes. He signaled
for the boy to be quiet and follow, and as they crept cautiously
back over the hilltop the sound of hammering stopped. When they
came in sight of the coach Bart was backing out of the doorway.
The flour sack was off his head, and he held it in one hand, partly
filled with the gold from the Wells Fargo box.

McConnell snatched the rifle from Jimmy's hands, and fired twice
in quick succession, but both shots missed. Bart whirled and ran
for the bushes on the downhill side of the road, clutching the flour
sack with both hands. Jimmy Rolleri grabbed his rifle back from
McConnell, shouting, "Let me shoot! I'll get him and won't kill
him neither." He fired, and Bart faltered for an instant, looking as
if he were going to fall, then slipped away into a thick stand of
manzanita.

When Reason and Jimmy reached the place where Bart had
disappeared into the brush they were too excited to pick up the
fresh trail and follow it. They hitched up the horses, galloped
them all the way to Copperopolis, and reported the holdup.

Ben Thorn, the sheriff at San Andreas, was an intelligent and
highly observant man. After questioning Reason McConnell thoroughly he did a little reasoning of his own: If the highwayman
had been watching the coach as it approached the bottom of the
hill he could not then have been in his hiding place at the roadside.
He would have had to be high on the crest of the hill, with enough
elevation to get an unobstructed view across the bush tops, and

near enough to the scene of the holdup to get there before the horses could climb the hill. After reaching the holdup scene the sheriff stood a minute or two studying the hilltop. Near the crest and a hundred yards back from the road the dome of a great boulder showed above the ragged fringe of bushes. He made his way straight to it, and his reasoning proved good.

Behind the boulder Thorn found a case for field glasses, a blanket, belt, magnifying glass, razor, and two flour sacks. In one of them he found three dirty linen cuffs and a handful of buckshot tied up in a linen handkerchief. Carefully marked in indelible ink at one corner of the handkerchief was F.X.O.7. In the other flour sack there was a pound of sugar and a paper bag with a few crackers in it.

When Sheriff Thorn took the evidence to Wells Fargo's San Francisco office, Jim Hume was interested only in the handkerchief, for he knew the letters to be a laundry mark. If, as he had long suspected, Black Bart lived in San Francisco, the mark should lead quickly and directly to him.

In 1883 there were ninety-one laundries listed in the San Francisco directory. It was weeks before Jim Hume discovered the right one and learned that the handkerchief belonged to Mr. C. E. Bolton, a gentleman with gray hair and a large white mustache who lived in room 40 at the Webb House, a small hotel at 37 Second Street. A search warrant was secured, and in the room was found all the evidence necessary for conviction: laundry bearing the F.X.O.7. mark, the suit Bart had worn when making his last holdup, and the famous linen duster. But most interesting of all was a worn Bible, on the fly leaf of which was written in nearly obliterated lead pencil, "This precious Bible is presented to Charles E. Boles, First Sergeant, Company B, 116th Illinois Volunteer Infantry, by his wife as a New Year's gift. God gives us . . . faith to believe. Decatur, Illinois, 1865."

Whether Bolton, Boles, or Black Bart, Wells Fargo had no wish to send the old rascal to the penitentiary for life, which could easily have been done with the evidence in hand. The firm's only desire was to recover what it could from the last holdup—the only one that had amounted to more than $500—and to see that the old fellow got just enough punishment to discourage others from trying the same stunt.

Hour after hour Jim Hume and his assistant, Harry Morse, talked to Bart, urging him to confess the Funk's Hill holdup and return the gold. And hour after hour Bart insisted that he did not have the gold, that he was a gentleman mine owner and couldn't possibly have been the robber. Then he suddenly turned to Morse and said, "Mind you, I do not admit that I committed this robbery. But what benefit would it be to the man who did do it if he should acknowledge it?"

Morse told him that if he would confess to the Funk's Hill holdup and return the stolen gold, or tell where it was hidden, Wells Fargo would not press charges on his other twenty-seven holdups.

"Supposing," Bart asked, "that the man who did commit the robbery should do this, would it not be posssible for him to get clear altogether?"

"No," Morse told him, "but it would go much easier for him."

"Well," Bart said, rising, "let's go after it!"

At Funk's Hill he led Hume and Morse down into a gulch a quarter mile below the road. There he kicked a pile of leaves away from the end of a hollow log, reached in, and pulled out the flour sack he had used as a mask for the holdup. In it was the full $4815 worth of gold he had taken from the Wells Fargo treasure box. When they asked him how he was able to get away from the scene of his holdups without leaving a trail and how he had known when the large shipment of gold amalgam was to be made, he answered, "Why that's easy. Any man who likes to watch wild creatures has to learn to walk quiet through the woods; it gets to be a habit. It was no trouble to find out when the shipment would be made. I just stopped at Tuttletown a few days and made friends with the folks who were shipping it. They told me when it was going out and that the box would be bolted down."

On November 17, two weeks to the day after the holdup, Bart appeared before a judge of the California Superior Court, entered a plea of guilty, waived trial, and asked the court to pronounce sentence. The judge, taking into consideration that the defendant was being accused of only the Funk's Hill robbery, that the entire amount of the theft had been returned, and that in his long career as a highwayman he had never harmed anyone, set his sentence at six years in the state prison.

Black Bart was the last of the colorful highwaymen who for a third of a century held up stagecoaches bringing gold down from the mining towns of California's Mother Lode or silver over the summit of the Sierra Nevada from Virginia City. And by the time of his forced retirement most of the colorful reinsmen who had driven those stagecoaches during their heyday in the '50's and early '60's had passed on, been killed in action, or hung up their whips and found some less rigorous occupation. Among them was Charlie Parkhurst, fondly known throughout the entire region as

Old Charlie, and though not the most colorful of that skillful and courageous breed, certainly the most amazing.

Charlie Parkhurst is reported to have run away from a New Hampshire poorhouse at a very early age and to have found a job as stableboy for Ebenezer Balch, keeper of an inn and livery stable at Worcester, Massachusetts. Charlie undoubtedly was born with an affinity for horses, learned as a stableboy to love and understand them, and had extraordinarily nimble fingers with a very sensitive touch. Nor is there any doubt that Ebenezer Balch was an accomplished reinsman, for he quickly recognized the natural aptitude of his new stableboy, and over a period of years schooled the youth thoroughly in the art of reinsmanship.

When, in the early 1840's, Balch moved to the What Cheer House at Providence, Charlie went with him and soon became known as the finest reinsman in Rhode Island, but after a year or two went to Georgia with another driver, and did not return until shortly before Jim Birch and Frank Stevens set off for California in the gold rush of 1849. Two years later Jim Birch, desperately in need of expert reinsmen for his rapidly growing stage lines, induced Charlie to come to California and go to work for him.

Parkhurst soon won the reputation of being one of the fastest and safest stagecoach drivers in California, and being by that time nearly forty years of age, was given the nickname "Old Charlie," for there were numerous stage drivers named Charlie and most of them were striplings.

Outlasting Jim Birch, Frank Stevens, Warren Hall, Jared Crandall, Louis McLane, and most of the other greats of California stagecoaching, Old Charlie drove stagecoaches on nearly every route in the Mother Lode country, back and forth over the "big hump" to Virginia City on the Pioneer Line, and between all the cities of central California before the building of the railroads.

Charlie smoked cigars, chewed tobacco, drank moderately, played cards and shook dice for cigars or drinks, and was always cheerful and agreeable, but always reticent about personal matters, and was unique among stage drivers because of never using profanity under any circumstances. No more than five feet seven inches tall, Charlie was broad-shouldered, smooth-faced, and sun-browned, and had gray-blue eyes and a rather sharp, high-pitched voice. It was said that in more than twenty years no highwayman had dared to hold up a stagecoach with Charlie Parkhurst on the box, for the first two who tried it had been shot dead in their tracks.

One of the greatest honors to be extended to a man was an invitation to ride on the box beside Old Charlie. J. Ross Browne, California's most sensitive author of the 1860's and '70's, was given such an invitation on a trip from Placerville to Virginia City, and in writing of it left a poignant portrait of the venerated driver:

It was 5 o'clock P.M. . . . . when we took our places on the stage, and . . . I was the lucky recipient of . . . the seat of honor. The driver was Charlie—that same Old Charlie who has driven all over the roads of California, and never capsized anybody but himself. On that occasion he broke several of his ribs, or as he expressed it to me, "busted his sides in." I was proud and happy to sit by the side of Charlie—especially as the road . . . over which we passed after dark, branches off over hills, and along the sides of hills, and into deep cañons, and up hills again; dark, dismal places in the midst of great forests of pine, where the horses seem to be eternally plunging over precipices and the stage following them with a crashing noise, horribly suggestive of cracked skulls and broken bones. But I had implicit confidence in Old Charlie. The way he handled the reins and peered through the clouds of dust and volumes of darkness, and saw trees and stumps and boulders of rock, and horses' ears, when I could scarcely see my own hand before me, was a miracle of stage driving. "Git aeoup!" was the warning cry of this old stager. "Git alang, my beauties!"

"Do many people get killed on this route?" said I to Charlie, as we made a sudden lurch in the dark and bowled along the edge of a fearful precipice.

"Nary a kill that I know of. Some of the drivers smashes 'em once in a while, but that's whisky or bad drivin'. Last summer a few stages went over the grade, but nobody was hurt bad—only a few legs 'n arms broken. Them was opposition stages. Pioneer stages, as a genr'l thing, travels on the road. Git aeoup!"

"Why, I have read horrible stories of people crushed to death going over these mountains!"

"Very likely—they kill 'em quite lively on the Henness route. Git alang, my beauties! Drivers only break their legs a little on this route; that is, some of the opposition boys did last summer; but our company's very strict; they won't keep drivers, as a genr'l thing, that gets drunk and smashes up the stages. Git aeoup, Jake! Git alang, Mack! 'Twon't pay; 'tain't a good investment for man nor beast. A stage is worth more'n two thousand dollars, and legs costs heavy besides. You, Jake! Git!"

"How in the world can you see your way?"

"Smell it. Fact is, I've travelled over these mountains so often I can tell where the road is by the sound of the wheels. When they rattle I'm on hard ground; when they don't rattle I genr'ly look over the side to see where she's agoing."

"Have you any other signs?"

"Backer's another sign; when I'm a little skeer'd I chew more'n ordinary. Then I know the road's bad."

"Don't you get tired driving over the same road so often?"

"Well, I do—kalklate to quit the business next trip. I'm gettin' well on in years, you see, and don't like it so well as I used to afore I was busted in."

"How long have you been driving stage?"

"Nigh onto thirty years, an' I'm no better off now than when I commenced. Pay's small; work heavy; gettin' old; rheumatism in the bones; nobody to look out for used-up stage drivers; kick the bucket one of these days, and that's the last of Old Charlie."

"Why, you must have made plenty of friends during so long a career of staging."

"Oh yes, plenty of 'em; see 'em today, gone tomorrow! Git alang!"

At the close of the 1860's Charlie Parkhurst quit driving and opened a stage station and saloon on the road between Santa Cruz and Watsonville, made a few thousand dollars, then rented the station and went into the cattle business in Santa Cruz. Because of sciatic rheumatism, the curse of early-day stage drivers, Charlie was obliged to give up ranching, and for a few years lived quietly and alone near Watsonville, the rheumatism growing more painful and cancer of the tongue developing.

On the last day of December 1879 a couple of neighbors dropped by and found that Old Charlie had died a day or two before. When they prepared to dress the body for burial they discovered to their consternation that Charlie Parkhurst was a woman, and upon examination by a doctor it was definitely established that she had been a mother. Her financial and legal affairs had been carefully taken care of, and all the papers had been simply signed C. D. Parkhurst.

Charlie Parkhurst was not only the most skillful reinswoman the world has ever known, but typified the devotion to calling, the pride in accomplishment, and the determination of all the drivers who made it possible for stagecoaching to play the glorious role it did in the opening and development of the American West.

Bibliography

BOOKS, ARTICLES

Athearn, Robert G., *Westward the Briton*. New York: Charles Scribner's Sons, 1953; Lincoln: University of Nebraska Press, paper (Bison), 1962; Gloucester, Mass.: Peter Smith, 1963.

Bancroft, Hubert Hugh, *California Inter Pocula*. San Francisco: The History Company, 1888.

———, *History of California*, Vol. 7, *History of the Pacific States*. 39 vols. San Francisco: The History Company, 1882–87.

Banning, William, and G. H., *Six Horses*. New York: The Century Company, 1930.

Barnes, Demas, *From Atlantic to Pacific, Overland*. Princeton, N.J.: D. Van Nostrand Co., 1866.

Barsness, Larry, *Gold Camp*. New York: Hastings House, Publishers, 1962.

Beck, Warren A., *New Mexico, A History of Four Centuries*. Norman: University of Oklahoma Press, 1962.

Beebe, Lucius, and Clegg, Charles, *U.S. West; the Saga of Wells Fargo*. New York: E. P. Dutton & Co., 1949.

Bennett, Estelline, *Old Deadwood Days*. New York: J. H. Sears & Co., 1928.

Billington, Ray A., *Far Western Frontier: 1830–1860*. New York: Harper & Row, 1956.

Boggs, Mae Hélenè Bacon, comp., *My Playhouse Was a Concord Coach*. San Francisco: priv. printed, Howell-North Press, 1942.

Bolton, Herbert E., *Rim of Christendom*. New York: The Macmillan Company, 1936; Russell & Russell, 1960.

Bradley, Glenn D., *The Story of the Pony Express*. Chicago: A. C. McClurg & Co., 1913.

Brown, Dee Alexander, *Fort Phil Kearny*. New York: G. P. Putnam's Sons, 1962.

Burton, Richard F., *The City of the Saints*, ed. by Fawn M. Brodie. New York: Alfred A. Knopf, Inc., 1962.

Casey, Robert J., *The Texas Border*. Indianapolis: The Bobbs-Merrill Co., 1950.

Chapman, Arthur, *The Pony Express*. New York: G. P. Putnam's Sons, 1932.

———, *The Story of Colorado*. Chicago: Rand McNally & Co., 1925.

Clark, Dan E., *The West in American History*. New York: Thomas Y. Crowell Company, 1937.

Cleland, Robert Glass, *Cattle on a Thousand Hills: Southern California, 1850–1880*. San Marino, Calif.: Henry E. Huntington Library, 2nd ed., 1951.

———, *From Wilderness to Empire: A History of California*, ed. by Glenn S. Dumke. New York: Alfred A. Knopf, Inc., 1959.

———, *History of California–the American Period*. New York: The Macmillan Company, 1939.

Clemens, Samuel, *Roughing It*. New York: Harper & Brothers, 1903; paper, New American Library, 1924.

Codrington, Thomas, *Roman Roads in Britain*. London: Society for Promoting Christian Knowledge, 4th ed. reprint, 1929.

Conkling, Roscoe P., and Margaret B., *The Butterfield Overland Mail, 1857–1869*. Glendale, Calif.: Arthur H. Clark Co., 1947.

Corle, Edwin, *The Gila, River of the Southwest*. New York: Rinehart & Co., 1951.

Davis, Jean, comp., *Shallow Diggin's*. Caldwell, Idaho: The Caxton Printers, 1962.

Dick, Everett, *Vanguards of the Frontier*. New York: D. Appleton-Century Company, 1941; Lincoln: University of Nebraska Press, paper (Bison), 1964.

Dillon, Richard H., *Meriwether Lewis*. New York: Coward-McCann, Inc., 1965.

Driggs, Howard R., *The Pony Express Goes Through*. Philadelphia: J. B. Lippincott Co., 1936.

Duffus, R. L., *Santa Fe Trail*. London: Longmans, Green and Co., 1930.

Dunbar, Seymour, *History of Travel in America*. Indianapolis: The Bobbs-Merrill Co., 1915.

Eggenhofer, Nick, *Wagons, Mules and Men*. New York: Hastings House, Publishers, 1961.

Estes, George, *The Stagecoach*. Troutdale, Ore.: George Estes' Publications, 1925.

Foreman, Grant, *Marcy and the Gold Seekers*. Norman: University of Oklahoma Press, 1939.

Foster-Harris, William, *The Look of the Old West*. New York: The Viking Press, 1955.

Frederick, J. V., *Ben Holladay, the Stage Coach King*. Glendale, Calif.: Arthur H. Clark Co., 1940.

GARDINER, DOROTHY, *West of the River*. New York: Thomas Y. Crowell Company, 1941; paper (Apollo), 1963.

GHENT, WILLIAM JAMES, *Road to Oregon*. London: Longmans, Green and Co., 1929.

GOETZMANN, WILLIAM H., *Army Exploration in the American West, 1803–1863*. New Haven, Conn.: Yale University Press, 1959.

GREELEY, HORACE, *An Overland Journey from New York to San Francisco*, ed. by Charles T. Duncan. New York: Alfred A. Knopf, Inc., 1963.

GREEVER, WILLIAM S., *Bonanza West, the Story of the Western Mining Rushes, 1848–1900*. Norman: University of Oklahoma Press, 1963.

HAFEN, LEROY R., *The Overland Mail, 1849–1869*. Glendale, Calif.: Arthur H. Clark Co., 1926.

HARLOW, ALVIN F., *Old Post Bags*. New York: D. Appleton-Century Company, 1934.

———, *Old Waybills*. New York: D. Appleton-Century Company, 1934.

HEBARD, GRACE R., *Washakie*. Glendale, Calif.: Arthur H. Clark Co., 1930.

———, and BININSTOOL, E. A., *The Bozeman Trail*. Glendale, Calif.: Arthur H. Clark Co., 2-vol. ed., 1922; 1-vol. ed., 1960.

HERRMANN, PAUL, *Conquest By Man*. New York: Harper & Row, 1954.

HOLLON, W. EUGENE, *Southwest: Old and New*. New York: Alfred A. Knopf, Inc., 1961.

———, *Great Days of Overland Stage*. American Heritage, Vol. VIII, No. 6, 1957.

HUNGERFORD, EDWARD, *Wells Fargo*. New York: Random House, 1949.

INMAN, HENRY, *Great Salt Lake Trail*. Topeka, Kans.: Crane & Co., 1941

JACKSON, JOSEPH HENRY, *Anybody's Gold*. New York: D. Appleton-Century Company, 1941.

———, *Bad Company*. New York: Harcourt, Brace & Co., 1939.

JACKSON, W. TURRENTINE, *Wagon Roads West*. New Haven, Conn.: Yale University Press, 1965.

JOHNSON, WILLIAM G., *Overland to California*. Oakland, Calif.: Biobooks, 1955.

KELLY, CLYDE, *United States Postal Policy*. New York: D. Appleton-Century Company, 1931.

KNOWLAND, JOSEPH R., *California, A Landmark History*. Oakland, Calif.: Tribune Press, 1941.

KRAENZEL, CARL F., *The Great Plains in Transition*. Norman: University of Oklahoma Press, 1955.

LAVENDER, DAVID S., *The Big Divide*. New York: Doubleday & Company, 1948.

LECKENBY, CHARLES H., comp., *Tread of Pioneers*. Steamboat Springs, Colo.: Pilot Press, 1945.

LEWIS, OSCAR, *The Big Four*. New York: Alfred A. Knopf, Inc., 1938.
———, *Autobiography of the West*. New York: Henry Holt & Co., 1958.
LOCKWOOD, FRANCIS C., *Pioneer Days in Arizona*. New York: The Macmillan Company, 1932.
LONG, MARGARET, *The Smoky Hill Trail*. Denver, Colo.: the author, 1932.
LUCIA, ELLIS, *Saga of Big Ben Holladay*. New York: Hastings House, Publishers, 1959.
MAJORS, ALEXANDER, *Seventy Years on the Frontier*. Columbus, Ohio: Long's College Book Co., 1950.
MANDAT-GRANCEY, EDMOND, *Cowboys and Colonels*. Philadelphia: J. B. Lippincott Co., 1963.
MONAGHAN, JAMES, *Overland Trail*. Indianapolis: The Bobbs-Merrill Co., 1947.
MOREHEAD, CHARLES R., JR., "Personal Recollections," in *Doniphan's Expedition*, ed. by William E. Connelley. Kansas City, Mo.: Bryant & Douglas, 1907.
MORGAN, DALE L., *The Humboldt: Highroad of the West*. New York: Holt, Farrar & Rinehart, 1943.
MORSE, FRANK P., *Cavalcade of the Rails*. New York: E. P. Dutton & Co., 1940.
NADEAU, REMI, *Ghost Towns and Mining Camps of California*. Los Angeles: The Ward Ritchie Press, 1965.
NEWMARK, HARRIS, *Sixty Years in Southern California*. Boston: Houghton Mifflin Co., 1930.
ORMSBY, WATERMAN, ed. by L. H. Wright and J. M. Bynum, *The Butterfield Overland Mail*. San Marino, Calif.: Henry E. Huntington Library, 1942.
OVERTON, RICHARD C., *Burlington West*. Cambridge, Mass.: Harvard University Press, 1941.
PADEN, IRENE D., *The Wake of the Prairie Schooner*. New York: The Macmillan Company, 1943.
PATTIE, JAMES OHIO, *The Personal Narrative of James O. Pattie*, ed. by William Goertzmann. Cincinnati, Ohio: 1831; Philadelphia: J. B. Lippincott Co., 1962.
PAUL, RODMAN, *Mining Frontiers of the Far West, 1848–1880*. New York: Holt, Rinehart & Winston, 1963.
PEATTIE, RODERICK, ed., *The Black Hills*. New York: Vanguard Press, 1952.
PENCE, M. L., and HOMSHER, L. M., *Ghost Towns of Wyoming*. New York: Hastings House, Publishers, 1956.
PERKIN, ROBERT L., *First Hundred Years*. New York: Doubleday & Company, 1959.
PHILLIPS, LANCE, *Yonder Comes the Train*. Cranbury, N.J.: A. S. Barnes & Co., 1965.
POURADE, RICHARD F., *The Silver Dons*. San Diego, Calif.: Union-Tribune Publishing Co., 1963.

RICHARDSON, ALBERT D., *Beyond the Mississippi*. Hartford, Conn.: American Publishing Co., 1867.

RIESENBERG, FELIX, *The Golden Road: the Story of California's Spanish Mission Trail*. New York: McGraw-Hill Book Co., 1962.

RIPLEY, HENRY, and RIPLEY, MARTHA, *Hand-clasp of the East and West*. Montrose, Colo.: M. Ripley, 1914.

ROOT, FRANK A., and CONNELLEY, WILLIAM E., *The Overland Stage to California*. Pr. by W. Y. Morgan, Topeka, Kans., 1901; Columbus, Ohio: Long's College Book Co., 1950.

RYUS, WILLIAM H., *The Second William Penn*. Kansas City, Mo.: Frank T. Riley Publishing Co., 1913.

SANDOZ, MARI, *Cheyenne Autumn*. New York: McGraw-Hill Book Co., 1953.

SETTLE, RAYMOND W., and MARY L., *Empire on Wheels*. Stanford, Calif.: Stanford University Press, 1949.

SMILEY, JEROME C., *History of Denver*. Chicago: The Berkeley Printing Co., 1901.

SMITH, WADDELL, *Stage Lines and Express Companies in California*. Pub. by Pony Express History and Art Gallery, 1965.

SPRAGUE, MARSHALL, *The Great Gates*. Boston: Little, Brown & Company, 1964.

SPRING, AGNES WRIGHT, *Caspar Collins*. New York: Columbia University. Press, 1927.

———, *Cheyenne and Black Hills Stage and Express Routes*. Glendale, Calif.: Arthur H. Clark Co., 1949.

STANGER, FRANK M., *South from San Francisco*. San Mateo, Calif.: San Mateo County Historical Association, 1963.

STONE, WILBUR F., ed., *History of Colorado*. Chicago: S. J. Clarke Publishing Company, 1918.

STRAHORN, CARRIE ADELL, *Fifteen Thousand Miles by Stage*. New York: G. P. Putnam's Sons, 1911.

TRUMAN, MAJOR BEN C., "Knights of the Lash," *Overland Monthly*, 1898.

TWITCHELL, RALPH E., *Leading Facts of New Mexico History*. 2 vols. Albuquerque, N.M.: Horn & Wallace, 1963. Vol. II.

VESTAL, STANLEY, *Old Santa Fe Trail*. Boston: Houghton Mifflin Co., 1939.

VILLARD, HENRY, *Memoirs of Henry Villard, 1835–1900*. 2 vols. Boston: Houghton Mifflin Co., 1904.

———, *The Past and Present of the Pike's Peak Gold Regions*. Princeton, N.J.: Princeton University Press, repr. 1860 ed., 1932.

WARE, EUGENE F., *The Indian War of 1864*, ed. by C. C. Walton. Topeka, Kans.: Crane & Co., 1911; New York: St. Martin's Press, 1961; Lincoln: University of Nebraska Press, paper (Bison), 1963.

WEBB, TODD, *Gold Rush Trail and the Road to Oregon*. New York: Doubleday & Company, 1963.

WILLIAMS, ALBERT N., *Rocky Mountain Country*. New York: Duell, Sloan & Pearce, 1950.

WILSON, NEILL C., *Treasure Express*. New York: The Macmillan Company, 1936.

WILTSEE, ERNEST A., *Pioneer Miner and Pack Mule Express*. San Francisco: California Historical Society, 1931.

WINTHER, OSCAR O., *The Great Northwest*. New York: Alfred A. Knopf, Inc., 1950.

———, *Old Oregon Country*. Stanford, Calif.: Stanford University Press, 1950.

———, *The Transportation Frontier*. New York: Holt, Rinehart & Winston, 1964.

———, *Via Western Express and Stagecoach*. Stanford, Calif.: Stanford University Press, 1945.

W.P.A. FEDERAL WRITERS' PROJECT: *The American Guide Series*
> *California, Guide to the Golden Stage*. New York: Hastings House, Publishers, 1939; rev. 1954.
> *Colorado, a Guide to the Highest State*. New York: Hastings House, Publishers, 1941; rev. 1951.
> *Idaho, a Guide in Words and Pictures*. Caldwell, Idaho: The Caxton Printers, 1937.
> *Kansas, a Guide to the Sunflower State*. New York: Hastings House, Publishers, 1939.
> *Montana, a State Guide Book*. New York: Hastings House, Publishers, 1949; rev. 1955.
> *Utah, a Guide to the State*. New York: Hastings House, Publishers, 1941; rev. 1954.
> *Wyoming, a Guide to Its History, Highways and People*. New York: Oxford University Press, 1941.

HISTORICAL MAGAZINES, ETC.

Arkansas Historical Quarterly
> IX, 1950: IRWIN, RAY W., "The Mountain Meadows Massacre."
> XV, 1956: ROSE, F. P., "Butterfield Overland Mail Company."

California Historical Society Quarterly
> II, 1923–24: HAFEN, LEROY R., "Butterfield's Overland Mail."
> XIII, 1934: WINTHER, OSCAR O., ed., "Stage-Coach Days in California—Reminiscences of H. C. Ward."
> XVI, 1937: BLAKE, ANSON S., ed., "Working for Wells Fargo—1860–1863."
> XIX, 1940: ELLISON, M. H., ed., "Memoirs of Hon. William M. Gwin."

Quarterly of the Society of California Pioneers
> VII, 1930: VISCHER, EDWARD, "Stage Coach Days."

Colorado Highways
> April, 1925: HOOVER, EDWIN HUNT, "The Smoky Hill Route."

Colorado Magazine

II, 1925: HAFEN, LeROY R., "Early Mail Service in Colorado, 1856–60."

IV, 1927: SHIELDS, LILLIAN B., "Relations with the Cheyennes and Arapahoes in Colorado to 1861."

VIII, 1931: BLISS, EDWARD, "Denver to Salt Lake by Overland Stage in 1862."

VIII, 1931: HALL, J. N., "On the Westward Trail."

VIII, 1931: HAFEN, LeROY R., "Zebulon Montgomery Pike."

IX, 1932: SANFORD, ALBERT B., "Mountain Staging in Colorado."

IX, 1932: HAFEN, LeROY R., "Claims and Jurisdictions over the Territory of Colorado Prior to 1861."

XII, 1935: COLFAX, SCHUYLER, "Detained at Virginia Dale by Indians."

XII, 1935: LONG, MARGARET, "The Route of the Leavenworth and Pike's Peak Express."

XIV, 1937: ALLEN, ALONZO H., "Pioneer Life in Old Burlington."

XV, 1938: HAFEN, LeROY R., "Cherokee Goldseekers in Colorado, 1849–50."

XVI, 1939: BURGUM, EDWIN G., "The Concord Coach."

XIX, 1942: BLOCK, AUGUSTA HAUCK, "Old Burlington."

XX, 1943: HAFEN, LeROY R., "Colorado's First Legislative Assembly."

XXII, 1945: SPRING, AGNES WRIGHT, "Food Facts of 1859."

XXII, 1945: DOWNING, FINIS E., "With the Ute Peace Delegation of 1863, Across the Plains and at Conejos."

XXIII, 1946: GOODYKOONTZ, COLIN B., "The People of Colorado."

XXVIII, 1951: COVINGTON, JAMES WARREN, "Federal Relations with the Colorado Utes, 1861–1865."

XXVIII, 1951: BOLLINGER, EDWARD T., "Middle Park Stage Driving."

XXIX, 1952: CUMMINS, D. H., "Toll Roads in Southwestern Colorado."

XXX, 1953: PERRIGO, LYNN I., ed., "H. J. Hawley's Diary, Russell Gulch in 1860."

XXXII, 1955: BOND, I. W., comp., "Old Trails in Reverse."

XXXIII, 1956: ATHEARN, ROBERT G., "Colorado and the Indian War of 1868."

Kansas Historical Quarterly

I, 1931–32: WYMAN, WALKER D., "The Military Phase of Santa Fe Freighting, 1846–1865."

XII, 1944–45 and

XIV, 1946: ROOT, GEORGE A., and HICKMAN, RUSSELL K., "Pike's Peak Express Companies."

XV, 1947: HENDERSON, HAROLD J., "The Building of the First Kansas Railroad South of the Kaw River."

XV, 1947: SCHEFFER, THEODORE H., "Following Pike's Expedition from the Smoky Hill to the Solomon."

XVI, 1948: MOLLHAUSEN, H. B., "Over the Santa Fe Trail Through Kansas in 1858."

XIX, 1951: SAGESER, A. BOWER, "Along the Line of the Kansas Pacific Railway in Western Kansas in 1870."

Mississippi Valley Historical Review
> V, 1918–19: COTTERILL, ROBERT S., "Early Agitation for a Pacific Railroad, 1845–50."
> XII, 1925–26: HODDER, FRANK H., "The Railroad Background of the Kansas-Nebraska Act."

Missouri Historical Review
> XVIII, 1923–24: BEIBER, RALPH B., "Some Aspects of the Santa Fe Trail, 1848–1880."
> XXVI, 1931–32: SQUIRES, MONAS N., "The Butterfield Overland Mail in Missouri."

Montana Magazine of History
> III, Summer 1953: FLETCHER, BOB, "Virginia City."
> III, Autumn 1953: KUPPENS, FRANCIS XAVIER, S.J., "Christmas Day, 1865, in Virginia City, Montana."
> III, Autumn 1953: FLETCHER, BOB, "Last Chance Gulch."

Nebraska Historical Magazine
> XXI, 1940: DENNEY, ARTHUR J., "The Pony Express Trail: Its Dramatic Story."
> XXVIII, 1947: HAGERTY, LEROY W., "Indian Raids Along the Platte and Little Blue Rivers, 1864–1865."
> XXIX, 1948: MANTOR, LYLE E., "Stage Coach and Freighter Days at Fort Kearny."

Historical New Hampshire
> XX, No. 3, 1965: SCHEIBER, HARRY N., "The Abbot-Downing Company of Concord."

New Mexico Historical Review
> XXVI, 1951: WALLACE, WILLIAM SWILLING, "Short-Line Staging in New Mexico."
> XXXII, 1957: WINTHER, OSCAR OSBURN, "The Southern Overland Mail and Stagecoach Line, 1857–1861."
> XXXII, No. 2, 1957: WALLACE, WILLIAM SWILLING, "Stagecoaching in Territorial New Mexico."

Chronicles of Oklahoma
> VI, 1928: WRIGHT, MURIEL H., "The Removal of the Choctaws to Indian Territory 1830–1833."
> XI, 1933: WRIGHT, MURIEL H., "Historic Places on the Old Stage Line from Fort Smith to Red River."
> XII, 1934: WYMAN, WALKER D., "Survey of a Wagon Road from Fort Smith to the Colorado River."
> XII, 1934: WRIGHT, MURIEL H., ed., "The Journal of John Lowery Brown, of the Cherokee Nation en route to California in 1850."

Oregon Historical Quarterly
> XXXVIII, 1937: BEALS, ELLA A., "Oregon to California by Wagon, 1872."
> XL, 1939: WINTHER, OSCAR OSBURN, "The Development of Transportation in Oregon, 1843–49."

XLI, 1940: WINTHER, OSCAR OSBURN, "History of Transportation in Oregon, 1843–49."

Quarterly of the Oregon Historical Society
I, 1900: YOUNG, F. G., "The Oregon Trail."
XIII, 1912: BAILEY, WALTER, "The Barlow Road."

Pacific Historical Review
III, 1934: WINTHER, OSCAR OSBURN, "Stage-Coach Service in Northern California, 1849–52."
XI, 1942: RICE, WILLIAM B., ed., "Early Freighting on the Salt Lake–San Bernardino Trail."
XXVI, 1957: BOYD, WILLIAM HARLAND, "The Stagecoach in the Southern San Joaquin Valley, 1854–1876."

Pacific Northwest Quarterly
XXXVII, 1946: SCHMITT, MARTIN F., ed., "From Missouri to Oregon in 1860: The Diary of August V. Kautz."

Southwestern Historical Quarterly
LIX, 1955: McMILLEN, KATHRYN SMITH, "A Descriptive Bibliography on the San Antonio–San Diego Mail Line."
LXI, 1957: WILLIAMS, J. W., "The Butterfield Overland Mail Road Across Texas."
LXI, 1957: MAHON, EMMIE GIDDINGS, and KIELMAN, CHESTER V., "George H. Giddings and the San Antonio–San Diego Mail Line."

Utah Historical Quarterly
IX, 1941: ACKLEY, RICHARD THOMAS, "Across the Plains in 1859."
XXII, 1954: MABEY, CHARLES R., "The Pony Express."
XXIV, 1956: ANDERSON, BERNICE GIBBS, "The Driving of the Golden Spike: The End of the Race."

Washington Historical Quarterly
XIV, 1923: BEMIS, SAMUEL FLAGG, "Captain John Mullan and the Engineers' Frontier."

Annals of Wyoming
XI, 1939: TAYLOR, INEZ BABB, "Career of Cheyenne–Black Hills Stage Line Owner, Colorful Story of the 'Old West.'"
XIII, 1941: SPRING, AGNES WRIGHT, ed., "Old Letter Book: Discloses Economic History of Fort Laramie, 1858–1871."
XV, 1943: WILSON, RICHARD HULBERT, "The Sweetwater Stage Company—1869."
XV, 1943: WILSON, RICHARD HULBERT, "Letters of 1862 Reveal Indian Trouble Along the Overland Mail-Route."
XV, 1943: RINER, WILLIAM A., "The Old Trail to an Empire."

Harper's Monthly Magazine
XXXV, 1867: WYMAN, WALKER D., "A Stage Ride to Colorado."
LXXXIII, 1891: CLAMPITT, JOHN W., "The Vigilantes of California, Idaho, and Montana."
CCI, 1950: DEVOTO, BERNARD, essay in "The Easy Chair" editorial section.

Journal of American History
   III, 1909: ELDREDGE, ZOETH S., "First Overland Route to the Pacific."
PRIVATE LAWS, TERRITORY OF KANSAS, 1860–62.
PRIVATE ACTS, COLORADO TERRITORY, 1866.
U.S. Congressional Globe, 1855/61.
The Westerners' Brand Book, Denver Posse
   1951: PARKHILL, FORBES, "Decline and Fall of the Stagecoach Empire."
   1952: BEMIS, EDWIN A., "Wagon Master."

UNPUBLISHED MANUSCRIPTS, ETC.

Early Stage Lines in Colorado–1859–1865. A thesis prepared in July, 1959, by Jimmie Lee Frazier, University of Denver.
The Smoky Hill Trail. A Thesis Submitted in Partial Fulfillment of the Requirements for the Degree of Master of Arts of the University of Denver by William Crane Johnston, Jr., A.B., University of Denver, 1924, Denver, Colorado, 1927.
Malcom Campbell, Sheriff. A Manuscript in the Western History Department of the Denver Public Library by Robert B. David.
By Russell's Line from Leavenworth. A Monograph in the Western History Department of the Denver Public Library, reprinted from *The Bennington Banner*, Bennington, Vermont, 1859–1860 by Libeus Barney.
Staging in Central California, as Related by Henry Ward. This holographic manuscript, the recollections of one of California's earliest stage drivers, is preserved in the Bradford Collection in the Manuscript Department of Stanford University Libraries, Stanford, California.

NEWSPAPERS

CALIFORNIA

Sacramento	*The California Farmer*
	Placer Times
	Sacramento Times
	Sacramento Transcript
	State Journal
	Union
San Francisco	*Alta California*
	Bulletin
	California Courier
	Call
	Herald
	Pacific News
Marysville	*Marysville Herald*
San Diego	*Herald*
Shasta	*Courier*

Stockton	*Stockton Republican*
Visalia	*Mariposa Democrat*
Yreka	*Yreka Union*

COLORADO
Denver	*Denver Post*
	Rocky Mountain Herald
	Rocky Mountain News
Central City	*Central City Register*
	Tri-Weekly Miners Register
Aspen	*The Aspen Weekly Times*
Canon City	*Canon City Times*
Dolores	*Dolores News*
Fort Collins	*Fort Collins Express*
Georgetown	*The Colorado Miner*
Gunnison	*Gunnison Review*
Steamboat Springs	*Steamboat Pilot*
Trinidad	*The Trinidad Enterprise*

ILLINOIS *Chicago Tribune*

KANSAS
Atchison	*Daily Free Press*
Leavenworth	*Leavenworth Herald*

MISSOURI
St. Joseph	*Catholic Tribune*
St. Louis	*The Missouri Republican*
Independence	*Commonwealth*

NEW YORK *New York Herald*
New York Times

OREGON
Oregon City	*Oregon Spectator*
Portland	*The Oregonian*

Index